PRISM OF THE NIGHT

PRISM OF THE NIGHT

A BIOGRAPHY OF

ANNE RICE

KATHERINE RAMSLAND

A DUTTON BOOK

For Steve and Lori,
who believed

DUTTON
Published by the Penguin Group
Penguin Books USA Inc., 375 Hudson Street, New York, New York 10014, U.S.A.
Penguin Books Ltd, 27 Wrights Lane, London W8 5TZ, England
Penguin Books Australia Ltd, Ringwood, Victoria, Australia
Penguin Books Canada Ltd, 10 Alcorn Avenue, Toronto, Ontario, Canada L3R 1B4
Penguin Books (N.Z.) Ltd, 182–190 Wairau Road, Auckland 10, New Zealand

Penguin Books Ltd, Registered Offices:
Harmondsworth, Middlesex, England

First published by Dutton, an imprint of New American Library, a division of Penguin Books USA Inc.
Distributed in Canada by McClelland & Stewart Inc.

First Printing, November, 1991
10 9 8 7 6 5 4 3 2 1

REGISTERED TRADEMARK—MARCA REGISTRADA

LIBRARY OF CONGRESS CATALOGING-IN-PUBLICATION DATA:
Ramsland, Katherine M., 1953–
Prism of the night : a biography of Anne Rice / Katherine Ramsland.
p. cm.
ISBN 0-525-93370-0
1. Rice, Anne, 1941– . 2. Novelists, American—20th century—Biography. 3. Horror tales, American—History and criticism. 4. Erotic stories, American—History and criticism. 5. Vampires in literature. I. Title.
PS3568.I265Z86 1991
813′.54—dc20
[B] 91-15904
CIP

Printed in the United States of America
Set in ITC Galliard
Designed by Leonard Telesca

"The Night darkens the spirit,
but only to illuminate it."
—St. John of the Cross

"It was the poetry of darkness
and she loved it."
—Anne Rice, *Exit to Eden*

CONTENTS

INTRODUCTION ix

CHAPTER ONE
KATHERINE AND HOWARD 1

CHAPTER TWO
FOUR GENIUSES 11

CHAPTER THREE
CHANGES 45

CHAPTER FOUR
A DREAM OF FAMILY 78

CHAPTER FIVE
MICHELE 117

CHAPTER SIX
THE VAMPIRE 142

CHAPTER SEVEN
THE BILDUNGSROMANS 177

CHAPTER EIGHT
THE DIVIDED SELF 210

CHAPTER NINE
LESTAT 245

CHAPTER TEN
LIBERATION 272

CHAPTER ELEVEN
THE GUISE OF EVIL 294

CHAPTER TWELVE
THE GREAT FAMILY 318

CHAPTER THIRTEEN
THE PRISM 345

NOVELS BY ANNE RICE 353

CHRONOLOGY 354

SOURCE NOTES 359

INDEX 373

INTRODUCTION

Exploring a writer's life to shed light on culture and creativity is a complex task. Cause-and-effect relationships are never exact and it is tempting to oversimplify. When that writer changes names, styles, subjects, and genres as Anne Rice has repeatedly done, and when the writer is still alive and writing, the complexities multiply. Nevertheless, the themes of her novels remain consistent and evolve toward a vision that provides a crossroad between author and audience.

Why Anne Rice, and why now? Anne Rice is unique among authors. She writes in genre images that capture mainstream readers. Her first novel was heralded as an "event," though it was ostensibly about vampires, because it seemed to tap into the spirit of a culture seeking new myths. She detailed the breakdown of the structures of a self based on traditional values, which fed into a contemporary thirst for exploring such a process. Although her protagonist wasn't destined to offer a stronger moral vision, à la Nietzsche, he did exhibit the preservation of moral integrity and he examined the notion of a power within himself that could deliver him from despair. The story touched a social nerve, and out of nowhere, seemingly against all odds, Anne Rice became a best-selling author.

That novel continues to sell some fifteen years after its initial publication. Nevertheless, Anne Rice's success has been controversial. She has been praised by critics for her literary accomplishment as well as sullied for her "lurid" prose and choice of subject matter. Her writing has had a widely variable effect on readers as well, which seems to demand a study of who she is. A biography of how her life issued into such compelling and provocative images would offer not only a chronicle of creativity but also a means by which to look at ourselves.

Anne Rice is a curiosity. She doesn't just stick to "what works" or what feels safe for her as a writer, but instead follows her imagination wherever it takes her, even if that means risk. She has written under three names, from "supernatural mainstream" to contemporary erotica, from historical subjects to "elegant" pornography. Her most popular novels are about vampires, and while avid fans may be aware of her other subjects, they often do not realize how rich those books are. Nor do they realize that the novels offer a progression from Anne Rice to A.N. Roquelaure to Anne Rampling and back to Anne Rice that reveals the journey of an author toward a sense of personal clarity and ever greater experiments with creative expression. The more popular she becomes, the more curious people are about her and about their response to her work. A biography would reveal the subliminal ways in which she evokes strong feeling.

Anne Rice is as comfortable with philosophical depth and psychological dynamic as she is with a lighthearted romp through Edwardian England or with creating a sexually explicit fairy tale. She can address the cosmic implications of morality as easily as the craving for symbolic violence. While one novel moves with the dense thoughtfulness of a Russian writer, another of the same length changes style so dramatically that it reads in a fraction of the time. What does it mean for an author to explore so many diverse subjects, to write in so many voices? Why would an author who has garnered popular success with mainstream fiction risk it by writing pornography? Does her life shed light on these questions?

Anne Rice grew up in New Orleans amid a broad spectrum of physical and artistic stimulation. She was raised in an unusual manner and exposed to high ideals that gave her a sense of personal specialness. Her imagination took over and she populated a fantasy world, responding to dark mystery and the supernatural. Although her sense of nuance and her southern and Irish heritage may have influenced her style enough to have made her a successful writer, it seems to have been the dramatic events in her life that gave to her work the emotional richness that has captured so many readers.

Anne experienced a series of losses, including her mother's death, that threatened to fragment and crush her. She felt the tug of surrender to despair as well as the urge to resist, paralleled by her desire to get educated in an era when such values were suspect to people her age. From childhood, she felt different from others, never quite matching social expectations. She wavered between wanting to be accepted and wanting to be herself. Each time she asserted herself, she became stronger, but life seemed darker.

In her twenties, she wrote pornography and erotica, fascinated with the freedom of male experience and with her own masculine qualities. It would take another tragedy, however—the loss of her five-year-old daughter—before she found the subject that tapped the pain, intensity, and imagery of the crush of life experiences and lost values: the vampire.

Noting the compulsion and sensuality of the vampire mythology, Anne utilized her own physical intensity to draw out erotic qualities. She put her vampires into relationships that paralleled the gay experience just when being gay meant exhibiting the courage of political pioneers. Expressing her personal desires and experiences through metaphor, she connected with establishment and renegade alike.

People responded to the psychological depth and philosophical explorations in the search for values on the part of a creature who hovered at the boundaries of humanity. This was no genre novel, where the vampire represented a dark force that had to be annihilated by a fearless and holy vampire hunter. Anne took the point of view of the vampire as an outsider who possessed human emotions and the need for answers and acceptance. The questions about immortality were disguised questions about mortal life. The book chronicled deep grief and the search for inner resources.

Buoyed by her success, Anne explored other subjects that obsessed her, blending aspects of her life and values into the lives of her characters. Her next two books traced the breakdown of structure once again, but were not as successful. Anne had to consider whether to yield to what editors told her would sell or to stick with her own visions. Since conformity had never been high on her list, she decided on the latter.

Whenever she considered subjects that would sell, something deep within took over and steered her toward some other idea to which she connected so intimately that she couldn't *not* write about it. From vampires to castrated opera singers to sexual rebels, she decided that if something interested her, maybe it would interest others. She allowed her intelligence, education, experience, and subconscious to work together to satisfy her as well as to tap subliminal elements that could speak to a popular audience. Autobiographical elements emerged in symbolic ways as Anne experienced personal growth while indulging in sensuality. These books showed a pattern of development rooted in, as well as transforming, her more "acceptable" novels.

To friends she seemed inhibited, but in her imagination she proved to be daring and provocative, giving expression to a secret fantasy life that felt genuine enough to grip her readers. Her vulnerability and strength combined to add a paradoxical dimension to the psychology of her characters, especially those exploring the relationship between dominance and submission.

Anne Rice's work reflects her life. She searches for clarity of expression as a way to establish clarity of values. She uses her novels to push herself closer to an intimate contact with the essence of life, including the socially forbidden areas. Her life gives authenticity to her characters, but her work also includes mythic qualities. Having lived through a decade of social unrest and possessing the facility to channel into her writing much of what she has observed and experienced, she gives something of us to ourselves—something we might otherwise miss. A biography of Anne Rice would invite us to see how the universal and highly contemporary elements in her novels can broaden our own self-understanding.

Biographies can serve many functions and take many forms, from a strictly historical chronology to simple vignettes. A biography is a *perspective,* developed from a variety of sources and employing a specific style to weave it all together to present a portrait. That portrait captures not only the *subject* but also the creative process that goes beyond a particular life to provide sources of identification for readers.

My approach combines psychological interpretation with philosophical themes. As I read the novels, I looked for qualities that transcended genre, while also developing autobiographical sketches. I cannot count the number of times I changed my mind on what made Anne "tick," and may yet change it again, but this book is the result of an involved and sincere attempt to trace in her writing elements of literary creativity manifested in psychological sources. I am convinced that Anne Rice possesses a guiding motivation that comes through in her work and that an understanding of that motivation can enhance the experience of reading her novels.

While I believe that subconscious forces emerge in a writer's work, I do not accept the view that those forces determine the writer's outlook on life. What authors write may flow forth from inarticulate places deep within the self, but they have the capacity to make choices as well that will be reflected in how and what they write. I believe in the "willed self" as an expression of who a person is and that although patterns may emerge, causal attribution must be flexible and loosely formed.

The greatest frustration in writing this book was, inevitably, the limitations of space. Each of Anne's novels deserves much more attention than I was able to give. I selected aspects that I felt contributed most to a coherent biographical theme.

Writing an account of another person's life always involves people associated with the subject. I am deeply grateful to many people who willingly offered their assistance and support.

Foremost, I want to thank Anne for her gracious, patient, and detailed cooperation. She answered questions, gave me names, photos, and phone numbers, and clarified inaccuracies, but exerted no influence or control over my artistic vision. It is always a risk to give over the telling of your life to another person, and I appreciate Anne's courage and generous spirit.

Members of her family were also generous with their time. Her husband, Stan, and son, Christopher, were always helpful and enthusiastic. Stan checked the initial manuscript for factual errors. Anne's father, Howard O'Brien, and her sisters, Alice Borchardt, Tamara O'Brien, and Karen O'Brien, provided important information on Anne's childhood and adolescence, and Tamara helped to get details straight on events in California. Anne's half sister, Micki Ruth Collins, and her stepmother, Dorothy, were also helpful.

Stan's side of the family assisted me with their perspectives on Anne. Thanks to Stanley Rice, Sr., Margaret Rice, Larry Rice, Cynthia Rice Rodgers, and Nancy Rice Diamond.

Relatives outside the immediate family—Billy Murphy, Allen Daviau, Patt Moore, George Daviau, and Gertrude Helwig—offered wonderful and important memories.

Anne also has many friends who added significant details. In alphabetical order, I'd like to thank Geri Peterson Arnold, Jim Bodishbaugh, Andy Brumer, Laura Chester, Cathy Colman, Carla DeGovia, Jack DeGovia, Betsy Dubovsky, Tony Dubovsky, Candi Ellis, Ann Fekety, Marjorie Ford, Blair Fuller, Jack Gilbert, Linda Gregg, Lucy Provosty Harper, Ginny Mathis Hiebert, Kenneth Holditch, Ann Bailey Johnson, Kathy Macay, Carolyn Doty Mein, Martha Nawy, Judy Murphy O'Neil, Robert Owen, Lynn Phelps, John Preston, Michael Riley, Jesse Ritter, Floyd Salas, Joe Slusky, Casey Sonnabend, Ed Stephan, Shirley Stuart, Leland van den Daele, and Annette Arbeit van Slyke.

People involved in the publication side of Anne's life were also willing to help. I'm grateful to Diane Ekeblad, Joni Evans, Pam Henstell, Richard McCoy, Lynn Nesbit, Phyllis Seidel, Antoinette White, Victoria Wilson, and Bob Wyatt for their comments.

People not already mentioned who supplied comments, information, photos, letters, reviews, articles, names, and addresses include Jeffrey Adams, Eric Bauersveld, Dave Campiti, Sister Lydia Champagne, Karen Colimore, Robin Gajdusek, David Geisinger, Michael Gonchar, Barbara Hall, Pat Holt, Barbara Johnston, Helen Knode, Stephen Martin, Bill Munster, Ed Olsen, Donya Papaleo, Muriel Perkins, Alisa Rice, Michael Rogers, members of Anne Rice's Vampire Lestat Fan Club (with special thanks to the officers), Liz Scott, Kevin Steiner, William Weigand, Stanley Wiater, Perla Wichner, Richard Wiseman, and Lloyd Worley. Thanks to each and every one.

I also appreciated the support of my family and the enthusiasm and patience of my husband, Steve.

People who waded through drafts of the manuscript deserve thanks for their critiques as well: Howard O'Brien, Stan Rice, Julie Holbrook, John Preston, Lori Perkins, and Steve Ramsland.

Thanks to Lori and the Barbara Lowenstein Agency for placing the manuscript, and to John Silbersack, my editor, whose vision for the book deepened and strengthened it.

CHAPTER ONE

KATHERINE AND HOWARD

1

The little girl played quietly on the bare wooden floor near the piano as she listened to the bustle of activity in the other room. She shook her long brown hair over her ears and pretended not to hear. She did not want to think about what it meant. If she ignored it, just maybe—

"Suzie! Howard Allen! Let's go!"

A chill of dread shot through her. She glanced up. Her mother stood in the doorway, hands on slim hips, waiting.

"Howard Allen, come along."

The girl sighed. There was no avoiding it. The first day of school, the first grade. Heads would turn when the other kids heard that embarrassing name: Howard Allen. It made her want to just stay home. Scrambling to her feet, she smoothed her pleated navy skirt and gave a quick tuck to her white blouse. Then she reached for her mother's outstretched hand.

At least *she* was going. There was always great comfort in her mother's presence.

But then class would start and the other girls would smirk at their classmate who toted a boy's name. It made her feel painfully different, awkward, when what she most wanted was to be accepted. Later they'd tease her or just look at her as if she were some bug that had crawled into their midst. She cringed at the thought.

The walk to school went quickly. Howard Allen kept one hand in her mother's damp palm and felt the moist "New Orleans sheen" rise on her own scrubbed skin. The end of summer was always so humid, but the heat magnified the wonderfully overpowering scent of crepe myrtles. Howard Allen breathed it in as she walked dutifully on one side of her mother, while her older sister, Suzie, walked on the other. They strode down the sensuous, sinister streets of the Garden District, shadowed so densely by towering live oaks. Huge, bulging roots broke up the sidewalks outside the magnificent Greek Revival mansions, many of which stood in sad disrepair. Howard Allen hung back to stare through windows, hoping to catch a glimpse of a spirit from former times. Nothing entertained her more than a good ghost story.

But Katherine was tugging at her hand, taking her past the spooky old houses, out Philip Street, until the buildings became the more ordinary, double "shotgun" houses through which one could see straight to the back door. The lingering scent of summer's night-blooming jasmine hung in the morning air.

They arrived all too soon at Redemptorist School, a square brick building in the Irish Channel next to St. Alphonsus Church, and went into the classroom. Girls clad in identical Catholic school uniforms milled about. Howard Allen felt herself being led toward a woman in a black habit and white wimple, knew the dreaded moment was at hand, and saw no escape. Other girls were already glancing at her. She came to a halt before the nun, who leaned toward her mother and asked, "What is her name?"

Katherine smiled, her mouth opening—

"It's Anne!"

The name came fast, confident. Howard Allen swallowed, wide-eyed at her own brash answer. The sister blinked at her, then turned questioning eyes to her mother, who shrugged and said, "If she wants to be Anne, then it's Anne."

2

Anne Rice, born Howard Allen O'Brien, adopted a nickname in the first grade that became the name by which the world would know her. Yet in New Orleans, nicknames were common. Everyone seemed to have a birth name as well as a moniker used by close friends, as if attempting to retain the European flavor of the city founders. Nicknames captured an informal intimacy reserved for friends and family not inherent in the

English-language customs of the rest of the country. Each of Anne's sisters had a nickname. Alice was Suzie, Tamara was Tiger T, and little Karen, the youngest and tiniest, was Mitey Joe. Anne's father, Howard O'Brien, was called Mike at the post office where he worked, and many friends knew Anne's mother, Katherine, as Kay.

New Orleans in the 1940s was an interesting place to grow up for a girl like Anne. Alive with motion and energy, the city had a distinct personality. With French, Spanish, and Caribbean influences, genteel and gleefully corrupt, there was no other place in America quite like it. Settled on the precarious banks of the Mississippi River, it harbored people of strong passion, manic aspiration, fragility, and deep despair. They partied hard and repented to excess. The public facade hid private communities, as New Orleans invited the world to celebrate Mardi Gras, where tourists were shown what they wanted to see, yet closed its tall shutters to outsiders for the more profound family traditions. Like the ironwork that decorated the houses, the citizens were both delicate and strong—imparting an atmosphere of ambiguity in which heat damned as "hellish" was tolerated for the sake of preserving fragile flowers that shed the aromas of heaven.

Contradiction was evident everywhere. Mansions of the wealthy sat next to economical shotgun houses. Buildings that once had housed churches became taverns. St. Louis Cathedral attested to a strong Catholic presence, yet sat in the midst of French Quarter bars, prostitutes, and transvestites. While Proteus, the god of change, reigned over holiday parades, century-old traditions, like having red beans and rice every Monday, provided continuity that preserved those traditions past their original purpose.

New Orleans culture was created by survivors. Fires had twice wiped out the city, between floods, hurricanes, and plagues of yellow fever and cholera. The dead were remembered in high style in above-ground tombs that could cost thousands of dollars. People without money to buy elaborate monuments rented their burial space—and if the rent wasn't paid, they'd be removed until someone came up with the money!

It may be due to the specter of death that extreme frivolity developed as a tradition in the city that ignored Prohibition; or perhaps the gleeful excesses were due to the fact that New Orleans seemed fated to erode into the ocean, but the pleasure-seeking, day-at-a-time atmosphere could not be denied. Steamy, dark, and mystical, home to voodoo queens, jazz musicians, and gamblers, the essence of the "Big Easy" in those years was not easily grasped in rational terms. Appearances were often other than what they seemed in a city where the sun rose on the West Bank, and where there never was a canal on Canal Street. Even the original French name—Nouvelle Orleans—is said to have been feminized as a joke on the duc d'Orleans, a man who sported women's underwear beneath his clothes. As the rest of the country moved toward the "left hemisphere," New Orleans leaned toward the right, relying on easy sensuality and eccentricity to grant it a special status as the most unusual city in America. Such an atmosphere could not help but leave its mark on an impressionable young girl.

3

Anne was familiar with the entire city, from the Mississippi to Lake Pontchartrain, eight miles away. The swamp-drained land had been built into a roughly organized system of unique neighborhoods, and she would describe it in detail in her future novels. The French Quarter—the oldest part—had a distinct Creole architecture and was laid out in a neat six-by-twelve-block graph pattern. Uptown was an upscale Victorian neighborhood bordering two major universities—Tulane and Loyola. The Garden District, once the American sector, offered to Anne visions of Greek Revival mansions and huge magnolias. Bordering it was the notorious Irish Channel, where immigrants formed communities to support one another through extended families and religious ties.

Anne's father, Howard O'Brien, was a son of the Irish Channel. He grew up fighting to preserve his dignity against the name with which he was saddled. "Howard, Howard, little girl coward!" the other boys taunted him, so he learned to be tough.

In his day, segregation laws were strictly enforced, and the poor Irish were regarded as just a step or two above blacks. "When a black boy got within ten feet of me," he said, "he went out onto the street and gave me the sidewalk." Such a tenuous social structure relied on rigid class hierarchies, and people knew you were from the wrong side of Magazine Street by your accent.

Howard came from a large family. He was the middle boy between four sisters and four brothers, and one of his aunts had been married to the son of a man who had served time in the Confederate army during the Civil War. His mother, the eldest of twelve children, was the family historian, and he recalls how she gathered with her sisters to talk about private matters intended for family ears only: who was homosexual, who was divorced, who was getting married and having babies. She loved to sing, and instilled in her children an appreciation for classical music and for songs from the 1890s. Howard's father was uneducated, but possessed a love for calligraphy, and Howard learned the art of beautiful handwriting by imitating his father's each night on homework assignments. Howard had a good mind, with an ability to form in his head the structure of what he wanted to say so that it flowed out the way he intended. Growing up among Irish storytellers, he learned the rhythm of rich and sure expression.

Irish Catholic traditions provided a clear structure to Howard's life—interspersed with Lutheran influence from his German-Jewish grandmother, who married "Big Jim" Curry—and for six years he studied for the priesthood at a local seminary. He gave it up to get a job when his family needed money. He also wanted to be a journalist, but instead served in the merchant marine. Eventually he took an exam to work for the post office.

Howard had a friend named Pete who was an insurance adjuster and a drinking buddy. At the bar, Pete talked animatedly about his dates with a girl he called Kay. Howard was impressed. Kay sounded like a brilliant girl and he was anxious to meet her.

Kay was Katherine Allen.

4

Born in 1908, Katherine came from an old and respected Irish family. At five foot, six inches, she was thin and beautiful, with full, dark hair and brown eyes that gave her an Indian appearance. Her mother, Alice Allen, had given birth to eight children, only three of whom survived to maturity—Katherine, her sister, Alice, and her brother, John—known as Mickey. Katherine was the youngest.

She was a storyteller. As a child she went with her mother to housekeeping jobs and read Charles Dickens out loud, over and over. Knowing by heart the plots and entire scenes of such stories as *Oliver Twist, David Copperfield,* and *The Old Curiosity Shop,* Katherine learned to weave a good story herself, and relate it with a mesmerizing delivery. She had a disciplined memory, but disliked reducing her imagination to writing, so she developed her talent for expression into a remarkable ability to recount accurately books she had read and movies she had seen. "Katherine was with movies," Howard recalled, "as so many people today are with television. She associated with so many characters, and she had an extraordinary facility for exact memory for whole segments of dialogue. She would build up the story just as it had been developed in the movie." She also acquired the skill of palm reading, and found herself in demand.

Charming, gregarious, and sensitive, Katherine always had something positive to say. She possessed a terrific sense of humor, loved to laugh, and despite austere Catholic beliefs, was fond of risqué jokes. She had high ideals, a wise saying for every day of the week, and was never afraid to show affection.

Yet she had known tragedy. Her father had been thrown out of the house because of his excessive drinking, and had died from tuberculosis and alcoholism at the age of forty-eight in a charity hospital. It was to make ends meet that Katherine's mother had humbled herself to work as a domestic servant in the Garden District.

For the family, an alcoholic was a social shame, which resulted in a sense of secret poison that invaded the lives of each person involved. One of Katherine's brothers had died at the age of six from stepping on a rusty nail, and it was felt that had Father been sober, Mother would have had more time to attend to the children: the tragedy would never have occurred. Alcohol was a deep and deadly evil. The fear and guilt, and the atmosphere of pain it created in the family, gave Katherine an intense desire to follow in the ways of the church and to devote herself to being good. Purity and absolute perfection became her goals.

Mamma Allen took her marital problems in stride. Short and wiry, she possessed a dominating spirit that inspired others and gained her many friends. One of them was a wealthy German woman named Mrs. Franz, who owned several houses on prestigious St. Charles Avenue—bordering the Garden District and on the Mardi Gras route. At 2301 Philip and St. Charles stood a two-story white house with double porches, called "galleries," on both floors. French windows opened onto the front porches, one of which was screened. A purple flagstone walk graced the front yard to the street, and the garden on the side sported a symmetrical yew tree. On the other side was a chinaberry tree, grown in earlier times to ward off plague. A Japanese plum and a large oak tree completed the landscaping. Mamma Allen moved in with her three children, and John and Alice took jobs to help with the rent.

Her relatives, who were content to live in the much more humble Irish Channel, looked at her askance. They felt that she was putting on airs. "Lace curtain Irish" they called her, in contrast to their own curtains, made from flour sacks.

"Aunt Ali didn't have anything," remembered Gertrude Helwig, a niece, "but you would never know to look at her. She always had a nice black dress and a little black hat that she had all the years I knew her, and every year she'd put a new ribbon on it." Mamma Allen had manners and she aspired to more social status, even if it meant having only the *appearance* of it. For a brief time she was even able to hire a full-time maid. "They were role models," Gertrude explained of the Allens. "They always strived for something better."

The two daughters, Alice and Katherine, were popular, beautiful, and bright. Alice was shorter than Katherine, and more practical. They were encouraged to take every opportunity to better themselves, like going to college—rare for women in those days. They were educated and imbued with a sense of grace. Katherine was an honors student in high school, and her forte was Latin. After college Alice went on to law school and was the second woman—by an hour—to graduate from Loyola School of Law.

However, they were working against the Depression and people did what they could to get by. Alice worked at the Standard Oil Corporation across the street, then went to a law firm. Katherine became a secretary and a notary public. To help pay household expenses, Mamma Allen took in boarders. Her house was narrow but long—plenty of room for renting out space. She let the first floor and a room in the back that had been part of the kitchen. A section of the pantry became a bathroom with a tub but no sink.

One of the boarders was George Daviau from Chicago, who was taking a degree in 1935 from the business school at Tulane and working at Johns-Manville. His memories of Katherine were fond: "Kay had plump, big cheeks. She looked just like a Salvation Army girl with a tambourine in her hand. She was adventurous and always happy. I never saw her do anything but smile and enjoy life." He stayed eighteen months, dated Alice, and asked her to marry him. They went around the world on their honeymoon and settled in Los Angeles.

Katherine was left alone with Mamma Allen. She had been out to Hollywood briefly, working for Texaco, then Boron, but had returned to New Orleans. She gave George the tip he needed to land a job in Los Angeles, then got serious about her own future.

5

It was her hair and eyes that caught the attention of Howard O'Brien. She was older than he by ten years, but he was daunted less by that than by the fact that she was already spoken for by his friend. He spent many hours in the company of Pete and Katherine, yearning for just such a relationship.

"She's going to marry me," claimed Pete one day. "The insurance company is giving me a raise. Wants to send me out of state. Kay'll go with me!"

Howard was unhappy. He knew he would miss the conversations that often sent sparks into the air. But he would especially miss Katherine.

Pete left and time passed. Aching for their company, Howard imagined Pete and Katherine happy together somewhere. Then he heard a surprising piece of news. Katherine had not married Pete after all! It seems, he was told, that Pete had a drinking problem, and Katherine was not about to get entangled with *that* after what her family had been through with her father. For Howard there was still hope.

He spotted her at church and asked her to be in an Easter play he was writing for the young people of the Catholic parish. It changed the course of their lives.

"Katherine was cast in the role of the Virgin Mary," he recalled, "and I wrote myself in as Peter. The makeup people had put talcum powder on my hair to make it white. After I had denied Christ three times, I threw myself at the feet of his 'mother.' All the powder flew up into Katherine's face, and the Virgin Mary had a terrible sneezing fit. She grabbed me by the shoulders, and that was our first intimate contact."

Howard began to call on her and discovered that she had once lived in Hollywood. She told him about boarding with a family whose son had worked with Jackie Cooper in the movies. He sat in rapt attention as she told stories about places she had seen and movie stars she'd heard about. They often talked on the front stoop until two or three in the morning, sometimes reading together from Latin texts, sometimes just dreaming of the future. Having felt pressured by her mother to achieve good grades, Katherine entertained a more romantic notion of education for her own future family that entailed a free and spontaneous atmosphere. She was determined to raise healthy children who would be *geniuses,* all of them. These children would never know that their grandmother had been a housekeeper. They would have pride in themselves and become something special. Male or female, they would have every opportunity she could give them. Toward that end, she and Howard read Dickens, studied Shakespeare and theology, and argued about the concept of genius.

Howard was thoroughly entranced with Katherine's brilliance and mystery, but sometimes she unnerved him. One night, out on the steps in the sweltering air, Katherine confessed that she expected to die when she reached her prime. Howard believed she possessed some degree of vision with her palm reading, and her words chilled him. He asked that she never mention it again.

At the end of their long evenings, they often made a date to meet for seven o'clock Mass that morning. When Katherine went in, Howard watched from First Street, a block away, until her light was out.

"One night I realized I didn't even feel my feet," he recalled. "I was walking on air. It occurred to me I had to be in love! I danced all the way home."

After Mass, they breakfasted with Mamma Allen, then Howard went to work, looking forward to the next evening's discussions. He felt very good about being included in this household, perceiving how their education had helped to better their circumstances. He also enjoyed the attention that had been more widely dispersed in his own family among his many siblings, and Mamma Allen appreciated having a man around.

Howard loved Katherine's ambitions and her religious devotion. She was always finding a cause to work for, like being involved in a Big Sister program at the orphanage.

"Everything about Katherine was mysterious," said Howard. "She always had some secret project going. In the days when elevators had operators, the girls had to stand up all day. Katherine started a crusade, and within two years, she had chairs for those girls." She practiced her Catholicism with strict adherence, and demanded of herself severe asceticism. She attended Mass and Communion daily.

They dated for five months while Howard waited for his job situation to improve: It was 1938 and he was a temporary substitute for the post office. He never knew from day to day if there was work, and he could not ask Katherine to marry him until he felt secure. The goal was to become a regular substitute, because that meant employment every day.

In October, he achieved his goal with a salary of sixty-five cents per hour. They set the wedding date for November 25, Thanksgiving Day, at 5:00 A.M., during Mass.

Katherine was nervous. Many of her relatives did not approve of this marriage. She was thirty years old, Howard twenty, and the unusual arrangement further alienated her in the eyes of those who already saw her as different because of her education. The thought that no one would attend frightened her. She was also nervous about marriage, period. She had dated many men before Howard and had loved being popular. Now she was uniting with one man for life. That they shared a common religion and a common vision was important.

The wedding morning arrived. Katherine rose early and put on the white dress that she had made with the help of her godmother, Gertrude Sheppard. She had sewn orange silk flowers into the skirt, under the tulle. As she listened to the driving rain outside, she tried to reassure herself, knowing the bad weather would provide an easy excuse not to attend. She closed her eyes to seal off the tears. No one would come, she just knew it! Her wedding would be embarrassing, painful. How had she allowed this to happen? Then she steeled herself against disappointment: all the better if no one came. It would be quiet and intimate, as a wedding of two serious souls should be. But tears formed again and soon she was weeping. She had wanted a beautiful wedding and instead it would be humiliating.

By the time she arrived at the church, Katherine had found inner control. She glanced up at the unmatched twin brick towers of St. Alphonsus and felt good. This was her church, where she had daily put herself into the hands of God. If it was rainy and cold, then she and Howard would find out who really loved them! Anyone who braved that kind of weather at that hour in the face of familial disapproval would *have* to love them. And if there was no one, well . . . they had each other.

She stepped into the church. Dampness magnified the chill of the solid stone beneath her delicate slippers. She breathed in and allowed the atmosphere of holiness to envelop her. Someone standing near the inner doors turned and beamed at her. Curious, she moved forward to peek through the crack. Her eyes widened.

The church was packed! It was five in the morning on a rainy Thanksgiving Day, and everyone was there! Katherine could hardly believe it.

Soon the music started and the doors opened. She swept into the spacious sanctuary to begin her walk down the aisle. A huge overhead mural of the saints against a blue sky gazed down at her as if in approval. She smiled, then felt something at her feet. Looking down, she saw that an orange blossom, so carefully sewn, had broken free from her skirt. Others were missing and she sensed she was leaving a trail of pretty flowers as she stepped forth to meet her smiling groom. They stood together at the altar as Aunt Josie burst forth in her operatic voice with "The Angel Serenade." It was more beautiful than Katherine had dreamed, and for Howard it was the happiest day of his life.

After the wedding, they left on their honeymoon, packing Alice's wedding gift, a volume of the collected works of G. K. Chesterton, inscribed specifically for "honeymoon entertainment." Upon their return they moved into the spacious house at 2301 St. Charles with Mamma Allen.

One year later, they had their first child, a daughter. They named her Alice Allen to retain Katherine's family name. When George Daviau declared she looked more like a Suzie, she gained a nickname (which she rejected in favor of Alice in her late teens).

Two years after that, on October 4, 1941, a second daughter came along. Thinking back to the days when his own name had been associated with girls, and perhaps in an effort to give it away, Howard named the little girl Howard Allen Frances O'Brien.

CHAPTER TWO

FOUR GENIUSES

1

In 1942, when Anne was still in diapers, Howard consulted with Katherine and decided to enlist in the navy for a three-year hitch. "It was the wonderful and the right thing to do at the time," he said. Pearl Harbor had been bombed months before.

Howard was weary of the post office and he wanted to see some action. His plan was to get into radio school to acquire the experience he needed to return to the merchant marine as a radio operator when he got out of the navy. He would earn more than he hoped to make staying where he was. It was his dream to serve on a ship with sixteen-inch guns. However, his transfer to the Fleet Marines was cancelled and he ended up in Bethesda, where he was trained as one of the navy's first electroencephalography technicians, reading brain waves. Then he was stationed in Idaho and finished up in California. He came home on leave only three times, each time for a week.

At the same time, Alice's husband was in officers' training on Treasure Island in San Francisco, so she came to 2301 St. Charles to have her baby, whom she named Allen. Mamma Allen went back with her to California, and Katherine found herself alone with her two daughters, ages one and three.

Never in her life had she been faced with such responsibility. Mamma Allen had always run the household, and Katherine was not nearly as organized. She understood what was expected of her—to be brilliant, independent, and a proper southern lady, even when she had no money to finance such gentility. Her mother was highly regarded, and Katherine knew she had a tall order to fill to keep up social appearances. When faced with buying things for her home, she found reasons why she should not have them—like claiming that rugs were destroyed if they were cleaned—that masked financial inability. Katherine was a charming hostess who could organize an impressive party, but managing a household was something else. Nevertheless, the pressure to carry on did not evaporate with Mamma Allen's absence.

Katherine wanted badly to prove herself. She wanted to be a good daughter, a good wife, and a good mother, but forces seemed to conspire against her. She felt that she just did not measure up. The house under her direction seemed always in chaos, with piles of laundry, dishes, and books scattered about. So she strove harder. But she did not possess the physical strength to take care of two children and a large house for an extended period of time. The chores were endless and conveniences that eased the workday of other women were not part of her world.

"She had few or no appliances," explained Anne. "She washed clothes in the bathtub, and swept and mopped bare floors. There was no air conditioning in those days, and dust came in through the old screens. She worked the way people did in the last century, the way her mother had."

The worst of it for Katherine, however, was being alone at night. She was afraid of the dark.

After tucking in the girls each evening, she took refuge in her own room to read. The light stayed on the rest of the night to keep her company—a habit that became permanent, even after Howard returned. Katherine also started to drink.

"Katherine was having a terrible time," recalled her cousin, Patt Moore. "Nothing in her life had equipped her to raise children or to be alone. She had so few options. I remember going over and seeing her, and she seemed very sad. My mother told her that everything was going to be all right, and I remember her telling my mother how frightened she was."

Mamma Allen spoke to Katherine on the phone and knew she was in trouble. She cut short her visit with Alice and came home. The house was soon put in order, but the strain of those lonely, frightening weeks did not evaporate for Katherine, and she continued to drink.

Howard believed his absence may have also contributed to Katherine's desperation. "In subsequent years," he said, "I realized what a terrific burden I had placed on her." At that time, however, no one anticipated that using alcohol to cope might turn into a serious problem for her.

It was a common practice among the Irish of New Orleans to drink away their problems, and it was viewed with tolerance. Excesses were quietly absorbed into the family system. In the mid-forties in the South, serious alcoholism was misunderstood as a weakness of the will, a personal dysfunction that was under one's own control—bordering on sin in the Catholic church when it got out of hand. Families did what they could—which was very little—to help the alcoholic in their midst. Only extreme mental illness or people contemplating suicide were considered as candidates for psychotherapy. An alcoholic situation was not discussed, not even within the family, as if ignoring it would somehow make it go away. Relatives fell easily into patterns of secrecy and protection, especially where the appearance of gentility and propriety was emphasized.

Katherine was fortified by Mamma Allen, who possessed a powerful, charismatic presence that commanded respect. Anne remembered her as a thin woman with gray hair, braided regularly each night. She wore wire-rim glasses and had a built shoe to support a hip that had been twice broken. "She was a tireless worker," said Anne, "who cleaned all the time. She was always doing laundry in tubs in the kitchen on scored boards, and carrying it in huge wicker baskets to hang outside. Other people had wall-to-wall carpeting and vacuum cleaners, but she mopped the bare floors." The elderly matriarch saw that the children had regular meals and a clean house.

She was also a moral model to her grandchildren, refusing to indulge in prejudice. "We are all God's children," she would say in response to discussions about blacks. Her tolerance, however, did not extend to governments. Influenced by her deceased husband's former occupation as a labor organizer, she felt that governments were inherently evil and repressive, and that the children should be taught self-reliance. Katherine agreed.

They frequently sat together at the kitchen table to talk over tea about neighbors and family, captured in a story Anne wrote years later, called "October 4, 1948." In the next room Anne and Suzie carried on a similar conversation.

"My grandmother and mother had tea every day at four o'clock," said Anne. "We imitated them. We would sit at the dining room table and drink water and pretend it was whiskey."

Together Anne and Suzie played out fantasies that they made up. "We had a couple of fantasies that we shared," said Anne. "One time we were pretending to be Mary and Madine Slickery, these two characters in our dream world, and one of them said, 'Ah, now we can afford salt in our whiskey.' They laughed in the kitchen.

"Madine had something like one hundred children, that they called the Slickery children. I was Madine and Suzie was Mary. They would move all over the world building castles, and they could build them very fast because there were so many Slickery children; each one would take a brick, and that's how fast it would get done. I loved castles. We used to play that endlessly in the dining room. I don't remember what the Slickery children were always doing, but they went places and built castles."

The Slickery fantasy developed early, before Anne was in school, influenced by a Saturday morning radio program called "Let's Pretend," that taught children fairy tales. Anne and Suzie also spent a lot of time building palaces out of playing cards. "We had these two decks of cards," said Anne, "which sort of find their way into every novel that I write. One deck was French and one was English. We bent the English ones for the posts. The French ones were beautiful. They had a fleur-de-lis on the back, and all the face cards were in a Marie Antoinette style. We'd build the floors with them. In our fantasies, we always had people playing solitaire with beautiful cards and living in correct houses. That was a big deal to me."

Later the girls developed another shared fantasy. "We had this whole world," said Anne, "that revolved around a television show called 'The Space Patrol.' Suzie had seen it when she visited Aunt Alice in California. We were those characters, Commander Corey and Space Cadet. She'd tell me the plots, and we'd do those characters and create adventures."

"Anne made up the stories," said Alice. "Mostly I just laughed."

Anne also immersed herself in a solitary fantasy world. "I've had these dream worlds since I was a kid, and they were very active. When it started, it was about children and parents and great big houses with lavish interiors, and it was sort of a fairy tale kingdom. Then it got more developed. There's one in ancient times and one in modern times, peopled with dozens of people, and it's really violently ongoing, and involves all kinds of people. They're so vivid. Sometimes they involve gangsters and crime and shooting–about the same amount of violence that weaves itself into a soap opera. They have conflict and drama and love relationships. Things happen in them that seem almost inevitable, and I can't stop them. I finally placed one in Canada because I had to place it someplace. It evolved from the time I was five years old, and so the people dressed differently than normal people. It started as a troop of children having adventures, and as I got older, they grew into people. The ancient one I sort of set in Greece or Rome, and it's much more limited. The one in Canada has had the same characters since I was five, and there are dozens of them. I could write reams on it. It mirrors my interests, and exists for my pleasure and preoccupation. I sink into it in waiting rooms or when I'm trying to fall asleep." She would later describe the fantasy of ancient times, set in Greece, in her novel *Exit to Eden.*

Waking dreams were more a part of Anne's fantasy life than were dreams while asleep. However, when she was four years old, she had a dream that would influence her tenth novel, *The Queen of the Damned,* for its lucid, surreal quality: "I saw a woman who was completely white, like marble, and she was walking down Philip Street, behind where I used to live, next to this old house. It was frightening because it had no paint and was very dilapidated. She had a prayer book in her hand and someone said to me, 'That's not your grandmother, that's your Regis grandmother.' I had never heard the word *Regis* and I did not know the meaning of it. It was a very frightening dream."

The fantasy world stayed with Anne as she matured, branching out and changing dimension as her own life and concerns changed.

2

Katherine strove to raise healthy, perfect children, each of whom would be a genius. To be a good mother, she believed, was to be the operative force behind a brilliant child, and that meant allowing them the freedom to express themselves in whatever way appealed to them, and encouraging their imagination. She treated them like adults by having them call her and Howard by name, rather than referring to them as Mommy and Daddy.

"Katherine believed," said Howard, "that children shouldn't be caused to feel that they were just little people. They should be encouraged to feel that they were part of a unit and could ask any question they wanted, and listen to any story they wanted, and speak like adults. When we had company, the children were allowed to join in with the adult conversations."

"She was a wonderful mother," said Patt Moore. "Katherine definitely did not believe that children should be seen and not heard. They were everywhere, anytime. It was a household with little structure, but that was the way Katherine wanted it."

A typical example was when, one sunny day, Anne and Suzie went running outside into the fenced backyard without any clothes. A neighbor called to alert Katherine to the situation. Instead of being upset, as the neighbor had expected, Katherine responded with "That's why we have a fence! Just don't look out your window. They're children, and that's what they want to do!"

When relatives heard about the incident, they were outraged. They could not understand why Katherine persisted in raising her family in such a manner. It went against the grain of both social propriety and the church, and did not appear to be producing superior children. Anne and Suzie were too outspoken, doing and saying what they pleased. Katherine was just not like other mothers! She was too educated for her own good and too unconventional. Attracted to artistic types, there was even a touch of the bohemian about her, as she sported a beret. "The whole household was like something out of a Tennessee Williams play," said one relative. "It was chaotic."

The undisciplined household seemed confusing to others but meant a great deal of freedom for the children. "We were allowed to draw on the walls," Anne explained, "and paste our pictures all over, and play everywhere in the house. We'd drag out the china and crystal and play with it, and crawl around inside the big lower chambers of the sideboard."

They were also allowed to sleep in any bed they chose, and they changed sleeping arrangements from night to night. "Often I bunked in with my mother," said Anne, "when I got afraid or just didn't want to be alone."

"The main thing that Katherine stressed," said Patt Moore, "was to do what you wanted to do, and be all that you could be. Don't be limited by the fact that you're a girl."

The children had a head start on developing a sense of nuance in language. In the Irish community, storytelling was a favorite pastime, especially when the alcohol flowed. Part of the fun was attending to the shape of language as a dramatic vehicle, using phrasing and timing to convey the playfulness and morbidity that was part of the Irish character.

Toward that end Katherine made up poems for each of her daughters, and after prayers were said each night, she had them recite to her as they went to bed. "I remember her reading to us when we were little," said Anne. "She wanted us to hear poetry read so that it would give us a sense of rhythm." When they were in bed Katherine would sing a chant to put them to sleep. Modern psychologists corroborate Katherine's innate sense of how to inspire children. The developing brain is susceptible to properties of sound and rhythms of words before responding to meaning, and early verbal play develops linguistic flexibility and sharper perception for elusive qualities—a trait that served Anne well when she started to write.

Katherine also enticed them with stories from her voracious reading. She was especially fond of telling a good ghost story, like the one about a woman who burst into flame as she brushed her long blond hair. The girls heard all about the bloody deeds of Lucrezia Borgia and Macbeth. They also heard local tales about a haunted Jesuit rectory and about a spirit at Mercy Hospital, where Anne had been born, who visited a student nurse in her cubicle in the night. "It was very vividly told," said Alice. "Katherine talked about the curtains and the way the girl was dressed. The supernatural was very close to us. The people around us believed all kinds of things. Even with the church, it was as though the unseen was always present."

As a storyteller, Katherine was gregarious and loved to laugh. "She would read jokes out of the *Reader's Digest,*" said Anne, "or parts of Jerome K. Jerome's *Three Men on Wheels,* a British novel she adored. We would all laugh together." She was a model to Anne, who later became known among family and friends for her own wit and her practical jokes, despite the serious nature of much of her later writing.

As Anne learned to read, she made her way through one Nancy Drew mystery and a child's version of Greek mythology, but she read slowly and preferred listening to others tell the tales.

The emphasis in the home was on the classics—those that the Catholic church listed on its official register of acceptable books. Having learned many of the plots of Dickens's stories, Katherine passed them along orally to her children. "She told us stories all the time," said Anne. "She told us the entire plot of Dumas' *Count of Monte Cristo,* and sometimes the tales came from the movies she'd seen. She told us all about great writers like Dumas, Dickens, and the Brontës—how the Brontës had written their great works under male pseudonyms, and how shocked everybody in London was to discover they were women. Years later, watching the late show on TV, I'd realize I was seeing a movie my mother described, blow by blow."

One of her most memorable stories, according to Anne, was about the way the writings of Charles Dickens affected people. When he was writing *The Old Curiosity Shop,* installments came to America by ship and people crowded on the pier waiting for each one. At a crucial point in the story, rather than wait for the ship to dock, they yelled out to the captain, "Is Little Nell dead?" The captain yelled, "Yes," and the devoted readers sat down and cried.

"I heard later," said Anne, "that they tore the pier apart. It was a lovely story about the emotional impact of fiction. I wanted to affect people that way."

There was no television in the O'Brien household until Anne was a teenager, and the predominant form of entertainment came from the radio or from movies. Katherine's enthusiasm for movies was contagious. "On the average," Howard recalled, "Katherine went to movies about once a week." Anne and her sisters were introduced to such films as *Caesar and Cleopatra, Hamlet,* Marx Brothers movies, and *Casablanca.* They also saw movies they might never have otherwise discovered, like *The Red Shoes* and *Rebecca,* as well as foreign films. Anne was infatuated with the screen images of Errol Flynn and Laurence Olivier.

"*Hamlet* was the first movie I ever saw," said Anne, "and the only scenes I remember are the ghost scene and the scene where Ophelia floated on the stream with the flowers coming out of her hair after she died. Seeing that in a dark theater in the days before television *must* have had an influence on me."

Katherine possessed a dramatic flair that not only made her an entertaining storyteller but also filled her imagination with ambitions she could not attain, spilling over into her daily life. New Orleans was run by elite social clubs, and she longed to be part of the romantic atmosphere. When Howard returned, Katherine tried to impress her sister, Alice, by describing how she dressed in a long gown every night for a formal dinner with her husband, who wore a suit. It was not true, but it demonstrated for her children a rich imagination that was to be used to one's own advantage.

When Suzie eventually started school, Anne grew lonely. Katherine enrolled her in a public school for a half day, and it was there that she realized the horror of being called Howard Allen. Already shy with strangers and self-conscious about her differences, she found the experience of being scrutinized because of her unusual name excruciating. Her formal education that year did not last long, and soon Anne was back with her mother, listening to stories and poetry.

"I think I received my real early education purely from her," said Anne. "School was a boring supplement."

Part of Katherine's theory about raising geniuses included the complete lack of corporal punishment in the home. She exercised restraint herself, and later demanded Howard's compliance. He was not allowed to raise his hand in anger or discipline, and he found it difficult at times to keep his temper. Suzie seemed especially wild at bedtime, and he felt she needed firm guidance. "One night," he recalled, "I went in to give her some pops on the pistol pocket, and Katherine flew in and cried, 'No! No!' " The children were to follow their own whims. If that meant staying awake all night, so be it.

Katherine seemed to have a natural instinct for many of the conditions for encouraging genius. In a noted study on creativity by Silvano Arieti, a list of important factors for fertilizing genius is laid out. The list confirms many of Katherine's practices, some intentional and some inadvertent. She provided a variety of stimuli for her daughters—especially in the liberal arts; she encouraged individual development and stressed the process of being special; she made available, within her means, ways for them to pursue their talents; she instilled a sense of freedom; and she encouraged intelligent interaction by her willingness to talk about any subject they raised.

The creative process is a synthesis of motivation, detailed perception, vision, attitude, circumstance, and the ability and perseverance to transform primitive stimuli into specific concepts or images. It involves enlarging experience, developing disciplined and focused mental habits, stimulating mobile subconscious energy, and tolerating "omnivalence"—multiple levels of contrary meanings. Katherine may not have understood the terms, but she did seem to grasp the need for a breadth of experience and an immersion into long traditions of classical thinking. She also provided a sort of "ordered chaos" that fed the developing psyches of her impressionable children.

It was Katherine's intent to liberate them from social restrictions that produced mediocre people and to guide them toward the mental lucidity that she had known in her short time in college. She was alert to their budding inclinations, and without explicitly realizing it, she provided an additional source for spawning creativity: restrictions—in this case, of a rigorous religious discipline. What Katherine wanted was for her daughters to be geniuses, yes, but *Catholic* geniuses. "My mother was a very strict Catholic," said Anne. "The Catholic religion at its most dogmatic was her faith completely. She used to get us up for Mass and daily communion every morning. It never occurred to me to miss Sunday Mass unless I was bedridden. She would say, 'Go to Communion! The body and blood of Christ are on that altar two blocks from here!' " Through Katherine's influence, the church became for Anne a symbol of structure and security, and later of enveloping mystery and transcendence.

For Katherine the church provided a foundation of goodness and purpose, so she emphasized freedom, intelligence, and education within those rigid demarcations. "There were all kinds of things we couldn't see or read," said Anne. "You knew it was a mortal sin to read anything on the index of forbidden books. You weren't allowed to read anything by Dumas but *The Count of Monte Cristo.* The church condemned the others because they were about dueling, which was a sin. My mother's idea of being a genius was to be like G. K. Chesterton. Her thoughts did not come too much in contact with the avant-garde in art. Her picture of great writing had to do with the past. Art existed for God's sake. Anything that did not conflict with those values was fine."

Looking back on this Catholic atmosphere Anne likened her parents to French Catholics, referred to as "immigrants of the interior"—they knew their religion but had little interest in the culture around them. The Catholic community was sufficient for them and for their children. "Anyone outside the church was like a charlatan," Anne said. She would give a similar tone to the characteristics of fictional parents in a novel written decades later, called *Exit to Eden.* About the father she would say, "There is this awesome intellectual weight to everything he says, this constitutional puritanism." The mother is just as guarded.

"And my mother so disapproving as she made out the list for the communion breakfast, saying what people needed was to go to confession, and there didn't have to be psychiatrists."

The mix of freedom and censorship in the home was reinforced when Anne eventually went to school by juxtaposing the discipline of parochial education against a free-spirited household, deepening the tensions of paradox.

Anne's first experience with Catholic education was at Redemptorist, the poorest white school in the city. In the neighborhood across the street was the massive St. Mary's Assumption Church. The children witnessed early the effects of ethnic and religious segregation by the German and Irish Catholics, who would not be seated together in the same church. Anne's family, with one German Catholic, had more mobility, and in yet one more way, a bit less restriction. She would return to Redemptorist for the early years of high school, but from the fourth to ninth grades she went several miles across town, near Loyola and Tulane universities, at Holy Name of Jesus school on Calhoun Street.

There were two orders of nuns in the parish—German nuns who were the Sisters of Notre Dame, and the Irish Sisters of Mercy. Anne was taught by the Sisters of Mercy until high school. Some of them were masculine, and in second grade she heard about one nun who could open Coke bottles with her hands. There were stories of cruelty, tyranny, and brutality, some of which Anne captured in her twelfth novel, *The Witching Hour*. Her later associations between women, humiliation, and humorlessness can be partly attributed to the domineering atmosphere.

The school day had a strict discipline that increased in restriction as Anne grew older. "If you didn't walk silently and if you chewed gum, you were told you couldn't learn," Anne said. It was an environment of rules, reflected in the conformity and anonymity of required uniforms.

The girls wore white blouses with triangular patches sewn on the left pocket. The patches were blue, sporting religious symbols like crowns. Navy skirts matched navy beanies, and white socks with saddle oxfords completed the outfit. Everything had to be clean and unwrinkled. The boys wore khaki pants and leather shoes, their shirts tucked in. On their sleeve was the school insignia, and ties were tucked between the second and third shirt buttons.

A typical school day began with eight o'clock Mass, lasting forty-five minutes. Each child had a specified pew, girls with girls and boys with boys. They were expected to arrive early and to say the rosary quietly until Mass began, learning by heart Masses for various occasions for which they were cued by the liturgical color of the priest's changing vestments. If Communion was taken, the child was required to fast the night before to purify the body.

At nine o'clock, the children assembled in the classrooms for lessons. They greeted their teachers courteously, and if the principal entered the room, they stood up to say in unison, "Good morning, Sister." Typical lessons consisted of religion, math, and reading in the morning. Then Anne and her sisters went home for lunch. At noon, they stopped whatever they were doing to listen for the church bells that announced the Angelus, a Latin prayer to the Blessed Virgin. Then they went back for other subjects. It was a very regimented day.

Katherine's program for genius was thus filled with contradiction. Be free, within limits; have your thoughts and behavior dictated at school, then come home to anarchy. Reacting to her own mother's rigorous expectations, Katherine rarely pressured Anne to do homework, allowing her to skip school whenever she felt like it.

Katherine's determination not to follow in her mother's footsteps, however, merely blinded her to the fact that in some ways she was treading the same path. Lack of pressure about schoolwork was not lack of pressure altogether, and the children felt the burden of it. Anne was developing a character attracted to excess and the urge to be special, while Suzie was beginning to withdraw. "We were expected to behave," Alice remembered, "in a manner inconsistent with our age and the environment we were growing up in." Whether it was the impetus to produce genius or just a delayed rebellion against her mother, Katherine quite deliberately set herself and her family apart.

Anne felt this difference most distressingly at school. Unfortunately, as for many who are chosen for a community rather than choosing it themselves, the experience was alienating. Anne always felt estranged. Although she did not question the authority or the rituals, the rules of the church did not seem to touch her very deeply.

"I wanted desperately to fit in," she said, "and was very upset by being an outcast at school. We felt the other kids ridiculed us for our book reading and our vocabulary. The nuns accused us of trying to be different. I was a bad student, I daydreamed in class, I wrote stories in my notebooks. I learned the basics, but most of my active intellectual life was outside of school. It was acutely painful because we *felt* different, like misfits. Our individuality was almost irrepressible, but I wanted to fit in."

Whenever she drew attention that made her feel freakish, she was horrified. Once she accidentally wore mismatched shoes, a black pump and a brown penny loafer, and she met a former teacher who stopped to talk. Everything was fine for a few moments, but suddenly the teacher seemed to want to get away. Anne saw the shoes and thought it was funny. Then she felt the stares of people passing by. "I really thought I was going out of my mind," she said, "that I could do something like that. It was a terribly traumatic incident."

Another time Suzie pulled a black veil over her face to get a different perception of the world and forgot to remove it. She and Anne walked down the street and drew looks that made Anne feel as if people thought there was something mentally wrong with them, like some kind of congenital insanity. Despite Katherine's urge to make her children "special," Anne longed to be normal and inconspicuous.

In addition, there were financial restrictions on how much freedom could actually be allowed to pursue talents, and the encouragement to be creative frustrated the children when they could take it only so far.

Thus, they developed early a capacity to accommodate opposing ideas simultaneously—another condition of creative genius on Arieti's list. The experience of freedom coupled with suppression and frustration can produce an explosion, like pouring bicarbonate of soda into a glass of vinegar. By emphasizing freedom but restricting its expression on several levels, Katherine gave momentum to a spontaneous force within her daughters that, with compression, would build into an intense and complex creative energy that would not be easily contained along the paths that she had set.

3

Howard's return from the service added to the artistic chaos as he set up a table for his wood sculptures. For him, these were the "golden years," although he worked at two jobs and Katherine was drinking more than he thought she should. He returned to the post office, another daughter, Tamara, was born, and things seemed to be on track as Anne and Suzie settled into school.

Howard introduced the girls to classical music. "We played it all the time," he said. "I used to stand up and conduct for the family—Beethoven's Violin Concerto. I also played the harmonica." He borrowed records of *Swan Lake* and the *Nutcracker Suite* from the library and kept the house filled with majestic sound.

A piano stood in the front room near the marble fireplace, and the girls tapped out tunes in the evenings. Anne danced around with a broom for a partner, and on occasion she picked up her baby sister and waltzed as she sang, "Casey, he danced with the strawberry blond as the band played on!" Suzie would take off her shoes and spin on the bare floors until Katherine finally said, "We have to give them a chance to work this out! We have to get that girl someplace where they'll put toe shoes on her!"

Suzie and Anne both wanted dance lessons. Howard found free lessons in City Park, but Anne wanted to go to a real dance school.

"I begged my mother to let us go. I even went to the dancing school on Jackson Avenue to watch." Her mother refused, saying that such places were rackets and would con her into buying costumes. "She just wouldn't approve of it," said Anne. The truth of it was that there was no money. Katherine was trying valiantly to raise her children in a sophisticated atmosphere without the funds to go all the way, and it looked as if Howard's return to the post office had capped her dreams of eventually escaping her true economic status. She continued to drink.

Katherine drank alone, mostly at night in bed while she read, until she passed out. She was not a steady drinker but tended to go on binges, as if in some repetitive, compulsive effort to acquire security by satisfying this craving. For some alcoholics, the first soaring experiences of drunkenness are like a union with a higher force. It is not surprising that Katherine, with her yearning for holiness and perfection, would find alcohol seductive, especially with her roots so deeply embedded in an institution that encouraged unattainable perfection. Her attraction to it was magnified by a family history of alcoholism, by an excessive Irish society, and by her own demanding ideals.

Katherine's decision to have perfect children was, perhaps, her way of purging herself of the imperfection that children of alcoholics often feel about themselves, and of numbing her disappointment that she could not achieve all that she desired, intellectually or economically. Some part of herself may have seemed to her unacceptable. Yet the illusory resource of liquor fragmented her true resources. She fed parts of herself at the expense of other parts—those that her family needed for continuity and reassurance, which might have won for her the emotional and social nurturance she sought.

For the children, this meant dealing with feelings of guilt, secrecy, depression, helplessness, and insecurity over their mother's unpredictable affections. At times she overflowed with emotion; at others, she withdrew. They never knew what to expect, although it would be a few years yet before her drinking became an unending source of anxiety, tension, and embarrassment.

However, unsatisfied needs in children only increase in intensity. If they must be repressed for the sake of the family status quo, they become motivating forces, feeding into the ways in which the children later direct their lives. The inner chaos of dealing with an alcoholic parent can be emotionally crippling, or it can yield independence and strength, depending on the child's resources. It was within the alcoholic family system, coupled with the tensions of freedom and restraint, that Anne first developed the ambivalence between self-sufficiency and the need for love that pervaded her life, her secret fantasies, and later, her art.

4

Howard was a significant literary influence on Anne. He read to the children from Shakespeare, Edgar Allan Poe, and Oscar Wilde. He also wrote a novella for the girls called "The Impulsive Imp," and read chapters to them. Using an incident when a spark had ignited a wooden sliver in the fireplace, he transformed it into an imp with a barbed tail. The chapters detailed the imp's adventures. "He roamed the house," said Howard, "and climbed onto the icebox in the kitchen to let the shade up, and when people came in, he had to hide on top of the kitchen cabinets." A black rat became his steed, and watching over the children became his task. The story ended with a fire, and the imp warned Suzie so she could get the family out.

Howard also wrote poems, dating back to high school, that he kept in a desk. Anne discovered them one day. "I thought they were beautiful and romantic," she said. "My father was a terrific influence on me. He was always reading and writing. I see elements of his story that later appeared in my work. He was living proof that a person could write. He made that a possibility." When she grew up, she bought him a book by Eudora Welty and inscribed it, "To the first writer I ever knew, my father."

Despite the continual exposure in the home to intellectual subjects, Howard worried about Katherine's emphasis on free structure. After Suzie had been in school for a year and still seemed unable to read, he said to his wife, "You're raising a hell of a kind of genius here." Katherine insisted that it would happen in time. Behind the scenes Mamma Allen lent a hand. She insisted that Suzie could read if she wanted to and sat her down to the task. One day Howard came home, and to his surprise, Suzie was able to read. "I put a copy of Tom Wolfe in her hands," he said, "and she sounded out the words." He remained mystified as to how "Katherine's" system had actually worked.

In addition to intellectual stimulation, the children were exposed to the heavily sensual atmosphere of the New Orleans climate. Howard and Katherine loved to take walks. When Anne was small, Katherine sometimes took her and Suzie to Audubon Park, several miles down St. Charles Avenue, across from Loyola University. It was a huge park, filled with massive oak trees dripping with Spanish moss, and it stimulated Anne's romantic imagination. Howard took his daughters more often to another park a few blocks from home. As he pushed them on the swings, he'd sing a song that he'd made up for them:

"Swing me high, I'll tell you why,
I like to fly up to the sky;
Swing me long and swing me strong

And I will promise, I'll not cry.
My hair whips out and I laugh and shout,
And I go swinging high
The leaves fall down and touch the ground,
And can't fly as high as I."

Sometimes these outings frightened Anne. In the evenings, the park was a dark, mysterious place. "I wanted to go to the well-lighted drugstore, for a Coke," she said.

The penchant for walking passed from father to daughter as Anne grew up exploring the streets for long distances after school, gazing at old Victorian houses. She'd spend her bus money on Coke and just wander. Anne loved the pulsing, palpable heat that was so present it seemed able to support her should she trip. With cicadas singing in her ears, she experienced a rich intersensory connection along the shaded streets, smelling the summer rain on dusty pavement, listening to the rumbling streetcar, watching trees burst into color, noticing small changes, like a green fence painted black. Highly color-sensitive, she especially loved the violet sky at sunset as streaks of red and gold shot through the puffy clouds. Different areas of the city had their own special moods that fed an emotionally coded awareness of the physicality of her world.

She had favorite houses. One was the deteriorating Nellie Fallwell house, captured in Anne's first published short story. Another was a rose-colored Greek Revival with French windows and Corinthian columns, described in *Exit to Eden.* She also kept her eye open for the house where the devil lived with his mistress, and another one inhabited by a beautiful quadroon spirit. Walking through the Garden District, she dreamed she belonged there and would one day live in a mansion. To her, houses symbolized whole worlds.

Howard was also fond of taking her through cemeteries—often at dusk—where they read the history of the city through the inscriptions. They pinpointed former city limits, determined times of plague, and counted how many firemen had lost their lives to devastating blazes. Anne loved these "cities of the dead," and the one nearest her house, Lafayette, would become the site in her fiction where the vampire Lestat hid his valuables and where the Mayfairs owned a family vault. "I thought the cemeteries were beautiful," she said.

New Orleans cemeteries are unlike graveyards in the rest of the country. European architectural influences coupled with a high water table have inspired tombs that are predominantly aboveground. Even those considered "in the ground" have a retaining wall that allows burial only as deep as three feet, and rest partially above the ground. Old caskets were made of cast iron hermetically sealed against water at the time of interment; however, when the water table rose in times of heavy rain or hurricanes, they tended to float and the tombs broke open. As Anne wandered, she sometimes saw bones spilling out, but the sight did not upset her. Like other natives of New Orleans who whitewashed family tombs each year on the Feast of All Saints, she understood death to be part of life. She attended many family funerals and was not disturbed by them, although, as a result of misunderstanding a Catholic doctrine, she was afraid of being buried herself whenever she died.

"I had a childhood fear," she explained, "that we would all be in our graves, in the darkness, not moving until Judgment Day. That fear has persisted, that there's life in dead bodies, that it's locked in there and can't get out." She gave this fear to the character Jesse in her novel *The Queen of the Damned*: "When I was little, I used to think it would be like this, death. You'd be trapped in your head in the grave, with no eyes to see and no mouth to scream."

The fear never quieted, even when she realized her mistake.

5

The neighborhoods of 1940s New Orleans were interesting to a stimulus-sensitive child like Anne. Although most of the colorful street vendors from earlier years had disappeared, the few that were left impressed themselves on her memory. "There was a vegetable man who came by in a truck and parked at the corner. My mother would go out to buy tomatoes and get into terrific arguments with him. His name was Mr. Serio, and he also sold shrimp and crabs. I also have faint memories of a banana man who passed on a wagon, singing, 'Ba-na-na-na-na!' We had milk, pie, and bread delivered, and the ice cream man would walk by with his little cart, pushing it by hand, ringing the little bell."

As in most southern traditions, family was an important part of the O'Briens' social dynamic. Across the Garden District in the Irish Channel lived many relatives. Anne understood the importance of family. "She would get on the phone," said Tamara, "and pick their brains for hours."

"I don't remember a time," Anne admitted, "when I didn't care about family. I cared about who they were. I was very hungry to have a family and I was envious of kids who had large families that they were in constant contact with. I wish we'd had more contact with ours." Anne became close with a cousin on Howard's side, Billy Murphy. With her sisters, she spent a lot of time at the Murphy residence, since Katherine was frequently ill from her dependence on alcohol and Howard often worked late.

Together, the cousins listened to radio shows like "Inner Sanctum" and "The Shadow." Billy remembered how the programs scared Anne. "She was afraid of things that came from the imagination—the things you couldn't see."

He also recalled a Halloween party. "There were about fifteen or twenty kids, and we made our own costumes, so there were lots of sheets. Anne and Suzie dressed as gypsies." The party ended at nine-thirty, but Howard was scheduled to work until eleven, so Anne and Suzie stayed behind with Billy. It was an unusually cold Halloween night. They turned out the lights in the front room and gathered around an ornate gas heater to tell ghost stories.

"The ghost stories were about local places like the Garden District," said Billy, "where huge old houses were run down. There was even Spanish moss on the trees, for atmosphere. We would try to see who could top the other—who could make their story scarier." Suzie, equipped with numerous stories that she had read in the library, outdid everyone, while Anne mostly sat quietly and listened. At least she seemed to be listening; but, said Billy, "When she *did* tell stories, it would make your eyes jump from your head. Anne had all the creepy tales from the crypt. She told one that Halloween about someone rising from the grave. I had dreams of someone coming back from the dead and knocking at my door and wanting to come in."

Their love of ghost stories took them to the old public library on Lee Circle, first introduced to them by Howard. "That was the most wonderful thing that ever happened," said Anne. It was a dark place and cool in the summer. Anne went to the desk and asked for books about big houses and creepy things. The cousins discovered *Frankenstein, The Phantom of the Opera,* and Sherlock Holmes. Eventually they moved on to Algernon Blackwood and M. R. James. This kinship led Anne to predict a future for them that would have supernatural overtones. "We were eleven or twelve at the time," Billy said, "sitting out on my front porch. We decided that one of us should write stories about ghosts and another of us should be a ghost hunter." As it turned out, Anne wrote the stories and Billy eventually became an amateur ghost hunter.

Anne was still a slow, thoughtful reader, feeling that she could never match Suzie's voracious pace, so she listened as Suzie told her what she'd read. Anne did discover two stories, however, that especially gave her chills: *Jane Eyre* and *Great Expectations*. Dickens became a favorite author. Paying keen attention to character and to the struggle between good and evil, he modeled for Anne complicated mixtures of ambiguous images, showing that true goodness can be achieved within oneself, that evil and good are never pure, and that even in triumph there can be loss.

Even the school day provided dark mystery. The pre-Vatican II Catholic church emphasized mysticism and immortality through a bloody Christ who promised kinship through salvation. Each day involved rituals of dark and violent spirituality. The emphasis was on a just and avenging God, and reminders of sin were rampant in long lists of impure thoughts and behavior that made the blood race. Everything was black or white, and the dark side of the human soul was presented as potentially dangerous and menacing. Purification was available only through ritual penances and surrendering oneself to God. The physical body was frowned upon, hidden for the "holy ones" by long habits that made the priests and nuns appear asexual, and the atmosphere was solemn, vibrating with the tension of the forbidden.

The Mass was chanted in secretive Latin and included Holy Communion—the central dramatic event, called Transubstantiation, where the bread and wine transformed into the physical flesh and blood of Christ. The *essence* of the physical substance was mystically changed and made holy. It was not a symbolic gesture but believed to be a genuine physical event. Its centrality commanded attention, and for a child, gullible and attuned to the frightening and seductive mystery, the ceremony left its mark. Anne incorporated this powerful imagery into much of her later fiction.

6

When Anne was twelve, she was confirmed in the church. She was to take a new name, and she followed family tradition by adopting the name of a saint coupled with the name of an aunt, who was a nun: Alphonsus Liguori. She became Howard Allen Frances Alphonsus Liguori O'Brien. "I was honored to have my aunt's name," she said, "but it was my burden and joy as a child to have strange names."

Taking a new name was not that unusual for her because she had been doing it since first grade. She once had adopted the moniker Gracie Lee, then Ellen, and her father had called her Frances Thursiderry for fun. "I changed my name in grammar school all the time," Anne admitted. "I thought it was glamorous. I think I quit changing it by the fifth grade. I don't know how I settled on Anne. I remember just liking the name and taking it."

Billy Murphy had resisted. "Anne used to come over and say, 'I want to be called this today,' and I'd say, 'Knock that off. You're Howard Allen.' " Others had admired her independence. Her Aunt Alice had supported her.

The other sixth graders joined Anne for the auspicious occasion of taking her official religious names. "It was called the Big Communion," Anne offered, "because you wore a white dress, veil, and a wreath similar to what you wore on your First Communion, or Little Communion. We wore very fancy white dresses and carried prayer books and rosaries, and little bags made by relatives. Usually the rosary was given to you as a gift and you carried it in your bag. The bishop came, and you'd go up the aisle, one by one, and be anointed and declared a soldier of Christ. Then you were given the additional name."

The church year spun out in similar rituals, and there were moments of excitement for the children. May Day featured a May procession, and the Feast of All Saints followed Halloween. At Christmas the most colorful vestments were donned by the priests for the midnight Mass. The boys wore red cassocks for procession and the girls wore white. The ceremonies left a vivid impression on Anne, which she described later in several novels.

Between Christmas and Easter was Mardi Gras. It was not a religious holiday, but had loose connections to the church, since it allowed the citizens of New Orleans to party hard before the days of solemn meditation brought on by Lent. Anne's family invited cousins to watch the Mardi Gras parade that came down St. Charles Avenue in front of their house. "We had an annual thing," said Patt Moore. "There were few parades that came quite that far, because most of them stopped around the Lee Circle area [about a mile down St. Charles]. One particular parade came past their home on Sunday afternoon." The children often made elaborate costumes, but Anne recalled only one: "It was a little princess costume made of pongee or silk, with a crown that was still wet with paint when I put it on my head. It was painful to get off because my hair stuck to it."

Anne was afraid of the Comus parade, which went out at night with drums beating and floats surrounded by flambeau carriers with their blazing torches. She stayed in the house, trembling, while the others went out. She was afraid of fire and was certain that the flambeaux would incinerate one of the floats. Later, her fear of fire became even more intense.

Easter lasted three days, and the mystery of Christ was stressed. The statuary in the church was draped with purple jersey between Ash Wednesday and Holy Saturday—the day before Easter Sunday. The Lenten ritual, lasting six weeks, included extra chanting on Fridays after Mass and "making the nine churches," a ritual in which Anne participated once. Penitents went around the city and visited nine designated churches. "The crucifix of Christ would be on the altar," Anne explained, "and people would come up and kiss it. Then the priest would wipe it with a rag, and the next person would kiss it." Lent was broken by renouncing the devil and celebrating Easter.

To intensify the mystery, the priest faced the altar and did things only the altar boys witnessed. He was like a magician. Life-size statues of the saints stared from vantage points throughout the church and made a deep impression on Anne: "Being good always seemed to interest me.

I loved the saints for their excessiveness, their going out on a limb, their willingness to fight everybody, the misjudgment they endured."

She also became intrigued with the blend of masculine and feminine in the sculptures and stained glass portraits. "Most people who grew up in a Catholic environment didn't pay any attention to the church. I was always fascinated. I would look at the figures of the angels in the church—those huge marble statues in the back that looked like both woman and man combined. Androgyny is everywhere in the Catholic religion. Most of the saints are androgynous. In fact, most representations of Christ present him as androgynous, weeping, with hips that are defined. Over and over you're confronted with it. The stained glass windows contained pictures of very feminine-looking male saints and men who weep over and over again. The priests and nuns are very androgynous figures, and the nuns who taught the boys were masculine-looking. A lot of it comes from the Renaissance obsession with androgyny in art that got blended into Catholic traditions. The Italians dreamed up the androgynous, ideal male, and I grew up in a parish that was run by an Italian order, so I think I got more of that than people who grew up in a Jesuit parish."

Her attunement to the ambiguity of sex may have prepared her for becoming a novelist, since creative personalities often exhibit great tolerance for androgyny.

Being exceptionally alert to physical stimuli, and having an active fantasy life, Anne felt sexual stirrings toward the dark and lurid images that confronted her every day in her spiritual exercises. "You sit there and you imagine what Christ felt as he walked down the street carrying the cross," Anne explained, "or what the thorns felt like going into his forehead, or the nails into his hands. You had to use your imagination to make the leap." In the hushed room, excited by colors and music, aroused by the priest's covert activities and the alternating Latin rhythms, listening to the bells, smelling incense, feeling the warmth of candles contrasting with the cryptlike coldness of stone floors, putting her body in various positions of humility, imagining the extremes of Christ's suffering, Anne began to experience an erotic connection to the rituals that initiated her into this contained world. There was a magic to the ceremonies that excited her, especially with the promise of spiritual transcendence and union with the infinite. The excitement mixed with thrills of fear to provoke a special physical tension. It fed her fantasy world with sexual overtones, even though she had no experience with explicit sexual imagery. "It was always there in one form or another," she admitted.

Later, in the novel *Exit to Eden,* Anne would have her protagonist, Lisa, say, "I've had the feeling most of my life that I was a little more physically there than most people." Lisa, who experienced an orgasm at the age of eight, adds, "I couldn't figure out what childhood was supposed to be. I had dark, strange sexual feelings when I was very little. I wanted to be touched and I made up fantasies."

"That was sort of based on me," said Anne. "although I did not have an orgasm when I was eight. I always felt that I *was* more physically there, even as a child. I had a great feeling of sensually and sexually responding to things."

It was in the sixth grade that she was introduced to sex education. The priest came to religion class and spent a half hour with the girls while the boys played outside, then spent half an hour with the boys. They were taught that sex was beautiful but also tainted. There was no context in either church or family for understanding a child who experienced strong sexual stirrings and fantasies. Anne was made to feel unfeminine, as if it were inappropriate for girls to experience what was natural for boys.

"I was pretty repressed," she admitted. "If they said it was a sin to have dirty thoughts, I'd agree with them. If they said it was sin to touch yourself, I'd agree with them. All of this was repressed, except for a couple of occasions when I discovered things, but then I just went to confession and that was the end of it. I never dreamed of discussing things with children my age, so I had no idea what they were feeling. My mother always said such feelings were normal but sinful and I shouldn't do them. She taught me that I should never kiss a man unless I was married to him. Maybe she stressed this out of fear, but she seemed to mean it. Yet she also insisted that sex was beautiful and natural, and she could be amazingly tolerant. I remember her being angered by the furor over Marilyn Monroe posing for a nude calendar. My mother thought people were being unkind, that what Marilyn had done was understandable."

Such double messages from home and the church proved to be both a deterrent and a stimulant. Anne understood that she was sinning, and took pains to suppress her feelings and imagination, but she also found such thoughts entertaining. As a result of the excitement and dread of participating in the forbidden, and anticipating possible punishment, she had sexual fantasies with a masochistic flavor. "I've had those fantasies since I was very little. I think lots of children do. Some children find that stuff sexy right off, and some don't."

7

What sort of children emerged from such an unusual atmosphere? Suzie and Anne had received the benefit of Katherine's sole attention for several years before Tamara was born, during Katherine's most steady, visionary period, and their personalities developed in different directions.

"Anne was feisty and intense," Patt Moore remembered. "When I asked her why she had changed her name, she looked at me as if I were some sort of idiot, and said, 'I just did.' "

"Anne fought back constantly," Alice said. "She fought everybody—the teachers at school, me, my mother, my father. She could con any of them, too. She was afraid of a lot of things, and her reaction to fear was to attack. She liked to dominate situations that threatened her. She was also a line-drawer. She drew a line, went only that far, then turned and walked away."

"She was always full of the most startling expressions," said her father. "For example, once she and Suzie and another little girl were playing in the backyard, and I heard wailing and weeping. I ran back to see what was the matter, and Anne was standing there with her hands on her hips, and she said, 'I'm playing with them and I don't want to be an Indian, but they make me be an Indian, and even though I'm an Indian, they won't let me be bullet-proof!' "

As feisty as she was, Anne did not play roughly. She resorted to reason to win an argument and relied on her intelligence. When she wanted to learn chess, she borrowed a book from the library. Proud of her effort, Howard bought her a chess set, and within two weeks she was able to beat him soundly.

Curly-haired Suzie (Alice) was a wild and boisterous child, described by Howard as "a creature of impressions and feelings," who was always ready to climb the yew tree in the yard and shoot at imaginary Indians coming down the street. She knew about football and baseball, and proved her mettle once by beating the devil out of a boy in the neighborhood who had yet to be bested by any of the other boys. Anne was more timid, despite her audacious temperament. She yearned to follow her older sister up the tree but could not. "Suzie would stand at the top, screaming and yelling," said Anne. "I wanted to climb, and it was very frustrating. I tried but I'm not physically obstreperous. I don't like heights."

Suzie was also fond of horseback riding, but Anne discovered right away that she was afraid of horses. "Suzie would save her money and go ride," said Anne. "She fell off and injured herself once, and got right back on. The one time I rode, the horse began to run and I jumped off."

Howard interpreted Anne's reticence as disinterest, even as an expression of her softer femininity, but it was actually fear. Anne was like her mother in that respect. While Suzie brazenly went about her business, Anne suffered from inexplicable terrors.

Often her parents sent her down the block to pick up something from the local store. On windy days Anne stood in front of the house, too frightened to walk past a slender palm tree in a doctor's yard that bent over with the force of the wind. "It always looked like it was falling," she said. Sometimes Howard walked with her, but other times she braved it and walked alone, setting precedent for the way she would eventually approach her fears through fiction. At the corner, in front of the store, an old man sold newspapers. He'd invite Anne to put her hand into his change pouch to jingle the coins so that she wouldn't be so afraid. It always made her feel better. Him, too, no doubt.

Like her mother, she was also terrified of the dark—the realm of things threatening and forbidden. She and Suzie were both afraid of ghosts. But nothing gave her a scare like a good monster movie.

The old Granada Theater was two blocks behind the house, and Anne and Suzie were frequent customers, sometimes with their mother, sometimes alone. There was a movie house downtown and they dressed in their Sunday best—hat and dress, white socks, and black, patent-leather shoes—but the Granada was their home base, where all the kids in the neighborhood went.

"I thought about being a movie star all the time when I was little," said Anne. "I remember in first grade wanting to be a movie star, and I'd have lengthy discussions with people about it. That lasted through the second grade. I wanted to be *everything*. I wanted to be an explorer and go to the Amazon, be a mad scientist, and go in a rocket ship to the moon." Yet it was the darker film images that left the deepest mark.

When Anne was seven, she and Suzie went together to the movies. The special feature was the 1932 black-and-white film, *The Mummy,* starring Boris Karloff.

The two girls paid their money and settled into the front row—a habit Anne adopted for life. On the screen a whirling globe announced "Universal Pictures," followed by an ancient Egyptian pyramid. Credits rolled by, backed by eerie music, hieroglyphics, and pictures of Egyptian women with their arms angled away from their bodies. Across the screen flashed the words, "This is the Scroll of Thoth. . . ."

Anne stared, breathing hard, as three men appeared on screen, discussing their find at the archaeological dig that day. They crossed over to a mummy in a coffin leaning against a wall and speculated from the contorted face beneath the rotting bandages that it had been buried alive.

Buried alive! A thrill of horror shot through Anne, tugging on her fear of the grave.

The men dusted off a box and read the curse that warned of death to any man who dared to open it. Two of them left to discuss the implications of this curse, and the third grew too curious to wait. He opened the box and discovered a scroll. Over his shoulder Anne could see the mummy in its case. She sensed something coming. The music intensified. The mummy opened its eyes, then moved its arms, lurching toward the unsuspecting archaeologist. Anne burst into tears and fled to the lobby.

Suzie was shocked, then angry. She stomped out after her sister to drag her back in before she missed much more. Anne resisted. She wanted to go home. She even refused to stay in the lobby with that creepy music coming through the doors. Suzie had no choice but to take her home. The same thing happened with the next mummy feature, and Howard came and rescued her.

For Anne, the mummy had been firmly implanted in her subconscious as the monster to be most feared. Even into adulthood, she would be unable to conjure up images of a corpse wrapped in tattered rags, shambling along, without a trace of the same terror she experienced in the theater that night.

8

When Howard was promoted to a training position, he began teaching personnel officers in employee and management relations. It meant he had to travel, but it also increased his enjoyment of his job. During one of his absences, Katherine visited her sister in California.

"Kay came out with Suzie and Anne," brother-in-law George Daviau said. "She never wrote a letter or called. She just walked in."

Anne was impressed with her aunt's house. "Our house was cold, chaotic, and gloomy, and she lived in a modern house where everything was bright and cheerful. She had a big, sunny backyard. It was a better life altogether. Uncle George drove a nice car and they'd royally entertain us."

Aunt Alice also introduced Anne to beautiful dolls, something she wanted but did not get from her parents, who had to watch their money. "My aunt would send us these pretty little storybook dolls when we were little," said Anne, " and they always got broken. I don't recall ever having other dolls, but I remember loving them." The childhood desire would one day become an obsession to collect dolls.

In 1949, when Anne was eight, another daughter was born. Karen was tiny—only three pounds at birth—and there were complications with her health. Katherine had continued drinking throughout the pregnancy and felt guilty. She believed her relatives were critical of her behind her back for having a child so late in life, and this suspicion was confirmed in her mind when family members came frequently to check on the child's health. Katherine threw herself into a protective frenzy over Karen, following her around with food to get her to eat. However, she also continued to drink, and her blackouts caused periods of terrible neglect, despite her intentions to give her baby the best treatment.

Then tragedy struck. Mamma Allen died.

In her eighties, she had been ill for some time, and Alice had come from California with young Allen to be with the family matriarch in her last days. She had received many visitors and Katherine had taken charge to see that no one taxed her mother's strength. "I got a sense of this incredible social structure," said Allen. "These ladies were movers and shakers in their community." Mamma Allen had rallied, and Alice had gone back home. A few days later, however, Mamma Allen died.

"I remember her funeral quite vividly," said Anne. "It was at Leitz-Egan's on Magazine Street. I remember kissing her good-bye and going to the cemetery. I don't think I knew what death really was. I remember later realizing she was dead and crying. I think my mother was terribly upset. I recall her saying, 'Take the flowers or people will steal them as soon as we're gone.' So we took some of the flowers from the grave."

It became clear at once that Mamma Allen had been the organizing force in the household. Things fell into greater disarray as Katherine became more dependent on the bottle to deal with her anxiety over raising her children. To make matters worse, she sensed people talking about her, and she took pains to hide her problem and pretend that everything was all right. Yet in the intimacy of the immediate family, things were not all right. Katherine could not always be trusted to make meals regularly or to keep up discipline, and Howard began to work longer hours, staying away. He took a second full-time job with Western Union, working from six o'clock in the evening until three the next morning.

For the girls, this freedom was an advantage. They could do whatever they pleased. "Since we were four girls with no brothers," said Anne, "and there was no emphasis on housekeeping, we did not grow up with any notion of ourselves as lesser because we were female, or people who had to be servants to men."

Their freedom soon expanded to include the entire city when Howard bought a black three-speed bicycle. "Once they got wheels," he said, "the entire city of New Orleans became their hunting ground. I just let them take off."

"I felt New Orleans was safe for me," said Anne, "and I could go anywhere I wanted. I never got in any scrapes. I never was scared."

Anne had a friend named Lucy Provosty, who ran around with her all over the city. She was an easygoing girl from an old plantation family in Louisiana. They met at the trolley stop when they were both ten years old. Lucy glanced over at the girl in the dark bobbed hair, recognized Anne's school uniform, and introduced herself. They began to walk home from school together and soon were riding, two on a bike, around the city and out as far as Lake Pontchartrain. Frequently they visited the docks on the Mississippi to watch men unload fish.

They became best friends and confidants, and Anne told Lucy about characters in her dream worlds. "We were close," Lucy recalled, "but we were also kind of separate because that's the way Anne wanted it." Lucy perceived that Anne lived by a strict moral code and was always well informed. "Anne's parents never held back information," she said. "If I wanted to know something, Anne was always my best source." Anne thought it strange that Lucy couldn't just go ask her own parents. She did not realize how progressive Howard and Katherine really were. From Lucy's perspective, Anne appeared to have a closer relationship with her mother than did her sisters, although Anne did not get the high grades Tamara got and could not read as fast as Suzie—qualities Katherine admired.

Anne read Lucy stories she had written. "Anne wrote one every day," said Lucy. "We had talk time and story time." Together they made up adventures, with Anne encouraging Lucy to go along. "She could sell snowballs to Eskimos," Lucy said. Once they went downtown to the Monteleone Hotel and came up with an idea to write a threatening note. Anne wrote it and dropped it on a desk. Then they took seats in the lobby. "Pretty soon," said Lucy, "all these people were running around. We thought they would know a kid wrote it, but they had no idea. One guy was really frantic. We felt bad, but we couldn't go tell."

Another time they spotted a mysterious man while they sat in a park on Magazine Street. The man had an unusual face, so they followed him, tracking him to a bar and waiting across the street until he came out. He moved fast and they ran after him until he disappeared into a greasy-spoon restaurant, emerged with a package, and returned to his starting point to eat his dinner. The adventure was over, but the man's activities and identity continued to plague Anne's imagination.

The girls took their religious training seriously. They were going to follow the example of St. Therese, the Little Flower, a young French nun who proclaimed the "little ways" of achieving union with God. She had been a martyr and had subjected herself to self-inflicted brutality to gain a higher spiritual state. "Anne was really taken with this," said Lucy. Anne had also read about St. Rose de Lima and St. Teresa of Avila and had become so passionate about prayer that Howard turned a dysfunctional, three-by-five-foot bathroom in the back of the house into an oratory. He painted the walls gray and Anne installed a prie-dieu, mounting red, blue, and white statues of the saints on doiley-covered tables. Anne did not keep her own room as neat as she kept this private place. "She would spend long hours in there," said Howard, "kneeling and praying."

"Her oratory," said Lucy, "was a place of peace, somewhere she had to get away to and a place where she suffered a lot. It was a cheerful, peaceful, and necessary retreat."

Anne remembered it as a time of intense meditation, although it developed in her the desire to devote herself to religion. Her fantasy world was soon filled with religious figures. "All the characters were going into convents," said Anne, "or they were religious brothers or priests." One character was a boy named Chris, who had been a child-genius and who possessed priest-like qualities.

Some relatives believed Anne would follow two aunts who were nuns and a cousin who was a priest. "I wanted to be a nun," said Anne. "It was part of my going to extremes. I believed I was going to be a Carmelite and a saint." She stayed in her oratory late into the evening, until, according to Lucy, her phobia of rats and roaches took over and drove her out.

"Anne's temperament was such," said Howard, "that when she embraced something, she had to exercise real restraint not to become a zealot or fanatic."

She would transplant these traits into a character in her first published novel, who spent hours in his own oratory. "Prayer was what mattered to him," she wrote, "prayer and his leatherbound Lives of the Saints."

Later, she would develop the character Lestat around the same intense urge to be good. He knelt on the floor with his arms in the form of a cross and told God he would do anything, suffer any torment, if only God would make him good.

Lucy was not quite as keen as Anne on the idea of becoming a nun. "I tried to hang in there with her when she wanted to be a saint, but I was pretty much on the outskirts." One thing she did know was that Anne's obsessions ran their course. "Anne's interests and moods went through what I would call time frames. If you didn't like where you were, you could at least be sure that changes were coming." The phase did eventually pass for Anne, but lasted a year.

Suzie became involved with the Little Sisters of the Poor, a religious order that observed a vow of poverty and opened a home for indigent and elderly people. Anne begged to be taken along and became enamored of the organization. It was clean and orderly, in contrast to her home, and she was instantly the center of attention. Each day after school and sometimes in the mornings, they went to the home to take care of the elderly. Occasionally Lucy came along. "What amazed me," said Lucy, "was the really good communication Anne had with the nuns. She was always able to talk to grown-ups about the things she was interested in."

Howard felt the intense commitment to good works was a redemptive act for Katherine, but he was unprepared for Anne's zeal. She begged him to allow her to enter the order. He resisted. "I told her to wait until she finished high school. She didn't become a Little Sister of the Poor."

9

One day Howard brought home a tape recorder and it soon consumed everyone's attention as he invited each of his daughters to take turns singing into the microphone. Anne became the director, letting each of her sisters know when it was their turn. She herself sang with confidence and recited poetry with a clear, strong voice. During one recording, Katherine had to break in and gently point out, "Everyone should have a turn. Karen has had one turn, Tamara two, Suzie two, and Anne has had fourteen." They sang religious songs that they knew from school and had a great deal of fun playing them back and listening to their voices. Howard also recorded records from the library.

Anne loved music, and as she grew older, she developed musical aspirations. She plunked out notes on the piano, but it was the violin that caught her attention. "It struck me," she said, "as the most poignant, the most searing, the most emotional instrument." Hearing Isaac Stern in concert, she became obsessed with becoming a musical genius. "My idea was to be a violinist," she said, "but the early expression of it was to read every book in the library about violins." She finally bought a used violin from a pawnshop and took lessons. "It was a terrible struggle. I didn't have a good ear. I would go every Saturday for the lessons, but I didn't have the discipline to practice. The teacher was very generous. She went on giving me lessons when my father no longer wanted to pay for them. But she told me that if I really worked, by the end of high school I could play in the orchestra. That wasn't enough for me. I wanted to be Isaac Stern."

Her father also discouraged her. "I was premature," he admitted. "I told her she did not have enough strength in the fingers of her left hand. I should have let her discover it for herself. She had such an indomitable drive that when she makes up her mind, she wants to go forward. I should have let her go. She would either have learned how to play or given up on her own." Her teacher also told her that she could not read quarter notes. Thwarted by so little encouragement, she withdrew from the lessons. "It was a crushing disappointment," said Anne. She sold the instrument back to the pawnshop, but the beautiful sound had invaded her subconscious and filled her with longing. Her love for the violin would emerge in her novel *The Vampire Lestat,* and, more autobiographically, in Michael from *The Witching Hour*. It also would be the impetus behind Anne's discovery of the subject for her third novel, *Cry to Heaven*.

Anne also took art lessons one summer. She became quite adept at drawing and painting, and even painted a portrait of her sister Tamara. Her first published story, years later, was about herself as an art student.

Primarily, however, Anne was exploring her talent for writing. She had written a "novel" at the age of five, composed of one sentence spelled by her grandmother: "LeeLee was sitting in her chambers." Later she put together a family newspaper and became a playwright. She cajoled her sisters into acting out the parts. Suzie was reluctant, but Tamara played any role and even ad-libbed. "I would always play an emotionally charged role," said Tamara. "Like someone caught in a conflict. I was also the beautiful girl. I loved those plays and I could go with them; there was a lot I could do with them. I don't know that any other family would play them with the intensity that we did. We'd spend hours on them."

The girls sold tickets to Howard and Katherine, and sometimes Lucy came to watch.

"Tamara and Karen were very eager," Howard said. "Tamara would always ask Anne to write a part so Karen would be her little slave." Karen was too little to memorize parts, so Anne often dressed her in a raincoat with the sleeves hanging over her arms to make her look like a ghost or a mummy. "There was always a dead mummy in the next room," said Tamara, "that would get up and walk, and I was always some horrified attendant."

One of the plays was called "The Mummy Ghost." Another was based on the fairy tale "Rapunzel." "Tamara would bring in Mitey Joe [Karen]," said Howard, "and she was supposed to climb up Rapunzel's hair. Only it was changed to 'Repulsive, Repulsive, let down your hair.' "

Anne ended every play by killing the actors. "We didn't have curtains," Anne explained. "My father got very critical of the violence, but it seemed the best way to end it."

"We heard," said Alice, "that this is why Shakespeare killed everyone in the last act." Since *Julius Caesar* was the inspiration, it was a logical step.

In the fifth grade, Anne wrote her first work of length in a notebook. It was about two people who lived on Mars. "They were grown people," said Anne, "Mark and Maureen Michael. They were brother and sister, and they lived in this very elaborate castle-like house. They had a spaceship and they went to earth and picked up this guy named Jimmy. Then they let Jimmy off—he was a good friend—and drove their spaceship into the sun. The terrible secret was that Mars still had slavery. So these two committed suicide. They just couldn't live there."

She also wrote a story called "Caesar's Ghost," which she read to her sister Alice. "There was no real plot," said Alice, "just a series of episodes. Anne placed the ghost of Lucrezia Borgia in a haunted castle. She invented Caesar's ghost, which was the ghost of two or three of the more corrupt caesars. He looked like a bed sheet. He was continually ending up in someone's wash. One time he hitched a ride on an airliner—on the wing—and he arrived in a very disheveled condition. Lucrezia was always rescuing him from some kind of situation, when he was hung up on a line or getting used as someone's cleaning rag or something like that."

"For as long as I can remember," said Tamara, "Anne wanted to be a novelist. Her head was filled with stories to tell. She came home and wrote, and it got her through every experience. She's as thorough a writer in her heart and soul as anyone I've ever met."

Howard and Katherine were delighted, and they watched over Anne's new direction with a critical eye, which startled Suzie. When they judged her efforts by adult standards, urging her toward betterment, Suzie felt they were too harsh, but Anne always asked what they thought and continued to write. It seemed that this form of self-expression came closer to her fantasies than did music, and thus became for her a more natural and intimate way of dealing with her world. Later she would say of writers, including herself, "We dramatize our psychological problems in terms of stories."

She wrote a story in seventh grade based on a movie she had seen that had starred Stewart Granger. It was about a safari. "They were going after some big jewel," she said, "and when they got the jewel, it opened up, and the elixir of life was inside." That same elixir would show up in her eleventh novel, *The Mummy*. Anne passed this story around to her friends at school. She also wrote about the effect on a family of an unnamed hurricane from 1947 that had taken down several large trees, one of her special fears.

Suzie would bring books home, and one day she read to Anne a story about a vampire called "The Renegade," in which the vampire was presented as a sensitive protagonist. However, it was another vampire story that left an impression on Anne strong enough to recall after her own published successes.

When she was eleven years old, she heard the family discussing a story called "Dress of White Silk," by Richard Matheson. It was told in first person, from the point of view of a child who wants to show her mother's treasured white dress to a friend. When the friend shows disgust, the child's vampire nature is revealed in her revenge. "I never forgot that story," said Anne. "I thought it was quite wonderful. I didn't actually read the story, I just remember everyone talking about it. I wanted to get into the vampire. I wanted to know what it was like to be the interesting one—the point of view of the person right in the center of it all."

The vampire image was strengthened later when she saw the 1936 film *Dracula's Daughter,* starring Gloria Holden. "That's the first time I saw vampires as a kid. I loved the tragic figure of Dracula's daughter as the regretful creature who didn't want to kill but was driven to do it.

The tragic dimension is at its fullest, most eloquent and articulate in Dracula's daughter because she herself was articulate and intelligent."

10

Katherine was getting worse. She was often on binges, drinking herself into insensibility, and eating aspirin by the handful.

"She did all her drinking secretly in her room," Anne remembered, "and we would know it was happening because she would be completely passed out. I never knew her to party, to have drinking buddies, or to enjoy a beer with anyone. She just drank in secret, and she would be like Sleeping Beauty, lying there day after day, out cold. We'd find the bottles, but I never really saw her doing it."

However, Katherine's night drinking did extend into the daytime, and the girls never knew what they might find when they came home from school. They felt like they were harboring a terrible secret. On several occasions Katherine smoked in bed and set fire to the mattress. They'd discover it burned, smelly, and wet from water used to douse it. Once Suzie had to put out a fire herself.

Perhaps because of the uncertainty and danger inherent in Katherine's behavior, Anne was deathly afraid of fire. This had started as a child when a fire burned down a house across the street. She had seen huge flames in the windows of the green Victorian as the fire engines gathered, and the scene gripped her with such fear that she became hysterical. "I remember screaming and screaming and crying, and people bathing my forehead." Later she overheard her father observe that the house was so dry, with such bad wiring, that it could go up at any time. The comment settled uneasily in her mind, underlined by her mother's carelessness with her cigarettes.

This phobia peaked late one night when Anne was in sixth grade. A friend of Suzie's named Kay Johnson came over. She was an artist living in the French Quarter and they called her Woody. She began to describe an incident she had heard about.

"They were discussing the measles epidemic that took over a hospital," said Anne. "Woody mentioned that even the burn cases had gotten it. A shiver of horror went through me. One of them lit a cigarette and I couldn't even look at the match."

Anne took to her bed for a week. She remembered "shivering and crying and being afraid." She immersed herself in books about Raggedy Ann and Andy to take her mind off the horrific vision of burned skin. "I kept seeing images of Tamara and Karen trapped in the living room, and the living room on fire, and my mother drunk, trying to get down the hall and coughing. They were screaming on a couch surrounded by flames. That image produced such paralytic terror that I kept seeing it over and over again. I was terrified that a fire engine would pass by the house and I'd see it or hear it and go crazy."

Katherine sat with her and explained that there was nothing to be afraid of. Anne eventually recovered, but the fear of fire did not leave her.

"Other times it would just get a hold of me," she said. "There was a movie campaign during Fire Prevention Week, and they kept showing this horrible image of a skeletal horseman riding through the night with a torch in his hand. I was horrified by it. I couldn't shake the feeling of gloom or depression that would come over me."

Fire is a prominent feature of many of her novels. The vampires are destroyed by fire, and they use fire as weapons against one another. Cleopatra is consumed by a ball of flame and burned in *The Mummy,* but Anne faced her greatest challenge in *The Witching Hour,* where she had to describe how witches were burned alive during the Inquisition.

There were other tensions in the home. Suzie and her mother bickered and fought, and sometimes Katherine threatened things she did not mean, or accused Suzie of activities with boys that she only imagined.

"I said dreadful things to her," Alice remembered, "and regretted them as soon as I'd said them. It was nightmarish. I loved her and pitied her; I identified with her struggle."

One particularly vicious argument was over Suzie's need for glasses. The way Suzie perceived it, Katherine could not bring herself to admit that any of her children had deficiencies and would not allow Suzie to get a pair. Her resistance may have been an unconscious sense of deficiency as the daughter of an alcoholic, now as out of control as her father had been, and for whom a lack of money exacerbated the deficiency. In her children she could believe that the poison had dissipated only if they were perfect. Howard finally saw that Suzie really did need glasses, and he relented and bought them. But wearing the glasses did not ease the strain. "I always had the feeling," Alice said, "that she wanted something from me and that I could not deliver."

When relatives visited, Katherine often excused herself. They'd hear the refrigerator open and notice that when she returned, she smelled like Listerine. She became more paranoid and began to hide money around the house. Anne was quick to defend her. Despite the deteriorating conditions, she'd say, "Look how beautiful she is. You don't know what she used to be like!" She was steadfastly loyal, even though she, too, was growing weary of the constant anxiety over her mother's drinking. Something had to happen to bring this nightmare to an end. It was a miracle that Katherine was lasting as long as she was.

She was not sleeping at night and often Alice read science fiction to her. "She'd lie there," said Alice, "and I'd finally fall asleep, but she wouldn't turn out the light."

"I can remember," said Anne, "waking up in the middle of the night, wandering into her room, and seeing her there, smoking and reading on the bed. It was as if she never slept at all. She just read all night."

Katherine's condition may have influenced Anne's later affinity for vampires, who crave the warmth of blood. "I have a vague memory of talking with her about it a couple of times," Anne recalled. "I think she told me it was a craving in the blood, that her father had had it, and his father. She asked me to say the rosary. She seemed scared of it. This is such a dim memory and so unusual that I've never been quite sure of it. She and I lying on the bed, saying the rosary together, and her telling me that about the blood."

Katherine exhibited soaring, enraptured moments followed by depression, as if drained by a vampire. Gertrude Helwig, Katherine's cousin, described this inconsistency: "She would act like she was on top of the world, and she'd always manage to tell me something good, and then a phone call would come from Katherine and I'd know that things were not so good." Howard tried everything he could think of to get Katherine to stop. He tried pleading, turning his back on her, and drinking with her, but nothing seemed to work. Sometimes he lost all patience and their relationship was strained. She joined Alcoholics Anonymous briefly, but something always triggered another binge.

Things had changed. This was not what Katherine had expected from life. Perhaps the tragedy of her addiction was the result of changing times and an emphasis on domesticity for women; perhaps it was due to an unconscious identification with an alcoholic father, or to a genetic predisposition, although no one knew about such causes at the time. Katherine did not know where things had gone wrong, and slowly she became a victim to her inability to control whatever compelled her.

Howard still had two jobs. He handled the mail for the American Bank, and it required long evening hours of sorting. He was not around much to help.

Suzie withdrew, feeling that she had not lived up to Katherine's vision and, as a consequence, that she caused Katherine to drink to drown her disappointment. Having no clear sense of validation from either parent, feeling adrift, she anchored herself in books. "The environment hurt me," she explained. "I was protecting myself."

It was Anne who took charge. She tried without much success to get her elder sister involved in the household. "I was in charge all the time," Anne said. "I became the older sister because Alice was buried in books. If anyone cleaned the house, I did, or my father did, but not very much." Later, she would give to her character Lestat the self-reflection that was true of her: "I've always been my own teacher. . . .

And I must confess, I've always been my favorite pupil as well.'' But she was not happy about the responsibility thrust upon her.

She turned her attention to the younger girls and became what Howard described as ''the cohesive force,'' teaching her sisters to read and play games. She played school with Tamara, who was a good student and showed early signs of becoming a poet.

''She read to me a great deal,'' said Tamara. ''She read history, about the ancient Egyptians and mummification. She'd ask me questions and I'd give her answers.''

''I remember just absolutely loving the books I got out of the library on Egypt,'' said Anne. ''I loved the pyramids and the pharaohs and Egyptian art—the whole idea of the country.''

''I think one of the reasons Anne and I got along,'' said Tamara, ''was that her intellect was more accessible to me than anyone else's in our home—the scope of her interests and her articulateness greatly influenced me.''

They also played a game in which Tamara was Anne's ''secrumtary'' and Egyptian scribe. ''I would take notes on things she said or run errands,'' said Tamara. ''She always played the role of mentor for me.''

When Katherine's drinking got so bad that Howard finally felt that he was unable to handle it himself, they moved to 2524 St. Charles, four blocks away, where they were closer to help from the church. A massive, graceful house with pillars in front, it was owned by Catholic priests. There were three bedrooms downstairs and four upstairs, all with hardwood floors. It had been a school, a convent, and a rectory. In the front room, a former chapel was closed off. Now the house was vacant and falling apart. It was Anne and Suzie who convinced the father in charge of the house that someone should move in. ''They went over,'' Howard said, ''and told him how sad they felt about that big house. Somehow they planted it in his mind that he should ask me to rent it.'' The rent was reasonable and Howard was to keep it in good repair.

It was about this time, when Anne was fourteen, that she experienced the intrusions of adolescence. She was beginning to realize that being a girl was very different from being a boy, and it frightened and angered her. She looked to her mother, so ill and thin, and found no help.

Then one day, two months before she turned fifteen, her world was shattered.

CHAPTER THREE

CHANGES

1

It was a Sunday night toward the end of a hot July. Tamara was in the hospital with a ruptured appendix. Howard was unsure whether she would pull through, so he took the other children with him to stay with her. Katherine had been on a long binge with frequent blackouts, and Howard did not trust her alone at home while he shuttled from work to the hospital. She seemed to want to dry out, but she needed constant attention which he could not give while Tamara was sick. He asked Gertrude Sheppard, her godmother, to take her in. Gertrude and her husband, Arthur, agreed.

Katherine lay in bed all the next day, asking for beer. That was all she wanted, a nice cold beer. Gertrude was hesitant. She recognized that her godchild was in very bad shape. Katherine couldn't even keep down a mouthful of food and had become horribly thin. Finally Arthur said, "Give her a beer. What difference can it make?" So Katherine got her beer.

At three o'clock in the morning, Howard received an urgent call from Gertrude, so he went over. "I'd seen Katherine like that before," he said, "so I told Gert that, yes, she's sick, but she would get better." He returned home. A few hours later, Gertrude called again.

"I'm pretty sure Katherine is dying," she said. "Katherine herself says that she's dying."

The tone of her voice was so solemn that Howard ran to get a priest to administer Last Rites just in case. Katherine's frightening prediction that she would die in her prime spurred his feet, but by the time he arrived, she was dead. She had died in the arms of the woman who had made her christening dress, as if going full circle back home. She was forty-eight years old, the same age at which her father and grandfather had died.

Howard collapsed in shock. It seemed impossible! What had become of all their youthful dreams? He confided in Gertrude what he'd been through with Katherine's addiction, insisting that he'd loved her through it all but that it had been an incredible burden. He looked at the wedding ring on her finger as she lay on the bed and realized it was all she owned; Katherine had divested herself of all her personal possessions save that ring, in a sincere response, he felt, to the ascetic teachings of the church. She had succumbed to alcohol, yes, but in other ways she had been as devout a wife, mother, and Christian as any person he'd met. Her death was a terrible waste, a tragedy.

He delivered the news to his children. For them, it was a shock and a source of anger, grief, and shame. Katherine had been slowly killing herself for a long time and death had seemed inevitable. Yet alcohol abuse was regarded in those days as a character flaw. A person so out of control was humiliating to the families that suffered with and because of them. The children had deeply loved their mother, but what she had become had been too painful to bear. In some ways, her death was a relief—for her as well as for them.

"At that point," said Anne, "everyone wanted that situation to end. There was no hope that she'd ever stop. She was much too far gone mentally into denial—and hysteria when she was sober—and her last bender just seemed to go on forever. There was no place for her to go. She was going out of her mind. Her world had become totally unlivable for her."

"Our mother was such a victim," said Tamara. "I think the message she sent to us was 'Don't die of self-inflicted wounds like me, and don't succumb to wounds inflicted by others.' "

Despite her relief, Anne was devastated. She had not realized until her mother was gone what had been ripped from her life. "She gave me so many wonderful things," Anne said, "but above all, she gave me the belief in myself that I could do great things, that I could do anything I wanted to do. When it came to accomplishments in the world, to manner of dress, to intellectual curiosity or achievements, she gave me a sense of limitless power. She put no premium at all on conformity. I never doubted she loved me or was interested in me."

A child's union with a mother is a source of gratification and a sense of security and wholeness, as it had been for Anne in the early years. Her mother had provided structure in a world into which Anne had not been easily accepted. The sudden separation at an impressionable age, even from a mother whose love has become increasingly erratic, resulted for Anne in anxiety, anger, and a deep sense of deprivation. Living for years in an unpredictable situation beyond her control; remembering the love there once had been; developing the inevitable insecurities and needs that accompany increasing chaos; struggling to find a way to adjust and create a secure world—only to have it all climax with a loss that she could not prevent but felt she *should* have—was unbearable. Anne was left with a fragmented world that had once seemed clearly to have answers, even if they had been held together with fragile threads. How could the all-powerful God presented by the church have allowed this to happen? And why? How could a woman with such high ideals go spiraling out of control? There were no answers.

The subconscious is universally dominated by fears of loss, and coping for some individuals takes the form of holding on to the past by locking part of the self into the pre-tragedy experience. Anne wanted to remember her mother in a positive light and kept reminding herself of those earlier days. It buffered the pain while she searched for ways to recover aspects of herself blown away in the explosion accompanying the revelation of her loss. Yet unspoken fear and anger inevitably intruded. Living on a double track of past and present may provide a degree of emotional integrity during intense conflict, but soon such people feel pulled in more than one direction. Anne's memories may have spared her from facing the full force of the pain, and thus given her the resources to survive it, but suppressed suffering often returns in other forms.

There came an edge of darkness to Anne's world, an anxiety typical of children who lose a parent. It might have remained nothing more than a separation neurosis had not other events, still looming in the future, forced her further toward the horror of her loss. Eventually her inner world would unfold in novels that revealed the need to regain her mother's presence and a desire to conquer death. Many of Anne's early themes would involve young people suffering through sudden change, tragic mother figures, or the doomed embrace of a mother and child lost together, juxtaposed against immortality and other forms of power and triumph. Like Dante's hero, Anne had a journey ahead that would require descent in order to transcend.

More immediately, however, she found other ways to deal with what had happened. Although the past had been cut off as if with the brutal chop of an ax, she responded by using her intelligence and imagination to adapt. Anxiety over the lack of predictability inevitable with an alcoholic parent contributed a layer of richness and continuity to Anne's fantasy world. It had always been there for her as an expression of her active mind and now it offered a refuge, an outlet for frustration over being unable to change what had happened. She could control what went on with her characters, developing "safe" ways to express anger and resistance. Her imagination provided for her a womb in which to hide and heal, and eventually became the source for saving herself in the future from pain that threatened to overwhelm her.

The final diagnosis of Katherine's death was inconclusive. She had died of coronary thrombosis, perhaps from malnutrition, alcohol withdrawal, or from aspirating fluid into her lungs during a convulsion. Howard felt that had he been able to care for her himself, she would not have died that night, and now he had to live with that regret.

Katherine was interred in the Connel plot—her mother's family—in St. Joseph's Cemetery, after an Irish Catholic wake that lasted all day and night. Years later, Anne described such a funeral in her novel *The Witching Hour,* in its morbid beauty, with a dark-haired woman in a coffin, dead at the age of forty-eight. It was clearly the reawakening of an event through fiction that had left its mark. When the wake for Katherine was over, the family took their leave of her privately, then went to church for communion.

Howard asked the children not to discuss the situation with friends, and he withdrew from relatives on Katherine's side. They would grieve by themselves.

Anne's friend, Lucy, however, had been to the funeral. She observed about Anne afterward: "It was as if she were alone for the first time. She would be very sad and then she'd get very busy. She felt she had to be independent, so she started working on ridding herself of her fears. She learned to give herself a big hug. She would wrap her arms around her shoulders and whirl around."

Anne also took walks at night, even in the rain, and sometimes Lucy went with her. "She really felt like she was on her own," said Lucy, "and that she had to do it all. She was very thin, very tired and couldn't sleep." Anne had read about someone who overate to "compensate for a lack of affection" and she and Lucy took up the expression as a bemused comment on the state of their own lives.

Anne continued to take over household responsibilities. While not explicitly aware of how her vision was forming at that young age, she would soon resonate to the notion found in Dostoevsky and Dickens of the inadequacy of the guidance of parents and the need for self-reliance. As she later matured in her literary scope, she expressed a deeply held belief that one must become one's own parent. The theme became an emotional anchor, influenced by a mother who had fallen tragically short of her own high ideals of motherhood. Like one of her favorite characters from Dickens, David Copperfield, Katherine had been faced with the question of whether to be the victim or hero of her life. Perhaps trying too hard to be a conqueror, she had succumbed all the more easily to the other extreme of being a victim. Anne, too, would feel the pressure of this question in years to come, and her own strong personality would shade into gradations of dominance and submission that would become for her two complementary sides of a single perspective.

The summer passed as the family mourned, and then a new school year began.

2

It was 1956. A disquieting fear of teenage sex filtered into advertising and movies, and Jack Kerouac was writing *On the Road*. Although Anne was unaware of these events, they would eventually meet her head-on as she became a young adult in a decade of sweeping changes.

It seemed that life would settle now into a routine, although the familiarity of school and home was to be short-lived. During that year, however, Anne became involved in high school activities and started to go on group dates. She was in tenth grade, going back to Redemptorist High School. She took up the oboe in the school orchestra for its "exotic sound," then took piano lessons. As with the violin, neither instrument held her attention for long because it was clear to her that she would never become a great musician, and anything less was unsatisfactory.

Anne was now taking many classes in a coed atmosphere. Boys were attracted to her and she enjoyed a degree of popularity, although she was self-conscious about being small and looking like a little girl. Nevertheless, she was feeling more accepted. The sophomore class numbered about one hundred thirty students, and the teachers were the Sisters of Notre Dame.

"The Sisters of Notre Dame were very sophisticated," said Anne, "and I loved them. They were sympathetic to, and supportive of, me and Alice." It was a welcome change.

Anne stood out to classmates at Redemptorist as being highly intelligent, but since education had not raised the status of the O'Brien family economically—made obvious from their clothing—they were sometimes mocked for being pretentious. Some of the girls, however, were attracted to Anne's qualities. She made friends with Ann Bailey and Judy Murphy, who recalled what she was like.

Anne had made the first move. She'd scooted her chair back to lean on Judy's desk and talk before class, and they'd learned that they shared the same birthday. They also soon shared a crush on their homeroom teacher, a young man fresh out of Loyola.

Judy's first impression of Anne was that "she was very small, and her hair was long and dirty blond. She had a round face with a pouty bottom lip. I remember her feet being long and narrow for her body. She was different, articulate and bright. She talked about things other than boys. I'd go to her house and it made an impression on me because I'd see her father sitting in this big easy chair and there was classical music playing throughout the house. It was a different type of family."

Ann Bailey had a similar impression. She lived outside the school district, in Metairie, and she and Anne walked together to the streetcar lines on St. Charles Avenue. "She was fairly quiet and introspective," said Ann Bailey, "polite and sensitive. She knew she was out of synch with her surroundings, but I don't think she blamed her surroundings or herself, which for a teenager is pretty astute. I didn't fit with my environment, either, and I felt a bond with Anne. She was a cut above most people in the school in terms of moral sensitivity. I thought she was like an isolated ray. I felt that she knew what she was talking about."

Coming from a working family and a shotgun-style home in the Irish Channel, Judy was impressed with the large, elegant house at 2524 St. Charles. She observed, however, that the family was not wealthy. "It was obvious they did not have much money. Anne wore hand-me-downs. I remember her wearing an old, ill-fitting coat."

"Anne was very thin," said Ann. "Her clothes were not really unkempt, but it looked like a child doing the effort."

Anne and Suzie began to give parties, something they might never have done had Katherine survived, and the front room was turned into a dance floor. "It was one of the zanier parties I went to," Ann Bailey recalled about one such event. "It was a crowded party, but Anne told me that most of the people there were friends of her sister's. There were people doing the jitterbug, swinging in all directions. It was a Catholic area and some people were uncomfortable with that."

During another party, Anne showed Judy around the house, and she noticed a mural in Anne's bedroom of pastel pyramids and palm trees. Anne admitted she had painted it. There was another painting upstairs, inside a large fireplace, created by the whole family. Honoring Katherine's traditions, they still expressed themselves by using the walls of their home as canvases.

Anne's father chaperoned the gatherings and her friends were impressed with his polite manner and his involvement with his children. Neither Ann nor Judy knew where Anne's mother was because Anne did not tell them. She was quiet about her family life. "You didn't dare ask anything personal," Judy said.

Ann Bailey thought Anne seemed sensitive about her family, even a bit angry. Once she asked to stop in the house for a drink of water and was refused. "Anne indicated that this was not appropriate, as if they were not allowed to have people in when her father was not at home."

Anne was also involved in school projects. The school was raising money for a gymnasium, and students were asked to participate. Judy was impressed with Anne's enthusiasm. "We had cans given to us that said 'Redemptorist Gym Fund.' She walked through the Garden District to my house, past all these spooky trees, and we'd go up and down, knocking on doors, asking for loose change. The homerooms competed to get the most money, and the night we went out, our homeroom won the prize."

Going door to door, however, was not enough for Anne. She had another idea—not surprising, considering her later predilection for vampires. "That's when blood banks were buying blood," Judy explained. "Anne suggested the kids go home and ask their parents to sell a pint of blood and donate the money."

The kids were wild about the idea, and they went home full of optimism, calculating how much money they would raise. The adults, however, were less enthused. "We couldn't get any parents to go along with it," said Judy.

It was in high school that Anne began to feel uncomfortable with the school philosophy about women. Her mother had taught her that being a female should never stop her from doing what she wanted—that she was equal and valuable in her own right as a person. However, Katherine was no longer there to buffer Anne from the tide of chauvinism and double standards that now confronted her. "I was learning all those dreary Catholic rules," she said, "that you weren't supposed to let boys do anything or they'd think you were cheap. There was not a thing in it [Catholic sex education] geared to attending to what women were feeling; it was all about how to play your cards right so boys didn't think you were a whore. No one ever said anything about whether you were entitled to any kind of pleasure, or whether your desires represented anything other than something you weren't supposed to give in to."

Girls were not allowed the privileges of boys, and if they took them, they were mercilessly punished by horrendous peer pressures. Anne remembered when a girl in her class went parking with a boy at a place called Devil's Point. Later at a school entertainment, the girl stood up to sing a song. Anne was shocked at what happened next. "All the boys hooted from all over the auditorium, and the nuns could not shut them up. What they hooted at her was 'Devil's Point.' She had been fool enough, according to their code, to let them do things with her. I remember sitting there and being absolutely horrified." She realized at once that women weren't entitled to do what men did and get away with it. "I understood perfectly at that moment." It became more apparent that the physical intensity from her childhood was not an acceptable experience for girls.

"In early childhood," Anne said in a later reflection, "when you're sexually undifferentiated, before all this crap descends upon you, that's when you are a pure character and heading towards strengths that will manifest themselves as an adult. Adolescence is a treacherous period where all of that can fail. Up to that point in my life, I had been a free spirit and could do anything I wanted. When I was fourteen or fifteen and saw what adolescence was, it was like a storm descending. And I was horrified."

In the novella *Katherine and Jean* that Anne would write for her master's thesis, she would capture this atmosphere: "Never had anyone or any book told me that the male body was beautiful or enticing. The girls at school felt you loved a man first, and then tolerated his body. You fell in love with him because he was 'cute' and 'wonderful' and then you giggled and turned red talking about the size of the bulge in his trousers."

In her ninth novel, *Belinda,* Anne would portray a young girl who has a lesbian affair at the age of twelve and, maturing quickly, recognizes the oppressive irony that adolescents are criminals. They are not legally allowed to do what their bodies urge them to do, not even if they are emotionally equipped to handle it.

Anne might have described her adolescence at this time the way she has a character in one of her later erotic novels describe the protagonist, Lisa: "I could see that a powerful sexuality had shaped you, perhaps even embittered you." Lisa acknowledges this, that "some vital imprinting had never taken place, some message about sex being bad had failed over and over to reach its destination in my head."

There were other inequities that rankled Anne. The boys were prepped for college, but it was assumed that the girls would get married and raise families, or become secretaries or nurses. They took home economics, while boys were ushered into shop, mechanical drawing, or higher-level intellectual subjects. It was inconceivable that a girl would run for student council president. And when the gym was finally built—with funds raised by the girls as well as the boys—the girls discovered that they were allowed to use it only when the boys were finished. Anne's sensitivity to this gender bias never diminished, although it also never blossomed into a manifesto. It would eventually move her toward an attraction to relationships in which equality was the rule. However, at the moment the issue concerned her future.

In a discussion with Sister Caroline, one of the nuns Anne liked, about what she ought to do with her life, Sister Caroline insisted that one should strive to be good in everything. To Anne that was the formula for mediocrity and she intended to be *anything* but mediocre! She was not about to settle down and become just like the girls around her. She was going to get educated and *be* someone!

"I was very much into excess then," Anne recalled. "I wanted to excel at one thing!"

It was her determination to become great that kept her going in the face of social and religious pressures to succumb to submissive female roles. Already intense, she was now becoming more independent.

3

Howard was about to meet his next wife. While he was riding the streetcar to work, he spotted a woman who attracted his attention. He did not know her, but he wrote a letter explaining his interest and asking her—if she would allow him to take her to lunch—to wear the pin that he had enclosed with the note.

The woman's name was Dorothy Van Bever, and she was visiting her sister in New Orleans. The note intrigued her, so she wore the pin. After the first date, she went home to tell her sister, "This is the man I'm going to marry."

They continued to see each other, but there was a problem. Dorothy was a divorced Baptist. Such a match did not sit well with friends and family who felt that Howard should remarry in the church. However, he was happy to have found good companionship with Dorothy and he resisted the pressure.

Soon the O'Briens had to move out of the house at 2524 St. Charles and Howard found a small apartment on St. Mary's Street. One change demanded another. The place was crowded and Anne was expressing her weariness at playing mother to Tamara and Karen. "I really didn't want the responsibility," she said. "It was an enormous job. We didn't own a washing machine or a regular vacuum cleaner. And I resented taking care of them. I wanted to go out on dates."

A boarding school seemed to Howard to be a good solution. The three girls would be there five days a week getting regular meals, a good Catholic education, and staying overnight. Over Anne's protests, they were sent to St. Joseph's Academy on Ursulines Avenue, near Esplanade. It was a four-story brick building, and the boarding students slept on the top floor.

"It was like something out of *Jane Eyre,*" said Anne, "a dilapidated, awful, medieval type of place. I really hated it and wanted to leave. I felt betrayed by my father. I thought he chose it in haste. He didn't shop around." She also found many of her teachers to be rather strict.

Sister Lydia Champagne, in charge of discipline among the boarders at that time, remembered some of the rules: the girls could not leave the premises without permission or unaccompanied by one of the sisters; study halls were obligatory, although daily Mass was voluntary, since it began at 6:00 A.M.; meals were taken under supervision; uniforms were required; and the nuns kept a close eye on letters that passed to and from their charges. They questioned Anne closely about what her father wrote to her of his activities with Dorothy. It had an effect on Anne which she later fictionalized: "The fear that someone would take anything I wrote had been firmly implanted at the convent, where even my mother's letters to me were read."

The girls also performed chores like dusting and keeping their own space tidy. No rumpling the bedspreads! They were allowed to read anything in the school library, which had been carefully screened, and it was at St. Joseph's that Anne first heard of an author who would become a future literary inspiration: Ernest Hemingway. The girls had all gone to see *A Farewell to Arms* and were very taken with it. However, the nuns squashed their enthusiasm. Hemingway, they were told, was godless and immoral, not fit to be read. Anne did not return to him for several years.

Bedtime was at eight-thirty and a nun slept at either end of a long row of seventeen metal beds. Anne remembered that the girls were not allowed to take pictures of each other in baby doll pajamas, lest they provoke temptation among their schoolmates. Ironically, such rules probably gave the girls ideas they might never have otherwise had.

In the hallways they had to walk in perfect silence, with their hands at their sides. They were never invited to sit down with their teachers, and were scrutinized in their dress and makeup. As a matter of etiquette, they were to bathe each night and set their hair. Lipstick was allowed, but not too dark; if they wore excessive makeup or earrings, they were hauled into the principal's office.

"It was always like that," Anne insisted. "Always standing at attention and being mercilessly questioned about everything you did. Children were little beasts that had to be civilized. That's what the educational system was like."

She told Sister Lydia, then called Sister Peter, that she wanted to be a bohemian. The idea was shocking, since such a life was deemed immoral. Anne would write about St. Joseph's in *Katherine and Jean,* giving her protagonist, Katherine, the same rebellious streak, but it would not be until she wrote *The Witching Hour* that she would really let loose the pent-up anger she had felt about being at St. Joseph's. She hated the experience so much that she cried almost every night for a long time. One of her few pleasures was to sit in the swing in the pecan trees at twilight. "That's one of my most beautiful memories," she said. Otherwise, it was an experience she wanted to forget.

Anne had moved from a world of mingling with boys and going on car dates to one in which such activities were less accessible. She had grown close with a woman named Anne Cervini, who was married to a man who worked with Anne's father, and when she could, she biked over to see her. Anne Cervini had a brother named Dennis Percy, living in San Francisco, and she filled Anne's romantic imagination with descriptions of the city. Anne and Dennis were encouraged to become pen pals, and then Dennis came to visit. He was sophisticated for his age and laid-back. He read people like Hudson, Caldwell, and Wolfe, and was attracted to ideas. He and Anne liked each other right away.

"They had reciprocal minds," said Howard. "They could sit for hours and thresh things out."

"We had sort of a romance," Anne admitted. Dennis gave her a jade necklace that she cherished for years afterward. When he went back home, they wrote letters. Anne did not realize it at the time, but this friendship would have a significant impact on the direction of her life.

When she turned sixteen that October, she got her first job, although she had been hanging around stores since she was ten, seeking in vain to work. She waitressed on weekends in a drugstore on Canal Street and soon learned that if she had snags in her stockings, she'd get better tips because the men thought she was loose. Between boarding school and work, Anne saw little of her father, although he had made a momentous decision. He asked Dorothy to marry him.

They tied the knot in November 1957, and Howard's daughters now had a stepmother. Anne was relieved. "I hoped things would work out for them, and that he wouldn't suffer guilt." She felt it was good for her father to remarry, especially for the sake of her younger sisters, but she was not ready for what happened six months after the wedding.

4

The post office was undergoing a shake-up and was about to close the district office where Howard worked. He was offered another position in New Orleans as well as one in the Dallas regional office. He thought it over. He was estranged from the church, his mother had died of a heart attack, and few ties remained for him in New Orleans. He and Dorothy went west in May, realized they could afford to buy a house if they moved to Texas, and decided it would be nice to make a new life for themselves. In June, when the girls finished school, Howard took his family to Richardson, a suburb of Dallas.

Anne was shocked. First her mother, then boarding school, and now this! Texas! "I didn't want to be in Texas," she said. "It was very much against my will. I felt like I had been ripped out of New Orleans, and I felt homeless. I felt like I wasn't anything. I was very angry and bitter." New Orleans had been a place of pain, yes, but it had also been her world. It was where her mother had lived. She knew the landscape, the church. Things had been in place there, familiar and secure, and the differences between New Orleans—a sort of Caribbean outpost—and Dallas were striking.

The new house was a tract house with three bedrooms and a brick veneer. The rain came hard, not like the "soft Irish mist" of New Orleans, and brought with it heavy muds. There were no sidewalks, no trees, no Spanish moss. For a wanderer like Anne with a romantic imagination, this was a major disappointment. The greatest change, however, came with Anne's enrollment for her last year in high school. There were no Catholic schools.

Dallas was a Baptist area, and for the first time Anne found herself in a public school. To her great surprise, people laughed and talked in the halls, rather than walking silently, with their eyes ahead. She had been taught that no one could learn in such a chaotic environment, but obviously they could. Soon she realized that she liked it. "Everyone was very nice," she said. "They spoke better and dressed better. I wasn't afraid. I learned new things and it was liberating. I loved it, but I never loved Texas itself, never felt at home there."

Anne was now sixteen, going on seventeen. The beatnik movement was reaching across the country from California and it caressed her lightly in Richardson. She had bleached her hair blond in New Orleans, although it was closer to red. She was growing it out rather than dyeing it dark again, which resulted in a strange two-tone appearance. That was how she looked the first day she walked into Richardson High. She was conspicuous once again as one who did not belong with the popular crowd, but maturity, mixed with Katherine's attitudes, had given her a bit more security, and she attracted a gang of people who were outsiders like herself. They gave her a new sense of wholeness and worth.

"I really loved those people," said Anne. "We had a great gang going there."

Within that group was a quartet of girls, three of whom shared the same name, so they dubbed themselves A1, for Anne O'Brien, A2 for Ann Fekety, and A3 for Anne Ramsey. The fourth girl was Lynn Packard. Lynn was artistic, Anne O'Brien was a writer, and Ann Fekety had a scientific frame of mind.

"We were a crew of very odd people," said Ann Fekety, "for Richardson, which was small, conservative, and religious. Almost all of us were originally from out of town or out of state. We were not part of the Texas football mentality. We were relatively intelligent and not ashamed to be so, which for women at that time was not smart."

Anne dressed in a way that drew still more attention to her strangeness. She wore leotards under her dresses and had one outfit that her friends called "the pumpkin outfit."

"We were getting stylish," Lynn explained, "and Anne bought a green silk shirtwaist dress that was too big for her and she had pumpkin colored tights. You never heard her mention anything about being 'in.' She seemed to have a certain acceptance of herself, even though she was quite alien. She didn't seem to have the typical vanities that most teenage girls have. Fixing herself up wasn't an issue for her. She was the most self-possessed person in that age group, interesting and gutsy and assertive. I've always felt that Anne was comfortable in her outsidedness." Lynn was impressed that Anne called her father and stepmother by their first names, and sensed a freedom of expression that most teenagers do not enjoy with their parents. "They talked to each other. It wasn't like my home at all." That was the way Anne seemed to Lynn.

Anne, however, did not always feel as secure as she appeared. She observed girls who were naturally popular, understood that as a size three she was thin and underdeveloped, and sometimes still felt like "a shrimpy little kid." Yet she continued to attract attention from boys, many of whom did not even go to her school.

"She was very pretty," said her sister Tamara. "She never had a lack of dates. Her combination of charm and attractiveness made her popular. Men enjoyed socializing with Anne."

She inspired respect and trust, although she shunned sexual advances, feeling that sex was the province of marriage and that marriage required an emotional and spiritual bond.

She thought she saw the qualities she was looking for in a tall, thin boy she had set her eye on in a journalism class. He was a junior, a year younger than she, and he had just transferred to Richardson. He had a wild, creative look about him like a young James Dean, her hero. "He was the strangest, most otherworldly person I'd ever met," she said. He'd moved from the front of the class to sit next to her, saying, "I'm tired of sitting up there by myself." She'd been immediately attracted to him and learned that his name was Stan Rice.

Raised in Dallas, Stan had come from a blue-collar family, and his father was a plumber. He was older than his three siblings, a brother and two sisters. After a period of religious zeal in his teens, he grew disenchanted with a lukewarm Protestant religion that yielded no real answers and had become an atheist. He'd had little exposure to books growing up, and any mental stimulation he'd gained, he'd provided for himself, as with his discovery of classical music when he was fifteen. "I was enveloped in it," he said. "It seemed like the most complex, rich, full-of-possibilities sound I had ever heard, and I wanted to hear more. The same with poetry, which, in high school, was very much a private matter. I ran into a use of language that I thought was as immediate as experience itself—that put images right into my brain. When I bumped into the stuff that was doing this to me, I wanted to do it, too.'' He read what poetry he was able to find and kept his own hidden in a drawer. For Richardson High, he was as unusual as Anne.

''What Stan had going for him,'' said Tamara, ''was a fire in his eyes that very few men have. He was startlingly witty and funny.''

The age difference did not matter to Anne, and she hoped something might develop between them. Stan, however, did not share the romantic vision. Anne was not his type. He preferred popular girls who were less morally restrained and a bit more conventional.

''She was truly a weirdo,'' he said. ''She wore white loafers and a speckled skirt and a leopard-skin jacket. She had dyed her hair and had it in a ponytail that stuck out like a horse's tail. It was bright orange, and the rest of her hair had grown out so it was brown. It was a sight.'' Nevertheless, he found her stimulating. ''Just being around her was like being around a lighted sparkler.''

For Anne, however, Stan was *the man,* and she pined for him. Neither was aware at that moment of the series of events that would eventually turn the tables and make him chase after her.

Stan joined Anne's gang and dubbed her with yet another new name. She announced to her friends that she wanted to change her name, and henceforth she would be called Barbara forever. Stan said, ''Okay, Barbara Forever.'' The name did not stick, except as a joke.

Anne got involved with the school newspaper, *The Talon,* reading with avid interest the columns that Stan wrote as editor. She thought him witty and brilliant. She herself wrote short feature articles about local parties and continued to write short stories. Unbeknownst to her, she also found an audience in Stan. She wrote a story called ''The Thinker,'' about a tough gang leader who was intelligent. It was read out loud in class and Anne thought no one had liked it. Later she found out that one person had been very impressed: Stan Rice.

''She could obviously really write,'' he said. ''Other people were just cliché by comparison.''

In other ways, Anne showed an early facility for excessive language. Lynn Packard recalled a song that Anne made up, to the tune of ''Row, Row, Row Your Boat.''

> "Propel, propel, propel your craft,
> Placidly down the liquid solution,
> Ecstatic, ecstatic, ecstatic, ecstatic,
> Life is but an illusion."

Such verbal exercises often took place at slumber parties, a popular activity in Texas. The girls bought steaks for dinner, but since Anne was Catholic, at her house on Friday nights they cooked after midnight. At these events Anne exhibited an unusual modesty about her body. Lynn remembered that she changed her clothes in the closet—surprising for someone who would later write explicit pornography and erotica. But in those days she was still involved with the teachings of the church and with maintaining her purity, although she was opening her mind to other ideas.

Religion was still part of this school, despite being a public institution, and the students were assembled from time to time in the auditorium while Baptists came in to pray for them. The four girls, however, were questioning such things. "We had what we considered extremely esoteric philosophical discussions," said Ann Fekety, "about religion and philosophy." Anne was getting a broader education, but at home her father resisted anything outside Catholicism. He read literature and poetry that resonated for him with God's truth and that was good enough. Anne felt he did not understand why she needed more, and she grew increasingly frustrated. She'd attack the church's actions and Howard would defend them. "We had terrific arguments, pro and con," said Howard, "exercising the limits of our minds and our reading." Anne would capture the tone of this conflict in the relationship in her novel *Exit to Eden* between Lisa and her father: "Her dad was an old-guard Irish Catholic . . . always reading Teilhard de Chardin and Maritain and G. K. Chesterton and all the Catholic philosophers. . . . On sex he was Augustinian and Pauline as she described it. He thought chastity was ideal."

The year soon climaxed with graduation, and Anne turned her thoughts to college. During the school year she had worked in a restaurant with Lynn, then continued to live at home for the summer while working at Skillman's drugstore. She discussed with Howard where she should go, and Texas Woman's University appeared to be the best choice. It was affordable and within easy driving distance. Suzie—now called Alice—had moved to Dallas to attend nursing school, but the previous November, Anne's half sister, Micki Ruth, had been born. With three small children, Howard could not help much with expenses. Nevertheless, he encouraged Anne to get an education, as Katherine would have done.

During that summer, Stan came around, since he lived fairly close, and asked Anne out. She was ecstatic. Perhaps *now* something would happen. Both were restless to get out of Dallas, although Stan still had a year of high school, and one of their favorite dates was to go out to Love Field and watch airplanes take off to distant places. "We liked the building," said Anne, "and there was a big map of the world."

Anne wanted badly to take a trip back to New Orleans before she went off to college. Lucy Provosty, her childhood chum, had visited Texas, and one of Anne's friends, Joe Ramsey, had liked her. Anne proposed that she, Joe, and Stan go together to her old hometown. She wanted to show Stan her beloved New Orleans.

They went to ask Stan's parents for permission. He was sixteen, Anne seventeen. They were not married, and the trip would be unchaperoned. It was 1959. Morality was strict and Stan's parents were conservative. It was a bold request.

However, both Stanley Rice, Sr., and his wife Margaret liked Anne. "We thought she was a wonderful girl," he said, "and thoroughly approved of her." They gave permission readily, because of "the confidence we had in both of them" to observe moral decorum.

They went to Louisiana for a week. Stan and Joe stayed at 2301 St. Charles, refurbished as a boarding house. Anne stayed with Lucy. "It was all very proper and Catholic," Anne said.

Nevertheless, she was growing less conservative about her views on kissing, and Stan was honored to be the first boy that Anne kissed. Her recollections of the feeling were later captured in her second novel, *The Feast of All Saints:*

> Richard had just kissed Marie and she had never felt a physical sensation akin to what she'd experienced when he was holding her lightly, gently, as if he might break her, in his arms. His hands had spread out firmly against her back, pressing her to his chest so that the buttons of his frock coat had touched her breasts. And when that had happened, a shock had passed through her, so keenly pleasurable that she had let her head fall back, her lips apart, and felt that shock's consummation in one shuddering instant as his lips pressed against hers. . . . She had been obliterated in that instant, everything she had ever been taught had been obliterated, all that she was before had simply gone away.

For Anne, already easily stimulated by her physical world, the experience was highly charged.

"Anne was more exciting than ever," said Stan. "She'd lost her physical inhibitions and really came bursting out of the gate." However, their dating remained casual, and summer passed into fall without any real commitment. It was time for Anne to leave for college, but to her frustration Stan did not express interest in a long-distance relationship.

"I was brokenhearted," said Anne, "because I was still in love with him." Things looked bleak for her love life, but the excitement of anticipating college buffered it.

Dorothy, once a typist for the FBI, took Anne to get her first typewriter. She tested the typewriters at a junk store to find one that was fast. Finally she was satisfied and presented it to Anne. "It was a little black portable typewriter," said Anne, "with a wooden case. It was just as fast as it could be." She named the typewriter Oliver. With typewriter and luggage trunk in haul, she set out for Texas Woman's University.

5

It was a small campus of brick buildings and college traditions. To Anne, it was a wonderful new horizon.

"I loved college life from the first moment I was there," Anne declared. She was assigned into a co-op dormitory, a new concept, where the girls worked to help with expenses. They took meals in the dorm and helped to cook and clean up. It was perfect for Anne, since money was tight and she'd taken out a student loan.

In the dorm, four rooms opened into each hallway, and four girls were assigned to each room. Four desks and four bunks were built into the walls. The dorm mother was a slender, white-haired lady who served tea in the afternoons.

Lynn also went to Texas Woman's University, to major in art, while Anne Ramsey moved away and Ann Fekety went to Southern Methodist University. Lynn described how Anne dived at once into writing. "She used to write these stories, and they'd stack up. There were literally two feet of unfinished stories. They were weird, full of offbeat characters. Wally Bean was a character that came up all the time, and he got to be a joke. She was always banging on that typewriter."

"That's when I was hardly able to get two pages done," said Anne. "They used to tease me about my novels being a page-and-a-half long."

She also wrote long letters of generous affection to friends in other places. "I miss you like cream in my coffee," she insisted to Ann Fekety, admitting how corny she sounded. She described her new experiences with language picked up from bohemian influences. Sprinkled throughout were phrases like "Dig?" "Pad over if you can, man," and "I'm cremating a cancer stick." She admitted to drinking freely and was having a ball. "I'm beginning to really *live, live, live!*" she exclaimed in one letter. She also offered advice about men, talked about her dates or lack of them, and commented on serious books like *1984.* She repeatedly asked Ann to find some boys at SMU to invite over for a "blast," although she remained conservative about romance, fearing that sex would lead to pregnancy, then marriage and five kids, and she would be held back from achieving her goals to better herself.

It was in the dorm that Anne met Ginny Mathis, destined to be a close friend. Ginny was tall at five foot nine, with blond hair and large eyes. She had grown up in Oklahoma, and her father had died when she was young, giving her an emotional link with Anne. She was from a middle-class, Protestant background, and had started college the year before, at the age of sixteen. She and Anne got along like soul sisters.

"We ended up in the same room," Ginny explained, "and we hit it off instantly. She said that I was the first really educated person she'd ever met, which stunned me, because from my perspective she was the first I'd met at our age who was an intellectual. We liked and appreciated each other. We were lunatics together. We were both seventeen, both different, both restless, both seeking things. We had a lot in common."

"I think most of the friendships I've had over the years," said Anne, "have been with women who have been like allies or sisters. There was a shared sense of humor, the ability to laugh at similar jokes, and a kind of camaraderie."

They went through several sets of roommates. "I think we were obnoxious," Ginny admitted. "We disturbed the others. We were noisy, and we laughed at conventions, and stayed up late. We said what we thought and we bothered people." They nurtured each other through the ups and downs of college life. "We talked all the time about everything," said Ginny, "about religion, about what color our hair was, and other big philosophical questions of life. We were always interested in the essences of other people. Things were changing and people were changing, and we got caught up in that. We wanted to break the bounds of the conventions that we had been raised with."

Rules were strict, but the girls found ways to sneak out and walk around town, dressed in odd fashions. "Anne bought this wonderful fake fur coat," said Lynn Packard, "that was many sizes too large for her. She rolled the cuffs to her elbows and it hung to her ankles. Ginny wore a brass alarm clock around her neck, which was always going off, and I wore my leotards and trench coat with paint all over it. If we had gotten caught, we would have been expelled."

Back in the dorm, Ginny indulged in books, while Anne, still a slow reader, consumed movies. "She would go by herself," said Ginny, "and I'd read. She'd tell me the story of the movie, and I'd tell her what I'd read. I think we were nihilists for a couple of days when I was reading a lot of Nietzsche. We never tired of talking with each other."

They became each other's personal confidantes. "Anne talked a lot about her childhood in New Orleans, about her mother, and it sounded so awful, these girls never knowing what to expect. I remember the theme of sadness, mostly, because of her mother."

Being female was a common concern, although not yet in an explicitly feminist sense. Anne and Ginny talked about sex and attracting men. Anne confessed that she had been told since she was young that her mannerisms and desires were inappropriate for a girl, and that she was too aggressive and direct. She had also noticed how other girls had developed into women, leaving her behind and making her feel different. She had read in an opinion column that small figures were not sexy and had taken the idea seriously. "She worried a lot about her femininity," said Ginny. "I always thought she was bright and attractive, and I never could figure out why she worried. She had dark hair on her arms and legs, and she worried about that. She made jokes about being a spider."

Anne's fantasy world had kept up with her sexuality, and she had replaced childhood scenarios with romance. She had a secret place in the botanical gardens at TWU where she went to be alone, wearing a white dress and the jade necklace given to her by Dennis Percy. There she would dream. Her characters evolved into young men and women in college, and some of them, like the boy genius named Christopher, dropped from the picture.

A new element crept in, an attraction to love between individuals of the same sex, especially males. "If I go back to stories I wrote in high school," Anne said, "it was there. I just didn't know what it was. Anyone reading the stories would have seen how the males talked to each other, and the emphasis on their appearance, and a slight idealization of them. It was latent." This attraction would grow stronger, even after she married, into pornographic fantasies, but the element of equality between lovers was as strong as the sensuality.

Anne felt an affinity with sensitive or "feminine" males because she related better to the idea of gay men as an androgynous mix than to the more stereotypical "straight" populations of either sex. Her assertiveness was like a secret male part that as a woman she was not supposed to possess but did. Coupled with social standards that demanded of her physical features she did not possess, she felt inadequate on the one hand, and robbed of an inner treasure on the other. Inevitably, as she was told often enough that she did not act like a girl, and as she observed the freedoms and privileges of men, which she wanted for herself, she would gravitate toward a masculine perspective, fueled by a rage against fashion that did not allow her to be herself. It would stamp her as unique, not easily assimilated.

Having felt estranged much of her life, Anne developed sympathy for outsiders, especially sexual outsiders. One day she and a friend were in a park. Across the lagoon they spotted a man doing something strange. "We realized that this thing he had in his hand," said Anne, "was his penis. I thought it was hilarious and this girl went to pieces." Later, in an erotic novel, *Exit to Eden,* the event would become part of an observation about Lisa, the protagonist: "You told me that in a very real way you loved all the sexual adventurers who didn't hurt others. . . . You felt love and pity for the old flasher in the park who opens his coat. . . . You said that you were they and they were you. It had been that way ever since you could remember." These concerns would drop away, then return as Anne was increasingly confronted with gender-based political and social situations. Eventually she would make a bold statement in the form of erotica and pornography for women.

Anne worked as a waitress at the Gaslight restaurant just off campus, as much as fifty or sixty hours a week. She earned sixty cents an hour, which amounted to about twenty-three dollars a week with meals deducted. Since students frequented the place, the tips were skimpy. She also got up with Ginny once a week to do their dorm duty. "We had to sweep and mop and wax certain sections of the floor at six o'clock in the morning," said Ginny. "It was horrible. Usually we stayed up late and talked. We were not early morning people and we were both in agony."

Anne was taking twenty-one credits per semester, an overload that required permission from the dean and meant classes on Saturdays. She majored in journalism and favored courses in French, fencing, sociology, and history over math and science.

"I crammed the schedule," said Anne. "I was very good at listening to lectures and passing blue book exams, so I could frequently do that without reading the text. I was a slow reader, so there was no possibility that I could read everything assigned."

Ginny remembered her friend's long hours. "I think Anne was afraid she was going to wind up an uneducated person who had aspirations to get the good things in life."

Like her character Katherine in *Katherine and Jean,* Anne felt "right near the surface of the water with both hands reaching up for something, the sky. . . . If I didn't succeed, I was finished. I was drowned."

"My biggest fear in life," said Anne, "was that I would get sidetracked—that I would not go to college and not be a writer and not be anything in life." One of her inspirations was her Aunt Alice, her mother's sister, who had gone through law school in hard times. "I'd always heard how brilliant she had been, and she was a role model." Few others in the family had ever attended college.

She gravitated toward strong lecturers, echoing a trait she gave to the character Marcel, in her second novel, *The Feast of All Saints,* who felt that he needed to "learn how to learn."

"I think I was describing myself to some extent in him," Anne admitted, "his tremendous need for guidance and learning. I'd go only to classes generally where there was a tremendous amount of personal force on the part of the professor, a great force to shape the material, to give insights and to change us through lecturing. What I wanted to do was to suck up all the learning I could from these people who had been places I hadn't been and who had read things I hadn't read."

Nevertheless, Anne was exhausted. "I don't think anyone should have to work as hard as I did. To watch the college world through the café window while you're wiping tables fifty hours a week is a bitter experience. I survived it because I was very strong and had a tremendous ambition to succeed, not to be stuck cleaning that café table for life. What hurt me most was the lack of sleep. I remember sitting down and realizing that there was no night on the calendar when I could contemplate more than four or five hours of sleep. I would get almost panicky. But I would have done anything within my moral principles to succeed."

Class attendance was mandatory, but Lynn Packard recalled that Anne frequently would leave to go to the bathroom and just disappear. She suspected Anne climbed out the window and went back to the dorm for a quick catnap. She also remembered that Anne was forever sitting out of the 7:00 A.M. PE class.

"I hated them," said Anne. "I don't do anything at seven o'clock. I even flunked the written test."

It was in college that Anne discovered literary novels that had been kept from her reach by Catholic censorship. She spotted books by Carson McCullers in a newsstand in downtown Denton and soon became an avid reader. "I loved her wonderful storytelling ability, the ability to draw out all those characters and put them in motion. I loved *Member of the Wedding*. I thought it was the most beautiful, delicate book about the heart and soul. I liked the compassion she felt for her characters, and the compassion she felt for everyone—that's what came out: the really gentle soul."

By Christmas her first year, Anne was undergoing a crisis with her Catholic faith, caused by "a tremendous intellectual curiosity, wanting to read all kinds of books." Most of the titles in Voertman's bookstore that excited her were on the church's index of forbidden books. "I remember walking into a campus bookstore filled with trade paperbacks with wonderful covers, and there was Nietzsche and Kierkegaard, and I wanted to read them all—I wanted to find out what this existentialism everyone was talking about was—and it was all condemned and forbidden. A Catholic girl doesn't read that stuff!"

Anne questioned whether the church was really the foundation of truth, whether there was a heaven or hell. It was a shock to be thinking such things, but it began to open her mind to new ways of interpreting her experiences. She expressed her doubts to her father and he told her she was right to explore other ideas, but believed the church would stand strong against them. Anne felt she was losing Howard's approval and later expressed her uneasiness over this aspect of their relationship in a novel, *Exit to Eden:* "My father looking at the book on the bed, the new novels, the paperback philosophy. 'Lisa, you have never had any taste, any judgment, anything but a penchant for the worst trash you could find in a bookstore, but for the first time, I fear for your immortal soul.' "

It was not long before she threw off the religion that she had cleaved to as a child, wondering, "Does the priest really believe Christ is on the altar? Or is it just a matter of chalices and sacramental wine and the choir singing?" Although she lost religious conviction, she retained a sense of moral goodness that would see her through when the deeper emotional impact of this loss eventually caught up years later with her intellectual rebellion.

A priest told her that she would be unhappy with her decision. "You're the kind of person," he said, "who will be a Catholic all your life. Any attempt to give it up will lead to misery." She was not convinced.

"It's sad," said Anne, "that some people think other people are incapable of changing and evolving. The priest's prediction was completely wrong. It was good that he said it, because it liberated me." She was determined to overcome her upbringing in order to be the person she wanted to be, and such declarations only fanned the flames.

Even with the long hours of work and study, with Ginny's friendship and the wonderful new world Anne was exploring, she still thought about Stan Rice back at Richardson High. When the girls sat around and talked about guys, Anne talked about Stan. Swearing Ann Fekety to secrecy in a letter, she revealed a chant she had made up: "I love Spanish rice, fried rice and Stanley Rice."

"She was interested only in Stan," Ginny said. "I think a lot of people have things in their lives that are what I call an Absolute Certainty. One of Anne's was Stan. He was her destiny."

Anne wrote him letters but he did not write back. She went home occasionally and would see him, but he was not responsive. "It was very anguishing for me," said Anne, "because I was completely in love with him." Still, she realized it might be time to forget him. It was clear there was no future in sitting around hoping, so she got involved with a jazz musician named John Scarborough, who played at local clubs and dances.

Nevertheless, she was restless. It was evident that Denton was a dead end. She and Ginny talked about going somewhere like San Francisco, and Anne suggested they paper the ceiling with travel posters. They shared big dreams, but Anne was running out of money. She took out another loan to continue school into the summer session, still working at her waitressing job, but she was not very happy. Ginny went home to Oklahoma to work.

The next semester, Anne tested a new horizon by transferring to North Texas State University, a school with a famous jazz department that possessed an artsy atmosphere. Stan, too, enrolled at North Texas State, with an interest in studying law.

Early in the semester, he and Anne met in the street outside a movie theater where Anne had just seen *The Bicycle Thief*. Her heart lifted at the sight of him and hope was rekindled. They spoke briefly, but Stan showed no inclination to follow up.

"It was heartbreaking," said Anne. "He just didn't seem to be responding." Her boyfriend was playing at a dance close by, and Anne invited Stan to go over with her. She introduced them and they hit it off, later forming a discussion group called The Clan. When John was finished with his gig, Anne left with him. It seemed to her that things were pretty well finished with Stan.

6

Ginny was still in Oklahoma, and Anne realized that she could not continue where she was. Her funds had run out and there were no jobs to be found. She remembered how her mother had, as a young woman, gone out to Los Angeles to work. The old restlessness that had prompted so many late-night talks with Ginny inspired Anne to write to Dennis Percy, with whom she was still in contact, to ask if she could stay with his family in San Francisco until she found a job. He encouraged her to come. Her sophomore year at North Texas lasted six weeks. In October, just as she turned nineteen, she went to San Francisco.

She found a job working as a claims processor in an insurance office and discovered that working only thirty-seven-and-a-half hours a week allowed her enough money to afford an apartment. "It was like heaven!" she said. She urged Ginny to come. Ginny joined Anne later that month and they found a furnished apartment in the Haight district, at 625 Shrader Street. It was situated a few blocks from the University of San Francisco, an all-male Jesuit school that allowed women to take courses at night.

"Our apartment was the first floor of an old building," said Ginny. "It had big rooms that opened into each other. There was a living room, one bedroom, another room, a hallway, and kitchen."

They changed the bedroom into a dining room by moving the bed into the walk-in closets. "It's weird," Anne admitted in a letter to Lynn, "but we love it."

"It had a godawful bathroom," Ginny said, "with a tin box for a shower. But we didn't care. We were poor and we were on our own. We had a lot of books but nothing else. We thought we were grown up. We depended on each other. We shared toothpaste, we shared thoughts, we shared everything. I have a mental image of the two of us running headlong with our arms out, as fast as we could into whatever was there. We put a lot of energy into everything that we did. We wanted to taste everything!"

Of course they argued, especially when it came to keeping the place clean. "Neither of us ever wanted to clean the apartment when the other one did," Ginny admitted, "and neither of us did much cleaning, except in desperation!"

They were enthralled with their independence. Anne told Lynn that life was very different now with her "ludicrous, horrible, wonderful adventures in California." With youthful bravado and a sense of immortality, Anne and Ginny explored the city on bicycles by day and trolley by night.

Drugs like speed and LSD were available, but they declined to experiment. "I think we were smarter than that," said Ginny. "We never even got drunk at the same time. That was one way we protected each other."

When it was time for Ginny to look for a job, the employment agency sent her to the insurance office where Anne was processing claims, so they ended up working together. Because of the Beat movement, the people around them were suspicious of unusual clothing, and they had to be careful, although shopping in thrift stores did not allow them much choice. Once when it was cold, Ginny wore black tights, and she was called into the manager's office for fear she was becoming a beatnik.

Nevertheless, they wanted to experiment. One day, Anne convinced Ginny that she would look good as a platinum blond. At the time Anne's hair was dyed a reddish color (which she would later change to blond), and she had no qualms about making such alterations. "Anne could convince me of anything," Ginny said, echoing Lucy years before, "and she convinced me that she was an expert on hair color." They were going to the symphony that night to treat themselves, and Anne bought what she needed to give Ginny a new look for their special evening. They worked on it all day.

"When she was through," said Ginny, "my hair was the color of a brand-new copper teakettle. We both just fell on the floor laughing."

They realized at once that Ginny could not go to work looking like that, so Anne went out and bought more hair products to change the color.

"It turned out dusty green," said Ginny. Nevertheless, they thought it looked good enough, so they left it that way.

Anne continued to write and even did some drawings. "Strange things," said Ginny, "out of her imagination." They made up stories together, reading to each other. "That was another Absolute Certainty in Anne's life," Ginny recalled, "that she was going to be a writer. I had always thought of Anne's mind as baroque, because her imagination was rich and dark and ornate and elaborate."

At one point they decided they would write steamy romances and make a lot of money. Ginny described this venture: "Anne said what we needed to do was to walk around the red-light district of San Francisco.

So we did. One evening we took the bus to the Tenderloin district and just strolled around and observed. Nothing happened and we were disappointed. I don't think we wrote the stories, but it's a wonder we survived. That's a rough area, and there we were like idiots strolling around. No one bothered us. We probably looked hopelessly wholesome."

Anne was still interested in the existential philosophers, popular on college campuses. She and Ginny took night courses at the University of San Francisco, where she sampled Nietzsche, Kierkegaard, and Bergson. Her favorite existential writers, however, were Camus, for his clear expression of abstract ideas, and Sartre. "I'd put on long black gloves," said Anne, "smoke Camel cigarettes and read Sartre. It felt terrific. I think I understood Sartre rather completely, although I did not understand the French disgust for the middle class, or their alienation from the physical. That always puzzled me, and Sartre's work reeked of that." Many of Anne's novels would show this influence.

She was also reading Aldous Huxley. "I remember learning things from him, like he never described what people really looked like, and that was amazing. He always left it vague."

Living in San Francisco, Anne could do what she pleased and read what she pleased without the confrontations such exploration might cause at home. She did not have much contact with her family, feeling that there was no place for her there in Texas. She wanted to know who Yeats was, who Dylan Thomas was, and W. H. Auden. "I just wanted to be educated. I wanted to read and make up my own mind about things."

Anne loved her independence, but she also wanted to meet some men. For a brief time, she found company among a group of students that Dennis Percy knew from the Jesuit College. They met Jack DeGovia, who got them involved in a theater group called the University Players, making costumes and stage scenery. They also met Ed Stephan, a student who liked to discuss philosophy. Their apartment became a hangout. "We were 'sensitivos' together," Jack explained. "We were interested in the arts and in an environment that was not encouraging."

"Everyone we knew," said Ginny, "was a creative person, an artist or a writer—we were all fledglings. I think we were on the opening part of the wedge of the hippie movement—the first part of the artistic, free-spirited people." Others joined them, including a saxophone player with a collapsed lung, a cartoonist, and several actors. Their group was an artistic microcosm of the greater Haight district. Unbeknownst to them, the acid rock movement was taking its first breaths. Within blocks lived Janis Joplin, Big Brother and the Holding Company, Grace Slick, and the Grateful Dead.

"We all lived there," said Ed, "and didn't know what was going on. It was a fun place to live, but we lived there because it was cheap."

Ed was reclusive and wore glasses that gave him a serious air. He was questioning many of the doctrines taught at his Catholic college, something he had in common with Anne. "She was chewing on her Catholic faith and so was I." Anne was intensely attracted to him. One night, in the back of a '52 Cadillac the gang dubbed the "Big Green Weenie," Anne made her move. She hugged Ed enthusiastically to give him the message, unaware that he was exploring alternative possibilities for his sexual orientation. He did not respond. "I liked her a lot, but I couldn't commit anything at all. We didn't know enough about what being gay meant in those days, but I think I knew I was." Anne also unnerved him a bit. "I liked her mind and her intensity, but I was also afraid. She was *too* intense, and awfully strong. I've always been afraid of very strong people."

Anne was disappointed. "It just didn't work out. It was like two conversations. It never got off the ground." She never quite realized the effect she had as an independent, sexually aroused young woman at a time before a formal feminist movement encouraged such traits. She had the same effect on another young man—one that she already knew.

Along with Ed one evening came Lee van den Daele. Lee was flamboyant, a student of psychology who liked to analyze people. Years before, he'd heard about Anne through Dennis and had stolen her address. He described their relationship in a letter.

"I cribbed it in one of her correspondences to him," he wrote. "I was sixteen or seventeen and Anne was fourteen or fifteen. We corresponded on and off for four years. I believe we had a long-distance crush on each other. She was idealistic in her appraisal of my characteristics; she wrote that I fascinated her and was intellectual. My letters to her were replete with 'posturing' and affected erudition. I wanted to impress her. I suspect for a while we provided a projective landscape to one another, two adolescent souls who needed desperately to make sense of a world which did not add up."

In her letters, Lee had noted a "profoundly Catholic sensibility," even when she spoke of her own agnosticism. "Anne appeared concerned about 'temptation' and 'the loss of innocence.' "

When Anne spent time with Lee face to face, the meeting jarred them both and their relationship burned out quickly. Lee remembered the evening:

"The apartment was a sparsely furnished Victorian with a cavernous living room, ample hallways and entrance, shadowy with too few pools of light. The atmosphere in the house was charged with sexuality and an almost palpable hysteria. The flesh-and-blood Anne could neither be relegated to some role of intellectual affinity, nor assimilated to any ready category of proper Catholic womanhood. Anne, I think, was in heat. The same seemed true of her friend. Together they supercharged the air with forebodings of secret delights, tempestuous excitation, and fleshy exploration. They were thoroughly bohemian: gypsies in dark, street tones, iconoclasts that shucked off authority, anarchists that sought the Tree of Knowledge, even if it meant banishment."

He was not so sure he was going to like his involvement with Anne. "I felt the undertows of emotional urgency, hunger, and anguish that issued from Anne. It was too much the undisguised enticement of flesh, the soft amnesia of touch, and dark emotions better tethered to some underground place." What Lee wanted were "everyday requirements for everyday rewards." Anne threatened "nemesis, engulfment in the shadow world."

Anne had a different perspective on why things did not work out. "Those boys believed that if you were really cerebral and interested in passing your courses, you stayed away from women. Coming from the South, where we went on car dates at the age of thirteen, this was bizarre to me. I was from a rich heterosexual world, and we didn't have this division between men and women. I was totally unprepared to be treated that way." She admitted, however, that she was a "wild, undisciplined person. I got drunk a few times and they must have been shocked. I must have represented chaos to them. There I was, reading Sartre, smoking cigarettes and wanting to be an existentialist, and here were those crazy boys talking like it was a sin to go see girls on the weekends, when they should be studying Aquinas."

She was also displeased to learn that, as a woman, she would not be allowed to contribute anything to the school newspaper. Her irritation was an extension of problems she had already encountered with male chauvinism in her Catholic schools, and the more independent she got, the worse her status as a woman seemed to her. She listened to her male friends talk about how dumb and shallow women were, how they did not do things like read Dostoevsky or think for themselves. What they thought of her with her intellectual aspirations, she had no idea. She figured they regarded her as a loose woman, and that coming to her apartment meant for them, "going off the deep end." It confused her.

"I was suffering from being alone out there, cut off from my family and New Orleans, and cast adrift in a strange world." She wanted acceptance and was not receiving it. The lack of acknowledgment became a sore spot that was destined to get worse as her liberal ideals deepened. She longed for a time when men and women would be granted equal status and equal opportunities. She also wished for a relationship with someone who would return her intense affection, respect her mind, and encourage her ambitions. There appeared to be no such man.

7

Back in Denton, Stan Rice was going through his own changes. He had made contact with older students who showed a serious commitment to their ideas, and it gave him courage and direction. He read T. S. Eliot, Dylan Thomas, e. e. cummings, and James Joyce. "The real explosion in my head," he said, "came when I found a copy of an anthology called *New American Poetry 1945–1960.* It was a seminal volume bringing together for the first time the Beat poets and non-academic poets of that era." He became enamored with the philosophy of Susanne Langer, who wrote *Feeling and Form.* He was impressed by the notion of "significant form" as a quality of the mind, and believed that the "felt life" was conveyed through poetry, revealing the subjective universe. His new perspective made him think again about Anne.

"My life began to catch aflame, and I realized that the only other person I knew who was inflamed was Anne O'Brien." He'd been impressed with her independence and had not realized that he might be attracted to that sort of woman. He decided to see if he could salvage their former relationship. It was just after Thanksgiving, and he called on one of her friends to ask where she was.

"She's gone to California," he was told.

"California?" The news slapped him hard. It seemed so far away. "It was like night coming," he remembered. "My heart just stopped. It was a staggering shock. I'd let her get away!"

He got Anne's address, sat down and wrote her a long letter.

When Anne received it, she was jarred back to the love and longing she had once felt. She had not forgotten about Stan, with his presence and the qualities she admired, and she was delighted to hear from him. She answered his letter right away and they took up a correspondence.

"Anne's letters were wonderful," Stan recalled. "They were ten or twelve back-and-front yellow legal pad pages, and they just swept me off my feet."

He had made friends with Michael Riley, seven years his senior, when they worked together behind the scenes at the State Fair Musicals. Staying at Michael's apartment over Christmas, Stan made several long-distance calls, the earnest tone of which struck Michael as significant. "It was clear," he said, "that Anne's unexpected departure had shaken him."

Stan and Anne talked about the possibility of seeing one another, but scheduling and funds made it difficult for the next few months. Anne decided to return to Richardson for Easter break. In a letter to her high school friend Lynn, she asked, "Have you seen Mr. Rice? I haven't yet told him I'll be in Dallas for Easter. I'm sort of afraid it will scare him to death or something."

She called him and he rushed over to her house to pick her up. "When she walked into the room," he said, "I was a goner. She had this luster of a woman who had gone out into the world."

Stan's youngest sister, Cynthia, who was nine years old, remembered Stan bringing Anne home. "My first impression was how different she was from me. She had dark hair, dark eyes, and a hearty laugh."

Another sister, Nancy, two years behind Stan, recalled, "She was shy around my parents at first. She would sit back and observe and size up the situation, then assert herself later."

"She wore a somber, solemn brilliance," said younger brother Larry, "a warm, welcoming light. She was definitely not what one would call stylish, but my first impression was of the sound of her voice, crisp and articulate, and her lovely smile that charmed me from the beginning."

Anne confessed to Stan how she had been secretly in love with him for a long time, and how horrible it had been for her to suffer through that. He told her how he'd felt when he thought he'd lost her forever.

"We fell madly in love again," said Anne. "It was a very torrid, romantic year of wonderful letters changing hands."

8

Back in San Francisco, Anne and Ginny moved to a new apartment in the same general area. It was on a fourth floor, with no elevator, but the building was nicer, and they continued to give parties.

In January, Anne's cousin Allen came to visit. He had just been thrown out of Loyola University for failing to study, so he drove up with a friend to see her. "We shared a great admiration," he said, "for the quote: 'The accused, guilty or innocent, but always on the side of the accused.' We always felt we were both the accused."

There commenced, according to him, a weekend-long party. "It was wild, and people were passing out where they stood. Stan's name was in the air, but my impression was that Anne had taken her life in her hands, and that whatever happened, she was going to be out on the Coast."

When school was over for the semester in June, Stan arrived to spend a week with Anne. "He came," said Ginny, "and we all kind of tiptoed around him in awe." He had to return to Texas to go to work, and nothing was actually settled as to where he and Anne would go from there.

Ginny and Anne moved back with the Percys, and by August Ginny realized that the party was over. The Absolute Certainty in *her* life was that she wanted to be a healer. She had applied to a nursing program in Oklahoma and was accepted. It was time for her to leave. It was an emotional parting for both of them.

"I was really sad to leave San Francisco," Ginny said. "It was a very intense, magical time." She boarded a bus and Anne waved good-bye. As the bus went over the bridge, Ginny began to eat a sandwich. That was Anne's final image of her in San Francisco.

Anne continued to live with the Percys while she worked at the insurance office during the week and at a cafeteria on weekends to make money to go back to Texas to see Stan again. She felt things were happening quickly between them, but was not sure what to do.

One morning at seven o'clock as she was getting ready for work, she received a special delivery letter. She tore it open. The letter was from Stan. "It was a long letter," she remembered, "just saying, 'I want you to be my wife.' "

9

Anne called him right away. He was starting his sophomore year at North Texas State and he asked her to come to Denton. Although she preferred San Francisco, she wanted more strongly to be with him, and she joined him in time to sign up for classes. They set a wedding date in October, just after Anne would turn twenty.

Stan was still eighteen, but was to turn nineteen in November. "I was underage," he said. "I couldn't get married without my parents' permission, so my mother had to drive up fifty miles to this little town and give her permission." It was an embarrassing moment. The clerk issuing the license wrote Anne's legal name, Howard. She thought Stan was Howard and Anne was Stanley. Stan's mother burst out, "Howard! Her name is Howard?"

October was chaotic, as Anne and Stan kept changing the wedding date. Anne's sister Alice came to see them one weekend, but they did not tie the knot. Stan had gone to Howard to formally ask permission to marry Anne, and Howard had felt honored, but he refused, to his later regret, to attend the wedding. They had decided on a justice of the peace instead of a church wedding, and Howard saw no point in their getting married at all if that's the way they were going to do it. Although he himself had married out of the church by marrying a Baptist, he still insisted that religious ritual be part of the ceremony. Anne and Stan felt otherwise and went ahead with the plan. Tamara and Karen were too young to come on their own, and Alice had been with her the week before, so Anne was married without the presence of her immediate family.

Almost two dozen people attended, including faculty from the English department. Stan's family came, bringing his friend Michael Riley. Ginny was there, and so was Lynn Packard.

The ceremony was simple. It took place in the old-style Texas home of Stan's English professor and mentor, Dr. Jesse Ritter. Jesse was known by his students as a provocative, free-spirited man, "an existential, avant-garde, way-out professor." He was heavily involved in the integration movement, inspiring Stan to care about the issues, and was glad to be of assistance.

"He was a favorite student," Dr. Ritter said, "and we tended to shepherd bright students and socialize with them." His wife, Lorna, baked a cake for the small reception afterward.

Anne surprised Ginny at the last minute by telling her that she was to be the maid of honor. "She didn't tell me ahead of time," Ginny explained, "because at that time I didn't approve of marriage. She thought if she told me, I wouldn't do it. But it was okay for them to be married, because in my mind they had always been married. The only thing I was worried about was whether they could free themselves of Stan's background and set of conventions."

Anne wore a blue brocade shirtwaist dress with long sleeves and a flared skirt, size five. Stan wore a suit.

The JP was a one-legged Baptist who walked with a crutch and held a Bible in his free hand. He was warm and open, enjoying the unusual setting. The wedding party stood in front of a large fireplace, and the Ritters silently prayed that the occasional scorpion that came down the chimney would not show its face. "It was very moving," said Ginny, "very peaceful. There was a kind of glow in the room."

Being up close, Ginny missed what was evident to Stan's youngest sister, Cynthia. "Anne's knees were shaking uncontrollably, vibrating like two inches!"

The ceremony contained a few tense moments. Stan had warned the JP not to call Anne by the name Howard, and when the moment arrived where he was to ask Anne, "Do you take this man as your husband?" he hesitated, as if he could not remember what to say. Everyone waited as he struggled to get the license from his pocket, but one hand was occupied with the Bible and the other with his crutch. Stan groaned. "It was a comedy of errors," he said, "because if he had gotten it out, all it would have said was 'Howard.' " Stan's knees began to weaken, so finally he blurted out, "It's Anne." The JP went on with the ceremony.

He closed with the words, "In the Name of the Father, Son, and Holy Ghost . . ." and Anne froze. They had selected a JP because Stan was militantly atheist. Anne thought, "Oh no, this is it. He's going to leave the altar!" But Stan stayed and they were pronounced man and wife.

As Anne turned around, Stan's mother hugged her and said, "We're glad to have you." It was a moving moment that Anne would later remember when she needed family to turn to. "She seemed to need the love that we shared," said Larry Rice, "and wanted to belong."

Someone took pictures, but they were dropped off at the drugstore for developing, then forgotten.

Anne and Stan now had to concentrate on their schoolwork. They reveled in their new life together, although they had little money. Stan had been working since he was thirteen at the State Fair Musicals, but had quit in September. He found a job at school with the English Proficiency Testing program making fifty cents an hour, and Anne graded papers and worked as a research assistant.

They took an apartment, and Stan's parents, unable to help financially, loaned them furniture. They had two single beds that they pushed together, and close friends recalled that those beds were frequently broken. Their relationship burned hot as Anne finally found the sexual outlet that she had daydreamed about and craved since early adolescence.

Neither of them was domestic, although Stan tried to help out around the apartment. Anne would sprinkle clothes for ironing and put them in the refrigerator to keep for later, but frequently the clothing mildewed to the point of having to be thrown away.

Stan's sister Nancy described their Christmas tree that year. "It was just a bunch of branches from a tree that they'd stuck into something and hung balls on."

They took many meals with friends including Lynn, now married. One evening, they paid everyone back by making pizzas. The evening moved along until Lynn noticed that Anne and Stan had disappeared. Then she realized that the bathroom door was locked, and no one could get in. "They finally came out," she laughed, "just grinning."

When the semester was over, Anne and Stan decided it was time to leave. Stan's teacher Dr. Ritter counseled him to go to San Francisco, where the intellectual climate was more liberal. Anne was all for it. They got a truck from a service that allowed them to drive for free to get the vehicle across the country, and packed up their few possessions.

"They seemed very young," recalled Stan's sister Nancy, "but they had a great sense of adventure. They didn't know what was waiting for them at the other end. They were just going west, like a stagecoach pulling off across the prairie."

They had no jobs and no apartment, but they were in love, together, and heading for an exotic city of excesses that resonated with their mutual tastes. Stan drove all night himself because Anne did not drive. They hit the LA freeway at 6:00 A.M. in the middle of a traffic jam and began to laugh.

CHAPTER FOUR

A DREAM OF FAMILY

1

Anne and Stan were making a major change in their lives at a time when the entire country was about to erupt in change. They did not know it, but they were heading straight into the heart of it, back to Haight-Ashbury. Like many others, they were seeking direction and meaning for their lives.

In 1962, the U.S. Military Council was quietly established in Vietnam. Around the country the youth were becoming disenchanted with the trappings of the material affluence for which their post-Depression parents expected them to be grateful. They were alienated from the propaganda that America offered the best of all possible societies, and were hungry for experiences and for evidence that personal action counted. Available were the excesses of freedom and the exuberance of individuality. Anything seemed possible—even annihilation. The Cuban missile crisis signaled a vulnerability that alchemized into anger at authorities who could bring such things to pass. The spiritual gap between generations widened as children of the fifties, enamored of "rebels without a cause," shook off Cold War fears to search for peace, justice, and equality. According to existential slogans, humanity was deserted by God, and the true gods were those who shouldered the task of making new meaning. In the universities, the New Left formed from influences in the Beat underground, and rock 'n' roll became the poetry of disaffected, physically charged youth. San Francisco proved a beacon to the artistic community.

It was also a place of liberal ideals. Anne was thrilled to see a black man enter a restaurant there, because such a thing was unheard of in New Orleans while she was growing up.

Anne and Stan started school the day after they arrived, taking night courses at the University of San Francisco. It was less expensive than out-of-state tuition at a state university, had no residency requirements, and they were allowed to pay by installments. They stayed with friends until they found a place to live.

Their first apartment was at 820 Ashbury Street. "Living in the city," Anne wrote to Lynn (Packard) Phelps, "means expense, apartment dwelling, and people people people all around you blowing their noses, bumping into your car, crossing in front of you, closing the door on your hand, yelling over your head, etc. But it's nice." She loved the architecture. "I used to walk around going mad over the Victorians." As in New Orleans, she was fascinated with fine detail and thought about becoming an architect. She was not really sure what she wanted to do with her life, and there seemed to be so many possibilities.

Stan started to paint, using the bright colors and childlike forms of the primitive style of Picasso. He had a taste for the avant-garde, but wanted his art to be comprehensible to a wider audience. He took to the ocean and collected shells and driftwood to decorate their home. Soon it was filled with what they fondly termed "aesthetic clutter."

Dennis Percy and Jack DeGovia were still around, and the newlyweds got involved briefly with Jack's theater group. For the first time Anne would be on stage instead of behind the scenes. The play was a musical version of *Cyrano de Bergerac*. Dennis played Cyrano, Anne was a tavern girl, and Stan was a drunk who slurped continually from a wineskin. At the end of the play Anne also portrayed a nun.

"Anne was trying it out to see how it was," Jack recalled. "She was beautiful as the nun."

Nevertheless, acting did not agree with her. "I was scared to death," she said. "I don't like being seen. I didn't like being on stage; it just didn't bite." For her the experience crystalized a reluctance to be conspicuous. Going about invisible in the world would grow into a personal preference, despite the fact that becoming great at something—with its concomitant public recognition—would continue to be a powerful motivating force in her life. The theatrical experience also served Anne well for future fictional images in her first novel of the infamous Theater of the Vampires. "I got a lot of mileage out of a very brief experience," she admitted.

Stan and Anne found full-time jobs to support themselves while they continued with their night courses. They were pleased to be making the minimum wage of $1.25 per hour after what they had earned in Texas. Anne worked in an office and Stan became an accountant for Western Union. They had little time to pursue outside interests, and Anne's motivation to write diminished.

They wanted children, but agreed that their education came first. They were deeply in love and committed to a future with artistic direction. They wanted to try out a lot of things, moving through the world as equals, encouraging and supporting each other. However, their intense, dramatic personalities clashed at times. They both possessed the eccentricity and demands on others that can accompany bright, ambitious minds.

"Anne's a very strong-willed person," Stan explained, "and kind of indomitable, and I am, too. We disagree about things pretty strongly, but we never really fight. People will be with us when we're having an argument and they'll be afraid that there's some kind of awful thing going down, but it won't last five minutes. Our relationship has always been a wrestling match between two strong wills. It's exciting and there are no hard feelings." Anne was not one to settle for a woman's role, despising double standards, and Stan was pleased that the independent spirit that had attracted him had not cooled off with marriage. A pleasant androgynous quality settled into their relationship, with Anne exhibiting masculine traits and Stan developing poetic sensitivity, so their personalities took on broader dimensions and interaction became more interesting and exciting for them both. It became a relationship that would confuse future acquaintances who expected a more traditional marriage.

Whether they agreed or argued, they were able to talk things through and no subject was taboo. What Anne admired about Stan was his ability to stand firmly on his self-willed beliefs. "He's a model to me," she insisted, "of a man who doesn't look to heaven or hell to justify his feelings about life itself. His capacity for action is admirable. Very early on he said to me, 'What more could you ask for than life itself?' "

"I think what ties them together," observed Stan's youngest sister, Cynthia, "is a strong absolutism and passion—being able to discuss anything that they want in whatever kind of way they choose, and having the other person let it be okay. They have the strength to handle that and not be threatened."

"I've never seen such an intensely supportive marriage," said Jesse Ritter, who had sponsored their wedding.

Anne and Stan were each other's best friend. They respected each other and believed in each other—a bond that would see them through rough times ahead.

Soon they applied for school at San Francisco State College (later a university). The extension program there also did not require residency, and they were able to continue their education while working full-time, until they met the minimum requirements for enrolling in daytime classes.

Anne loved her courses and eagerly settled in for another two and a half years of college. One of her favorite professors was Dr. Richard Wiseman, who taught her the poetry of Yeats and Rilke. "He talked a lot about how they confronted the nothingness," she explained. "I remember one student raised his hand and said, 'What is this nothingness and why would anyone want to confront it?' I laughed because I realized it was impossible to explain if they didn't understand it." She had recently read *All Quiet on the Western Front,* a novel that brought home to her what war was about to an entire generation. "When you read that book, you could understand better when people talked about the void, nothingness, and death. One lecture just sent me through the week, off to think about things. He just overwhelmed me." The theme would leave its mark on her imagination, although reading about it in books did little to prepare her for her own eventual confrontation with the void.

She detested professors who exhibited no passion for their subjects—who felt their function was to analyze, define, and categorize. She expressed this disdain later in her second novel, *The Feast of All Saints:* "My teacher . . . handles books as if they were dead! . . . someone flesh and blood like ourselves wrote those lines, they were alive, they might have gone this way or that with a different word."

Much as Anne had wanted to write, she avoided English classes and majored instead in political science. "I enjoyed the courses and they were easy for me," she explained. "I couldn't read fast enough to pass English courses. I couldn't read Middle English at all. I was not ready to read Shakespeare at that age, and I had a great talent for research in history and political science." Although she took a few stabs at short stories, she had no clear direction and was criticized for lengthy sentences. "I don't think I had the dream of being a writer at that time."

It was Stan who majored in creative writing, having published his first poem in the USF literary magazine. While Anne took a detour, he dived full force into what he most wanted to do. It would not be long before his reputation as a poet mushroomed.

Anne's sister Tamara visited them, amenable to the TV dinners Anne served night after night. Tamara had been writing poetry since childhood and was ready for a more serious atmosphere. She liked what she saw and returned a few years later to take courses at San Francisco State. Stan's brother Larry would also leave Texas for San Francisco, given a boost by Anne and Stan, as would Anne's sister Karen.

The Rices spent most of their time that year working and studying. They had little time for socializing, although they had a small group of friends who shared their aesthetic visions.

In 1963, the counterculture was stunned by Kennedy's assassination. If someone so powerful and popular was vulnerable, then who wasn't? Certainties once taken for granted seemed to crumble, and an uneasiness pervaded as Lyndon Johnson took Kennedy's place.

Nevertheless, there was movement in the artistic community, as if something were coming to life, not yet defined but palpable. Everyone seemed to feel it. Poets, artists, and musicians gathered into supportive communities, and in North Beach coffee houses the attitude was nurtured of voluntary poverty, simple dress, free sex, and the merging of art with life. People meditated over jugs of wine on what could be achieved with such an abundance of energy and talent. A convergence of sympathetic spirits seemed at hand, beating like hearts ready to explode.

Anne and Stan responded. Although they felt strongly about their education and took responsibility seriously, they also rejected the conformity and mediocrity of the middle class. They preferred excess as a way of nurturing the imagination and the soul, and felt that middle class values stifled that.

Allen Daviau, now a film enthusiast saving to buy his own movie camera, came up from Fresno. He felt the excitement. "You had a sense of something happening in the artistic community," he said. "I came very close to moving there. Art was in its heyday and seemingly developing toward something socially significant."

The Rices moved to another apartment at 531 Clayton Street, a few blocks away, which eventually became a free health clinic for hippies. They were pleased with their new "digs." In a letter to Lynn Phelps, Anne described it as "the funkiest pre-hippie pad ever consistently maintained by a married couple for two years." The kitchen leaked gas and had a broken window, but they were unconcerned. Anne eventually painted the kitchen floor yellow. "It was my dream," she said, "to get it a bright, fathomless yellow like the stripes in the street, but I could never get it right." The living room was cozy, with a desk for Stan and room for his paintings.

With their move to day courses, Stan changed jobs. He worked in the library on campus and at a textile warehouse. Later he washed dishes at a girls school, Sacred Heart Convent, bringing home steaks and lobsters. Anne attempted to devise a budget, but neither of them was disciplined about money.

She bought her clothes at Goodwill, dressing in conservative schoolgirl outfits, with white blouses and dark skirts, but yearning for something more flamboyant. She loved long, brightly colored dresses with scooped necks. Eventually she bought two dresses for their "traffic-stopper" qualities to wear to parties. "I didn't go out of my way to costume up," she admitted, "but every now and then I would go out and get something. I had one dress with big patches of color that looked like something from the Minoan culture. And another I had bought at a bridal salon and it was trimmed in lace. I would love to dress up in those."

While the Rices worked hard to finish their courses and graduate together, the apartment gradually became a hangout for friends, many of whom had an artistic influence on them. Jazz and candles ornamented the atmosphere. Parties were glued together with jugs of wine and discussions about politics and what works and doesn't work in poetry, film, and music.

"Whatever they were doing," Jack DeGovia remembered, "they did all the way. Stan had an incandescent mind and was wonderfully verbal. They would think about anything and carry it through to its conclusion. There was nothing that was finished."

Anne drank to get high and preferred to be by herself. "I'd be fine if I was left alone," she said. "But if a fight broke out, I'd pass out. I remember being very vulnerable in that regard. I could be sitting alone in my house and drinking and having a wonderful time, and then someone would come in and pick a fight or start an argument. I couldn't handle it."

Stan met another poet, Casey Sonnabend, whose work he greatly admired. Casey had been part of the Beat movement since 1957 and had a carefree attitude that challenged Stan to loosen up and look at life differently. Casey felt it was important to make art out of the horrors of life and insisted that it should keep changing its form and directions. Together Casey and Stan devised exercises for improving their poetry, like tossing coins on a table or sloshing some beer and challenging each other to "spell the sound." Anne sometimes joined them.

"I think the most fascinating and successful exercise," said Stan, "was where one person would be at the typewriter and the other would pick a book and sit beside him or behind him and read the book aloud. The idea was to write a poem that uses what you're hearing as a springboard, but if something gets cooking in there, you go on that chain of associations until you run out of steam, and then you listen again. You get an imprint of both what's been said and what it triggers in your mind. The idea is to get as loose as possible while having some discipline feeding you in the background."

They frequented Casey's apartment in Sausalito, situated over a bookstore, although Anne was not always happy about the amount of time Stan wanted to spend there. Not being a poet, or having any other clear artistic direction, she felt left out, even intimidated.

Through Casey, she and Stan met other poets, like Linda Gregg, a beautiful blonde with a twin sister. The relationship between twins fascinated Anne, and she spent hours with Linda asking questions. Linda liked the Rices. "They really *talked* to each other," she said. "Anne would tell Stan exactly what was on her mind. She had intelligence and this richness, this desire to know things. There was somebody *there.*" She was amazed at how energetic and obsessive Anne's mind was. "Once she set out to learn about refrigerators and learned everything there was to know about refrigerators."

Jack Gilbert, a friend of Linda's who taught courses in writing at San Francisco State College, also noted this quality when he met Anne. "An idea would enter her attention, and she worked hard to find out all kinds of stuff about it for no professional use; it was just the appetite of a dynamic mind."

Although Anne was not writing, it was clear that she had a strong and insatiable intellect, an ability to retain details, and a drive that eventually would be channeled in ways that few among her acquaintances foresaw in those early days.

As Stan developed, moving them toward circles of writers and poets, Anne grew frustrated with her own lack of direction, especially as graduation closed in. She was discouraged when she thought about people like Carson McCullers, who had produced great novels at an early age. She was nowhere near ready for that, had no idea what to write about, or whether to even pursue writing. Nevertheless, she continued to support Stan's career.

In 1964, they finished their courses and took their college degrees—Stan in English, with an emphasis in creative writing, and Anne in political science.

That same year tensions escalated around the country over Vietnam as students proclaimed the Freedom Summer. Civil rights organizers were arrested on Berkeley campus, inspiring "sit-ins." Neither Anne nor Stan felt inclined to get politically involved. He looked toward the Ph.D. program at Berkeley, while Anne considered a variety of directions, including law school. She had gotten the materials to apply to Bolt, but contented herself with graduate courses in art.

2

Stan was twenty-two when a poem of his was chosen for the twentieth-anniversary commemoration of the founding of the United Nations in San Francisco—his second published poem. He was soon in demand for readings and began publishing in local literary magazines. He also began to dress in the style of a romantic poet, in suede jackets and neck scarves. His wild, youthful look, combined with the vigorous content of his poetry, caught people off guard. He exhibited power and presence as he read his work under the lights, emphasizing a phrase in a surprising way or filling out a line with dynamic emotion.

"Stan was an exceptional reader," said Anne. "He would read in a beautifully resonant voice that had tremendous range, with such dramatic intensity and immediacy that you could hear people breathe if they dared. He would stand and declaim, and the audience would fall back. It would be like a violinist knocking everyone dead with a few riffs from Paganini. He interpreted his poems in a way that few poets were able to do. He made them available to the rank and file."

Stan read in the coffee houses and was eventually invited to join name poets like Ferlinghetti. People gravitated to him, thinking him "cool" and "hip." Anne was proud of him and they dreamed of the day when he would acquire a national reputation. Doubleday showed interest in publishing his work, but the terms seemed too strict, so Stan decided to seek another publisher. Grove Press made an offer, but then went bankrupt. Stan went on with his readings.

He developed a unique style. "I'm a raw-meat, spontaneous, immediate poet," he said, "with roots in expressionism and the Beat movement, and yet someone who believes that emotions must be accurate, too. There's also a sort of scholar in me that's not interested in just emitted howls that are written down on the page."

In an interview years later, Stan spelled out his philosophy of poetry. "The poet," he explained, "is trying to understand life the way philosophers used to do—how to act, how to respond to the environment." Poetry, he felt, went beyond just description. Clarity of expression was his guiding concept. "If you trust the words, they'll do the work. If you trust the rhythm, the sense will follow." Forcing meaning into a few words condenses it, he believed, makes it heat up.

"I am one organism," he said in the interview, "and when I write I am putting together the conscious and unconscious just by every gesture. I have to consciously remember language, that *dog* doesn't mean *carrot,* but at the other end, I am trying to move quickly and associatively to maybe congeal the *carrot-colored dog*—that's an unconscious juxtaposition that just jumps out of your brain from somewhere." This idea is captured in his poem "Eating It."

> Can't eat death
> Like teacake shadow,
> Can't eat that.
> Chomp Chomp of russian novel
> Can't eat russian novel snow-on-horseflesh
> Nor vodka eyeballs of madman eat
> No no.

Can't eat brain itself & can't eat
Thoughts of mom-milk, gone, all gone,
Hush now.
Yet the banquet goes on.
Yet the banquet goes on.
Can't eat sleep.
Sleep eats me.
Day it eats
What Time can't be.
Dread is what we can't eat most. It tastes like
It won't stay down.

It is a matter, he explained, of recognizing patterns where no one else sees them.

Although he'd been an English major, Stan had taken more courses in literature and philosophy than most literature majors did to give substance to his writing. He also studied science because he believed it was the brain that made people what they are, and thus creative expression must be anchored in the physical.

Anne supported Stan's work, but they frequently argued over the merits of poetry versus prose as different paths for creating human feeling, sometimes becoming exasperated with each other's viewpoint. "Stan thought in images," explained his friend from Texas, Michael Riley, "stunning words that lit upon something no one else had thought about or seen. Anne thought in terms of stories and plots." Anne had learned about poetry from her parents, but Stan gradually enhanced her feel for the rhythm of this form of expression. She listened to him read, noting how he emphasized and timed certain phrases, learning from his gestures and voice inflections. She was impressed with the way he could move a room full of people in an almost hypnotic way.

"I've been influenced a great deal by Stan," she admitted. "It's not just the poems of his I've heard at readings, but it's the ongoing dialogue we've had about language. Through the readings I gained an understanding of modern poetry. In the beginning it was difficult for me. I remember trying to read Wallace Stevens and I'd say, 'What the hell does this mean?' Now it seems clear to me. Stan won me over from a point of almost hostility to poetry in general to deliciously looking forward to hearing what he was going to do. I think a lot of Stan's rhythms, phraseology, and music are deeply ingrained in my own writing—just ways of breaking off and saying things. I can hear the cadences of poems by Ginsberg and others as I'm writing."

Stan was a purist, believing that art, while it should be accessible, should not mingle too closely with the public mainstream lest it become diluted. Anne, raised on Dickens, felt art could be popular and still succeed as art. She'd always been a fan of movies and *Classics* comic books, and felt there was no necessary division between entertainment and art.

"We share the idea," said Stan, "that the work should be understandable to other human beings, that we're not alchemists in cone-shaped hats sitting in our parlors dreaming up codes that only other semiologists can understand. Spontaneity is important to both of us." It would be evident to them only in the years to come how close they were in their approach to the way they wanted their art to express their ideas.

Anne took a crack at writing again. Her cousin Allen had introduced her to the writings of Nabokov, calling him a "cinematic writer," and she wanted to let loose her own style into the excessive language in which she had reveled with *Lolita* and *Speak, Memory*. She withdrew from the parties to go sit in the back room and type.

Stan encouraged her, which baffled people in his circles that did not take her efforts seriously. They did not understand the closeness he shared with Anne. In that climate the male was designated as the inner pilgrim and the female supported him.

"Usually people responded to one or the other of us," Anne said. "There was a tendency for Stan's friends to protect him from me, to see me as a threat. It's amazing how many friends we had who really thought a woman's role was a stereotypical role of cooking and cleaning for a man, and maybe holding down a job and giving him money. I was perceived as the talentless square, and it was my function to come home after work and cook a meal for those people."

Yet Stan believed that Anne had talent that would one day surface. He was amazed at the complexity of her fantasy life. She had told him about the imaginary worlds that she had developed since the age of four, and they were still going strong, taking on elements of the adult world. She indulged in them during the course of the day to entertain herself when she was waiting for an appointment or walking or riding a bus. She could not shut off her active mind, and it seemed to naturally populate itself with fantasy characters.

The imaginary world set in Rome had become much more sexual, with slaves and masters, and each world had a full cast of characters with complete biographies. Stan was incredulous, especially whenever Anne expressed surprise over the developments. He had trouble keeping the characters straight, so one day he pushed a sheet of paper toward her and told her to write down the names of the people in her Canadian world. As he watched, she filled two columns, on the front and back, with one name after another. He was astonished. He knew she was working through problems in these worlds whenever she asked him hypothetical questions like, "What do you think, if a young man had a brother and one of them left home when he was twenty years old and went off to Europe, and the brother stayed home and worked in his father's business and they got rich off the business, should the first brother be able to come back and ask for part of the inheritance?"

"I'd know these things were happening in her dream worlds," Stan said. "She had to work out these ethical problems. If I see her sit down somewhere and she's sort of looking off, I know she's with those people. Sometimes she kills them off and then brings them back to life because she can't stand the fact that they're missing from the dream world. Sometimes I ask her what's happening to so-and-so."

Eventually Anne's efforts at the typewriter paid off as she finished several stories. One was about her alcoholic grandfather, but she was chagrined to realize that it was imitative of Tillie Olsen. "Her story was about a drunk," she said, "and it featured a poem. So did mine." She put her story away. She also wrote one about a creature she called Brenner the Shapeshifter, yet once again saw how strongly it resembled someone else's work—an episode from "The Twilight Zone."

Anne had an aversion to having her work sound like anyone else, even though she knew that she was influenced by people like Nabokov. In the late sixties she began to keep a diary, partly to assure herself that if an idea showed up somewhere else simultaneously with anything she had written, she could prove that she had created it free of inspiration from the other source. "I tend to have a very good memory, and I go back and sabotage my work," she admitted. "At the outset of writing, I decide it's too much like something else and I get very depressed. Then I go ahead and write. Then I tear out everything that I think is reminiscent of something else."

Sometimes she tormented herself that what she was writing might mean nothing, that it was an empty exercise. When she tried to get "The Thinker," her story from high school, published in *Transfer,* the college literary magazine, she was told it was not a story. The negative evaluation hurt her confidence. Yet she persevered and soon her work lengthened into novellas.

Jack Gilbert, Linda Gregg's friend, took a look at some of Anne's writing. "Anne was a natural writer," he said. "Her style had already a baroque quality, a decadent quality, almost a New Orleans quality, but very clear. Her sensibility was not like an American sensibility. She operated from a generative source rather than from having learned the craft."

Anne tried her hand at different subjects, but nothing gelled enough to take her very far. One day she and Stan were visiting Casey and she went downstairs to the bookstore. A friend handed her a copy of *The Evergreen Review* and told her to go over in a corner and read where no one could see her face. Anne was delighted with this clandestine instruction and turned to the page the friend had pointed out. It was the first chapter of a pornographic book called *The Story of O.*

Although Anne had no qualms about sexually stimulating material, she found the story too sinister, the way it punished sexual freedom with death. "There was something frightening about the way it took itself seriously," she said. She wanted something to read that would satisfy her strong passions, but wanted it less grim, so she wrote her own pornography in response, called *The Sufferings of Charlotte.* The novella was intended strictly for entertainment, to circulate among a few close friends. Written quickly, it was set in the nineteenth century and emphasized the idea of being forced to surrender to feelings. "Charlotte got dragged off against her will," Anne said. "It was either be executed for murder or join this cult. The idea was to provide some form of consent for the heroine that was still captivity." The theme of easy capitulation enveloped Anne. The masochistic fantasy gave her a chance to express the submissive, surrendering victim's perspective and she liked it. She felt the piece was quite a breakthrough for someone considered by acquaintances to be square, and she was proud of it. She loaned her only copy to friends and it was stolen from their apartment. Her first work of any length, and it was gone.

"I was pretty upset," she said. She set about to rewrite it but could not sustain the effort. Although she took a few stabs at pornography again, it would be almost twenty years before the themes worked well enough for her to develop into a full-length series of novels, and by then her ideas had evolved to a level of psychological sophistication. It is impossible to tell what *Charlotte* must have been like from the books written under Anne's pseudonym, A. N. Roquelaure.

Anne also wrote a romantic novella that she called *Nicholas and Jean,* about a man and a boy. Jean was named for a woman friend who worked with Anne and who often described for her the adventures of one of her gay acquaintances. Anne was entranced with the image of this man falling in love with a boy who had violet eyes. "That's what inspired me to write it," said Anne. "It gave me an image. I created this boy with violet eyes and imagined a man in love with him, and then the story came out of the subconscious."

Set in a castle on an island–a favorite image–it was typed single-spaced on seventy-five pages of flimsy newsprint; typewriter ribbon, Anne felt, showed up darker for a longer time on newsprint, thereby saving money.

"I was really letting my language go," said Anne. "I wanted to achieve something with Jean, this little boy figure, like Nabokov had achieved with *Lolita,* and I was madly pursuing my obsession."

The protagonist, Nicholas, is a photographer in his twenties and he narrates the story in the first person. He is allowed by a count to use a private, castle-like house, but when he arrives one night, he discovers Jean, who thrives on champagne and has a passion for velvet.

In this story Anne develops her flair for creating androgynous characters, begun as early as high school. Jean possesses "the red velvet jacket, the black leather gloves and those delicate features of which a girl might be proud." He is vulnerable and has become a sex object for rich men. He has been used, pampered, then imprisoned by one wealthy eccentric after another, running from each since the age of ten. Vulnerable and pretty, he presented for Anne a way to affirm the feminine within herself without confronting its unacceptable associations with her mother and with restrictive social roles and gender expectations. Through this character she could live out the male side of herself that she felt strongly, but not lose completely the female side.

Nicholas allows Jean to stay with him, and is himself sexually attracted to the boy. Anne, who felt herself to possess male qualities and could thus identify closely with Nicholas, found such a relationship sexually exciting; she allowed her imagination to explore the sensuality. She eagerly described the male body, seeing it as a thing of beauty, although women around her denigrated it. She felt a bit out of step in her attraction but indulged herself anyway.

Nicholas takes care of Jean, but eventually Jean leaves him. He drives around looking for the boy, and is told that Jean "has gone with the bat to the Bat Cave."

Through connections Nicholas gets admitted to a bizarre place where he must follow a ritual. He discovers that Jean is drugged and is being used as a male prostitute for men of "particular" taste. Nicholas rescues him and thinks he should try to find Jean's parents, but also wants to keep Jean for himself. Nicholas finally makes up his mind. "If you would love me, Jean," he says, "I would let you stay here forever, but it must be me only." Jean rises "just the fraction of an inch that was between our lips," and their relationship is sealed.

The language of this story was clearly influenced by poetry, possibly as much by Stan as by Nabokov: ". . . he tumbled into me like a gentle hot bundle of soft and hard things; he folded into me like my mother part, and his long thin leg caught the sunlight of that lamp and was turned to metal." Anne occasionally indulges in lengthy sentences, and it is astonishing how long she can draw out a thought with only the pause of a comma here and there:

> One night a month later, when I had cleaned out several rooms, had hired a servant, had found a man who would deliver wood for the fireplaces, had gotten a gas refrigerator, and a gas stove, I was in my darkroom under the red light when I heard

> the steps on the staircase and opening the door and stepping out into the cold air, I looked up and saw the little head again at the end of the hallway which was an open window still without glass, a gaping mouth to the sea, saw the gentle slope of the little bird shoulders, felt the little hands then on my lapels, and put my arms under those little arms, drew the iridescent eyes close to my cheek where I could listen to the lashes rising and dropping, kissed him, held him and heard him say with a slight giggle, "The man died."

The reader is not allowed to rest, but is carried along in the continuity of the scene as it merges with Nicholas's external, then internal experience. Anne showed early an excessive style, for which she would later be both praised and sullied. Patience and careful reading is required of readers, to feel the lyrical rhythms that she used and would continue to use throughout her career. Her prose was imitative initially of writers she admired, but also was developed enough to show early indications of her distinctive voice. Psychological and sexual ambiguities that make her characters complex and that reveal much about herself began to emerge in this early story. Her talent for detail is evident with a strong metaphorical quality.

The story serves as an initial foundation for her later work with erotic language and images, for the idea of a male who can transform into a female, and for the notion of an older man becoming a patient sexual mentor to a person whose social categorization as a child belies his sensuality. More important, however, the exercise of writing about such a subject gave Anne a sense of freedom and momentum. Although it cannot be classed with the philosophically complex novels still in the future, nor does it utilize any literary traditions, the presence of androgyny as an image of transition and freedom from gender set an important tone and direction for Anne's artistic perspective.

As the story continues, Jean remains with Nicholas, but they have problems. "Nicholas made the mistake," said Anne, "of telling the boy that he'd been married. So Jean, who was a female impersonator, went off and got garbed in female clothing and came to seduce Nicholas. He then revealed who he was and their affair was destroyed. Nicholas sent Jean away to boarding school. He could never forgive Jean, although Jean forgave him for having [sexually] responded. It ended with two other characters from boarding school, with Jean saying, 'I want us to have a certain amount of time playing this game, but if you don't come to your senses, I'll leave.' "

Some parts of the novella were read out loud at parties, to genuine enthusiasm, and several close friends willingly made their way through the draft.

"People loved it," said Anne. "They were tremendously encouraging. They responded to the excesses and the rhythms and the obsessions of it."

Michael Riley, who had migrated to California for graduate work after reading Stan's enthusiastic letters, and who made a habit of spending holidays with the Rices, read *Nicholas and Jean* one evening. His own interest concerned the creation of self in art, and he was stunned by Anne's ideas.

"I've never read anything that shocked me so much," he said. "It was dazzling and utterly different from anything I'd ever read. I felt a shiver as I turned the pages that night in the midst of a room filled with other people talking about other things. It seemed archetypal in the fullest Jungian sense. Everything was there, and you couldn't read it without being pushed to the wall."

Stan was equally impressed. "I thought it was very good as writing," he said. "It met the test of something sincere, articulate, and deep. We all have an interior of sexual fantasies which we normally forbid showing one another, but when we see it, I think we have to acknowledge it as being one of the wellsprings of mental activity that never gets outside of our heads." He had no problem with Anne writing sexually oriented material, not even one with homosexual themes. He encouraged her to write more, happy to see her talent come forth.

Anne brought part of the story to a creative-writing class. Other students were writing about subjects like hitchhiking or Big Sur, so she requested that it not be read out loud. The professor appreciated the story's originality, but felt it needed work. Anne eventually agreed, although what she liked about it was that "it was filled with high-pitched scenes."

Despite the encouragement, she never rewrote *Nicholas and Jean* into a draft that could be sent to publishers. Eventually she reworked the first chapter into copy acceptable enough to be published in the school literary magazine, and the novella later influenced two of her published works, *Belinda* and *Cry to Heaven.*

Although she was writing, Anne was also working full-time at the Orpheum Theater on Market Street. "I went to school when I had time," she said. It meant she had little time for seriously pursuing writing.

Stan worked in the mornings in San Francisco and drove out to the University of California at Berkeley at night. He had applied himself in the Ph.D. program for several months, determined to become a college professor, but he was growing disenchanted. Courses were large and impersonal, and the teaching was often more mechanical to his mind than creative. He was getting a reputation as a poet, and he did not want to be steered away from his spontaneous style. One day after classes, he was walking out of the student union building when he realized that he did not want to go on.

"It hit me like a bolt of lightning,"he described. "My foot was about to hit the third step when I realized that what I needed to do was quit and devote my life to being a writer. It was like seeing the burning bush."

However, to quit the Ph.D. program now, he realized, would be a major move. He'd be throwing away loans, job security, and education at a school with a good reputation. He had been shining in his classes. There was much to lose, potentially. He went home and waited for Anne to finish work.

"I came home," said Anne, "and he was sitting on the couch. He told me he really hated the Ph.D. program over there. He was miserably unhappy."

Stan gestured toward the cardboard boxes, painted on four sides, that hung from the ceiling—a symbol of artistic expression. "What I really want to do," he said, "is stuff like that."

"Do it," Anne told him.

She was less worried about job security and their future than she was that Stan might get enveloped in a more conventional world of job concerns. The priority was to stay with art.

"I knew he would never hurt me," said Anne, "and there would never come a day when he would say, 'Well, I'm gonna go to law school now and throw all these books out.' What I was afraid of was people who saw writing and art as only a phase. With Stan there was no need to fear. He would always be the mad bohemian and the mad poet. And he turned out to be responsible in ways that are good. He'd never have gone down to work for a savings and loan, but within the academic world he was conscious of decisions and choices that had to be made."

She assured him she would support his decision and he decided to quit. "It was the best decision I ever made," Stan said. "I didn't want to be defined in that way. I knew that once I got out, I'd have to do work that was defined by what I had graduated in. I decided right then to define myself rather than have a conflict at the *end* of the Ph.D. program." He went back to San Francisco State, to a master's program run by faculty who already knew him and appreciated his directions. He got a job as a clerical assistant to the chairperson and continued to give poetry readings.

It was a good move on Anne's part to support him, because she would need the same support from Stan years later when she made a similar decision. And her decision, too, would be the best one she ever made.

3

In May 1965, when Anne was twenty-three, her backroom efforts at the typewriter paid off. She published her first short story in the college magazine, *Transfer,* called "October 4, 1948"—the date of her seventh birthday. More dense with description than *Nicholas and Jean,* it showed a keen sensitivity to physical detail.

The story opens as a young girl, Dahlia (obviously Anne), is called in from outside because of an impending summer afternoon storm, the tension of which carries forth throughout the story. Dahlia joins her friend Lucy in Audubon Park, where Anne and Lucy Provosty had played together in New Orleans. They take the St. Charles streetcar, standing, as Anne and Lucy liked to do, next to the driver. It was "their favorite place . . . a little dangerous when the door swung open, but a delightful vantage point from which to watch the tracks disappear under the car, and to pretend one was driving the car." Dahlia gets off at her stop and goes home to a house like the one in which Anne grew up. "The ivy spilled from the patches near the picket fence over the cement squares and rustled in the wind. . . . Behind the screened porch, Dahlia could just trace with her narrowed eye the shape of her grandmother, tiny specks of white light filtered through the screen from her gray hair."

Much of the story is the moment-by-moment point of view of the girl. Anne packs sensory impressions into phrases like "the dry hiss of a car," "the tinkertip of change on the galvanized table top," and "nets of spiders and fragments of their unstuck victims."

In the kitchen, the grandmother and mother, Catherine, talk over tea, just as Mamma Allen and Katherine had done. Catherine sends young Dahlia to the store and she gladly complies, knowing she will pass the mysterious ruin of the Nellie Fallwell mansion, one of Anne's favorite houses.

The huge old house harbors secrets that frighten and attract the girl. Dahlia slows her steps, feeling the chill all children feel in the presence of haunted houses. She does not dare to go inside the rotting rooms to explore. Yet returning from the store, she hesitates, then pushes through the fence, and climbs onto the porch, sensing she will find a "terrible spectre." The tension of the weather parallels the girl's nervousness as her eyes wander painstakingly over broken furniture. She stands there, studying items that once belonged in the lives of people, and realizes she is alone. There are no ghosts. Her discovery deflates her fear, "as very gently, without even a pitter of warning, the rain began to come."

Anne won praise from friends for this story, and she was gratified, although it did not mean for her, as it does for many aspiring writers, a first important step toward recognition. No one was taking her seriously, not even herself. "I was too unformed at that point," she said.

She continued to wander through graduate school, painting nudes and several studies of a Christ face, but the activity did not envelop her. She changed her focus from art history to German to creative writing, becoming obsessed with each one, working it through, then moving on. She badly wanted more education but was not sure what she wanted to do.

In graduate school she encountered Hemingway again and fell in love with his writing, despite the fact that he was on the other end of the continuum from the excessive writers she adored. "I think Hemingway is a great model of how to write," said Anne. "I find him a source of inspiration and I never cease to learn from him. Just to pick up one short story and see how he does it is totally inspiring to me. He was such a marvelous craftsman that there was always such a great storytelling ability behind it. I've read more of his work than any other single writer." What impressed her was Hemingway's emphasis on immediate experience. "You have to capture the moment right before the sword goes in," Anne explained, "if you want to describe how a bull is being killed."

She also discovered Virginia Woolf. "I learned a lot from her, but reading her was always a task. It's hard to concentrate on her sentences. There's a lack of tension in her writing. I loved *Mrs. Dalloway.* I learned a lot about the way she [Woolf] would go into the mind and soul of a character over and over again—the way she would slip into their interior thoughts and weave a web of it." Both of these authors, along with Shakespeare, would become the focus of her graduate work.

Jack Kerouac was another writer who would eventually influence her. He had been a hero to the hip counterculture, a spokesperson for the beat generation. "I thought *On the Road* was the most wonderful book," said Anne. "I fell madly in love with it. I thought he was a genius. What he gave me in particular is the fact that he would say anything he wanted to at any particular time. He would just break the frame of the book to put in his own conjectures. I also like the tremendous compassion he had for his characters, his great ear for dialogue, and his appreciation for people from all different levels." She was inspired by his sense of freedom, symbolized in the metaphor of the open road, and she would return to this book over and over to remind herself of that freedom in both the style and content of her own writing.

Still submitting her work to *Transfer,* the first chapter of *Nicholas and Jean* appeared the next year, in June 1966. A third story, however, called "Absolution," was declined.

"I thought it was the best of all," said Anne. "It was about a boy who lived with a man in a sexual relationship from the time he was very little. When he was nineteen, he ran away. He comes back after many years and wants absolution for running away. He visits the man, but the man is very cold to him. I loved the story, but they didn't feel it was as strong as the others."

Was the story indicative of a search for her lost spiritual roots? She claimed her work came from the subconscious. She had been in a relationship with the church that could be metaphorically construed as sexual with regard to the emphasis on union with God, and she had left it, "run away," as an adolescent. There is vulnerability evident, and fear that looking once more into the face of God would only result in feeling shunned. Yet the sense of security she had experienced as a child was not easily forgotten. Even the image of absolution is religious—a remission of sins pronounced by a priest in an act of penance.

It would not be the last time that Anne would feature a child in a sexual/spiritual relationship, or the last time she would use a character to search for metaphysical meaning and reinstatement in a past unshattered by disillusionment and change.

4

While Anne and Stan were developing their skills, they continued to have parties and to explore artistic outlets. Sometimes, with too much free-flowing wine and a mix of temperaments, things got intense. People were challenged, pushed, bullied. The approach that both Stan and Anne took to such confrontations was to outthink a belligerent guest. They used words, not fists, to bring things under control.

Friends were in and out, and often after a party the rooms were full of people who had passed out. One morning Anne found five people sleeping in the living room, "flopped out on the carpet in their clothes for the night." Since her mother's blackouts she'd been anxious about being in the presence of a sleeping person and the scene unsettled her. The effect was heightened when a piece of driftwood hanging from a wire broke and fell through the window, shattering the glass. "Not one of those people woke up!" she exclaimed. But she was willing to go along with the atmosphere of freedom, developing her liberal ideals and allowing people space to do what they wanted, as long as they granted that to her.

Smoking marijuana soon became popular, and it seemed to present new, exciting ways to perceive the world. Stan was eager to try it as an aesthetic exercise to enlarge the sensory experience. It went hand-in-hand with what he called "natural process," which he explained to their theatrical friend, Jack DeGovia.

"He would put an orange in the middle of the table," Jack said, "and let it dry out and turn blue and black and moldy. Each stage of the process was viewed as being just as beautiful as the fresh orange. It preserved itself, like a gourd. He'd just watch that happen—the scenes of process. It would get thrown out when he changed the idea."

"Stan was very big into rotting food," Anne said. "We had a refrigerator full of rotting food, and people would come in to check on the progress. It was an aesthetic interest. They were smoking a lot of grass and they were very interested in the way the colors changed from moment to moment."

"It's like sculpture," Stan insisted. "It's drying up and changing. I let a lemon stand for about five years and it still smelled like a lemon."

As artistically influenced as the notion was, it made for comical situations. Anne wrote in a letter, "I remember the window in the kitchen broke because it didn't have a sash and nobody ever fixed it until the day we moved. One time someone threw a slice of pizza through it to the fire escape and it rotted out there for about six months. Then someone threw another sliver out there and it rotted, and one of these slivers was named Smiling Jack."

At times, however, Anne had had enough. "I remember one morning," she said. "The apartment was filled with rotting food and flowers and silly paintings. No one else was awake. They had this silly human skull that one of them had copped from the medical school, and they called it Lucy Grange. They decided that she had been murdered by a drunken husband. I woke up and charged into the living room, and there was Lucy Grange. They had put paper eyes in her sockets and a cigar in her teeth, and her teeth were wired shut, and I was horrified! There I was in the midst of this complete madness—books to the ceiling and ashtrays overflowing and everyone asleep on the floor—and I couldn't stand it a moment longer! I pulled the cigar out of Lucy's mouth and the teeth went *clack!*"

The apartment was temporarily cleaned up, and Lucy went back to the medical school.

"I was always a bit scared of what they were doing," Anne said. She admitted, however, that scenes in her later books may have been influenced by the concept of process. One notable example is where the protagonist, Louis, from her first novel is transformed into a vampire and he watches in fascination as his body goes through stages of change:

> It was as if I had only just been able to see colors and shapes for the first time. I was so enthralled with the buttons on Lestat's black coat that I looked at nothing else for a long time. . . . When I saw the moon on the flagstones, I became so enamored with it that I must have spent an hour there . . . and with my awakened senses, I had to preside over the death of my body. . . . I simply regret I was not more attentive to the process.

Anne had already developed her own intense attunement with the physical world, so her attention to such dramatic details may have occurred without exposure to rotting food or descriptions of marijuana highs. Ironically, however, Louis's transformation was influenced by a novel that Anne read later which detailed hallucinogenic experiences.

Another interest in the Rice household related to process was "essence." Discussions centered around observations of people who passed through the apartment. Anne and Stan got a kick out of making new acquaintances, then discussing what seemed to be positive and negative about them. Friends who listened were appalled at their detailed criticisms, wondering how *they* fared out of earshot. But for Anne and Stan, this was how writers should look at life, with an observant eye for personality and detail. It was a way of getting close, yet retaining artistic distance. Their critique did not imply moral judgment or rejection. It was simply their way of penetrating "essence."

It was not long before the social circles that the Rices had developed introduced them to hallucinogens. Some thought that dropping acid was the only way to understand what was happening in San Francisco. It gave new powers of sight and comprehension. "I wanted to go all out," Stan said of this new experience, "and see what it really had to show me. Stretch me out and get intense. I took LSD four or five times and peyote once."

Casey Sonnabend introduced them to Annette Arbeit, who eagerly encouraged mind-altering experiences. "At that time," said Annette in a letter, "we all saw ourselves as truth seekers attempting to pursue the most expansive, creative life-styles. It was our mission. We were experiencing being turned on to life's possibilities."

"She was wonderful, a natural philosopher of hip," said Jack DeGovia about Annette. "She understood what it meant to live life with your senses, appreciating everything. For example, in order to understand her kitten, she gave it a bath with her tongue."

Annette loved the Rices: "Anne and Stan were larger-than-life individuals. They seemed like investigative journalists tracking down the ultimate in creative truths. Anne was an unadorned beauty. Her look was conventional and conservative. But when she revealed her thoughts, she quickly commanded one's full attention. Her intellect was razor-sharp, probing. Her imaginings were radical and bizarre. Her hunger for information and insight was vast." She was amazed at the way Anne's creative obsessions led her deep into subjects as diverse as Egyptian art, Roman history, and gay artists.

People took care to have a guide on their trips. They were attempting to expand their vision, not just hallucinate for escape or recreation, and they often took large amounts of acid. For Jack's initiation he and Stan went to the beach. "What I got into," Jack explained, "was process. Stan would pick up an abalone shell and realize that the abalone shell was the way it was because of everything that had happened in the universe up to that point. I was really digging things, seeing things for what they really are, how a candle melts, driftwood, flowers. Everything had meaning."

Anne was not eager to join her husband this far in his mind experiments, despite his arguments about the artistic value. One day she came home from work and saw Stan at the top of the steps. He was wearing a flowered shirt and seemed to be glowing. He'd just come back from Muir Woods, from a trip on acid, and had been disturbed by the redwoods.

"Don't ever take this stuff!" he warned her, his eyes wide and intense. "Don't ever take it! You can't get away from anything you fear!"

Anne needed no further incentive to stay clean. "I already imagined giant cockroaches coming in, and I was not going to touch anything that destroyed the barriers."

When they partied, she went into the back room to watch TV or write. "Most of the time I was frightened," she said. "I watched them on their trips, but I wasn't going to scramble my brains with that stuff! I was the square of whatever crowd we knew." Although she had considered herself somewhat wild her first year in San Francisco, it had been in the context of drinking around boys who observed strict Catholic protocol. She had not really changed, but the context had, and she appeared to be out of step once again, only in the opposite direction.

Nevertheless, she was curious about the effects. "She questioned us at length," said Annette, "about our experiences and revelations."

"She would watch us get high," said Stan's brother, Larry, "and seemed to take delight in our attempts to catch up with her. She was not sanctimonious, though she would sometimes jokingly refer to us as a bunch of lascivious profligates."

Anne refused everything except an occasional joint, which had an extremely powerful effect on her, although the results were not psychedelic as others described. "It made her paranoid," Stan confirmed. "Everyone in the room started turning into monsters." She smoked while she listened to music, but preferred getting solidly drunk. Nevertheless, she captured accurately the experience of being high in her unpublished novella, *Katherine and Jean:*

"It was as if," says Katherine, "I'd been sleeping for a long time, hours, and had awakened to find we were still passing these little cigarettes around and around. I began to laugh. It would go on forever. Then it seemed I'd been laughing for ages. . . . 'This is it, this is really it,' I said. But I couldn't hear my own voice. The words seemed to become some kind of noise as soon as they were spoken." Anne wrote about the experience for Katherine in a manner that foreshadowed what her fictional vampires would describe of their magically heightened senses. She articulated the sensation that marijuana often produces of mixed sensory impressions: "We were all laughing and our laughter looked to me like a lot of crumpled silver foil. I blinked to stop the sensation that he was flickering on and off like a light as he spoke."

At one point Anne had an inner confrontation provoked by pot that profoundly affected her. "I had an absolutely devastating experience with it on the Berkeley campus," said Anne. "I had smoked it and I suddenly realized that we might not even know when we died what this [existence] was all about. I was a basket case for six months. I could hardly function." She had firmly believed that one day things would make sense, eventually, somehow, that there would come clarity and knowledge with a higher, more holy form of existence. Brought up on strict doctrines modeled for her by parents who fervently believed them; having herself been so convinced that they were true that she'd once begged to be allowed to enter a religious order; having enjoyed the security of a child raised in a climate of belief accepted by family, friends, teachers, and the larger society around her, she was only just now realizing what it was like to possess no real answers for the ultimate purpose and meaning of life. In college Anne had loosened herself intellectually from what she regarded as religious superstition, but not emotionally. Now she *felt* the implications of that rejection of absolutes and divine purpose, magnified by the surreal experience of pot; she felt it to the heart of her being and it hurt; she was swimming in an agony of absolute loss. It was as if her mother had died all over again, taking with her the warmth, love, and security of Anne's youth.

She went for help to a campus clinic, but it proved fruitless. She called friends to tell them of her negative epiphany, but they failed to see why it was such a devastating insight. They already felt that way most of the time. So we don't know, they said. So what? Why was it such a big deal? But for Anne, the sense of consuming dread and emptiness had a major impact on her perspective. Nothing looked the same. She saw flesh and blood decay; she saw people dead. She felt herself swallowed into a void.

"I was just walking around saying, 'We're all gonna die!' I never got over it. I went to class, I did what I had to do, but I was a gibbering idiot. It never went away. I never again felt the same way about life and death."

She captured the hollowness and horror years later in several novels, most dramatically in *The Vampire Lestat*. The young Lestat is in deep discussion with his friend Nicolas when the "Dark Moment" drops on him the way a predatory cat might spring from above. What he says is what Anne felt:

> I realized aloud, in the midst of saying it, that even when we die we probably don't find out the answer as to why we were ever alive. . . . "We'll never know, and all this meaninglessness will just go on and on. . . . We'll just be gone, dead, dead, dead, without ever knowing!"
>
> There was no judgment day, no final explanation, no luminous moment in which all terrible wrongs would be made right, all horrors redeemed. . . . No one was ever going to tell us anything!
>
> No, I didn't understand it at this moment. I *saw* it! And I began to make the single sound: "Oh!" I said it again. "Oh!" and then I said it louder and louder and louder, and I dropped the wine bottle on the floor.

It was too close to her fear of the grave, too close to the idea of existing in a limbo state, half alive and half dead but ever aware that there was no way out. The idea is echoed when, in Anne's tenth novel, one character says, "I'll tell you what I fear. . . . That it's chaos after you die, that it's a dream from which you can't wake. Imagine drifting half in and out of consciousness, trying vainly to remember who you are or what you were. Imagine straining forever for the lost clarity of the living."

Like Anne, Lestat questions each of his acquaintances. He even consults a priest. No one has answers and no one wants to be bothered with his emotional upheaval. He feels the impact of his realization more strongly than others might, just as Anne felt that she did. For Lestat, as for Anne, this dreadful awakening never did pass, although it would heighten and diminish with events still in the future. "The world looked different forever after, and even in moments of exquisite happiness there was the darkness lurking, the sense of our frailty and our hopelessness."

Scenes such as this would later provoke critics of Anne's novels to charge her with melodramatic writing, but for her the emotions were not exaggerated; they were the result of a clash between once powerful beliefs in a solid foundation and deeply felt, unvoiced fears that she would fall through the holes. No doubt it was the mystery of what hovered in the darkness behind the lighted candles that had provoked in part the childhood devotion to God that had sent her to her knees for hours of prayer and meditation. And now the candles were snuffed.

"What caused it?" Lestat reflects. "Was it the late night drinking and talking, or did it have to do with my mother and her saying she was going to die?" A revealing question indeed! Was it the serious discussions among marijuana vapors that had penetrated Anne's secret dread, or had suppressed grief over her mother's death suddenly surfaced to smash protective illusions? Memories of her mother seemed inextricably woven into emotional struggles with the church.

Smoking grass also frightened Katherine in *Katherine and Jean:*

> I was cold with fear. I saw the end of the universe then, or what I thought was the universe and out beyond it was a great darkness, the darkness of *non-being.* That's what it was, dying, if there was no God. It was just ceasing to exist. Never knowing what it was all about, never knowing if the sufferings of the world were justified . . . A darkness without reason. . . . I was lying down on the bed moaning, crying, unable to speak. . . . I would never go through this pain again in my life. Never. If I had the choice. No drug, no love, no nothing could be worth this terrible pain that I felt then. I lost my immortality. . . . I felt my vulnerability and the humiliation of being mortal totally. And I was inconsolable. . . . And when I looked at Jean I saw all the blood and breath in his body . . . I saw them corroding. . . . I looked at my hands and I knew they would rot . . . and I screamed.

Anne felt alone with her metaphysical insight, and horribly vulnerable. She decided grass was too dangerous and she stopped smoking, refusing to risk her mind for the sake of heightening her awareness. All around her, people got high and dropped acid and seemed to her to lose their motivation to do anything.

"I would have defended those people to outsiders to the death," she said, "but inside, I thought it was a crock. I was totally out of water with those people, all of them. I was the one who wouldn't take acid and just drank—which they didn't. I was an old-fashioned person who wanted to make accomplishments. The hippie revolution was anti-intellectual and I had great respect for the intellect. I was in the process of acquiring a traditional education, and I didn't intend to let anything get in the way. So I was the one who came home from work in high heels and stockings. I not only got flak for being a square but for looking and sounding like a square and saying things that were extremely unfashionable. I didn't click. I was out of step, inhibited, uptight."

Nevertheless, she respected herself, despite the peer pressure, and did not see herself so much middle-class as simply individual. Later Anne would describe her resistance in a fictional character: "Like all strong people, she suffered always a measure of loneliness; she was a marginal outsider, a secret infidel of a certain sort. And the balance by which she lived might be upset if she were to question her own goodness."

"Anne was always incorrigibly herself," said Larry Rice. "She was impossible to pigeonhole. Every fad passed her by like it had never existed, as she clung to her conservativism."

In the midst of the artistic chaos, Anne anchored herself even more decisively in traditional values when she was promoted to the box office at the theater where she worked. "The job was a real coup," she said. "I earned more than anyone else as a ticket seller." Then she became pregnant.

5

She and Stan were thrilled. At last they were going to have a family! Nothing meant more to Anne, having since childhood been strongly attached to her relatives. Now she would have a chance to care for a child of her own.

"I'm very maternal," said Anne. "I was really looking forward to being a mother." She had plans for a large family, perhaps as many as five or six children, and she could hardly suppress her excitement. As her body expanded with the growing child, she dressed in high-waisted gold and magenta dresses given to her by a friend, and later in her pregnancy she wore a white lace jumper with flaming pink shoes. "I liked to dress up like a doll," Anne said. Eventually she quit her job, although she and Stan did not stop giving parties. It was believed at that time, according to Anne, that alcohol did not cross the placenta, so she enjoyed herself and looked forward to the approaching event.

Stan worked on his last courses in order to finish up, make more money, and achieve stability. He received a grant of a thousand dollars for his poetry. Then he took his master's degree and began at the age of twenty-three to teach at San Francisco State University. In spite of his youth, he was highly regarded and was put to work teaching upper-division courses. He proved to be as dynamic and energetic in the classroom as he was at readings, and became quite popular with students. "There was a lot of give and take in the room," he said, "but I had to get high off it, I had to get it zinging in my head. That's what made it fun." He was also appointed the assistant director of the Poetry Center, one of the largest and oldest poetry-reading organizations in the world. Later he became the director. By the age of twenty-seven, he would be a tenured professor at San Francisco State.

Stan enjoyed teaching. "It's all theater to me," he said. "It's a cross between evangelism, drama, and a live reading." He tried to bring information from philosophy, physics, and mathematics to use as analogs to show how language could get congested. To him, poetry was a very physical, tangible thing that cohered to experience, and he possessed an intuitive feel for what was wrong and what was right with a poem. He was able to convey that to students, and he settled eagerly into his academic career.

That same year, 1966, an International Day of Protest was declared against the presence of the United States in Vietnam. The police became brutal, using offense as defense, and rioting began on the campuses. Flower children poured in from all over the country to get to utopia—Haight-Ashbury—effecting an evolution in clothing and language. "I remember," said Anne, "the first time I heard someone call himself a hippie. I couldn't believe it. In Denton, *hippie* had been a derogatory word for someone who wanted to be hip and didn't know how. Suddenly these hippies were everywhere!"

Hippies were a collective of yearning souls out to change the world with peace, love, and drugs. Influenced by the Beats, they preached: no envy, no possessions, no pain. Don't define experience in words. Unclutter your mind. Trust no one over thirty. Haight-Ashbury was transformed into a circus. Acid, still legal, was available everywhere and people "dropped out" by the thousands. A theatrical group called The Diggers—"artists of the will"—paraded through the streets in animal masks, carrying coffins and distributing free food and services.

Anne and Stan still lived there, and one evening they were stopped in the street because of their hair and clothing. They felt they were becoming targets for harassment and decided to move to a "square" part of town.

They found a spacious apartment on Taraval among the stuccoed buildings, in a neighborhood off Nineteenth Street known as the Avenues. It was treeless and boxed in by constant fog and by ultraconservative neighbors, which often drove them off to Sausalito with Michael Riley to sit in the No Name Bar. They furnished their apartment as nicely as they could afford and lived on a tight budget. The move took them away from the bohemian cliques and provided a mainstream, middle-class atmosphere, which did not sit well with them. They found themselves depressed by the sunless, uptight atmosphere, although Anne enjoyed easy access to the library, just a block over, where she read Flaubert.

On September 21, when Anne was almost twenty-five, she gave birth to a daughter. Stan was present at the delivery, an unusual event at the time, but they had searched for a doctor that would allow it. In gown and mask he watched in awe. "It was fabulous," he said. "I wept."

It was a breech birth, and after twelve hours of labor Anne was given a saddle block to ease the pain. During labor they named the baby Michele. "We'd been going over names for a long time," said Stan. "Anne hit on it and I figured if she really got visited by a good one, this was the right time to take it." Stan took the baby to the nursery to be weighed and was mistaken for a doctor, since doctors were usually the only men seen in the nursery.

Michele was blond with brown eyes, and won the hearts of everyone who saw her. She earned the nickname "Mouse" for her large eyes and small face.

"She was smart and precocious," Anne said. "She was a very beautiful little girl. She had everything going for her in every conceivable way. People stared at her on the streets."

Stan willingly pitched in and changed diapers, another unusual activity for men in those days. He made many of the child-rearing decisions because he had very firm ideas about how things should be done. Anne yielded, expressing to friends that she knew little about raising children and that Stan was better at it. She loved to dress Michele, however, and went to Goodwill to buy little cotton dresses with puffy sleeves that she was forever ironing—not like the mildewing shirts from her college days. "Michele was always dressed like a little princess," said Anne.

Finding herself at home with time on her hands, Anne studied soap operas. "I decided to watch each of three soap operas for an extended period of time to see if they differed in their emphasis. I drew the conclusion that 'The Edge of Night' always had to do with crime, 'As the World Turns' was centered on family relationships, punishing those who violated them, and 'Love of Life' I couldn't figure out. It was sort of prurient. I wanted to see how they worked." Friends were amazed at how Anne's mind absorbed these dramas and how she could recite intricate details of plot and character. The television shows failed to influence her fantasy life but gave her ideas with which to tinker for possible writing projects.

She wrote stories whenever she was inspired by an image or an idea. Once after reading a story called "The Nose," about one man stealing the nose of another, she concocted her own humorous version of such an event, with a special twist. She wrote about seeing a beautiful gay man in a park and exclaiming, "That man has my body!" It was a common fantasy for her now, wishing she were a man able freely to admire the male physique of another, as gay men did. They inspired in her a strong feeling of kinship, of not fitting socially acceptable definitions. "I felt that the terrific response I had to men physically must mean that I'm a gay man trapped in a woman's body."

Michael Riley had confessed to the Rices that he was gay, and to his surprise, Anne not only accepted that, "but," he said, "she showed an absolute fascination with almost everything that had to do with being gay. It was remarkable to be discussing the subject with anyone, much less a woman." He appreciated their friendship more than ever. For Anne the interest was a natural extension of her tendency in high school to idealize equality and courage. Characters in her fantasy world were already "coming out of the closet." She saw homosexuality as a physical realization of that ideal and looked to gay men as figures that exhibited the erotic aspects of gender while transcending the negative aspects. A man who transcends gender, she felt, sees the world more clearly. Yet there was something about them that reached more deeply into her, having less to do with ideals and more to do with a complex sexuality that released her from becoming anchored in stereotypical feminine roles. Across the next two decades, Anne would utilize this connection in her writing to produce a broad spectrum of sexual and emotional bonds that would not only reveal her own obsessions but would touch a powerful nerve in millions of readers.

In 1967, the media sensationalized the hippie movement as the "Summer of Love." Seventy-five thousand hippies flooded Haight-Ashbury in anticipation of a "happening," and swept away the burgeoning art movement. Most wore the now mandatory uniforms of beards, beads, headbands, and long hair. Although LSD was now illegal, acid-dropping parties still prevailed. Androgyny pervaded the sexual revolution through hair and clothing, and personal pleasure became the password. Fifty thousand people demonstrated in Washington, shouting, "Make Love, Not War!" while eighty-three people were killed throughout the country in race riots.

Anne was influenced. She would later say that the slogan "Make Love, Not War" was the most important cliché of the century. She believed in secular codes of morality that could endure in a godless world, and felt strongly that love was the goal to be achieved as a basis for ethics.

The day after Nixon was elected president in 1968, students and sympathetic faculty staged a rally at San Francisco State College. Governor Ronald Reagan sent police to the campus.

"The state campuses," Anne remembered, "erupted in unbelievable violence, with people beaten up and police marching all over. What I saw made me mad. I witnessed it but was not part of it. I've always looked at things as if I hadn't been born in this century." Being a mother with a small child, she also worried about safety.

She watched confrontations, then noted how they were later mediated through television. "The horrifying thing about the news every night was that it cooled things off too much. It was nothing like being there and feeling the incredible electricity when people shoved each other and someone hit another person and there was blood on his face." She felt the students were provoked but were presented as the initiators of violence.

The clamor was continuous through January of the next year, when five hundred demonstrators were arraigned in court. Untenured faculty who had participated were let go. Stan Rice was not among them. He had been involved in desegregation movements in Texas but felt that many of those basic issues had been resolved in San Francisco. "You had to be a political type," he said, "to get into something heavy."

In Berkeley, across the bay, people developed an empty lot into People's Park, only to have the police fence it off. Fifty demonstrators were hit by bullets, one man died, and the area was occupied by the National Guard under martial law.

Later that same year, the United States withdrew the first troops from Vietnam and sent astronauts to the moon—only one month before half a million people gathered for the momentous three-day rock concert at Woodstock, New York, where nakedness symbolized innocence. Hopes for a new age of peace and love were soon shattered at the Rolling Stones' free concert in Altamont, where Hell's Angels killed a black man. In October, student riots overtook the campuses at Berkeley and Oakland.

Stan and Anne kept to their own little world, enveloped with raising a daughter and watching Stan's career blossom. He was asked to do readings for large fund-raisers because he was a crowd pleaser, and Anne was content to be a mother. Michele was the bright point of their lives. They delighted in caring for her, taking her on walks, and watching her interests follow artistic directions as she grew from an infant into a toddler.

"As soon as she could talk," said Larry Rice, "one knew she had inherited the genius."

"She was very bright," Stan said, "and very talented as a painter. She liked to sit and paint and draw for hours. She had a good sense of humor and was very witty. She kept her own counsel. She could be alone easily, and she was more visual than oral. We were very much alike. She liked going out on the beach and roaming. She could walk off by herself and she was never afraid." Like Stan, who'd had an imaginary playmate as a boy, Mouse developed a cool independence.

Anne and Stan read to her, and Anne took her once to a preschool to play with the other kids. "I felt," said Anne, "that we were giving her a tremendously creative environment. There was no doubt in my mind that she was getting terrific input. She was exposed to adults all the time, and wandered all around at every party we ever gave. I expected her to reach the stars."

"Mouse was their ultimate perfect creation," said Annette Arbeit. "They literally adored her every move and gesture. Her drawings, photos, and quotes were posted throughout their apartment, displayed as important artifacts. They both seemed obsessed with the cultivation of her purity and virginal genius. They perceived her as a living art form."

Anne tried to give Michele dolls, but she showed no interest. "I remember the first doll," said Anne. "She just threw it on the floor. I think she didn't like the strong vinyl smell. I couldn't figure it out. She didn't take to them. She never cuddled or played with them."

Nevertheless, she provided hours of great joy and they could not imagine life without her.

6

By 1969, they felt it was time to move.

"San Francisco struck us as polarized," Anne explained. "Hatred for the hippies caused people to stare with hostility at people with long hair. And in Berkeley we found a wonderfully tolerant atmosphere where shopkeepers were used to students who looked like hell."

She was also sick of the politics. People would come in and ask her why she was writing a novel, why she was hung up on linear structure. Why didn't she just go out and draw on the sidewalk or play a recorder in the sun? "Get out of here," she'd growl. "*You* go draw on the pavement and walk around barefoot!" She wanted to be left alone.

"I hated incense," said Anne. "I couldn't stand Indian music. I got sick of the rhetoric, of being told by the liberals what I should be thinking or doing. I hated the conservatives because I thought they represented oppression and they were doing stupid things, but I hated the liberals because they were absolutely fascistic. Because I had long hair, I was being spoken to as if I was supposed to go along with all of it, and I always thought it was a load of crap. The shallow thinking infuriated me. It's one of the few periods in my life where my personality formed through resistance. I had to just resist their judgments and do what I wanted to do."

Nevertheless, she was loosening up. She gave up the long dresses of the sixties and began to wear short cotton sundresses with no underwear. "I thought it was liberated," she said. "It felt very free." People no longer accused her of being conservative but thought she was a bit too free as she sat carelessly, with her feet up, oblivious to exposure.

They rented a house in Berkeley at 1621 Dwight Way with room for a garden. They filled it with Stan's artwork—now lead weights from fishing nets that he painted with bright colors—and with furniture, often picked up off the street. They framed pictures cut out from magazines or posters, and covered the walls with photographs of Mouse. Anne began to collect things to make her house the home she had never had, and ran up high bills on credit before she realized she had to slow down. There was plenty of space, which she soon discovered required a lot of cleaning. Anne planted a banana tree in the front yard to remind her of her beloved New Orleans. She'd missed the trees and heat of Louisiana, and Berkeley seemed a step closer than windswept, damp, treeless San Francisco. She loved the physical beauty, but mostly she loved just having a home. Stan willingly hitchhiked over to San Francisco State to teach.

Jack DeGovia got married that year, and he and his new wife, Carla, became friends with the Rices. They took long walks together in Golden Gate Park, and Carla was especially enamored of Michele.

One day the four of them went on a picnic to the Russian River. In the car, according to Carla, Anne asked everyone what they wanted from life. Carla said she wanted to be a better actress. Everyone else had equally career-specific dreams.

"I only want two things," said Anne. "I want to be famous and I want to be rich."

Carla was impressed with her confidence, although Anne had meant it in fun. She wanted money, people remembered her saying, in order to be free of the need for money—to have freedom for art without financial worries. However, the way she and Stan recklessly spent every penny, they would never be rich, not unless Stan gained the national reputation that seemed almost within his reach.

Soon Stan met Floyd Salas, a novelist and a poet who had won the local Joseph Henry Jackson Award for poetry in 1964. He became part of the Rices' circle, much smaller now that they were out of the Haight, and more academic, with many of their acquaintances coming from Stan's department.

"Floyd was very good about inspiring young writers," Anne remembered. "He'd say we were all going to be great." He was going to the University of California at Berkeley on a boxing scholarship, and he took Anne and Stan to amateur and professional matches. Anne was enthralled.

"Those were great experiences," she said. "I really loved going out into the world and seeing something different. I love any sport that involves one person against another person. It's an amazingly sensuous experience. They're bathed in this gorgeous light, and they come out with very beautiful bodies." She enjoyed the excitement, especially watching people place bets in the aisles. "The writer in me loves sitting there and observing what's going on. It's masculine pornography."

Floyd had a century-old cabin at Big Sur, and he invited Anne and Stan to join him for a week. He maintained a rigorous exercise schedule, and one morning Anne—who was always provoking him into a match—suggested that he box with Stan. He looked at Stan, who accepted the challenge, and they sparred a bit. Then Floyd turned to Anne and said, "Now you put the gloves on."

He helped her with a mask that he used with women, then laced on the gloves. "She faced me," he said, "and she started moving her arms back and forth, and the most beautiful smile came across her face.

She loved it, the competitiveness. She was a natural. She was a killer, a driver."

Anne followed the sport avidly and became a shrewd judge of the matches. George Foreman had won the world heavyweight title from Joe Frazier and was going to fight Muhammad Ali. Anne insisted Ali would win, but Floyd replied that Ali was not strong enough. Anne was vindicated when Ali won by outsmarting his opponent.

Floyd was one of the few people with whom Anne exchanged stories. "Anne always read carefully," Floyd recalled, "and gave back a comprehensive report." He often argued with her over what made literature good. Anne admired writers like Dostoevsky and Dickens, but Floyd pointed out that intellectual characters were not consistent with the American style. American writers like action.

Although Floyd thought Anne and Stan approached their work too intellectually, he did admire Anne's drive. "What Anne had," Floyd said, "was imagination, and the industry and will to succeed. She worked long hours and was determined. She thought you had to have talent, but I used to argue with her that a writer needed love. That's what she had. There was tension in her, the urge to survive, but underneath there was this love of what she does."

He and Stan would kid around about how famous they were going to be, since both possessed the impression of a star on their palms. They looked but found no such impression on Anne's hand. Like palm readers years before who had looked at Anne's hand and found no sign of creativity, Stan and Floyd were wrong about what was only a few years away.

During that time Anne decided that she would write one story each evening, from eight until ten, as an exercise. One of them was about a vampire with a cynicism reminiscent of Oscar Wilde. She took it out several times to work on it, then put it away, unfinished. Without realizing it, she held in her hand the story that would one day radically change her life. Fortunately, she left it unfinished, making it possible for future events to develop the story more powerfully than she was capable of doing at that time.

She also wrote a story called "Die, Die, My Darling," that had an autobiographical tone. "It was about a bunch of hippies watching TV and smoking grass," Anne said. "It was written from the first-person point of view of one of the hippie women. She complains about her intensity and how it puts everyone off. Every time she starts to talk to people, she gets too intense and they get mad. So they're watching this hokey movie called *Die! Die! My Darling,* and there's this scene where Tallulah Bankhead pauses on this gothic staircase, and she's about to try to murder her daughter-in-law. The hippie woman freaks out and says, 'That's me! I am that woman and I am on that staircase forever, and I am the daughter being killed. I am all those people in that movie. That's it! That's it!' "

It was a feeling that Anne was always trying to capture, a moment of supreme clarity—a sense of something *there* that she wanted to grasp and describe that seemed authentic and close to the core of meaning. She had experienced it briefly once when she had been very drunk and had walked into a room where Stan had been watching Jean Cocteau's version of *Beauty and the Beast.*

"The beast was standing there talking," she said, "dressed in his velvet clothes with his huge beast head, and I remember saying, 'That's it, that's it, that's absolutely it!' and then passing out."

Although she could not articulate exactly what she was after, the search for it intensified. Another attempt to capture it featured a gangster named Bernie and his girlfriend, Lucy, who sat on his lap in a black slip. "I tried to convey," said Anne, "that I was Bernie and I was Lucy, that I was both of them, sitting there in that room by the brass bed with the shade pulled down."

There was a weirdness in these stories that felt normal to her, something that others did not understand. Her writing was not merely a way to describe her world and her feelings but to search for something beyond the surface. That search was destined to continue as Anne fanned out into a wide array of subjects and styles.

She pushed on, determined now to discipline herself, even to assert herself when she had to. "Exploit any reason to write," she told herself. She did not have clear direction with what she wanted to write, but she was now more determined than she had been over the past few years to see what she could do. Once when Stan and his poet friend, Casey, wanted to write, they found Anne at the typewriter. Stan insisted she let them use it. Anne claimed she was writing a story. Casey was incredulous. Stan was the writer, he insisted. Who did Anne think she was? But she held her ground. She was developing the first glimpses for herself of what would later become a grand vision of being a writer.

Around this time Anne had several unusual and vivid dreams that she would remember years later. One was about being a god. "I was standing before this temple and my job was to call down the rain. The priest told me that at one point I would call down the rain and there would be snow and then I would die. I raised my arms and called down the rain, and there were these enormous snowflakes and everything was destroyed around me. It was a huge deluge and I remember seeing this temple with the peristyles sinking into the water and people were screaming and clinging to the top. An alligator was eating them. The priests said, 'Come with us,' and they took me down into an old Catholic chapel. There were old gods sitting in the back pew, and I realized that we didn't die, we just sat in the back pew and the priests took care of us." The dream struck her as unearthly, like a vision, and it may have influenced the way the character Marius took care of Those Who Must Be Kept in her novel *The Vampire Lestat*. The other dream, however, was more frightening.

"I had a horrible nightmare that my daughter was turning blue and collapsing because of the fluid in her veins. She was withering and dying. It was awful. It was like a premonition." Anne watched her daughter closely, but everything seemed fine. Still, she could not shake the dark feeling, not with a background like hers—raised in New Orleans by a mother who read palms and fervently believed in the mysteries of the incarnated Christ. What could such a dream mean?

7

Anne broke off her graduate work at San Francisco State to enter the Ph.D. program at the University of California at Berkeley. She was excited to be accepted and considered it a high point in her academic pursuits. She had been afraid that her poor high school record would keep her back. Now she was ready to take courses in Shakespeare, Chaucer, and Middle English, "which filled enormous gaps in my education." All she wanted to do was write and read the classics.

Anne soon grew disenchanted, as Stan had before her. There was a heavy emphasis at Berkeley on literary criticism and steep language requirements. Anne made excellent grades, vindicating herself as a bright person, but seemed to be going in scholarly directions that did not suit her taste.

Over the Christmas break, she rewrote *Nicholas and Jean* into a longer novella called *Katherine and Jean,* featuring a different period in the life of the bisexual boy, Jean, but with a female protagonist. She probed further into the world of S&M cults, about which she knew little, and addressed sexuality more explicitly. There was less emphasis on the older man/younger boy theme, although the heroine, Katherine, was a naive schoolgirl, fresh out of a Catholic boarding school, who became aware of the seedy world of sexual hustling. Much of the sexuality was presented through hints and innuendos, playing on erotic impulses rather than becoming full-blown pornography. There was also a great deal of humor as Anne invented scenes where people talked about making love with butter and cinnamon. The story had problems, however, since she did not have the knowledge she felt she needed about important details, like the workings of a hotel. She had to consult friends about the procedures for checking in before she could put Katherine and Jean into the Fairmont in San Francisco.

"I was trying to write about Katherine," said Anne, "and how backward she was, but I didn't even know things about room service. I wasn't prepared to write it. It was a novel about me yearning to know all kinds of secret things about life."

Nevertheless, she thought it was polished enough to enter in the Joseph Henry Jackson awards contest. It won honorable mention and praise from a few New York publishers. But Anne did not feel it was quite right to send out. "I loved it but it didn't really jell."

The experience of writing it, however, made her realize that she did not want to stay at Berkeley. Her Chaucer professor had inspired her by describing a writer's life as a feeling of being saved every day, of doing something significant. In another class, after studying Stendhal through literary criticism, Anne finally realized she wanted to *be* someone like Stendhal, not just criticize him. She decided to return to San Francisco State to work on her master's degree in creative writing.

That same year Stan won the Joseph Henry Jackson Award for poetry. He received fifteen hundred dollars and bought a red MG sports car. Now he was able to drive to work, and drive in style. He also met Laura Chester and Geoff Young, small press publishers who invited him to read poetry in New Mexico and published him in their magazine, *Stooge*. Stan spoke to them enthusiastically about Anne's writing, but Laura later admitted she had dismissed his remarks. Like others who viewed Anne in Stan's shadow, she was in for a surprise.

One person who supported Anne was Betsy Dubovsky, a poet and artist just arrived in Berkeley from running a fishing boat in Alaska. She took a poetry course with Stan and was impressed with his teaching. "He was so remarkably full of spirit and vitality," she said. She did not like to drive on freeways, so she asked him for a ride home. One evening he took her to meet Anne.

"It didn't take long," said Betsy, "before I was completely overwhelmed and won over by her. I thought she was an extraordinary person."

The meeting began an intense time for all of them. Stan picked Betsy up almost every day and brought her to the house. "We'd spend all day talking and drinking and carrying on," she said. "We talked about art and we'd read stuff to each other. They were just ecstatic exchanges! Anne understood the enraptured state. The atmosphere was passionate and spontaneous." Anne was pleased that Betsy was not intimidated by an argument, but could hold her own and come back for more. That was the kind of woman she liked. She also found in Betsy a kindred spirit in her appreciation for Tolstoy and Dostoevsky. Betsy influenced Anne's later writing by proposing the concept of the "Golden Moment" that occurs in her eighth novel, *The Vampire Lestat*. "We were all drinking," Anne explained, "and she said, 'There comes a golden moment when everything makes sense.' I think Colin Wilson describes it as a peak experience, when everything seems to be part of you and you're part of everything, and the world makes sense for one minute."

Betsy's husband, Tony, also remembered meeting Anne, getting a firsthand exposure to one of her obsessions. When he walked in the door, he encountered a veritable sea of pictures cut from issues of *Road and Track* spread all over the floor. "That was my introduction to Anne," he recalled.

"I did go on a kick of being obsessed with sports cars," Anne admitted. "but I never pursued it because there was no way to enjoy it. I found it very interesting and glamorous. I liked reading about the races around the world."

Betsy and Tony were part of the crowd of people who came to the Rices' parties, still ornamented with candles, jazz, and readings. Floyd Salas also attended, and another artistic couple, Marjorie Ford and Joe Slusky. Joe was a metal sculptor who would later inspire a character in Anne's novel *Belinda*.

Little Michele, nearing the age of four, wandered among the artists and writers, getting exposure to their language and their work—something Anne's mother would have wanted for *her* had the opportunities been available and unhampered by religious propriety. Michele also went along with them to Kip's, a pizza parlor, where she watched TV or fell asleep on the floor as they drank beer with friends and argued late into the night. They thought it was terrific for her to have the stability of a home, but with bohemian leanings. They looked forward to seeing how she would develop as she grew older.

Anne's witty side emerged at parties. "It was a delight," said Larry Rice, "to watch her double up and turn red with laughter. Her wit was sharp and her sense of humor a joy to behold. Her laughter was always close to the surface, ready to erupt."

However, Betsy noticed that Anne was mostly ignored by the people who came to be near Stan. "It was painful for Anne to be snubbed," she said, "by all these teachers and students."

Nevertheless, Anne found people to talk to. At one gathering Joe Slusky remembered Anne speaking to a man who worked at San Francisco General Hospital, and he overheard a remark that struck him as odd. "She had this breathless desire to see sickness," he said. "She wanted to experience firsthand what suffering was about." The remark was not so unusual for someone developing as a writer, but it would become tragically ironic within a short period of time.

Many of the get-togethers went late into the night, and Tony Dubovsky remembered the scenes at five o'clock in the morning when people were passed out all over the house. Daisy, the shorthaired German pointer, went around tipping over abandoned cans of beer, spilling the contents and lapping it up.

"As we lay in bed," said Anne, "we could hear it happening, can by can."

The Rices eventually moved to a ground-floor apartment in Berkeley at 1275 Bonita Avenue. Not far away lived Larry Rice and Annette Arbeit, now married, and their daughter, Alisa. Anne described the new place to a friend as a "Richardson-style apartment with wall-to-wall carpeting and modern appliances." They installed a desk in the bedroom, with bulletin boards, a chalkboard, and books everywhere. Anne put up pictures of ceremonial masks and of Hemingway and Fitzgerald alongside drawings by Michele. She also included pictures of the French actor Alain Delon, who had inspired the physical appearance of her character Jean.

"It seemed like a paradise," said Anne of the new neighborhood, "with big California pepper trees shading the corner and kids playing outdoors all day long." It was two blocks from Live Oak Park, one of the most beautiful areas in Berkeley, and there were other children for Michele to play with. Stan often took her to the park or the zoo in her pretty gingham dresses.

Anne continued with her writing, dipping once again into pornography, and to Betsy and Stan she read two chapters of her fledgling novel, *The Tales of Rhoda*. The story was set in the present with a young heroine who was brought into captivity voluntarily. She had been in a local bookstore in Berkeley and someone had walked up and invited her.

"It was hysterical," Betsy recalled. "One of the questions that we were interested in was masochism, or the woman's wish to be dominated—how women could be aroused by that. We plunged into it over and over as one of our philosophical questions."

For Anne, however, it was more than philosophical. She had experienced masochistic fantasies as a child and had been experimenting with various scenarios of consensual bondage since her first novel. She would continue to do so for some time to come. The images obsessed her and would acquire intensity and greater dimension as she realized the social prejudice that reserved symbolic sexual violence as a turn-on exclusive to males. She knew what excited her and was not about to allow anyone to tell her differently—not men or other women. However, the new novel did not get past the first few chapters.

"It never got off the ground," Anne admitted. She was not ready to take up pornography again, although she gravitated toward sexual issues. Her intense physical desire filled her fantasy worlds, but she was not really sure how to work it into her writing. So far her more sustained attempts at pornography had been about women, although in *Nicholas and Jean* and a few short stories she had discovered how much she'd enjoyed writing about relationships between men. Like the saints she had so strongly admired in her youth, gay men exhibited an excessiveness that excited her and courage in the face of prejudice. As people reinventing themselves from outsiders to insiders in gay communities, they were heroes, representing freedom, and would become even more prominent in her imagination as they began to fight for their rights in the next decade.

At the same time Anne also turned her searching mind to her native Louisiana, "to answer questions of my own that haunted me. I had been living in California for years with no prospect of going back and I wanted to read up on New Orleans." She took Michele along to the public library and the library on the Berkeley campus, going through volumes of the *Louisiana Historical Quarterly* for articles on all aspects of Louisiana in the 1700s and 1800s. She had a vague idea about a novel that might take place in this time period in her home state—something that would move her away from pornography—but nothing solidified. She continued her schoolwork and searched for an inspiring theme. She was twenty-eight years old, almost twenty-nine. If she was going to be a writer, she had to get moving. But something else happened that made a career seem a trivial concern.

Late in the summer, Michele complained of vague illnesses. She developed a fever and felt too tired to play. It was not a child's temperament and Anne was alarmed. She noticed dark circles under Michele's eyes and an uncharacteristic listlessness. A chill of dread shot through her as she gathered up the little four-year-old and took her to the doctor.

The diagnosis stunned her: acute granuleucytic leukemia.

CHAPTER FIVE

MICHELE

> . . . on hearing
> The diagnosis was leukemia I lay down
> On the linoleum and saw a door shut
> On what *is*.
>
> —Stan Rice, "Some Lamb"

1

Michele's illness threw Stan and Anne into a flurry of activity. The prognosis was gloomy for their beautiful little girl, since most people who contracted this form of leukemia did not live long. But Michele had always been so healthy and happy. Surely that counted for something! The days following the diagnosis were filled with anguish, disbelief, and the need to find a way to react to such a calamity.

"Stan decided," said Michael Riley, "that he would live whatever time Michele had left to the fullest. He ruled out anything like false hope. Anne, by contrast, decided to fight the disease with everything in her power."

Anne put her obsessive talents for research to work at the medical libraries and started up what became a voluminous correspondence with people who might help in any way. She resolved immediately to quit school and devote her time to her daughter, then had second thoughts. She had only two courses left, one for her orals and the other for her thesis preparation. She already had a good draft of *Katherine and Jean*. She could use that for her thesis. There was time yet to make the decision about quitting if it seemed necessary. Mouse was not showing too many adverse signs.

She had contracted a rare form of leukemia that usually struck adults. Her white blood cells were suddenly multiplying at an increased rate, causing an over-accumulation that invaded the bone marrow and would interfere with her internal organs and make her prone to serious infection. It meant constant tests to count blood cells, a bone-marrow biopsy, medication, and transfusions. It also meant a great deal of discomfort.

Her physician was Dr. Alexander King, a dignified, elegant man, who put her on a drug called 6 Mercaptopurine. Anne also fed her large doses of vitamin C, despite the doctor's skepticism of vitamin therapy. She had heard about the wonders of vitamin C and was eager to believe in anything that offered hope, even if it was a current health fad. She thought that Dr. King just might be ignorant about some of the latest findings in nutrition, and at the very least, vitamin C might help to prevent colds that could weaken the immune system.

Michael Riley came to visit at Christmas. "I'll never forget the way Michele looked," he said. "She was the most radiantly beautiful child. It was impossible to reconcile this terrible thing that was happening inside her."

The Rices felt they were getting good care at the hospital, although Anne was distressed that Dr. King offered few words of hope. When she reported that Michele had easily kicked a cold, he said it meant nothing for the next time. From across the room Stan often watched him scribble on his charts, then told Anne, whose eyesight was too poor to read it herself, that the doctor had written, "Doing very well." Nevertheless, the hospital was not involved in a leukemia-research program, and Anne armed herself with a battle plan, locating places where she could go if the services they currently used failed her daughter. She wrote to doctors all over the country. Members of her family pitched in and helped when they could, with information, support, and physical assistance.

One day Anne read an article in *Life* magazine about a Dr. Lincoln whose wife had leukemia. This man had been helping his wife with his computer. Anne's cousin Allen located Dr. Lincoln's address and found two computer programmers to stand by. Anne wrote the doctor a letter and he called her back. She learned that at the cost of thousands of dollars, he had transformed his computer into a simulation of blood and bone marrow, then had "fed" it a potent drug and monitored the effects. Anne told him about Mouse. He was sympathetic, but she hung up the phone less optimistic.

She could never begin to imitate what Dr. Lincoln was doing. His wife's illness was too different from Michele's, so his computer model would be of no immediate assistance. She would have to wait for the publication of his research results, which would be slow, since government spending on the Vietnam War had reduced money available for medical research. At least he had told her that Michele was getting appropriate care. She felt good having another doctor validate what she was doing. She also learned that there were other drugs available if her daughter did not respond well to what she was taking.

Anne soon felt the cruel impact of California's obsession with health. Among many of her acquaintances, illness was considered the result of some lack in the person, as if he or she had not jogged enough or not eaten the right foods. Compounded with it was a greater social inability to accept random events. That translated for Anne into a feeling that she had been irresponsible. She felt defensive. Had she done something wrong during pregnancy? She'd had X rays to check Michele's position. Could that have been the cause?

People approached her with the latest findings on leukemia, and some produced quack cures. Others offered hope by describing people they'd heard about who had survived leukemia and now lived normal lives. It made Anne feel optimistic but desperate. She asked Lynn Phelps, with whom she'd resumed a correspondence when she'd heard that Lynn's son had been similarly stricken: "Have you had any contact with Joe Ramsey and do you know if his brother had this thing? . . . I want to write out a list of people I've known who have had it and send this list to the researchers."

Friends were sympathetic but helpless. Some said they knew exactly how Anne and Stan felt, but such words were more painful than comforting. How could they know? Their children were not sick. New babies born to their acquaintances were a source of pain, increasing the desperation. Carla DeGovia remembered Anne saying, "Don't you have feelings that you just don't want to have, and you'd much rather just throw yourself out a window?"

Stan, too, was a target. Even if Anne was somehow responsible for Michele's condition, why couldn't Stan, the daddy, fix it, as men are supposed to be able to do? His role was to be the family protector, right? Why wasn't he doing his job? Such responses were projections from people who needed to know that *they* were not vulnerable—that it had to be something that someone was doing wrong, that there was a way to right the situation and move on—but the remarks still hurt.

Anne and Stan both experienced periods of guilt. Were they doing everything possible? Had they done anything wrong so far? Had they used the wrong drugs, the wrong doctor? Should they find another hospital? Was there a cure that they had not yet heard about? Were they linked to the right research avenues? There was no end to the reasons available for self-castigation, and no action that seemed clearly the right thing to do. Although they were ever alert, they suffered from a feeling of impotence in the face of a force that seemed larger than themselves.

"Everything that could be done was done," said Jack DeGovia. "I never realized how thoroughly people could do something. They did that the way they did everything else: thoroughly, completely, absolutely. There was no holding back."

"They were overwhelming as parents," Betsy Dubovsky agreed. "They dedicated their lives to her."

"We drew close together," Anne said, "and Michele went everywhere with us. We were a threesome. We packed a lot of living into those years."

Howard came to help out and was impressed with all their efforts. "Stan was wonderful with her," he recalled. "She was very fond of crabs, so Stan always made sure that in the morning she had four or five hard-shell crabs."

Yet there were stark moments. At times Mouse seemed to understand that there might be no hope. She watched for her goldfish to die, and sometimes asked about death. Increasing pain matured her. Once when she was looking through her viewfinder at cartoons of Sleeping Beauty, she startled her baby-sitter, Linda Gregg, by claiming it was her favorite fairy tale, as if the images of a long sleep were significant to her.

When the Rices found they could not pay their bills, they filed for Chapter Thirteen to get their financial situation under control. It meant putting themselves under the jurisdiction of the court for two years and paying extra fees, but they were conscientious about meeting their obligations. The priority, however, was Michele.

They tried experimental drugs that had terrible side effects. Michele's head and body swelled to grotesque proportions and she lost much of her hair, though it would grow back a little at night as if in defiance. They bought her a wig to wear. A doctor from Houston provided a drug which Dr. King administered at Kaiser. Anne found it more and more difficult to accept that her child was changing so drastically.

Michael Riley visited again for his annual Christmas trip, and Stan brought Mouse to the airport. She was wearing a little brown hat, and she pulled it off and said, "Look, I'm bald!"

"There are no words for that moment," said Michael. "The round cheeks of the cherub were now puffy with the signs of the treatment. Still, she remained wonderfully cheerful and animated, as beguiling as ever."

Michele occupied herself with drawing and painting. She did a picture for Anne and hung it up on the wall. A few days later, she had a stroke that sent her to the hospital. Her whole left side was convulsing. As she was wheeled into X ray, she said, "The pictures on the wall, Mommy!"

Leukemia cells had irritated the surface of her brain. As she lay there mute, convulsing and staring, Dr. King listened with his stethoscope and announced that he had failed to hear the sound of blood rushing, as in a hemorrhage. That was good news, and the image stayed with Anne, as if this doctor had a special ability to detect invisible conditions. She described it almost twenty years later in her novel *The Witching Hour*.

Suddenly Mouse began to move. The seizures stopped and she recovered quickly. She was put on an anti-convulsant, Dilantin, and she became more engrossed in her arts and crafts, spending hours at it and producing many drawings. She matured emotionally—becoming an adult trapped in a child's body. She seemed to understand what was happening to her and to resent it. The drugs affected her moods. She would sometimes scream out, which surprised those who knew her, but she also startled people with her cool, philosophical attitudes. "She had an otherworldliness about her," said Stan. "There was something in her eyes. She knew stuff that adults didn't know, because they hadn't been through compulsory medical tests. She had an ironic humor and saw the double meaning in things. She'd come back with some wisecrack that was way out of what a six-year-old should be thinking." Most of the time, however, she was the sweet, captivating child that everyone cherished, possessing an astonishing spirit to survive.

In the midst of this turmoil, Anne learned that her Aunt Alice, her mother's sister, was failing in health. She had once tried to move her to a rest home closer to San Francisco but had not succeeded. She felt helpless, unable to do anything for Allen, and he in turn could not help her.

2

Anne continued to be uncertain whether to pursue her education or devote herself fully to her daughter. The goal was so close, but Michele was not getting better. She decided to go ahead. She might need to find a job if Michele's expenses increased. The insurance thus far had covered the medical bills, but there had been many other expenses. An M.A. would help. Besides, Michele was used to Anne spending hours reading and writing. To finish her studies would not change the household routines that much. Her sister Tamara offered to baby-sit, as did their poet friend Linda Gregg. Thus, the time that Anne had fully intended on spending with her daughter was taken up with her studies. She felt bad, but the end was in sight. Stan was home three days a week and that relieved her somewhat, although both of them were physically and mentally drained.

Anne took her two-hour oral exams in Shakespeare, Hemingway, and Virginia Woolf. It had taken three years to complete all her reading, including fifteen books by Hemingway. She had not, however, read as much Woolf or Shakespeare, which she announced to the orals committee. "I just told them I was a slow reader. I don't know how the hell I got away with it. I told them, 'I'm here to be examined on what I've read.' And I got honors. I had a wonderful time. I had a lot of passion. They also knew it was a tall order."

Professor Robin Gajdusek, who served on Anne's thesis committee, recalled her special talents: "She was ever one of the most highly sensitive, responsive, alert people I have known. It was rather wonderful to have her in my seminar on the poetry of John Keats, where her sharpness and her special insights, her intuitive feel for the imagery, the deeper metaphoric action, the mythic structures—basically her sensitivity to the poetry—helped make the class (but especially her own work) forever memorable."

Anne submitted *Katherine and Jean* to complete her program for the master's in creative writing. Her thesis adviser for the project was Dr. William Weigand. Professor Weigand was already acquainted with Anne through Stan, since they were colleagues in the same department. Having first met Anne in 1966, he had thought her wholesome.

Anne had taken courses with him in novel writing and directed reading, and he was a natural choice to head her thesis committee. "Anne was always easy to work with," he said. "I liked and respected her work." He and Dr. Gajdusek looked at *Katherine and Jean* and suggested changes.

Anne was frustrated with her first experience of being edited. She disliked how the story evolved. She had intended it to be light, but it became serious. "The more it got read and interpreted," she said, "the more it lost its original spirit." She had originally made it outrageously funny and radical, but the final product, in Anne's eyes, was quite different. "There were too many people advising me," she said. "That was a lesson in learning not to listen. I had conceived of a strong kind of heroine and it got bogged down in sentimentality. By the end it was not recognizable. I remember very well the clean impulses in the beginning, but then there was all this input about making the heroine this and that—'we have to make her more compassionate,' 'we have to make her deeper.' There is a tendency to think that if a character is going to be sympathetic, he has to be weak and vulnerable." It was not the last time Anne would be faced with the same suggestions from people evaluating her writing, but it was the last time that she gave in so easily. Nevertheless, the final draft, submitted under the name Anne Howard Rice, shows a writer with a command of prose and with a flair for quirky scenes. The novella is both autobiographical and pure fantasy.

3

Katherine Kelly has just spent the last ten years in a restrictive Catholic girls' boarding school, St. Joseph's Academy in New Orleans, where Anne went for a year. Many of Katherine's thoughts about the school echo Anne's. Having been denied books and ideas that she wanted to explore, she is anxious to get out.

Anne toyed with how much of her adolescent experience she would give to Katherine. The physical description matched her, even to the extent that Katherine has not mastered the fine etiquette of making herself pretty according to current styles. Katherine is small and intimidated by girls her age who already look like women and who wear lipstick and torturous-looking high heels.

She and her mother share the same name, Katherine, the name of Anne's mother. Anne had thought her mother glamorous and it was her desire to attain glamour for herself. Writing herself into the plot by using autobiographical trappings and renaming herself Katherine allowed her that strong identification, whether she was conscious of it or not. It was also a way to stay close to her mother. Later in the text, another character alludes to this: "We create protagonists for a little drama in which we can be the star, and we aren't alone anymore."

Soon Katherine learns that her alcoholic mother has been killed by a lover. She is not really surprised, and the idea excites her because it means she can get her deceased father's insurance money and go to college. To Katherine, as to Anne, college means power and betterment: "I was sure at that time in my life," muses Katherine in an autobiographical paragraph, "that anyone who read books was wonderful and better than anyone who didn't. My life had been divided between those who read and those who did not and the two groups opposed each other."

Katherine's Irish working-class relatives gather to decide her fate, oblivious to her desire for education. She is seventeen, not yet legally able to live her own life despite knowing what she wants, and she feels helpless. This theme of oppression of intelligent adolescents by people who "know better" has found its way into much of Anne's work. "The tragedy," says one character, "is that the parents, the teachers and the priests usually win so early in the game that everyone loses."

Katherine makes a decision. She will now be a hero of her life rather than a victim: "I'd spent so long being acted upon; now I felt that I myself might act." Katherine eludes her relatives after the funeral and goes to her mother's bohemian apartment, modeled on the French Quarter apartment where Alice's friend Woody had lived. She knows she will find money because her mother, like Anne's mother, had been in the habit of stashing it in various places. She finds a checkbook and decides to withdraw the money.

At the bank she encounters Jean, the character from *Nicholas and Jean,* only a few years older. He teaches Katherine how to cash a check, but the windows close before he can get his own money, which he desperately needs for a flight to San Francisco. Katherine offers to pay his way if he will take her. She is feisty like Anne, but terribly naive, having seen the world only through glimpses allowed her at boarding school. She looks to Jean to help her find her way from one situation to the next, much like Anne, who felt the need for teachers in order to attain the sophistication she sought.

In San Francisco they go to the home of Lawrence Haller, an older man from *Nicholas and Jean,* with priest-like qualities. In the middle of the night, in a dreamlike scene, Katherine sees Jean dancing nude for Lawrence. It is her first exposure to the male body and she is entranced, although a bit confused about Jean's relationship to this man. The mystery is deepened when Jean suddenly flees with Katherine to Carmel, a California town that has had great significance for Anne.

"I've always loved it," said Anne, "and have always gone there at points in my life when I wanted serenity. It seemed like paradise to me. It was like the nearest I could get to the ambience of New Orleans and Florida sort of mushed together."

They settle into a rented house, and Katherine asks Jean to teach her the manners of a literate life-style. He gets books for her, including Sartre, against which he warns her of its nihilistic tone. They live together platonically, while Jean shows her around.

In one of the funniest scenes in the book, revealing a sharp sense of humor and a feel for eccentric characters that is never quite repeated in Anne's later work, Jean introduces Katherine to Mrs. Lawson-Roberts. She is based on a woman Anne once knew, complete with her lame cat. Grim events ahead would give Anne's writing more emotional power than *Katherine and Jean* possessed, and she would learn how to structure her books for a tighter plot—it is a loss that she left behind her sense of comic absurdity, which makes this scene so hilarious.

Katherine probes Jean's secrets and he tells her an elaborate story—a wild scenario of great imagination on Anne's part—that is a hoax. Hurt, Katherine walks away from him. Then the action picks up.

Jean's first lover, Richard, invites them to his house, where Katherine smokes pot. Anne records the details of her own experience and observations, and makes up innovative images, like living jewelry, inspired by the sensory confusion. The entire scenario is an impressive display of Anne's early talent for elaborate description, as well as introducing a homoerotic quality for which she would later become famous.

Jean learns of a death threat from an S&M club called Sandra's, and he returns with Katherine to San Francisco, where they don wigs and dresses for their entry into Sandra's to confront the owner. Anne found this kind of cross-dressing sexy and describes it in elaborate detail. However, she shies away from going too far into the S&M atmosphere, about which she knew very little besides what she could imagine.

Lawrence Haller is revealed as the owner of Sandra's, and he admits that he built the club from Jean's fantasies. He tells Jean he is free to go and that no one will kill him. Jean is so shocked he lapses into an inexplicable coma and Katherine takes him to New Orleans. As with many of her early stories and later novels, Anne is drawn back to her hometown setting. It is not as clear in *Katherine and Jean* as it would become in later work that she seeks something symbolized by the place where she grew up, and where many of her characters would become more fully realized.

Katherine's experience in New Orleans includes an observation Anne made on one of her own return visits. She sees the house where she had lived and the description matches 2301 St. Charles. "Everything was smaller than I remembered . . . the fear of death that I had felt on marijuana . . . came back to me like the visit of a stranger." The house decays as life decays. Childhood innocence cannot be viewed as a shell into which one can crawl like a turtle. A sense of gloom hangs over this part of the story.

Jean seems to be willing himself to die, but then revives and marries Katherine. She discovers she is pregnant. She goes to the cemetery and sees a woman claiming to be Jean's mother. She thinks it is Jean in female clothing playing a game, but discovers that the woman is really Jean's mother. The meeting, and Jean's revival, give her faith for a better future.

The thesis was not profound and the ending seemed to lose its force, but the story contained seeds for much of Anne's future work. For example, the psychology of masochism received some attention: "I was smiling, thinking how easy it is to know them [masochists] in every walk of life; they tell you the simplest anecdote and it revolves around a cruelty or a slight. The people they know are inhuman. The law is blind. Even insects are against them." Anne also includes her idea of evil as seductive rather than repulsive—a strong theme motivating later novels—in a phrase about the devil: "Let's go on believing that the devil is a charmer . . . a gourmet, a quoter of Shakespeare, something of a dandy."

Some scenes were cut from Anne's original draft, which disappointed her. Katherine and Jean had gone back to the island with the castle from *Nicholas and Jean* and had built an atrium with a velvet swing (inspired by the movie *The Girl on the Red Velvet Swing)*. Lines that Anne loved about making love with cinnamon and butter were removed, and with them, she felt, went most of the humor. The original ending came when Jean gave Katherine money for college, then left her, but was replaced by an ending that offered closure but no real catharsis.

The committee accepted the work. Dr. Weigand remembered that it captured something in the air in San Francisco in the late sixties, "particularly, the 'new' sense of the male as sex object." Lenore Kandel's published poem on the subject had created a stir in San Francisco when it was banned as pornographic. Anne also, Dr. Weigand felt, had "caught the mood of a dark and mythic New Orleans, and in the main male character that sense of the manipulator and the manipulated, of fascinating mischief, helpless, and beyond moral judgment." Dr. Weigand did not view the work as original, since Andy Warhol had already worked on the idea of the compliant, homoerotic male, but he thought it was well written.

Speaking more broadly, he saw how this thesis grounded Anne's later work. Her strength, he thought, lay not in plotting but in producing vivid effects. "She specializes in broad and melodramatic effects, Gothic and operatic by tradition. On a sexual level, the characters are at once sadist and masochist. She works in terms of intense scenes, and even more accurately, of 'arias' (since the characters must relate their primal adventures)."

In 1972, Anne received her master's degree. Finally finished with her studies, she turned her full attention to her daughter. But Michele was getting worse.

4

She was not responding to the breakthroughs happening with more ordinary forms of leukemia and had been to the hospital several times. Things were looking grim.

In her first published novel Anne would write a passage about one character's love for a child that clearly captures what she was feeling:

> I loved her so completely; she was so much the companion of my every waking hour, the only companion that I had, other than death. I should have known. But something in me was conscious of an enormous gulf of darkness very close to us, as though we walked always near a sheer cliff and might see it suddenly but too late if we made the wrong turn . . . as if a fault in the earth were about to open.

Stan, too, was feeling the weight. "What does an angel's skeleton look like?" he pondered in a poem. "Looks like the shadow of a bunch of chains."

Uncertain what the future held, they did everything they could to make Michele happy. Stan received one of the first grants given by the

National Endowment for the Arts, and he used the five thousand dollars to take her to Disneyland, where they stayed with Michael Riley, now a professor at Claremont College. As they drove past a grove of lemon trees, Michele quipped, "Man cannot live by lemons alone." The remark caught them all by surprise. She was still the wry wit despite her decline.

In the last stages of her illness, when chemotherapy had weakened her bones, she moved with painful, shuffling steps. Anne and Stan rented a red wheelchair and often took her outside to sit in the sun and watch friends play Frisbee in the street.

Eventually she was hospitalized at Stanford's Children's Hospital in Palo Alto. Anne and Stan had beds for themselves set up in her room. Friends and relatives helped out as much as they could. Anne's father, now retired, came for several months, and Stan's family offered comfort and assistance. His sister Cynthia rented a room in a hotel near the hospital so someone would always be there to keep Michele company if Anne or Stan needed to leave. A popular song, "Bridge Over Troubled Water," became Michele's special song.

There seemed no end to the child's suffering. Sometimes she got angry and, as sick children do, projected a sense that her parents were not helping her. The mental torment was great for the whole family. If there were truly no hope, should they wish for a speedier death to release her from her pain? But how could they go on without her? The three of them were a family. She had to get better!

"The rapid tenacious heart of the child," Anne was later to write, "beating harder and harder, refusing to die, beating like a tiny fist beating on a door, crying, 'I will not die, I will not die, I cannot die, I cannot die.' "

By August, Mouse was eating only crushed ice. Stan and Anne made plans with her to go once more to Disneyland, and Stan showed her a catalog where he could purchase a T-shirt with anything written on it. Michele asked for a shirt that said, "DAISY'S RIDER." The words puzzled him.

Carla and Jack DeGovia stopped in to see her that evening. Carla broke into tears, unable to believe such a sweet and beautiful child could really die. "I know she's going to get better," she assured Anne. That was what Anne believed, too, although she wrote in her diary that she had never before seen Michele as she looked that day. "I was really frightened," she said, "but I firmly believed she was going to make it."

It was a terrible night. Sometime before midnight, blood from the transfusion bottle spilled all over the bed, and Stan held Mouse in his lap while the nurse changed the sheets. Her mouth moved. He leaned closer. She said something that was difficult for him to make out, about doing something for someone.

"For who?" he asked.

"Me, your baby."

She was placed back inside the oxygen tent, and the intern assured Anne and Stan that they could go to sleep; the staff had taken care of many critically ill patients and knew what they were doing. Anne realized that she needed sleep in order to care for Michele the next day, so she and Stan lay down around four. Anne positioned herself next to Michele so she could see her face as she closed her eyes. A nurse sat on the other side, holding the child's hand.

At five, the alarm went off on the heart monitor. The jagged lines had gone flat. Anne jumped up and woke Stan. "Call her!" the nurse shouted as she tried to revive the stricken child. Stan squeezed the oxygen bag and spoke Michele's name over and over. An intern rushed in and started a prolonged attempt at resuscitation. Anne stood, frozen, her hand to her mouth in disbelief. It was happening! Mouse was dying and there was nothing she could do!

Stan continued to pump, ambivalent, silently willing the child not to revive to a world of more pain and lost hope. He heard a gurgle in her chest. The nurse continued to massage her heart while the doctor put a needle to her arm and gave her a shot of adrenaline.

"Can't we do anything?" cried Anne. "Isn't there anything else we can do?"

The doctor tried again, then again. Michele did not respond. Anne willed her to come back, stunned, helpless, castigating herself for falling asleep.

Finally the doctor stepped back. "There's no use kidding ourselves," he said. "She's gone."

The room was silent except for the noise of the now useless machines. Mouse lay still on the bed and Stan bent down to give her a goodbye kiss.

He later captured the moment in a poem.

> . . . Anne in her blue robe astonished, after two years, still,
> at the last moment,
> ASTONISHED,
> Fingers to lips,
> The oxygen tent ripped back, the cooler roaring for nothing, me
> Squeezing the rubber bag trying to find the rhythm of a
> breather sleeping
> That her heart might recognize, being again, all the time
> Saying to myself, "Don't come back Mouse don't come back,"
> her head
> Heavy on rubbery neck the veins I'm ASTONISHED

Rising to the surface of the skin like crazed lacquer,
    One Two Three
Shots of adrenaline straight into the vein,
No response
Me squeezing now the tears dropping bright on the black
    rubber bag No
    Response
The head nurse massaging the chest a deep gurgle like
    a clogged trap
NO RESPONSE
. . . and my head cocks sideways like the RCA Victor dog
& I bend over & her lips part easily & wetly & I give her
the long kept sexual kiss of father
to daughter, too late
Hello.

It was over. Their daughter was gone. One month short of her sixth birthday, she had barely begun to live. Anne and Stan were exhausted, broken. Michele would become for them now like the phantom limb of an amputee, a shadow in their lives, never there, never gone.

It would have done no good
Screaming in the scream-multiplying hospital linoleum
corridors
    O O O O O
would have altered not one eye turning

Although they had braced themselves for two years for such an event, it still seemed impossible. What gods could think up a more heinous torture than to give to parents a perfect little girl, then snatch her away in the midst of such drawn-out agony?

Look! she is dead: no cover can cover her: look,
her hands are dead just as her face is dead: all of her is
    dead
where is the soul? she looked no lighter on the pillow
    when it went . . .
surely this is not what she was meant for:
look! a shaft of light pierces the dustball: just
    that effortlessly

she went.

Something snapped that day for both of them as they saw Mouse lying so still. It was a moment of absolute loss. Their glances locked, each seeing in the mirror of the other's distraught face their failure to save their child. "I never forgave myself," said Anne, "for going to sleep." Stan wanted to ride out into the sunset and find the thing that had killed his daughter, but there was nothing at all that either of them could do now. Except prepare to bury her.

Had any vestige of Anne's Catholic faith survived the death of her mother, her intellectual doubt, then her emotional crises from years before, it was utterly destroyed now. The prayers of her family had been useless, empty. There was no God, or at least not one who cared. She rejected any heaven that demanded the sacrifice of a child—especially her perfect, beautiful little girl.

Two years later, she would put this loss into words through the character Louis as he said in despair:

> I looked up and saw myself in a most palpable vision ascending the altar steps, opening the tiny sacrosanct tabernacle, reaching with monstrous hands for the consecrated ciborium, and taking the Body of Christ and strewing Its white wafers all over the carpet; and walking then on the sacred wafers . . . giving Holy Communion to the dust. . . . God did not live in this church; these statues gave an image to nothingness.

He confesses to a priest, then kills him in a symbolic act of hopeless defiance. Another character in *The Witching Hour* would claim that if there is a God, he is the source of all pain and not worthy to be worshiped.

It was time now to make the torturous phone calls. Friends, family, and colleagues were invited to a wake at a funeral home.

Anne's sister Tamara and her boyfriend Michael shouldered the grim task of collecting Michele's effects from the hospital in Palo Alto, then went to the wake. Michael, a pianist, played slow, poignant movements of the "Gymnopédies" by Erik Satie and popular songs that Michele had liked, including Paul McCartney's "Michelle." Stan was pale and washed out, Anne on the verge of collapse, but they endured the grim ceremonies.

An open-casket funeral was arranged at a small Catholic church near Anne and Stan's home. A requiem Mass was said by a priest who had not known Michele. The sermon was short, emphasizing what death means as a transitory state. For Anne the words were a source of agony. Something she had once believed in so firmly, that should have been comforting, was now dry as dust.

Stan set the mood with a stoic appearance, speaking little and showing no dramatic reaction. Anne, too, was controlled, as if following his lead, although she had refused to be drawn into what she saw as the typical California sterility about death. People there, she perceived, preferred not to be exposed to death. But she had been raised in New Orleans, where the dead are honored. Howard was the sustaining presence, knowing exactly what needed to be done in the Catholic protocol and doing it. He felt it was a sad but significant time for family bonds.

The day was hot, like the day Katherine had been buried. That the sun was shining seemed an illusion in the midst of such emotional darkness. A small procession went to an Oakland cemetery, where Anne insisted, against ordinary funereal protocol, on waiting until the coffin had been lowered into the ground and covered with dirt. She was not going to leave while her daughter lay alone in some building! Stan described the simple funeral:

Love went riding in a hearse
With me behind her in the flower car.
We stopped beside a hole where she
Was put by men who could not see.

Tamara, overcome, walked over and put her hand on the hands of each of the grieving parents and asked, "What can I say?" There was nothing to say.

The grave was marked with a flat, uninscribed stone. Anne and Stan turned and walked away, into a sense of emptiness.

Anne asked Floyd Salas and Betsy Dubovsky to come over as a few friends gathered afterward at the apartment. "The mood," said Betsy, "was quiet and solemn." Stan talked with Michael Riley about a journal he had kept during Michele's final days, containing intimate expressions of grief, which he later turned into a book of poetry. Anne told of her regret. "I had failed to remember," she said, "that the tide goes out at that time of day, and I'd read in Dickens how people go out with the tide." She drank heavily and passed out in the bedroom. Stan asked everyone to leave. He did not realize that Anne had wanted them to spend the night. She was disappointed when she rose later and found the apartment empty. Too close to the echo of her heart.

In her novel *The Witching Hour* Anne would express her feelings about the death of a loved one: "We lose our witnesses, our watchers, those who know and understand the tiny little meaningless patterns . . . and there is nothing left but the endless flow." The loss of a witness meant the loss of substance and foundation.

It also meant the loss of matrilineal continuity. On one side, Anne's mother was gone; on the other, her daughter. She had twice been through the experience of having warmth, solidity, and security ripped from her, and she was left starkly alone. She felt she had no right to live.

Her child had died and she should have saved her, just as she should have been able to help her mother. Both had slipped away despite all her efforts. How could life just go on as before? Why did the sun come up each day?

Anne and Stan both had trouble sleeping for a long time afterward, although depression made it difficult to get out of bed. Whenever Anne closed her eyes, she envisioned the hospital. She saw herself doing things differently, trying to change what could not be changed, seeing her child come back to life. She wanted to wake up from this nightmare that threatened to explode her mind with burgeoning anguish, yet she did not want to lose the image of Michele from her memory. She wanted to run away from Berkeley and start a new life. Some days she just screamed and screamed in an effort to gain release. But there was no escape. Stan could go to work to fill the empty days, but she had nothing except the echoing house and Michele's clothing, artwork, and toys.

Many friends refrained from asking about Michele, and Anne felt they were acting as if she had just vanished like a thought. The attitude only deepened the grief. Joe Slusky was the one who gave them needed solace. He invited them to open up one night at a bar and they were grateful. It meant a great deal to be able to talk about their pain, though it did not ease. Michele may lie buried in a cemetery, but she was not gone, would never be gone.

Thus began what Anne and Stan would later refer to as their "Scott and Zelda" period.

5

They already had been drinking for many years, but now they threw themselves into it with the same energy with which they had cared for their sick child. They poured bottle after bottle of beer into the vacuum of their souls, seeking numbness from the realization that life's essential goodness was no longer a viable assumption.

"There were no rules for me after that," said Stan. "If *that's* possible [Michele's death], anything's possible at any minute, so just let it all out. It was a mixture of giving ourselves permission to do anything that we wanted to and trying to buffer ourselves against the psychic pain—wanting to be out of your skull, giving yourself this rule-breaking permission, also just having as much fun as you can have because that seemed to be the name of the game."

Anne started the day with two tall cans of beer and drank until she went to bed, sitting in morose, staring sadness and anger. A twelve-pack of Miller had to be in the refrigerator for the next day before she went to sleep. "Anne drinks," Stan wrote in a poem, "pregnant with novel, writes & screams / Ten twelve fifteen beers, never enough." Her friends watched her drink all day until she hit a quiet stupor, surprised that she never seemed to get really drunk. Anne made no connection between what she was now doing to herself and what her mother had done to escape her pain because of the difference in their patterns of drinking.

Stan stayed drunk day in and day out, withdrawing from the poetry readings that had meant so much to him. He had debilitating hangovers and bouts of depression which eased only when he drank more. "It never seemed to be any fun unless you went all the way," he said.

"I could see them destroying themselves," said Larry Rice. "And they were not blind to it. They were deteriorating day by day. I was helpless to ease their gnawing pain. They squandered their money without regard for the future, and they cared not a whit for this life."

Anne put on weight from all her drinking, which became a source of irritation to her. Once again she felt the lash of the California obsession with health when she was made to feel that being heavy was in poor taste and made her inferior. Some people were aggressive, making vicious comments. To defend herself, Anne said that the extra pounds weren't really her. She jokingly acknowledged only the parts from the wrist down and the neck up, but she actually suffered from acute self-consciousness. She began to dress more conservatively to counteract the harsh judgments, moving away from the colorful clothing she loved and covering herself with dark outfits.

She also experienced bouts of inexplicable fear, keeping the light on all night. She could not sleep or concentrate on anything, and her moods drifted into deep depression. Stan worried about her, fearing a nervous breakdown. Anne wrote about the experience later, describing a similarly debilitating period for the character Michael in *The Witching Hour*.

They berated themselves over what they had done or not done for their child, and sometimes Anne would just rant and rave. Should they have tried more experimental drugs? Should they have sought a better doctor, taken Mouse to Houston? Anne had wanted to, Stan had resisted. Now he was sorry. "Every death's a murder," he later wrote. "A million maybes."

Their relationship suffered, the aftershock of the earthquake, as they argued or endured each other in excruciating silence. The tragedy had changed them both, forcing them into contrasting patterns of fear and rage. They needed each other, but neither had the resources to help the other. Instead they experienced greater distance, angering each other and causing more pain. Although they were together, they were each terribly alone. They were unsure what the future held and wondered whether they could hold it together or whether, as with many couples dealing with tragedy, they would drift apart. Friends noticed a sharper edge to their remarks, and at one dinner party Michael Riley observed: "Anne and Stan were wound up like tops, and the conversation between them bristled on the edge of what seemed like what could be a terrible fight. They had always argued with great intensity, but I never felt that something dark was at stake. That night I did."

Stan busily collected his impressions and feelings in a series of poems, including the pain of being with Anne:

> . . . It's hard
> to keep on loving someone
> whose every mannerism reminds you
> of a thousand failures. Mine
> multiplied by yours until
> we even resent each other's pleasures. How
> can I make it right
> what I ruined?

And

> Fear, fear is what makes
> the trust between two people
> feed on all the rotten things
> we do.

Laura Chester, a poet and publisher who had encouraged Stan's career, had moved to San Francisco. Although she had not known Michele, she saw how the Rices observed other children with a grim sense of loss. "In just one look from Anne," she said, "I noticed the present tense of their tragedy." It seemed to spill over into every facet of their lives.

The mortal dread that had settled upon Anne years earlier had taken sure aim. Michele was dead. Why? There were no answers. The doctor had said, For all anyone knew her illness could have been caused by a cosmic ray. Maybe no reason would ever be revealed. She was in the ground now, her life force gone, although Anne was visited by her childhood fear that the dead are not really dead. Louis the vampire would say, "I dreamed of my brother, for instance, that he was near me in some state between life and death, calling to me for help." Was Michele calling out to her? She was frightened for her child, for herself, especially that there was no ultimate meaning or hope in the world. She would never really *know.* Neither Stan nor Anne could bring themselves to go within blocks of the cemetery, and Stan could not listen to the tape he had made of Michele's voice. They were helpless against the waves of grief that came to crush and separate them over and over.

In the novel *Interview With the Vampire,* Louis grieves over his dead brother in a manner similar to the way Anne was feeling. Louis had no direct hand in the tragedy but still felt to blame. "I could not forgive myself," he says. "I felt responsible for his death. . . . I sat in the parlor beside his coffin for two days thinking, I have killed him." Later, in deep mourning, he says, "I saw myself turning on a knife then, languishing in a day-to-day suffering which I found as necessary as penance from the confessional, truly hoping death would find me unawares and render me fit for eternal pardon."

Anne still talked about Catholicism, but with a strange, bitter yearning. Annette Arbeit remembered that Anne had once said that she had been happier when she had been close to the church. Without religious codes life was too uncertain, too much adrift. Martha Nawy, a neighbor, said that Anne often spoke about the concept of evil as they sat drinking and talking on the patio. She seemed to have withdrawn from the gregarious person she once had been and to be more concerned with darker subjects. Anne also said things that shocked people. She claimed that Californians were too inclined to divorce for petty reasons, there was too little emphasis on commitment. If the husband wanted a mistress, it was better to stay together as long as he did not stop being affectionate and responsible to the primary family. To hear such a progressive concept from a person so conservative and loyal to family as Anne seemed incongruous. No one knew what to expect from her.

She and Betsy Dubovsky pursued discussions about the afterlife and things of mystery. "We talked about beliefs in a metaphysical world," said Betsy, "in which spirit is the basic force and mover. Anne felt there was good evidence that people move on after death, and that death is a change, not an end." When Anne came across an article about a house purportedly haunted by the spirits of children, she told Betsy. "We both completely believed it," said Betsy. Anne also grew more intrigued with research on the possibility of an afterlife, an interest that would fuel her later novels and inspire her mythological directions for anchoring the supernatural in the natural. She was right in synch with a cultural movement in which people were leaving organized religion and seeking alternative approaches to both life and death.

When Stan heard these discussions, he was adamant about material reality as the only reality. But Anne was not persuaded. "My own feeling," she said, "is that there's a great deal to be discovered about telepathy and the occult. It revolves not so much around the existence of unprovable entities as perhaps around energy." She would refine this view through her writing, giving it the strongest expression in her twelfth novel, *The Witching Hour*.

Anne kept drinking and it made her tired. Finally she decided that she needed to get away to clear her head. She felt helpless, out of control, paralyzed. She wanted to get her life in order. "I had to get off the party," she explained, "and get out of Berkeley. I was really depressed and really strung out and really exhausted. I just needed to get away from everybody."

Stan's parents, living in Dallas, had a house with an attic bedroom. Anne asked if she could stay with them, feeling it would be a good idea for the sake of her marriage to stay close with Stan's family.

"We loved her," said Stanley Rice, Sr., "we wanted to help." They graciously invited her to come for as long as she wanted.

"Going there was wonderful," she said. She stayed three weeks, examining her life, thinking through her options. The constant struggle between being a passive victim acted upon by others and a person who acts became a pivotal concept for her, and she decided that she had to take her life in her own hands and pick herself up.

"Her innate sense of, and need for, family life," said Larry Rice, "kept her on track when the dangers of dissipation were so pressing."

She became stronger, but she did not completely escape her vulnerable side. She had become a victim to her own pain, had sunk into an alcoholic numbness, but had been able to pick herself up. She was not quite the "hero of her life," but she was not about to lose Stan along with Michele, or to give up on herself.

6

When Anne returned to San Francisco, she sorted things out with Stan, cleansing their relationship with a renewed commitment to each other. Eventually they talked about another child. Should they risk it? Neither wanted ever again to go through the experience of loss. Not like that. They decided to wait.

Anne got a job to keep herself busy. She worked eight hours a day as a copy editor for a law book company, but she couldn't stand the work. However, she also had no real identity as a housewife, since she disliked housework and possessed no domestic expertise. Nevertheless, she had only been working six weeks when she went to Stan to explain her misery. Maybe, she said, she could take another stab at writing. She was torn between having a job for financial backup and just going all out, even at the risk of failure. Writing seemed to be the only thing she did with any degree of competence or satisfaction. It offered a way out of the anonymity and mediocrity that threatened to engulf her.

"Quit," Stan told her. He was willing to support her if she really wanted to write, as she had been years earlier for him. He did not care if she did not want to work at a regular job, and he believed in her ability.

Still, she felt insecure. Stan had his job and a strong local reputation as a poet, but at age thirty-two, what did she have? A copy of *Katherine and Jean* with which she was basically unhappy. She had worked on it throughout Michele's illness, but it just had not come together. She worried that she was not writing something that would catch an editor's eye. She had tried to use her own life to write the realistic fiction that seemed to be in fashion, yet inevitably some character like the violet-eyed Jean would pop up and carry her away. Stan assured her that she was an "imaginativist" and that she should just do what she liked.

She still had dreams of greatness, thanks in part to a mother who had believed in her and had made her feel that anything was possible and that she was special. She was going to make it as a writer, she just knew it. She would redeem herself, she believed, in the eyes of everyone who thought she'd wasted her life. She had talent, she was sure. She just needed to get back to work.

That autumn Anne experienced trouble getting out of bed. She got some medication for what was diagnosed as labyrinthitis, an inner-ear problem that affected her balance. A few weeks later, the symptoms worsened. She went to Kaiser Hospital, thinking she'd had a stroke, and the doctor checked her over, then told her to raise her eyebrows. She thought she'd obeyed but actually had been unable to perform this simple task. She was diagnosed with Guillain-Barre Syndrome, a serious viral infection of the nerves. Called "mock polio," it affected her hands, face, legs, and feet with a mild paralysis and generalized weakness. The doctor thought the condition had peaked, but did not tell her that she still could go into respiratory arrest.

The illness lingered for months, which was both frightening and distressing. Half of Anne's face was affected and one side of her mouth did not move when she smiled; she had a shuffling walk and had to be helped out of chairs.

"Lightning has struck twice," Stan told Michael Riley in despair.

People shook their heads, believing it was an emotional reaction to Michele's death, which only added to Anne's distress. "One of the maddening things," she said, "was that some of our friends thought that it was entirely in my mind, that it was an imitation of Mouse. But it was not a hysterical illness."

Eventually things improved, although the pain in her feet remained for a long time afterward and she did not experience full recovery for years. She learned only later that she could have died.

As Anne recovered mobility, she made friends with other women who wanted to become writers. They attended writing groups and invited Anne to come, but she was suspicious. "Writing, to me, was serious," she said, "and I could not believe so many people going about it in the various groups were really as determined as I was to do something pure. I thought they were like suburban housewives' Tupperware parties."

She agreed to visit, going with a friend to Leonard Bishop's writing class, and was further convinced that she did not wish to participate. Although she liked Leonard Bishop personally and they later became friends, she disliked the way writing groups relied on rules; for every rule she'd found a published book—often a best-seller—that broke it. The groups, she felt, could also destroy motivation. "I believe criticism is a two-edged sword," she said. "It may inspire you to do something wonderful, or it can chop your head off." She asked the question many times of friends who continued to attend whether anybody in the groups ever told another participant that something was ready. "You can take in a chunk of *The Brothers Karamazov,"* she claimed, "and they'd tear it to pieces. That's their business." Anne also disliked what she witnessed of people talking about others outside the groups. "I felt the politics of these groups were intolerable."

What she preferred was sharing her ideas and manuscripts with close friends, on a one-to-one basis. "When you respected a person and respected that person's writing, you could exchange manuscripts and get something out of it. What I objected to was the random criticism that came out of groups. I don't think you need to clutter up your brain with opinions of people you don't respect." Even at smaller gatherings at the house of a friend who invited people to read their work, Anne declined to show any of hers. She listened politely but indifferently to the discussions. "I didn't take them that seriously," she admitted, "and I was a bit of a snob where they were concerned. I wasn't interested in their criticisms. I was very guarded about that kind of thing. I simply did not lay myself open to it."

Anne was fueled by "world-class" dreams. She wanted to write something that would have an impact and be widely appreciated, as had Hemingway and Fitzgerald. She believed that the way to sell was not to ponder the market but to turn on the passion, to "write what you care about, get yourself into your vision, and to give everything to it; if you find it interesting, maybe someone else will." She wanted nothing less than to write a book that would have only an elite readership; the small literary novel that made no difference to anyone was not for her. Her goal was to write what she cared about and to reach a lot of people in the process.

"I never wanted to be just a literary writer," she said, "any more than I wanted to be just a commercial writer. I used to say quite often that if we took Aristotle's prescription for a good drama—plot, character, spectacle, and meaning—and we applied it to the novel, that was the best rule we could go with. People have a right to be entertained and a great novel does not have to be boring and plotless." For her, greatness was important. She wanted to write something that kept her up in the middle of the night thinking about it. "I can't write something if I don't think there's a chance it's going to be great."

Nevertheless, Anne realized that many of the people from those groups were passionate about their work, and she was impressed by the dedication of aspiring writers who met all day, taking meals together and reading to one another. Years later, as one after another became published and critically acclaimed, she admitted that attending the groups had paid off for them. Yet she did not change her own position on the potential destructiveness of subjecting one's writing to a group.

As if in echo of the assertiveness Anne was showing in her own life, the feminist movement made its mark in the Berkeley area, giving women more freedom. Anne was pleased—initially. "I was very glad to see it happening," she said. "I would listen to talk shows about rights for women, and I thought it was marvelous. I was very impressed." She believed firmly in equality and liberal ideals, and Stan had always supported her in this. She also detested housework and the notion that it was the woman's job to be a manual laborer, refusing to submit to such expectations. She had argued against double standards ever since she'd been in high school, shocking friends who'd never before heard a woman assert herself against social expectations. "I think I was always a radical feminist," said Anne, "in believing totally in equality between the sexes."

However, she resisted becoming subsumed into a group identity, and her personal contact with women who proclaimed themselves feminists was invariably unpleasant. "It was always someone ordering me to do something—read this, or don't do that. The radical feminists I knew were very strident and very aggressive. They made a bad impression on me. My firm feeling was that they didn't much like women. I got a lot of being shoved around. They were like the nuns from school. They believed I should be writing about women's experiences. I believed a woman should read and write what she wanted to read and write. I could not subscribe to their gender-focusing garbage. I was appalled by their fascist approach." Her distaste for what she viewed as the suppression of one group by another kept her out of organized political activities.

Nevertheless Anne developed close friendships with women, like the bonds she had formed with Lucy and with friends in Texas. Interested in homosexuality, she wondered on several occasions what it would be like to be sexually involved with a woman but pushed the idea away. That was not what she really wanted. Not all fantasies, she felt, needed to be acted out. Although she was not politically active in a feminist movement, nor did she develop any creeds, her convictions about personal freedom, regardless of gender, would eventually emerge in her writing as she encouraged women toward open expression of their sexuality.

One of Anne's closest friends was Carolyn Doty. Carolyn had a bachelor's degree in painting and drawing from the University of Utah but wanted to write fiction. A mutual friend asked Carolyn to drive Anne home from a class, and when she took Anne to her apartment on Bonita Avenue, she was invited in. Over beers they got acquainted. Carolyn's son was mentally retarded, and she and Anne found a common bond. "We spent a good deal of time during the beginning part of our relationship," she recalled, "talking about the ways families and others respond to people who are in trouble." Their discussions, along with Anne's support, eventually prompted Carolyn to write a book about her son, published as *Fly Away Home.* She was also influenced by Stan's poetry to write a novel, *A Day Late,* about a man trying to deal with the death of his daughter.

Anne had dinner with Carolyn most weeks that Stan taught Thursday evening courses. "I think our discussions," Carolyn said, "centered around the concept of art and writing rather than the specifics of what we were working on at the time. What Anne did better than anyone I have ever known is talk about art and what it meant to her to write . . . to explore whatever might come along in terms of a discussion of the art of writing, the craft, the words. I was mesmerized by it all."

Carolyn found a family among her new writing friends, but Anne stood out. "My other writing friends, also great readers, were just not as intense as Anne was about her writing, and I was inspired by her dedication and her drive. She was always committed to succeeding as a writer–not just artistically and intellectually, but commercially as well. Nothing was more important than writing and talking about it or being around writers."

One of the writers that they discussed was Nathaniel Hawthorne, whom Anne had recently discovered through a collection of short stories. "I was very influenced by 'Young Goodman Brown,' " Anne said, "and by 'The Minister's Veil.' I loved his use of language and the way he treated darkness–the mood, the ambience, and the richness. The stories seemed macabre and bizarre. I felt a kinship to him and to Edgar Allan Poe, that those were American writers that I was somehow connected with. They were writers that had European-American voices. I felt they had a lot to teach me." She was not aware at the time that she would soon take her place among American storytellers of the supernatural.

Carolyn wanted criticism on work in progress, while Anne was more interested in a viewing of a completed project. She urged Carolyn to submit her work for the Joseph Henry Jackson Award, and wanted to get to work herself with that goal in mind. She had also heard about a contest at the University of Iowa and wanted to enter. Looking through her short stories, she collected together several that seemed to her to have some merit.

Around that time Anne met a student of Stan's named Cathy Colman. Cathy was awed by Anne. "She looked more alive than most people and was extremely witty and intelligent." For her the Rices were the arbiters of taste, steeped as they were in knowledge about art. Anne showed Cathy a thirty-page story that she had written in 1968 about a vampire. Cathy thought the writing was evocative and sensual. They talked about its potential as a longer piece and Anne thought about making another attempt with it. Cathy encouraged her.

What Anne most wanted was that her writing be about life, feeling it was the only kind of writing that was important. She looked over the story again. It was about a vampire being interviewed about his experience. She had taken the point of view of the interviewer, wanting since childhood to know what it was like to be such a creature. How did it feel to take another person's life? Was it erotic? Spiritual? More important, was the story about life? Yes, she decided, life as the vampire sees it. Being immortal, he offered a way for readers to see their lives from a fresh vantage point. And the image, in its eerie darkness, seemed to echo deeply within her.

Anne sat at her typewriter and began to write.

CHAPTER SIX

THE VAMPIRE

Some things lighten nightfall
and make a Rembrandt of a grief.
—Stan Rice, *Body of Work*

1

"'Do you wish to hold the interview here?' the vampire asked." It was the original opening line, later cut, of a story that would become familiar to millions of readers. Anne went on writing, pursuing a whimsical idea—a short story of interest to her that eventually turned her inside out as it unfolded. She wanted to look at the vampire as a tragic figure, a human who had made the mistake of choosing such an existence to his deep regret. She wanted to ask him questions about what it was like to stay the same while everything around him changed. She hoped it would be good enough to win a contest, perhaps even garner some interest from an agent. What she could not foresee was the magnitude of the change this story would effect in her life.

Anne had gone recently with Stan to a small radio station on Divisadero Street in San Francisco, and the memory of it flavored the setting for her story. The vampire looked out on Divisadero as he discussed his bizarre life with an incredulous young man seeking to broadcast such stories on the radio. He explained how he became a vampire, what it was like and the struggle he had with it. In Anne's mind her characters sat together in a room in one of the old Victorian houses in that area.

The story lengthened. The vampire got a name, Louis, and a home, New Orleans. The first-person perspective took on a Dickensian quality, as Louis revealed his faults yet sustained sympathy. His attitude about life echoed Hamlet, and his tone had the flavor of Oscar Wilde—an aristocrat humorously observing modern life. "He was supposed to be a sort of George Sanders type of character," Anne said, "world-weary and comical; the things he said to the boy were cynical."

Describing Louis's past threw Anne back into her childhood as she moved her vampire through the French Quarter and out to the plantations surrounding New Orleans. Louis's Catholicism drew her into the rituals and beliefs that had once encircled her. She touched an old grief, her mother's death, echoed when Louis describes the mysterious city: "It . . . was part of the great awful sadness of all the things I'd ever lost or loved or known."

Anne did not analyze what the story might mean or how events in her life might be fueling her words; instead she guided her writing through an inherent sense of authenticity—how it felt to her in terms of emotional credibility and intensity—and just let it flow. She poured her energy into her characters, imbuing Louis with the sensitivity to detail that made him feel pleasure and pain keenly the way she did. The colors and textures were vivid, the darkness compelling.

The Louisiana history Anne had been reading so intently was at her eager fingertips. She already knew what the nineteenth century in New Orleans would be like, the type of wallpaper, the gas lamps, the swamps—many of them now busy highways in the modern world. She had read the personal inventories from the plantations and knew what people would have owned. She was familiar with the French and Spanish architecture, the huge live oaks, and the southern climate, and she had chosen, almost inadvertently, the perfect setting into which a vampire could blend: "A vampire, richly dressed and gracefully walking through the pools of light of one gas lamp after another might attract no more notice in the evening than hundreds of other exotic creatures." Anne had tried before to capture New Orleans in its mystery and gloom, and through this vampire, whose fictionality buffered for her a raw exposure to painful memories, she retrieved beloved impressions of graveyards, Spanish moss, flower-scented air, and crumbling old mansions. The timeless quality of the city magnified the theme of immortality.

"I was a twenty-five-year-old man when I became a vampire," Louis says, "and the year was seventeen ninety-one." The tale begins with his pre-vampire existence as the wealthy owner of an indigo plantation south of New Orleans, supporting a mother, sister, and brother. The brother,

Paul, prays for hours in his private oratory, as Anne had. He claims he has seen a vision of Mary directing him to tell Louis to sell the plantation and use the money for God. Louis refuses, ashamed of his brother's fanaticism, and they argue. In a rage Paul walks to the top of the stairs and seemingly throws himself into the air; then he falls, breaking his neck. Louis is stunned.

At that point the story exploded emotionally for Anne. She felt alive to what Louis was saying and feeling. She knew intimately the grief, the loss, the regret. She began to write almost unconsciously, transferring herself from the perspective of the interviewer interested in knowing about a vampire's experience to that of the vampire experiencing it.

Louis is a man in the shadows, symbolized by his dark hair. He does not look willingly into mirrors, because his surface image confuses him: he sees what he cannot control. To him the surface is deceptive, a theme that continues throughout the novel. Anne explored Louis's vulnerability, his thoughts of suicide and his despair, so close to what she had felt in recent months. "I cannot live now that he's dead," Louis says of his brother. Like Anne, he dreams endlessly of changing things, of bringing his brother back to life, feeling the anguish of utter helplessness. Retreating into Louis, Anne allowed her feelings to be molded into words on a page that breathed with emotional resonance. A metaphor captures the feeling: "I lowered a lantern down, down through the rising vapor until the fire blazed right over the lapping waters; and nothing came to light on that heaving surface but the light itself." The novel absorbs into itself the horror of rending loss and the collapse of ultimate meaning.

In a way Paul's death was also the death of Anne herself: the intense person of faith that she once had been—that had been challenged in college, then closed, perhaps forever, into Michele's coffin. She had once heard that when Hemingway killed off a character it was because he could not face something or could not envision what the character could accomplish. Paul's death had a similar tone: Anne, the person of faith, dying metaphorically when she cannot—perhaps *will* not—explore what might have been for herself.

At the same time, the writing is full of highly charged sensuality. In a distinctive voice Anne used voluptuous language and imagery to create subliminal tension and release that mimics sexual orgasm. The novel is erotic without explicit sex, creating a bridge between the impulse toward life deep within the psyche and the sensual excitement that could reach an audience. Tapping the physical agitation that accompanies fear, Anne provided a romantic adventure tinged with dark emotion and mystery. Her style was purposely ornamented with excessive language to create an atmosphere of sensory magnification. The story is told through passive reflection, but it is full of restrained energy and movement.

She used the first-person viewpoint for intimacy, making inner states vivid, and writing in a free-flowing but controlled dream-like state akin to unconsciousness. "The control has to do entirely with the universe that is in the novel," she explained. "When I say I'm unconscious, what I mean is that I don't think about life, not the larger meaning of the word in terms of my own life, because that would just block me. So there's a very conscious shaping, like building suspense. All the conscious things that have to do with craft are always at work: how to build suspense, whether to get this information out now, is this believable about a character, whether it's clear why these two characters are attracted to each other, things like that. That's always working, whereas I'm shutting out the more obvious things about my life. The book takes on its total life, like a daydream world unto itself. Then there's a conscious memory about other people's writing, what's happening in their work. I have an excellent memory about where things come from. But I'm principally thinking about what the characters will do next, what really matters, what's authentic, what the plot turn will be. If I just concentrate on what's intensely interesting to me, the rest will take care of itself."

Her descriptions are exacting, showing attention to the fine nuances that charge a scene with intersensory stimuli: "A rat moving somewhere near the altar . . . The gold candlesticks shimmered . . . a rich white chrysanthemum bent suddenly on its stem, droplets glistening on the crowded petals, a sour fragrance rising from a score of vases." She exhibits an awareness of hidden realities in fleeting perceptions, noting a greasy fingerprint on a telephone or the smell of dust mingled with rain. Although she occasionally overuses some words and phrases like *preternatural,* the fault fails to mar the overall richness.

As Louis tells the story of his deteriorating mental and physical condition, he describes how he became the perfect target for a vampire. Unbeknownst to him, a vampire has been watching him and finally makes his move, attacking Louis on a dark street. The vampire's name is Lestat and he offers to make Louis into a vampire like himself, to acquire immortality. Louis surrenders and finds exciting the experience of having his blood sucked: "The movement of his lips raised the hair all over my body that was not unlike the pleasure of passion." Lestat offers his blood and when Louis drinks, he is a vampire.

Vampires are supernatural beings who suck the blood of the living in order to prolong their existence indefinitely. The image is a complex metaphor of seduction and submission to a higher mystery and power. They are monsters, making the sacred profane, confusing normal gender roles, and procreating by penetrating their own children; yet they are a bridge to another realm because they once were human and still look human. They represent the threat of the continuum: their kinship to us allows them to invade our defined worlds and frighten us with the possibility of becoming like them. Yet the popularity of the vampire myth indicates that we are attracted as much as repulsed.

Vampires may represent the dark, frightening impulses within us to do the things we forbid ourselves—the "monster within ourselves," as Anne would later describe it: total sexual license. They are associated with guilt-free surrender, bizarre sex, violence, and a godlike power over death—perhaps a disguise for our fear of death.

Then there is the blood, symbolizing life, family, and racial ties. Anne had thrilled as a child to priests drinking wine that was supposed to be magically transubstantiated into the actual blood of Christ. Vampires take on this power by making blood central to their essence and existence. They, too, are spirit coming into substance, transforming it into a fusion of spirit and flesh—no longer quite human, not quite gods. They magnify the mystery of life and mimic the Holy Communion in their union through the blood. In fiction previous to *Interview With the Vampire,* vampires were viewed as enemies of the church. In Anne's novel they are a perverse reflection of it. Just as there is an inevitable let-down following the promise of union with God in the drama of the Sacrament, so also is there disappointment for the vampires immediately following the drinking of blood from a victim.

Nevertheless, for the victim, sexual arousal heightens with the threat of annihilation: a vampire is the image of "dangerous sex" in which the greatest possible orgasm is achieved at the point preceding unconsciousness, but the risk is death. However, to survive is to experience a rebirth. The victims envision transformative possibilities, especially in the idea of conquering death.

Immortality—a concept from the church that still fired Anne's imagination. The church was unable to grant it in the flesh, but vampires held the power. Here was a way for Anne to buffer her fear of death and to ease her grief over those taken from her. Working through immortal characters gave her a safe place from which to ponder the fact of death. Although Anne had been fascinated with this supernatural creature since childhood and was attracted to the erotic element, the vampire she was writing about also represented archetypal horrors at a deeper level that gave to her monster dimensions not portrayed in most vampire fiction. The destructive nature of the vampire was evident in what alcohol had done to Katherine, what leukemia had done to Michele, and what Michele's passing had done to Anne. Herself divided between painful remembering and the desire to forget that betrayed those she had lost, Anne found a way to unify both in the flexibility and tolerance of fiction. In this novel she wold resurrect Michele. Later, she would do the same for her mother.

As Louis becomes a vampire, he experiences an awesome perceptual transformation: "It was as if I had only just been able to see colors and shapes for the first time." As it intensifies, his humanity drains out with his mortal bodily fluids, a detail of the vampire mythos original to Anne. The transformation echoes the notion of process that had engaged Stan in the sixties. "When I saw the moon on the flagstones," says Louis, "I became so enamored with it that I must have spent an hour there."

There was another influence at work as well, which Anne called on with full awareness. She had read the novel *The Teachings of Don Juan: A Yaqui Way of Knowledge,* by Carlos Castaneda, that had created great excitement in the counterculture. It is about a young anthropologist who apprentices himself to a Yaqui Indian named Don Juan to learn from him an avenue into alternative realities that challenges everything he has taken for granted. The teachings involve heightened states of consciousness in order to peer into the mysteries of an elusive world not available to ordinary vision. It means becoming light and fluid, rejecting the burdensome chrysalis of the self-important rational mind, and looking clearly at one's own nature.

"I really fell into that book," Anne said. "I was enthralled with the writing and the simplicity of the descriptions and with his tremendous love for the figure of Don Juan as a teacher. That is definitely in *Interview With the Vampire;* the whole concept of Louis learning to be a vampire was influenced by Castaneda."

People all around her in California were exploring ways to "go within" and find personal meaning, inner peace, and transcendence. Although Anne was not involved with these movements, she was writing about similar concerns in the guise of a supernatural creature; her expression of crossing boundaries into a new realm of excessive, magnified experience would meet up with an intense cultural hunger for just such uninhibited introspection and transformation. Her medium, the vampire, would be quickly embraced.

Anne's vampires hint that to become one of them is a much greater experience than mere human ecstasy has to offer. Vampires, she figured, have lost the opportunity for the everyday satisfactions of life: sex, food, drink. At the same time, their sensory awareness has increased. "Pain is terrible for you . . . you feel it like no other creature because you are a vampire." Thus, the experience of sucking blood from their victims takes on increased significance and sensuality. "Killing is no ordinary act," said the vampire. "It is the experience of another's life for certain, and often the experience of the loss of that life through the blood, slowly." They fall in love with their victims and mimic human coupling the way they penetrate and draw out the blood. "The sucking mesmerized me," says Louis, "the warm struggling of the man was soothing to the tension of my hands."

There was yet another aspect of this new breed of vampires that made them unusual: Anne's vampires exhibited androgynous freedom. The androgyne is a being who reconciles opposites and channels duality into greater power. The vampires achieved this on several levels.

"I've always loved the images of androgyny," Anne said. "They always have an intense emotional impact on me, whether it's a beautiful woman in the opera dressed as a man or rock stars changing and shifting, it just gives me chills. I see the androgynous figure as the ideal figure."

The relationship between Lestat and Louis, then between Louis and another vampire, Armand, has homoerotic overtones as male and female distinctions become insignificant, since vampires do not engage in genital sex. The new vampire is brought over into a dramatically changed existence with a gender-free perspective.

Anne wanted to write about a romantic relationship that would avoid the clichés attached to heterosexual couplings, and she was also enamored of the image of lovers as equals. "For me," she said, "the most erotic scenes in any book are those that take place between totally equally franchised human beings, so I always find a scene between two men much more erotic to write about or read about than a scene between a man and a woman." Having already written about homosexual attractions, the relationships between her vampires came easily and naturally. Gay populations were "coming out" and becoming a political force, giving Anne momentum.

Reviewers would later note the strong similarities between her vampire "subculture" and the gay community, citing the tone of guilt, alienation, and the struggle with their deviance from the culture at large. Anne admitted that Lestat's invitation to become a vampire was analogous to a sexual awakening, even a dramatic sexual conversion from one gender to the other. Becoming a vampire involves being taken to the edge of experience and beyond into new territory, which is both frightening and erotic. Her male characters exhibit a degree of femininity normally prohibited in "real men," allowing them a wholeness that reached past gender divisions into the asexual subconscious. Louis's development was influenced by Jean, from *Nicholas and Jean,* and gave Anne a means of working with dominance and submission without making of it a gender-specific issue.

"I meant to imply," said Anne in a later interview, "that the nature of the kill was sexual but not in an immediate genital way. I think I swapped the male orgasm for the female. The pleasure he gets in killing was an overall swoon like women probably feel, a surrender."

Readers were invited to experience the blurred distinctions, raised to mythical heights. Becoming a vampire involved a merging of like minds in a way prohibited to people with fundamentally different perspectives. Female readers strongly identified with Louis, and later with Lestat, because Anne provided for them a means to experience male qualities that society prizes so highly without a loss of the female-oriented perspective.

Anne was fully aware that women were being encouraged by the burgeoning feminist movement to value their own experience, independent from men, but she told one journalist, "I think I have a gender screw-up to the point that I don't know most of the time what gender I am, in terms of anybody else's thinking." As a result, the vampire imagery that she developed appealed as a sexual fantasy from various perspectives, from a heterosexual exploring a secret but socially forbidden allure in the perspective of another gender to a homosexual finding affirmation. Anne's erotic style gave these metaphors an added touch.

She wrote mostly at night at a desk in the bedroom, and Stan learned to sleep with the light on or on the couch. In the early morning hours Anne fell into bed only a few feet away. By day, she went to the library. Stan's former mentor, Jesse Ritter, saw her once on campus, and she told him that she was finally going to write that novel about New Orleans that had been in her head all these years. She researched the sparse vampire lore, reading mythologies from other cultures, as well as stories like Sheridan Le Fanu's "Carmilla." She tried Bram Stoker's *Dracula* but, stunned to see vampires portrayed in such an animalian fashion, did not finish it. She looked up a serious study written by a former professor, Leonard Wolf, and a biographical account of the real Dracula by Raymond McNally and Radu Florescu. She also watched a made-for-television movie called "Frankenstein: The True Story," and the images of the sympathetic monster swam in her head as she was writing. "I was fascinated by all that," she said, "and I know that my writing was seminally influenced."

Anne began to realize that there was a gulf between the vampire in nineteenth-century literature and the vampire in folklore. In many world cultures, she discovered, people had been afraid of the spirits of the dead between the time the body was interred and the time it decays. She was fascinated with the rituals devised to ensure that loved ones did not become vampires, although she gravitated toward the fictional accounts for developing her own mythological universe.

Hearkening back to a 1936 vampire film, *Dracula's Daughter,* in which a tragic relationship of trust was emphasized over gore, she saw vampires as cerebral rather than animal, with a "preternatural obsession" both tragic and erotic. Louis was presented as a demonic angel, feeding on the essence of life. Anne thought of vampires as images that emerged from a deep primitive consciousness, trapped by their nature in a psychological purgatory, and not as pure evil, the way Stoker had depicted Dracula. "I think the vampire," she said, "is the image of a person who takes a blood sacrifice in order to live and exerts a charm over people. I saw them as angels going in another direction, as finely tuned imitations of human beings imbued with this evil spirit." They had a conscience and suffered from guilt, loneliness, ambivalence, and many of the numinous questions of their former mortality. Anne enlarged their existence with a mythological context, stiffened with the starch of contemporary logic, psychology, and enduring philosophical questions.

Angels as evil, vampires as gods. The paradoxes pop up in the descriptions, conversations, and confrontations, increasing the crisis in logic already established with the proposal of their existence as the living dead. They talk to each other in polarities: "Believing in anything, I can accept that there is nothing to believe in"; "your evil is that you cannot be evil"; or "the measure of my hatred is that love." The contradictions are slippery, existing as puzzling possibilities rather than canceling themselves.

Coupled with paradox is the tension of paired opposites: light and dark, experience and innocence, good and evil. Anne utilized twists and blends of opposing concepts to flavor Louis's ambivalent moods, but she did not bring them to philosophical completion until years later. Nevertheless, the elaborate style serves a purpose. It was as much a psychological outlet as a literary device.

Anne moved deep within herself, into the darkness of her sensibilities. The opposites with which she was working emerged from an inner source—the frightening place of unconscious, preverbal images where vagueness at the borders of awareness defies precise articulation, where chaos reigns. It is a fertile disorder created by the onslaught to the senses of the multiple impressions of the full panorama of life; only those who can withstand it without reduction of the whole into some manageable part can emerge, transformed, into people of creative depth. Contradiction had been part of Anne's life, as had a responsiveness to a broad range of physical stimuli. Growing up in New Orleans, experiencing the unpredictability of an alcoholic parent, exposed to the tension of polarities in a religious atmosphere in which the natural touched the supernatural, it was as if she had been prepared to fully surrender to her shifting internal energies. Hers was a sensitive and active subconscious, compressed toward a hot inner core with the suppression of painul events. As she wrote, the inner dynamic merged with literary images and ideas, flowing into relationships and conversations that became layered with philosophical and psychological complexity.

For the plot, Anne wanted a new take on the vampire. She retained the "need" for coffins as a mere superstition, but defied the traditions in which vampires are killed by stakes, fear crucifixes, can become mist, and show no reflection in mirrors. Lack of reflection signified that their souls were in hell, and Anne did not want her vampires to have any more assurance than did humans that God existed. "What I wanted

Louis to experience," she later told interviewer Eric Bauersveld, "was preternatural power without explanation. So I eliminated those things which would have necessitated too logical an explanation that God or the devil was at work." Inspired by a poem by William Blake, she felt that light itself becomes God to the vampires, but they are forever barred from it. Nevertheless, the issue of possessing a soul remained in question. They could see themselves in mirrors, and what an appearance they presented!

> The vampire was utterly white and smooth, as if he were sculpted from bleached bone, and his face was as seemingly inanimate as a statue, except for two brilliant green eyes. . . . But then the vampire smiled almost wistfully, and the smooth white substance of his face moved with the infinitely flexible but minimal lines of a cartoon.

Initially the relationships between the vampires were based on need and control, with one vampire dominating another for companionship or slavery. They were outsiders, seeking community on the boundaries of human society and using similar forms of repression to exact conformity. They possessed a vivid and focused view of life. Freed from human illusions, they explored new capacities for power and bonding. But, as with vampires everywhere, the pinnacle of their existence was the kill, and the threat for them was to be seduced by the orgasm of the beating heart just before it stopped. To keep on drinking past that point was to risk annihilation. This idea was inspired by "Ode to a Nightingale," a poem by Keats:

> Now more than ever seems it rich to die
> To cease upon the midnight with no pain
> While Thou art pouring forth thy soul abroad
> In such an ecstasy!

"I would think it would be like that to drink after the victim died," Anne said, "to just glide out of existence, to go out with the tide. It would be to be seduced by death." It was an image that Anne had associated with Michele's death.

Anne worked on the novel every night for five weeks until she had a manuscript of more than three hundred pages. When she finished, she sat back. Louis's presence still seemed so palpable that she felt she need only turn her head to see him standing there. She wrote in her diary:

> It is just before four a.m. Monday morning, January 14 [1974], and I have just finished my vampire novel—338 pages. Even as I

> write this the flaws occur to me. Perhaps I'll go in and add something terribly essential. But right now I want to enjoy the moment of being finished: as I think I've expressed to both of them [Stan and a writing friend], I am too excited about it to say anything humble or modest. I feel that even the writing of this entry is important. I dream, hope, imagine that this will be my first published work. I feel ashamed of nothing in it—not even what I know to be flaws. I feel solidly behind it as though Louis' voice were my voice and I do not run the risk of being misunderstood.

She went back that morning for a couple of hours and corrected what she had perceived as flaws in the ending. She was now ready to show it to someone.

2

Lestat is a blond-haired, Shakespearean-mannered creature who has no qualms about religion, little sympathy for moral weakness, and exerts a strong will on those around him. However, he has a mortal father to whom he feels he must prove himself, as Anne had felt during her adolescence with Howard. Anne had thought Lestat was an old French name but later realized the actual name had been Lestan. Lestat was loosely based on the physical appearance and attitudes of Stan. While Stan was flattered to be the physical model, he also perceived that the novel revealed Anne's reaction to his tendency to exert control. When they had been trying to save their child, Stan had taken the masculine route of trying to manage everything, but Anne had been too independent to react well. It may be that her resistance, along with the marital discord following their loss, was channeled into the novel. There is a distinct uneasiness in the relationship between Louis and Lestat, increasing as the novel develops, though they are bonded by mutual attraction. Anne admitted that all of her work incorporated impressions of people, places, and events familiar to her; and it is clear that her relationship with Stan provided intense emotional tones for the book.

Lestat also can be construed as another side of Anne's personality, complementing and clashing with what she experienced as Louis. He is dominant and Louis is submissive, expressing the contraries of hero and victim between which Anne had found herself. Although Lestat comes across as a thoroughly uncaring and selfish creature from Louis's perspective, he would eventually become for Anne in a later novel the man she wanted to be.

However, it was Louis with whom she was obsessed. He was a victim, a character with whom she could identify easily, who could express for her the despair and darkness that she still felt. He allows himself to be used by Lestat and to be provoked into doing things he later regrets.

Lestat teaches Louis to kill, but Louis is appalled. He drinks from animals, although it never satisfies his thirst—a metaphor of empty church rituals in which a non-existent God is substituted for inner spirituality. Louis realizes that he despises this creature who made him, and that there is an essential difference between them that will forever separate them. "And what I felt, most profoundly, for everything . . . was respect. Lestat felt the opposite. Or he felt nothing." Loneliness settles in, magnified by a look into a future that stretches out endlessly. They were linked but divided.

Louis most despises Lestat's habit of killing young men who "represented the greatest loss . . . because they stood on the threshold of the maximum possibility of life." He expresses Anne's feeling of loss with regard to her daughter. Almost six, Michele had been on the verge of experiencing her life more fully when the vampire, leukemia, had claimed her.

When Louis and Lestat are forced from their plantation, they seek sanctuary with Babette Freniere, whom Louis has helped in the past. He had initially appeared to her as an angel, but Babette now sees Louis for the devil he is and turns away in horror. He despises himself, realizing there is no return to human innocence. Nor could he have ever really loved her: "For vampires, physical love culminates and is satisfied in one thing, the kill." She will grow old and die while he remains the same. It is another taste of the bitterness of immortality and with it comes the feeling of entrapment.

Louis accompanies Lestat to New Orleans, where they occupy a town house. Anne used as a model the Gallier House at 1132 Royal Street in the French Quarter. There Louis finally succumbs to his hunger for human blood and feeds on a five-year-old girl. Capturing the lust and intimacy of the blood thirst, Anne took the reader to the very neck of the victims to experience the gush, the urgent need, the slow satisfaction. "In that instant I had bent down and driven hard into her soft, small neck and, hearing her tiny cry, whispered even as I felt the hot blood on my lips, 'It's only for a moment and there'll be no more pain.' "

It is at this point that Anne most strongly portrays the vampire as a compulsive sinner, the thirst as an addiction, like the alcoholic for the bottle. The hunger rises to overtake reason, as a "string pulling me through the labyrinth." The craving is overpowering, and after killing, "a vampire is as warm as you are now"—a common sentiment among alcoholics. Anne's mother had once told her that her craving was "in the blood." The images of Katherine's helplessness and need had taken deep root, echoed in Louis's mannerisms: guilt, insecurity, helplessness, a sense of isolation and secrecy, low self-esteem, over-reaction to criticism, and intense sadness. The environment surrounding him—partially created by him—was one of anxiety, fear, disappointment, disillusionment, and frustration. "I knew peace," he claims sadly, "only when I killed." Lestat and Louis play out a public facade while they secretly dive into their addiction, then emerge uneasy with one another, like the family of an alcoholic. The vampire thus becomes an expression of the inner chaos through which Anne retrieves the confusion and pain of an alcoholic family system, transforming it into a fictionally safe and universally compelling symbol. Drawing a child into it established the metaphor more firmly.

Lestat makes the little girl, Louis's victim, into a vampire to keep Louis with him. Louis passively protests, but is happy to have her as a companion. She plays for hours with the dolls that Michele had spurned, and Anne at last had a child who loved dolls as she did. They live together as a family: a dominant father, a passive mother, and a beautiful child, although the roles are confused as Louis is also the child's lover, sleeping with her in the same coffin.

The child vampire is Claudia, and she is the physical image of blond-haired Michele. Once when Michele had worn her hair up and had spoken in a voice husky from a cold, Stan and Anne had thought she looked like the actress Claudia Cardinale, who ironically had played in the vampire film *Carmilla*. They sometimes even had called her Claudia.

The vampires remain together for years, and Louis notices a change in Claudia as Anne must have seen in Michele: "Yet more and more her doll-like face seemed to possess two totally aware adult eyes, and innocence seemed lost somewhere with neglected toys and the loss of a certain patience. . . . Her mind was unpredictable, unknowable." Claudia is growing up, becoming a woman, although her body remains tiny. Similar to Michele, it is also the image of Anne, forced to become an adult while still a child, and retaining a childlike vulnerability as an adult.

Anne later saw this image as both a reflection of herself and of women in general. Whenever she had been sexually appraised, she had felt conspicuous, horrified, and angry. Since childhood she'd felt secretly like a criminal over her sexual desires, and her body made her visible in a way that she did not wish to confront. Unable to deal with her rage in fiction, she had locked it inside herself, gaining weight in an attempt to hide the features of her gender. "Claudia," she admitted, "is the embodiment of my failure to deal with the feminine. She is a woman trapped in a child's body. She's the person robbed of power."

As a vampire Claudia is careless about who and where she kills, and Louis and Lestat find a woman and her child dead in an outside kitchen. Claudia was seeking mother figures, according to Anne, and when they did not save her, she destroyed them. Yet at another level it is Anne herself who destroys them by giving form to the images and writing the scenes in which they are killed. A dead mother and a dead daughter are too close to her own twin griefs not to have an obvious relationship to what she was writing. Her mother had been unable to save herself, let alone her children, and Anne as a mother had been unable to save her daughter. The mother church had been just as impotent in both situations, and bitterness was the result for Anne. Although she had loved her mother, she could not help but feel betrayed; later, as a mother herself, she believed Michele could be experiencing the same feelings about her. The expression of that mix of need, love, and anger comes out in Claudia's activities. In one scene, Claudia decides she wants her own coffin. Louis is revolted by the idea of a coffin for a child and cannot stand for her picking one out. The images confronted Anne with her own horror over Michele's recognition of death and, eventually, of having to view her in a tiny coffin. The feelings mingled in the dark regions of Anne's mind, where the ever active function of the creative process tapped them and brought them alive in her novels.

As the story continues, Claudia becomes curious about what she is. "Which of you did it?" she demands. "Which of you made me what I am?" It is an accusation as much as a question. Louis explains. She reacts in a rage that defies her doll-like appearance, and decides to kill Lestat so that she and Louis can flee and seek out answers to the riddles of their existence. She tricks Lestat into drinking poisoned blood, then hacks him up, urging Louis to help her drag him out to the swamps. It is not so easy, however, to be rid of a vampire.

Lestat returns, scarred but in one piece, and furious at their betrayal. Lamps are overturned, creating a fire, and Louis and Claudia escape to their ship. However, they cannot shrug off the feeling that Lestat survived the fire. The idea of such power is Louis's first realization that having immortality has diminished rather than increased the choices he had possessed as a mortal.

An image of her own sense of diminished power, Anne saw this theme as central to what she intended with the story. Louis had become immortal without really knowing what he was getting into, much like humans who make choices without any idea of the possible implications. "If there's one theme that you could boil it down to," she told Eric Bauersveld on the radio, "it's that we have no grasp of even twenty-five per cent of what we're doing." Louis had the capacity to make the decision to become a vampire, but he has no sense until it is too late of what he has done. This is an expression of the existential themes that had once captivated Anne, although she had not consciously structured the book to illustrate them. Her own experience of choice and limitation had validated the ways in which philosophers like Sartre and Camus had described the "human condition."

Louis and Claudia encounter disappointment in their search for vampires in Eastern Europe, finding only mindless monsters. Claudia decides they must go to Paris. At this point the original manuscript took a direction that was quite different from the way the story evolved in the published novel. Anne initially wrote the story as follows:

Louis and Claudia meet the vampire Armand, who exhibits the beauty of a boy, though his mannerisms are clearly supernatural. Armand, at the age of four hundred years, is the oldest vampire of Anne's universe thus far. He lives with other vampires in a large mansion in the Faubourg St. Germain. Louis and Claudia join him and they all stand around in a circle reciting poetry from Baudelaire and drinking blood from caldrons. Armand is a sweet, romantic, and lovable guy. He provides a beautiful woman in a bed for Louis to drink from, but has no answers about the ultimate questions of good and evil that Louis has been carrying around with him. He takes Louis up to a tower room overlooking the city, and they discuss Louis's despair. Later, they meet on a dark street and Armand convinces Louis to go off with him. Louis feels that "at last I have found the vampire of my dreams." Claudia joins some children who terrorize the citizens of Paris. Lestat never does show up and seems to have been killed in the fire back at the town house.

Louis ends his interview with the young reporter and turns his back. The boy grabs the tapes and runs, but when he reaches the bottom of the stairs, Louis is there. He asks the boy why he ran and reminds him that he has no intention of harming him. Armand appears and assures Louis that the boy will do with the tapes what Louis wants. Then they get into a cab and drive away.

The ending did not reach a cathartic pitch, but for Anne the vampire's story was finished. Symbolically, Michele was granted immortality.

It was this version of the manuscript that excited Anne on that early January morning as she wrote in her diary, although she would later make significant changes.

3

Anne showed the draft to Stan. As he finished the last page, he thought to himself, "Our lives have changed."

His friend Casey also read it. "I was very surprised," Casey said. "I was knocked out." He turned to Stan and said, "This sends us back to kindergarten." He told Anne it was as strongly written as any man could do. Casey and Stan both felt that they had underestimated her.

Encouraged, Anne took the manuscript to a friend's writing group and passed it around for comments. She had ignored faddish writing trends and she did not fare well. Too shy to read it herself, she allowed a friend, Lee Wagner, to read the first thirty pages out loud and received criticisms that seemed to her empty and unproductive—"stuff that didn't matter." The group wanted to know why Louis wanted to help the Freniere family, how he knew them, how a dead overseer had been bruised if there was no blood in his body. They also asked how Anne could carry the plot for three hundred pages, and how she would sustain their interest in vampires. In short, they thought there were too many problems to make the story feasible. Anne ignored them. "I'm very stubborn and self-motivated, and I don't believe you should listen to comments. You should write what you believe. You stick with your vision."

Anne sent a draft of the novel to the Joseph Henry Jackson Award competition, going up against her friend Carolyn Doty, who was submitting her first novel. Neither of them won.

She also sent a copy, full of mistakes and spelling errors, to Jack DeGovia, involved now in production design for motion pictures. He loved it and thought he might be able to interest some movie people in bringing the story to the screen, although he suggested she change the title from *Interview With the Vampire.*

"She didn't argue," he recalled. "She just said, 'Uh-huh.' "

Feeling confident, Anne sent the manuscript out to several publishers. She knew this was going to be her first published novel if she had to bind it herself and sell it on the streets as a "vampire cheapie." Over a period of ten months, she received only rejections telling her the novel lacked finesse, plot, and character. Some were so bad, she laughed at them. If she could not learn something from negative criticism, she decided, she would ignore it. She sent *Interview With the Vampire* to a contest, directing it to a particular judge, and learned that a reader had thrown it out before any of the judges had seen it. "There were moments," she said, "when my confidence suffered."

Gradually, in a backlash from the grief from which writing had given her a temporary respite, she began to feel as if she contaminated everything she touched. She did not want to prepare food or touch other people lest she infect them. At one dinner party she put salad on her plate, then, not thinking, replaced the salad forks. She was horrified that she had contacted food that others would eat. She and Stan took most of their meals out, and Anne washed her hands compulsively, feeling the need to get clean but despairing of the possibility. Over and over she checked the locks on her doors and windows. When more compulsions drove her behavior, she felt she was falling apart.

"I felt I was going crazy," she said. "It was gradual at first, and then it got worse and worse. There was a feeling of germs being everywhere. I would see people take a six-pack of beer from the floor and put it on a shelf, and I'd tell them, you know you're getting germs all over that shelf. I'd wash my hands over and over and then accidentally bump the basin, and I'd have to wash them again. What you see when you're in that state is every single flaw in our hygiene and you can't control it and you go crazy."

She sought out a psychiatrist, but did not like him. Someone suggested Dr. David Geisinger, a psychologist who worked with behavior, so Anne contacted him. She thought him an intelligent, eloquent man. Later, he clarified his approach to therapy: "In essence I believe, like Sartre, that we are *condemned* to be free and that this is both our burden and our pathway to liberation and redemption. In practice, I am more pragmatic. The truth alone (whatever that is) doesn't make us free—we need some techniques, ample support, and lots of hard work." Anne went to him once a week for over a year. "It was a mixed bag," she said. "I thought it did some good for me to talk with him each week."

Her grief over her daughter's death did not decrease, but going to a therapist seemed to reduce the irrational behavior and Anne recalled one statement Dr. Geisinger made that had an impact on her: "Beware the affect." He put the power into her hands to get herself out of black pits of despair over things other people said.

At the same time, Anne went to the library and looked up psychiatric definitions of compulsive behavior. She was surprised to find descriptions that matched her behavior so closely—the persistent ideas, the anxious dread, the extreme countermeasures taken to deflect it, and the overwhelming need to perform behaviors that one finds irrational and tries to resist. "Realizing that people the world over had exactly the same symptoms," she said, "that this was a pattern, that it was not to be taken literally, was helpful."

Then one night she called the Free Clinic in Berkeley because she was afraid she had taken too much medication, and a doctor named John told her that obsessive-compulsive hand washing was a way that the mind tricked itself into avoiding something else that was worse; you attached all your anxieties to washing your hands. "I found that single statement," said Anne, "to be one of the most helpful statements I received from anyone. It was a profound eye-opener that I have never forgotten."

Eventually the intensity of the compulsion burned itself out, but not until after a momentous event.

At a friend's urging, Anne applied to a writer's conference at Squaw Valley that summer, in August. After her experience with the rejections she did not dare to send her novel with the application form. Instead she sent three stories about her family, including the one about her grandfather, and was accepted with a full scholarship on the strength of her work. The fiction director was very impressed and thought her writing bore signs of genius. She was gratified but, feeling insecure, was unsure whether she wanted to go. Stan put her on the bus himself. Secretly she tucked her vampire novel into a suitcase, just in case.

Squaw Valley is a ski resort in the Sierra Nevada, secluded and full of fragrant evergreens. The mountainous setting is perfect for serious writers who need peace and inspiration. There were regular morning workshops, for fiction, nonfiction and poetry, limited to a dozen participants per session. Editors, agents, and staff ran the workshops and gave talks on publishing and other literary concerns.

At an evening cocktail party, Anne met Kathy Macay. Kathy had just graduated from Harvard. She was a student of fiction who had not yet committed herself to being a full-time writer. She spotted Anne, who appeared uncomfortable, and walked up to her. They hit it off immediately.

"I remember Anne as being shy and soft-spoken," she said of their first meeting. "The minute I started speaking with her, I was struck by her intelligence, her verbal ability, and her beautiful storytelling ability. She said she had a manuscript with her which was about a vampire telling the story of the last two hundred years of his life. I said, 'Oh, great!' "

Anne was apprehensive about the week, but Kathy reassured her. "Stick with me, kid, you'll be okay." They spent time together and Kathy learned from Anne what commitment to writing really was. "Anne exemplified that. She was a terrific inspiration to me. She felt it so strongly, it was contagious. She found stimulus in so many different areas and had an insatiable curiosity." They shared a dream of making a real impact in the publishing world.

Anne was scheduled to meet with Phyllis Seidel, who was just launching her career as an agent. They spent a half hour together and Phyllis asked her if she had any other pieces of writing with her. Shyly she produced the manuscript. Phyllis Seidel took it and read it over the next few days. She was impressed. "Anne is a great setter of scenes and a teller of tales," she said, "and I was delighted with her world of ghoulish iconography. The manuscript had an authority, a command that was indisputable." She agreed to represent it, seeing it as a book about power that would interest people. That same day on the phone, Anne learned from Stan that a letter had arrived from another agency also interested in representing her. "I never thought I would face such a problem," said Anne. She decided to go with Phyllis Seidel, nervously awaiting the outcome.

Anne and Stan continued to have parties, and one of their guests was Andy Brumer, a writer. Anne revealed to Andy that she had an agent representing a novel she had written about a vampire. He thought it sounded interesting, but Anne did not say too much about it, as if unsure of its potential. Neither of them had any inkling of what was about to happen.

Two months went by. Anne grew discouraged. She told a friend that she felt like a failure. She had pinned everything important that she wanted to say on a theme she was sure no one would buy. To distract herself, she began to read Dostoevsky's *The Idiot.*

Her father came out to visit and Anne handed him her manuscript. She knew he was a sophisticated reader and would not be disturbed by the erotic elements. What mattered to him were style and moral tone, and she saw Louis as a tragic moral hero. Howard did not care for vampire stories, but he agreed to give his opinion. At first he was disturbed by the spelling errors, but as he became immersed in the story, he was stunned. "I thought it was so beautifully written," he said. "Her literary style knocked me off my feet. I had considered myself a writer and I said to myself, 'I have to give this up. I can't compete.' " The sensuality of her writing did not surprise him. "From the time Anne was two or three, she was a very sensual person. She would put her head in my lap and ask me to rub her back in a circular motion."

Then one night in October, the phone rang. Anne answered and thought the person on the other end had asked for Stan. She handed the phone to him. He soon gave it back. It was Phyllis Seidel. "Would you believe," she said, "that Knopf has flipped over your novel?" She had sold *Interview With the Vampire* to Alfred A. Knopf for a $12,000 advance for the hardcover rights. The typical advance for first novels at the time was $2,000. Anne had done very well, and at the age of thirty-four she would be a published author with a prestigious publishing house.

She was ecstatic. She and Stan began to make calls.

Cathy Colman was on the list. "That's a lot of tacos!" she exclaimed, referring to Anne's great fondness for Jack-in-the-Box tacos. Stan called Carolyn Doty at about eleven o'clock. "When I hung up the phone," Carolyn said, "I went out into the middle of the street and shouted that Anne had sold her book."

By the time Anne got around to telling her cousin Allen, however, she was feeling some backlash. Not everyone had been as enthused as she had hoped. "I remember the night Anne called me," Allen said. "It had all happened so fast. My comment was 'Far fucking out!' and she said, 'It's so nice to hear somebody happy for me.' Evidently she had experienced a lot of jealousy."

"There were mixed reactions," Anne admitted, "and that surprised me. Later I realized it was unfair to expect all my friends to jump up and down for me—they can't help but think of their own lives."

Days after the phone call, Anne was still screaming with delight and disbelief. Stan sometimes heard her in another room just belting one out. She was so excited she could not get back into Dostoevsky, although she carried the novel around for months afterward. The only thing that marred her triumph was that her mother was not there to see it, or her daughter to benefit from it.

The editor at Knopf was Victoria Wilson. Ironically, she had been at Squaw Valley but had not met Anne. A brief encounter with Phyllis Seidel had established a contact, so Phyllis had sent her the manuscript. She had a knack for spotting unusual fiction and liked what she saw. "One doesn't usually remember the experience of reading a book," she said years later, "but in this instance, I do. As I was reading it, I was having the most amazing responses. One thing that's a sure sign with me is that my blood starts to quicken, and I kept saying to myself, this is the strangest book I have ever read in my life. It is either absolutely wonderful and absolutely brilliant or I have been completely blinded. I was just beside myself. I had never read anything as extraordinary and peculiar and seductive." The way the novel expressed deep cultural mysteries and traditions seemed to her quite powerful.

However, she wanted some minor changes. The ending drifted off, she thought. Anne agreed to rewrite. She skimmed but did not rewrite the first half, then threw out the last hundred pages and added enough new material to make a 530-page manuscript. It took her ten weeks this time, working as long as twelve hours a day, from early evening until early morning. The story was taking over once again, expanding itself way beyond editorial suggestions. Anne researched the theaters in Paris and looked up street names in a guide to flesh out the Parisian scenes. The changes resulted in several new and essential twists to the plot.

4

In Paris, Louis and Claudia are confronted by a coven of older, more powerful vampires. Instead of going to a mansion and reciting poetry, they are invited to attend a performance at a place called the Theater of the Vampires. They watch as a mortal girl is killed on stage, to the approval of a human audience who believes it is acting. The girl was physically inspired by Linda Gregg, the poet friend from the sixties, because, as Anne told her, she was the kind of person who "surrendered willingly." Anne saw the exquisitely drawn-out scene from Louis's perspective of longing rather than from that of the terrified victim, although it presented the horror she had developed at the idea of dying in front of people who felt no compassion.

The theater is a metaphor of illusion, signaling the ambiguity of appearances: a welcoming gesture to Louis from the vampire coven clothes suspicion; honesty is merely a means to betrayal; the chief vampire, Armand, has the sweet face of a child, but says of himself: "I am evil with infinite gradations and without guilt.'' Louis and Claudia are caught up in this mysterious, confusing world, dealing with the slippery meanings with uneasy distrust, although Louis is attracted to Armand. Armand in turn is attracted to Louis. ''It is for you that I've been waiting,'' he insists, starting a theme that would continue in Anne's novels, of the protagonists becoming highly desired and special in the eyes of others.

To his despair Louis learns that Armand has no answer about the purpose of their existence, as in the first version of the manuscript. He had expected to discover that he was a child of Satan and to be damned for it, but there was no one to do it. The discussion between him and Armand about the levels of evil echoes Anne's frustration with a church that condemned alongside murderers children who French kissed. Armand insists, ''The only power that exists is inside ourselves.'' To Louis, now nearly an empty shell of a self, the realization is a great shock. ''It was as I'd always feared, and it was as lonely, it was as totally without hope.''

Although he is drawn to Armand, he realizes that he must remain with Claudia. Torn in opposing directions, his conflict symbolizes real-life ambivalence for Anne: she wants to be with Michele and also needs to let go in order to get on with her life. The pain and indecision ring with authenticity. Her obsessive-compulsive behavior, it was evident to her later, had developed in response to her inability to allow the grief process its evolution. She had brought Michele back in fiction and had given her child life, but that was not the way things were meant to be. She had to let go. The pages she added to the revised draft of the manuscript chronicle this process. Armand represents a healing force.

In the presence of Armand, Claudia seemed to be dazed. Later she tells Louis that Armand draws life out of her into himself. '' 'Do you know what he said . . . that I should die,' she whispered. 'That I should let you go.' '' Louis does not believe her, unaware of how he is being forced to give her up. She demands that he make for her a vampire companion to take care of her. She has selected Madeleine, a doll-maker, shallow and doomed, who has lost a child. Louis refuses and Claudia confesses that she despises him for making her into a defenseless child—''to give me immortality in this hopeless guise, this helpless form!'' This cry against Louis is also a cry against Anne: it was she who gave Claudia, and thus Michele, ''this helpless form.''

Louis realizes that Claudia really does hate him for the pain he has caused. Her venom destroys him because he had depended on her love as a way to ease his self-hatred. She had said once to Lestat, in echo of Sartre, ''Hell is hatred, people living together in eternal hatred.'' Louis sees now what it means. He gives in and makes Madeleine into a vampire. Afterward

Anne as Howard Allen, age three.

Anne's mother, Katherine Allen O'Brien, in her wedding dress on November 25, 1938.

Anne's father, Howard O'Brien, in 1952. (*By permission of Tamara O'Brien*)

2301 St. Charles Avenue in New Orleans, where Anne lived as a child. (*Credit: Katherine Ramsland*)

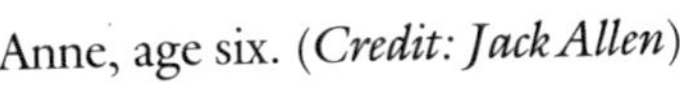

Anne, age six. (*Credit: Jack Allen*)

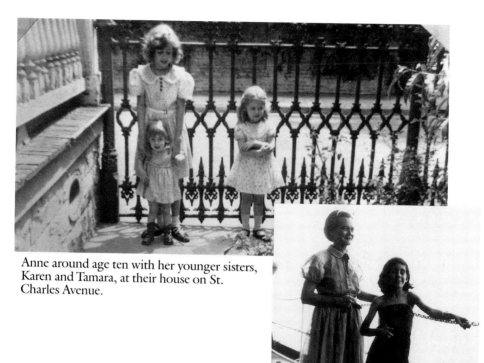

Anne around age ten with her younger sisters, Karen and Tamara, at their house on St. Charles Avenue.

Anne and her mother, Katherine, in 1951.

Anne with her girl scout troop at Holy Name of Jesus School in the fifth grade. Anne is in the second row, first girl on the left.

Lafayette Cemetery in New Orleans where Anne wandered as a girl. It was later used in her novels as the place where the vampire Lestat hid his valuables and where the Mayfair family had a vault.

Anne and her sister Alice. Anne is around eight and Alice is ten.

The towers of St. Alphonsus Church where Anne's parents were married and where Anne went to church. Next door, down the street, is Redemptorist High School where Anne attended tenth grade.

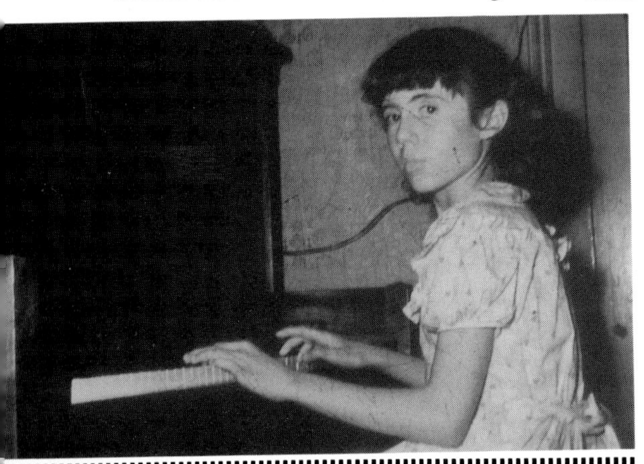

Anne, age eleven. (*By permission of Tamara O'Brien*)

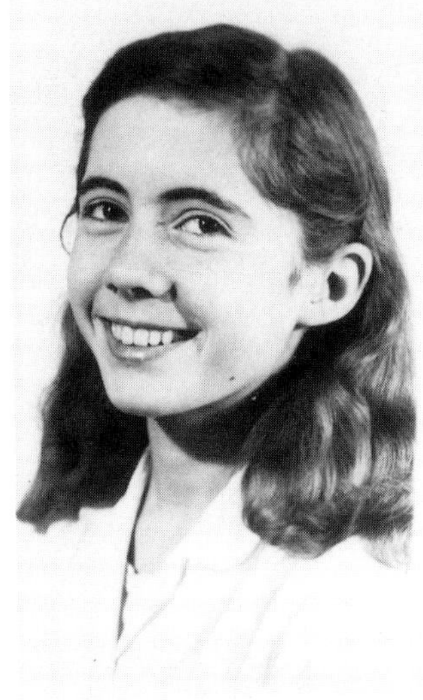

Anne in seventh grade.

Anne, right, age sixteen, with Alice and Lucy at the apartment on St. Mary Street in New Orleans.

Anne, right, and her friend Lucy Provosty in the French Quarter in New Orleans. Anne is sixteen.

Anne with her senior prom date, Jay Franklin, in 1959.

Anne, age seventeen in Richardson, Texas. (*By permission of Tamara O'Brien*)

Anne, age seventeen in Richardson, Texas. (*By permission of Tamara O'Brien*)

Anne with Joe Ramsey on the day she left Richardson to attend Texas Woman's University. She is seventeen.

Anne and Ginny Mathis near Fisherman's Wharf in San Francisco, June 1961. Anne is nineteen, with a preference for black clothing.

Anne and Stan, right, with Stan's family at their apartment on Ashbury Street around 1964. Left to right: Margaret Rice, Larry Rice, Stanley Rice, senior, and Cynthia Rice. (*By permission of Tamara O'Brien*)

Anne and her sister, Tamara, in San Francisco, 1964. (*By permission of Tamara O'Brien*)

Anne putting a wig on Stan, 1965. (*Credit: Casey Sonnabend*)

Stan, Anne, and Casey Sonnabend, 1965. (*Credit: Casey Sonnabend*)

Anne and Stan with Casey, right, and two friends, Anthony Durbin and John Stephens, left. (*Credit: Casey Sonnabend*)

One of the houses in Haight Ashbury where Anne and Stan rented an apartment. *(Credit: Katherine Ramsland)*

Anne and her sisters, Tamara, Alice, and Karen during the early seventies.
(*By permission of Tamara O'Brien*)

Michele, Christmas 1969.

Michele and Tamara, Thanksgiving 1970.

Anne and her family in the early seventies when Michele was undergoing medical tests. From left to right: Howard, Karen, Tamara, a friend of the family, Anne, Michele, and Stan. (*By permission of Tamara O'Brien*)

Michele and Stan just before she died of leukemia in 1972. (*By permission of Tamara O'Brien*)

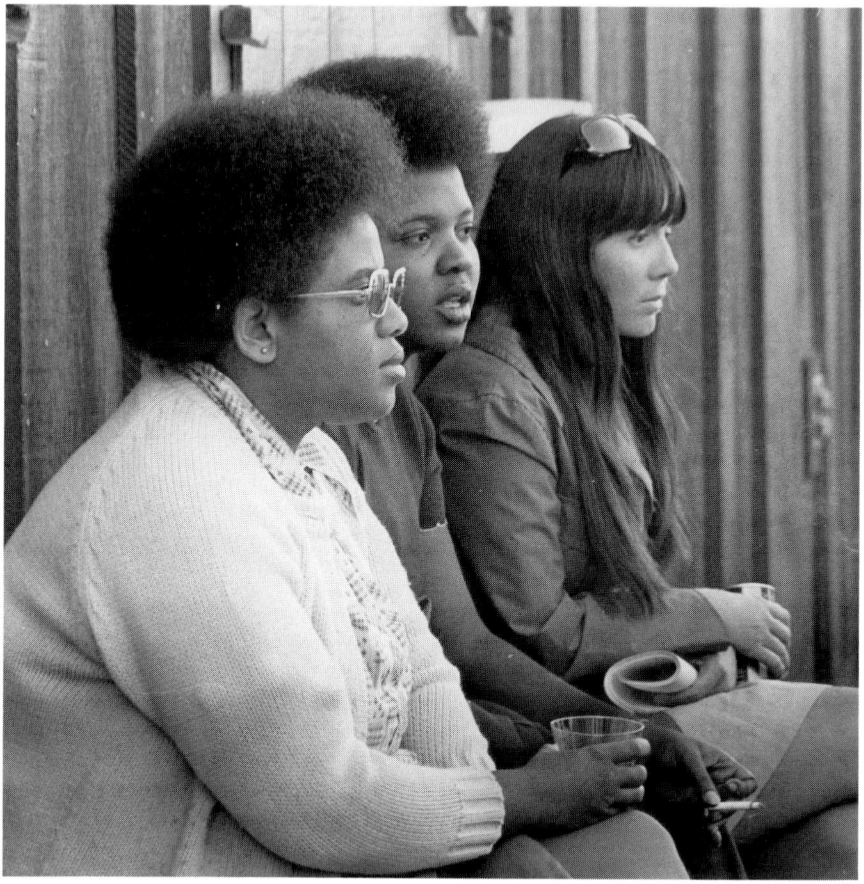

Anne at a workshop at Squaw Valley Writer's Conference where she met an agent who sold her first novel. (*Credit: Tracy Bailey*)

The house on Divisadero Street, right, that inspired the setting in *Interview With the Vampire* where Louis tells his story. (*Credit: Sue Quiroz*)

The Rices' house on Seventeenth Street in the Castro district in San Francisco. Anne wrote several novels here and made it one of the settings in *Belinda*. It was Jeremy Walker's house. (*Credit: Katherine Ramsland*)

Anne in her office in the Castro district Victorian. (*Credit: Katherine Ramsland*)

Christopher Rice, age six, with "Lestat's" mastiff.

The front of Anne's current home in the Garden District of New Orleans, where she moved in 1989. She set *The Witching Hour* here. Note the Egyptian "keyhole" doorway. (*Credit: Katherine Ramsland*)

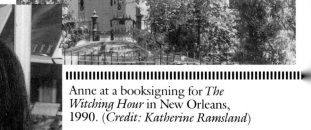

Anne at a booksigning for *The Witching Hour* in New Orleans, 1990. (*Credit: Katherine Ramsland*)

Part of Anne's doll collection. (*Credit: Katherine Ramsland*)

Stan, Chris and Anne with dolls, 1988. (*Credit: Victoria Rouse*)

Anne's half sister, Micki Ruth Collins, and her stepmother, Dorothy O'Brien, at a family reunion. (*Credit: Katherine Ramsland*)

Anne and Stan in 1988 at Monterey Bay in California.

Anne in her office in San Francisco, just before the publication of *Cry to Heaven* in 1982. (*Credit: Cynthia Rice Rodgers*)

he feels that he has lost the little humanity left him and has become as evil as Lestat ever was. Concepts of good and evil, once distinct, level out. There is no meaning, no moral foundation. Love and hate bleed together.

When Armand later confesses that he forced Louis to make Madeleine to get him to leave Claudia, Louis declares that he almost destroyed the very thing that attracts him—Louis's humanity and passion. It is a scene full of pain and the tenuousness of feeling. Armand believes, however, that the passion is still there and insists he needs Louis to tie him to the era. Otherwise he may succumb to boredom—the bane of immortals who remain the same through centuries of change. At that moment Louis reveals one more way that he is Anne as he exclaims, "I'm at odds with everything and always have been."

He is struggling, seeing in Armand the possibility of freedom from his guilt and pain. "It's as if," he says, "you've cracked a door for me, and light is streaming from that door and I'm yearning to get to it . . . to enter the region you say exists beyond it!" However, if he goes with Armand, he goes without Claudia.

Louis resists. "She's my child, and I don't know that she can release me. . . . I don't know if the child possesses the power to release the parent." Or if the parent possesses the power to release the child. Armand sees through him: "You feel an obligation to a world you love because that world for you is still intact." His accusation targets Anne. Slowly, as Armand works his spell, Louis moves away from Claudia, numbing himself against the guilt of betrayal yet still clinging.

Armand, however, presses relentlessly. "She's an era for you, an era of your life," he tells Louis. "If and when you break with her, you break with the only one alive who has shared that time with you. You fear that, the isolation of it, the burden." Louis senses the inevitable. "I can't continue to live divided and consumed with misery. Either I go with him, or I die." Still, he wants them both. He cannot make the decision. "You see Claudia slipping away from you," says Armand, "yet you seem powerless to prevent it, and then you would hasten it, and yet you do nothing."

Louis returns to Claudia for one last night and holds her on his lap—the image of a person who senses inevitable, irretrievable loss. At their weakest moment the coven attacks, dragging them to the theater. Lestat is there, accusing them of trying to kill him. Louis is sealed into a coffin, buried alive, forcing Anne, as the writer, to experience her own claustrophobia. He fights panic: "I told myself not to reach out for the sides, not to feel the thin margin of air between my face and the lid."

While Louis is sealed inside the coffin, Claudia is killed. She is trapped as he is trapped. Michele is buried, Anne buries herself. It is the bonding before giving over to letting go—tortured and painful. She must be sealed off in order to allow the healing to do its work, but the initial stages are excruciating, suffocating. Healing cannot happen as long as she has the power to prevent it. The coffin is her symbol of forced helplessness to eventually save herself.

Armand sets Louis free and he insists on going to Claudia. He finds her locked with Madeleine in an airshaft where the rising sun has burned them to ashes. It is the stark moment of confrontation with loss. "A cry rose in me, a wild, consuming cry that came from the bowels of my being." Louis lashes out, fighting with someone, then realizes that "the one I was struggling against was Armand."

Anne cries out here against senseless, absurd death, against letting go. A pair of images represent the double tragedies of her life. The mother and daughter found dead in the kitchen in New Orleans is Anne's first loss—*her* mother and part of herself. Then Claudia and Madeleine are burned together by the sun, a traditional symbol of God. This would be Anne and Michele, and the ultimate loss of faith. Something deep within Anne has died twice—as a daughter, then as a mother. The figure of Claudia is central to both images: she breaks up the family by killing, and she is the stricken child Michele, taking part of Anne with her.

Both losses were experienced by Anne as spiritual depletions, as irrefutable evidence to her that tragedies in life are cruel and random accidents. No outside power can be held responsible, because there is no outside power pulling the strings. Certainly no God that is truly benevolent as the church had presented him could do such things! There is no guarantee of ultimate goodness. Seeing her vampires as angels and gods transforms the image of God into that of a vampire.

In this scenario of symbolized grief, Anne expressed the guilt and isolation she experienced, and how she had to yield with gradual, reluctant steps, to the process of healing. She struggled against it, but also desired it, as Louis does with Armand. In the first version of the novel, written fresh inside her grief, she gave her daughter immortality. There was initial comfort in that, but it produced a psychological backlash. A year later with the rewrite, Anne was further removed. She was more inclined to get on with her life and to allow Michele to die. Armand's emotionlessness beckoned, a vampire "powerful and beautiful and without regret."

When Claudia is destroyed, Louis goes down into a grave to merge with his grief. "Closeted in that dark, smelling the earth . . . I gave myself over to everything that invaded and stifled my senses. And in so doing, gave myself over to my grief."

"There are moments," said Anne, "that feel so normal to me, like to write a scene like that."

Yet Louis's withdrawal is short-lived. It cannot be sustained. He is no longer the passive person he was, letting despair trap him. "That passivity in me has been the core of it all, the real evil." He acts quickly, decisively, burning down the theater with all the vampires save Armand inside—as Anne burned down the structures in her psyche where God might still have been living, suppressed but dormant, like a sleeping vampire. Claudia is gone, and so is the dependent, helpless part of Louis.

Later Armand joins him and they travel the world together but find little satisfaction in each other's company. Louis has yielded to Armand, looking for the promise of something good to replace his despair and found nothing of substance, no answers, nothing to replace the emptiness. He becomes a reflection of Armand. "You showed me," says Louis, "the only thing I could really hope to become."

Likewise for Anne, although the grief had subsided from its acute, suffocating form, the process of forgetting yields nothing—no emotional solace, no knowledge, no assurance. Just a letting go, a numbness. "I had made only one real plan in my life," Louis says of Claudia, "and it was finished." The rain, which has been continuous in the background, stops. Louis's vision clears, but he is left not with the joy of enlightenment but with the dull ache of disillusionment. He looks to art to find transcendence, but sees only cold, dead images cut off from their creators. "Now the human heart meant nothing," he says. "I did not denigrate it. I simply forgot it. . . . Like Claudia, severed from her mother, preserved for decades in pearl and hammered gold. Like Madeleine's dolls. And, of course, like Claudia, Madeleine and myself, they could all be reduced to ashes."

Louis returns to New Orleans and finds Lestat, a wasting, shriveled vampire who drinks from rats, dying from fear and paralysis. Armand confesses that he, too, is dying; he is bored. He admits, in an attempt to rekindle Louis's passion, that he was responsible for Claudia's death—he, the healing force, the betrayer—but Louis does not react. To be with Armand had required that he yield and change, yet he understands now that there is no substance to Armand, and that separation from Claudia and his unrequited need for goodness and love only made him as indifferent as Armand. Louis wanted purpose and Armand wanted passion. Cleaving to each other as vampires, they bled together into emptiness.

Louis ends the interview with the boy reporter, believing he has made his torment clear. The boy is aghast at his failure to see what a gift immortality is: "It was an adventure like I'll never know in my whole life!" He begs the vampire for it. Louis bites him, sucks his blood, and leaves him unconscious. When the boy wakes, he listens to the tapes for the description of Lestat's whereabouts and goes to seek him.

5

Anne sent this manuscript off, but was apprehensive. This was not exactly the novel that Knopf had bought. "There was a real change in tone," she said. "The Louis who opens the novel is not the same Louis by the middle. At the end Louis tells Armand to bug off. I remember wondering about that, and then I realized that the tone at the beginning was perfect for the tone at the end—but it was an accident. It worked out that the cold person who had started to tell the story had warmed up and then grown cold again." Still, the story had been substantially altered. What would they say?

But Vicky Wilson was delighted with the new version. She went over minor changes and the manuscript was ready. Anne later regretted some of the compromises. She had changed the original opening line, and she had removed a quote from Shakespeare, taken from *Macbeth*. Only later did she realize that it was not a senseless line as the copy editor had said, but was consistent with Lestat's character. "It's so important to fight for every small thing in a manuscript," she said. "I should never have given in." Anne also felt that Madeleine and some features of the vampire existence might have been more fully developed.

She dedicated the book to her older sister, Alice, to Stan, and to a writing friend, Carole Malkin.

6

Anne admitted that writing the novel had been cathartic for her. She had dealt with her pain and guilt by projecting them into the first-person point of view of Louis. People close to her believed she had "saved" herself from her grief. She'd felt guilty over her impotence and the possibility that she'd made a bad decision somewhere along the line with Michele, just as Louis had regretted ridiculing his brother's visions. She denied, however, that she had been consciously aware of any connection other than superficial between Claudia and Michele. Death by leukemia is hardly the sensual experience described by her vampires. If she had thought about a connection, she assured people who asked, she might not have written it. She would never have exploited her daughter in that manner. Friends were incredulous that she had not seen the obvious relationship between her character and her child, but she insisted that the book was about sensuality, pleasure, and satisfaction, and also had a strong moral purpose.

Anne soon grew to dislike her central character, Louis, having identified with him in a time of grief. The sale of her novel, she felt, had cured her more surely than any amount of psychotherapy, and she was able to move away from him as he had moved away from Claudia. "He was me at that time," she admitted. "I don't have a great deal of sympathy for a person who's that dependent and that vengeful toward people who won't fulfill his needs. To me the starting point is where he was sitting on the steps of the Theater of the Vampires after he's met Armand and he realizes, 'I hated Lestat for all the wrong reasons.' "

After the hardcover offer, Anne lived in tense anticipation of what was to come. Would there be a paperback sale? A movie deal? Her questions remained unanswered for over a year.

With the advance money the Rices made an extended, two-month visit in the summer of 1975 to New Orleans. Anne had taken trips in the past to piece together her family history. Little was known about her mother's relatives, but she'd found few people with memories vivid enough to tell her anything. The problem was that family scandals had been suppressed. Even her mother's cousin Gertrude, who held the deed to Katherine's grave plot, did not want to discuss Katherine's alcoholism.

In the meantime, Stan was published. *Some Lamb* was his first collection of poetry, published by his friends Laura Chester and Geoff Young, at their company, The Figures Press; it came out in 1975, when Stan was thirty-three. The following year he published *Whiteboy,* which was then considered by the American Academy of Poets for the Edgar Allan Poe Award in recognition of the work of a poet under age forty-five. To Stan's surprise, he won the five-thousand-dollar award. It was an important success for him in light of Anne's triumph, since the first published books for both of them concerned Michele.

Stan had channeled into *Some Lamb* his grief over Michele, taking it in a direction different from Anne's, and the result was a moving testament to both the depth of human emotion and the process of getting through.

"Our daughter's death," said Stan, "was a shared experience the response to which produced images that came from the same place. The history of a blood disease led into images of the vampire, and in my work to the book *Some Lamb*—the idea of the lamb that is sacrificed, the blood of the lamb. We started out in different places, but a lot of our ideas came together."

In a radio interview with Eric Bauersveld, Anne and Stan candidly discussed their separate responses to their daughter's death and the connection with their writing. Stan felt they were wrestling over being the guardian of Michele's spirit. Anne was surprised, but she understood it. "You wrestle," she said, "with who is in possession of the spirit of that dead person, who did right by that person, and who is going to have to keep grieving and suffering the consequences."

Peter Thomas, the Hollywood agent representing *Interview,* showed it to Richard Sylbert, vice president of production at Paramount Pictures. He was impressed with it, describing it as polymorphous sexuality, which pleased Anne. She hoped, if a movie was to be made, that Alain Delon would play Louis, since it required an actor who could exhibit a broad range of emotions. On January 11, 1976, Paramount bought the movie rights for an astonishing sum: $150,000, with escalators up to $250,000. The Rices went out for tacos.

For Anne this meant freedom to travel and to write without financial concerns. It also meant that her work would be available to a large audience.

Soon the paperback rights were auctioned. On the afternoon of the auction, Anne sat on her patio drinking a beer with her sister Karen and Carolyn Doty. The phone rang. Anne listened to the news: Ballantine Books had offered $700,000, a payment reserved for rare books considered very hot.

Soon the Literary Guild bought it as an alternate selection, and foreign rights were sold.

When Anne received her first hardcover copies of *Interview,* she distributed them to family and friends. Most of the recipients were enthused, although a neighbor expressed distress over why someone would want to write about evil.

Then Anne and Stan got on a plane and flew to Texas. They got in at five o'clock in the morning and waited in a truck-stop café, the Golden Eagle Drive-in, until she thought her father would be awake. Finally she went to his house and knocked at the door. When he opened it, she presented her first novel. He was thrilled. For Anne it was a show of respect—the respect that was so important to her. "It meant a lot for me to present it to him," said Anne. "He was wonderful. He was terrifically enthusiastic and proud. After that, it seemed like I felt more secure in his affections. I felt more confident."

Her first book signing was at Minerva's Owl, given by Blair Fuller. Blair was co-founder and co-director at Squaw Valley and was pleased by Anne's success. He had thought her writing interesting and that she was "terrifically talented," but had never anticipated the extent of her success.

Dressed primly in black and white, Anne went to the signing with a carload of friends—gathered for moral support—and cans of beer tucked in her purse. She wavered between fear and elation at the idea of people standing in line to see her. Suddenly fame was no longer an abstract goal. It meant being visible to many people, being the object of their scrutiny. Although she had made up her mind to be available to her readers, the encounters did not come easily for her.

Then the reviews came in. There were about seventy-five reviews across the country and most were positive. The *Philadelphia Inquirer* called the book a "supernatural thriller raised to the level of literature." Other adjectives abounded: enthralling, hypnotic, magical, sophisticated, lyrical, uncanny. She was compared with Proust, Du Maurier, Henry James, the Brontës, Mary Renault, and Oscar Wilde. People saw in her work ideas akin to Nietzsche and Dostoevsky. *Publisher's Weekly* said that it was "an extraordinary first novel," while *Library Journal* claimed that "Rice's talent makes Louis's story meaningful and moving."

Interview was also compared with *Rosemary's Baby, The Exorcist,* and *The Other,* which Anne did not appreciate, since she saw her novel as transcending genre, and not really as horror at all.

A few reviewers spotted the sexual elements. The *Washington Post* exclaimed that it was "unrelentingly erotic," while Jerry Douglas, noting that the recent popular gay novels had been written by women, said that the "calculated comparisons between vampirism and homosexuality . . . constitute one of the most extended metaphors in modern literature." Although Anne did not think of the novel as a gay metaphor while she was writing it, she agreed that the parallels were there. One of her former professors, Leonard Wolf, claimed that she had exploited the erotic elements in the vampire's embrace, which allowed all unions ordinarily forbidden.

Some reviews in important places, however, were fairly vicious. The vampire image was rejected as repulsive, and people did not want to be drawn into caring about a protagonist who lived off human blood. That so much money was paid for something so lurid seemed incredible. "They slammed it," Anne said. "It was panned in San Francisco, and the financial success surrounding the book was generally attacked." The literary community there, she felt, was alienated by her popular success. In the *San Francisco Review of Books,* praise was sparing, while the numbers were emphasized.

The *New Republic* accused Anne of contriving a plot that would contain the ingredients of a best-seller.

She was criticized by Leo Braudy in *The New York Times Book Review* for creating comic-book dialogue with an overblown, exaggerated style. "Too superficial, too impersonal," the reviewer said, "to touch the sources of real terror and feeling." He, too, saw the sexual tone. "Anne Rice exploits all the sexual elements in this myth with a firm self-consciousness of their meaning. . . . Homosexuality . . . is the hardly hidden mainspring of Rice's narrative, and her message seems to be: if you're homosexual, it's better to be unemotional about it."

Anne was not aware of what it all meant. She did not know about the way in which negative reviews in strategic places could hurt a writer's chances. The enormity of it hit her only later. She had no idea that to even get reviewed was rare, and even though the *Times* attacked her book, they had taken it seriously. Some of the people associated with its publication were surprised, but Anne was not. She thought it was a book that would endure. "Nobody understood it," Anne said. "It was an alienating experience. I wasn't prepared. I was devastated. I thought I was writing this great philosophical book that people were going to take seriously. I was just crushed."

Interview With the Vampire did not become a best-seller when it was released on May 5, 1976, as the people at Knopf had hoped, although it sold a respectable 26,000 copies. The following year, however, Ballantine made the paperback publication into an event, promoting the novel onto the best-seller list with a book tour, unique television commercials, radio spots, coffin-shaped book displays, plastic book bags, matchbooks, posters, and T-shirts that said, "I've got an Interview With the Vampire." George Walsh, editor-in-chief at Ballantine, was gambling on it being a "break-out" book, full of popular appeal.

Several social forces seemed to converge in the novel which assisted its success. On the heels of national instability with Watergate, people were seeking new myths and ideals, and the sexual revolution was in full swing. It was the gay golden age, before AIDS, and legalized abortion had freed women. Books like *The Joy of Sex* and *Fear of Flying* encouraged women to seek greater sexual pleasure (including bondage games and bisexuality), and *The Male Machine* urged men to get more in touch with their emotions and to experience the benefits of androgyny. The erotic, humanized vampire image was an invitation for growth for both sexes. "Tease television" hit a popular high, and both excess and androgyny were evident in changing fashions. The streaking fad, singles bars, and the encouragement of easy surrender for women affirmed the desire for uninhibited expression. People wanted to get beyond ordinary experience, to become larger than life. *Interview With the Vampire* expressed many of these developments in a way that made them fresh and unusual.

Parallel with sexual expression came spiritual explorations, perhaps as a reaction to an emphasis on technology. The quest for the divine collided with the search for self, issuing in a new age of self-actualization movements. "Use the power inside you," said Armand, a phrase that reverberated in the desire for transformation that originated from within. Reworking old myths became popular as people sought a new basis for morality and human potential. Est, rolfing, yoga, Transcendental Meditation, and Zen were called forth as tools. On the flip side, but with similar motivation, violence and androgyny increased in rock 'n' roll music, and Anton Levay made Satanism popular. Everyone, it seemed, was looking for meaning in some form other than those traditionally offered.

Anne understood that. "This book," she said of *Interview,* "is about stepping out of life so that you can better see life. You could see it as a drug experience itself. As religion loses its hold for people, they have to reinvent themselves in terms of new ideas." Even Armand saw the parallel, as he says of Louis: "Everyone else feels as you feel. Your fall from grace and faith has been the fall of a century."

There was also a renewed interest in horror and science fiction. *The Exorcist* in 1973, *Carrie* in 1974, and *Salem's Lot*—another vampire novel—in 1975 assisted the public appetite for the supernatural. In 1976 the success of *Carrie* and *The Omen* in the theater indicated what the public wanted.

But the question remained as to whether this book would have staying power, whether it would last and be understood as more than just a vampire novel. Some reviewers had granted literary acclaim, others had panned it. Yet it seemed to have an emotional resonance that made even the most reluctant reviewers allow it a smattering of faint praise. It also seemed to work on diverse levels of style and content, and revealed a unique voice and perspective. The vampire image tapped nineteenth-century literary traditions, but also reached beyond literature to ancient folklore, providing a rich metaphor and vivid imaginative states that other monster images failed to capture. Giving the vampire human feelings provided a new way to look at life.

Anne had gone within herself, into an abyss of inarticulate, painful subconscious images, surrendering to them to formulate characters who represented complex realities typically relegated to the dark, secret places in the psyche. The novel is a chronicle of seduction, with suffering as a central element. The vampires magnify human nature, not only in its capacity for sensory stimulation and eroticism, but also for loneliness, boredom, and vulnerability. They bring with them into eternity their psychological baggage, and there is no escape from self, not even through transformation. To clarify her own life Anne had forged the first elements of a moral vision. She sought purpose and goodness apart from Catholic doctrines, and that vision coincided with a humanistic movement that would celebrate itself into the next decade, giving *Interview* cult status.

Anne had also found the perfect medium through which to deal with questions about good and evil. "There really isn't any abstract evil," she said, "it's just whatever causes suffering. The only way we can turn away from it is to alleviate suffering." She gave that sensibility to Louis, who agonizes over his compulsion. "You die when you kill," Armand observes about him, "as if you feel that you deserve to die." As if in response to Albert Camus' assertion that to be human means to refuse to be God, Armand suggests that it is the vampire who is God. Thus, no sin really achieves evil. Louis objects. "If God doesn't exist," he declares, "we are the creatures of highest consciousness in the universe. We alone understand the passage of time and the value of every minute of human life. And what constitutes evil, real evil, is the taking of a single human life."

With Sartre and Camus, whom Anne had read years earlier, she concludes that if there is no God, life is all we have. For Louis the search for salvation through a religious framework is over. "Once fallen from grace, I had confidence in nothing." Vampires are neither holy nor demonic. They are merely vampires, killing over and over again to sustain their existence. It sends a message to people who justify themselves within religious systems.

Anne was also working out a theme of community that would continue throughout her work and make it stand out from the genre novels to which she had been compared. The vampires are prototypical outsiders, pried loose from their natural human habitat, shunned by human society, alienated from God, and contaminated by the blood of their victims. They seek protection and companionship with their own kind, just as do ethnic groups, gays, mental patients, alcoholics, and other social outcasts who need care and understanding. "I'll travel the world if I have to," Louis tells Lestat, "to find other vampires."

Anne illustrates the impetus in the human heart to seek others, but she also notes the tendency of wanting to bond with others so strongly that those who find community seek to force others to follow rules. When Louis first sees how other vampires dress themselves in black, he observes, they "had made of immortality a conformist's club." Anne herself disliked conformity and believed in the preservation of individual rights. However, she also understood the pull to be with others, to be inconspicuous, which meant to follow rules that divide insiders from outsiders. Thus she shows how the notion of community becomes a paradox, fed by the urge to dominate others and make them so like oneself that firm bonding can take place, validating the rule makers.

Yet the real self, as seen to some extent in Louis, is the constructive force within individuals to discover and express their uniqueness rather than to conform to an ideal formed by someone else. Groups divided into categories betray the richness of experience. People who seek community are often forced to compromise their urge to grow and attain self-fulfillment. As individuals they feel alienated from the community. As a member they are displaced. They will only be rejected if they persist in being themselves but, as individuals, cannot conform and still be unique. As Rousseau said, to be in a community is to be divided. Natural freedom is shackled when uniformity is imposed, and finding a home within oneself is the primary source of alienation within the community.

There is both gain and loss in either direction, isolation or self-sacrifice. Louis understands this, as Anne did. He does not fit with the other vampires. "Weak vampires are feared," he is told. "That you are flawed is obvious to them." He has yearned so long for community and now that he has found others who appear to him to be "made from the same material," he cannot find acceptance. The theme is an important expression of how individuality lies at the heart of creativity. Anne had had to assert herself over and over against various communities in order to retain her vision. If she had not had the strength of her individuality, *Interview With the Vampire* might not have been the book that it is. It speaks to that basic human urge and contradiction, giving her characters substance.

Besides content, Anne also concentrated on mirroring her themes in the fictional environment, as she had learned to do from classic novels and films. Louis and Claudia must cross an ocean—the unconscious, the sea of life, the gap—to try to find answers. The barrenness of the countryside in Eastern Europe reflects the lack of answers there. The use of the theater amplifies the deceptiveness of appearances. Even the weather was employed to emphasize psychological moods. Her language is ornate, an echo of the exaggerated sensory experience of the vampire.

In both style and content, then, Anne had attempted to write a novel that was not meant as just another vampire story. Whether she had succeeded in gripping readers at these other levels would be decided in the years to come.

7

Vicky Wilson asked Pam Henstell, the West Coast promotion assistant for Knopf, to send Anne a bottle of champagne. Pam delivered the bottle herself in order to meet Anne.

"Anne is so psychologically sophisticated and complicated," she said, "and yet there's also a matter-of-fact part of her. She described herself as a Catholic schoolgirl who had grown up."

One of the first publicity events that Anne wanted to do was to appear on a Saturday night horror-movie program called "Creature Features." Pam was confused; it was not a show she would have considered but she agreed to book it. The host, Bob Wilkins, willingly interviewed Anne during breaks.

"I was thrilled to be on," said Anne. "As I left, I shouted, 'More mummy movies!' "

Joan Rivers read the book and sought Anne out for a guest appearance on the "Tonight Show," where she was guest-hosting.

"She plugged the book every commercial break," said Anne, "and I came on at the end. She was charming."

"Anne wants more than anything to be taken seriously as a writer," said Pam. "What was working against her was the popular interest in her subject matter."

It was not long before Anne heard comments from her acquaintances that stung. Some of them hinted that she had sold out; she'd compromised the artistic vision of the literary writer for crass commercial success. She was hurt, especially when one of her closest friends grew suddenly cold. She sent copies of *Interview* to former professors, hoping they would see how serious her work was, but some, she felt, were rather ungracious. One man said he respected her too much to read it. "Never," she said, "did I develop a social life as a writer with the people I had grown up with there in San Francisco."

What shocked and saddened her was what happened with Stan. People stopped calling him for readings. "His career was interrupted," said Anne, "the way a journey is interrupted when a load of rocks falls on the road. The publicity surrounding *Interview* changed the perception of him in the minds of those who knew him." So much of the publicity surrounded how much money Anne had received, and friends began to treat them differently.

Stan, too, was saddened by what he described as the "fragility" of their friendships. "They were sarcastic about rich people," he said. "They made us feel it was not hip to be rich." Nevertheless, he did not want Anne to feel any less satisfied with her accomplishment. He had encouraged her to write and he was happy for her.

Anne felt that some people viewed her as controlling and selfish when she did not offer to support other artists with large amounts of cash. She wanted to help, but she did not want to be taken advantage of. She also thought her money was better spent on family than on friends, setting up a self-publishing venture called Full Fathom Five for a book of Tamara's poetry, called *Squaw Valley*.

Anne deeply appreciated friends who remained loyal and did not pressure her or thumb their noses, yet she began to withdraw. Success was not all that it had seemed, on the one hand, yet she refused to be made to feel guilty or unhappy about it.

She sent a copy of her novel to Richard Wiseman, the teacher who had so impressed her, and he read it and responded with an involved analysis. He thought the novel was an allegory of evil and had captured the transience of life in a dramatic fashion. "I couldn't shake the feeling," he later recalled, "that all of this was a mask, that she wasn't interested just in that story at the surface level but it was a way of getting at something that she maybe had not even articulated to herself. It fascinated me to think of it as a way of stating something that couldn't otherwise be stated." Anne was gratified by his thoughtful response.

She was generous with aspiring writers, financially and with literary contacts, allowing people to use her name as an introduction to publishers. Carolyn Doty, in need of money, was hired to sew Anne's dresses, and she made a series of colorful velvet jumpers for her. "Anne took me out to dinner," said Carolyn, "more times than I can count." Anne also helped her to get on her feet after a traumatic divorce and introduced her to Phyllis Seidel. "I don't know of any writer," said Carolyn, "who was or is more willing to help a beginning writer in terms of contacts. This is a *generous* act for a successful writer, and Anne was exceptional here."

Stan's sister Cynthia called from Hawaii, where she was living. She wanted to get out and had no money. Would they help? Stan invited her to come. "I was welcomed into their home with open arms," she recalled. "It was a time of great elation for them, and disbelief." They allowed her to live with them and encouraged her to return to school. They took her to dinner and always picked up the check. "That really characterizes the way they handled their wealth," said Cynthia.

Soon they prepared to move out of their rented apartment on Bonita and into a new house. For Anne it was a bittersweet time. She dreaded the thought of taking down pictures that Michele had pasted on the walls. It was sad to dismantle a life, but a new house meant starting over in a big way.

They bought a Federalist Georgian-style house in South Berkeley and went around purchasing antiques. It was a dream come true for Anne, a way to reconnect with the glamour she had been raised to appreciate. This was not a house in the Garden District of New Orleans, but it was huge, had a pool, and lots of elegant French doors. They proceeded to throw bigger parties. The old jug-wine intellectual get-togethers were populated by old friends as well as by new acquaintances: editors, agents, other writers.

"A guest could sit in the sun room," Carolyn Doty described, "and listen to a discussion on the aesthetics of death between a poet and the literary critic for the educational radio station, or have your palm read in the dining room by an aspiring novelist. Upstairs, there was a pool table and a game in progress always. The food was fabulous. Anne demonstrated over and over again her cooking skills. Lots of southern cooking."

People asked Anne what she would write next. Given the success of her first novel, the expectation was that she would follow it with a sequel. However, she was not ready to get back to vampires. The critical attacks had cooled her interest, and she was not eager to be classified as a horror writer. The main reason she did not go back to Louis's world, however, was that she was obsessed with another subject set in New Orleans. On her wall she had pinned up a motto from *Othello* that served as a theme: "But I do love thee, and when I love thee not, chaos is come again."

For Anne, writing a novel meant finding subjects that helped her to channel and express her obsessions. She wanted to know how people dealt with the fact of death, especially exceptional types of people, and she wanted to explore ways of taking characters through change. But there was something else tugging at her as well. She wanted to return in her writing to her home town. The experience of writing *Interview* had given back to her so many memories of the textures and traditions she had known so well, but had not satisfied her longing altogether. She had also become enamored of the nineteenth century, and she had found a way to work with both. Another novel was already in progress.

CHAPTER SEVEN

THE BILDUNGSROMANS

1

Anne realized that she had gotten some terrific breaks as a writer. Her first novel had been sold to a prestigious house, optioned by Hollywood, and translated into several languages. Now her success was up to her. She had the right contacts in New York and she had an audience. As Armand had said to Louis, the power was within herself.

While she was writing her new novel, she was asked to work on a script outline for the movie. Richard Sylbert had hired a scriptwriter and Anne offered suggestions. To Anne's dismay, she felt that Louis's passivity made him almost invisible, so she decided to give him more anger and to make him into an avenger who killed other vampires wherever he went. She liked the idea, but it did not come to fruition as other problems cropped up to put the project on hold. Richard Sylbert left Paramount and was not allowed to take the property with him. It fell into the hands of people who were not sure what to do with two adult males and a child vampire. Anne eventually agreed to write another script, but not until several years had passed with no results.

Anne grew unhappy with Phyllis Seidel and decided to find a

new agent. Vicky Wilson suggested Lynn Nesbit, so Anne contacted her. She agreed to represent Anne's next novel. "I thought Anne had a very original point of view," she said. "Clearly she was doing something that no one else was doing. Her books have a truly archetypal drive to them. I think they have a deep mythological level that touches people and arouses real passion."

Anne got back to work on the novel that had formed from her intensive research of Louisiana. In addition to the journals at Berkeley, she had visited the libraries at Tulane and Louisiana State University. In one book she had spotted an article about the first literary magazine in the state, *L'Album litteraire, journal des jeunes gens, amateurs de la litterature*. She was surprised to discover that it had been created by the *gens de couleur libre*—free people of color—a group who hovered socially between the established white population and the denigrated slaves. They were the freed offspring of African slaves and Spanish and French traders, and many had emigrated from Haiti. Anne read through the poems and essays, written in flawless French, and wondered at the education of these black men during the days when slaves were being treated as property. They were free to pursue their trades, to get a good education, to dress like whites, but were allowed few rights. They could not vote or insult a white man. The women, famed for their beauty, often became mistresses to white men, who advanced their status by setting them up with a house and slaves of their own.

Anne also found a rare collection of personal items belonging to a free man of color, William T. Johnson, including extensive pre-Civil War diaries, letters, and financial papers.

Although a few friends questioned whether she could empathize sufficiently with blacks, Anne was drawn right away to this fragile society. She perceived them as a people who could be the subject of a tragedy and felt compassion for them. They had been misunderstood, maligned, and hindered from exercising their freedom to choose how they wanted to live, and yet they prospered through many generations—the outsider's urge toward community. Their situation clearly had universal significance. She tried to imagine the problems such people would face. Tracing back their history to Haitian race wars, she knew she had to go there to get a feel for the place.

Anne and Stan decided to travel. In the fall, he took time off from teaching and they went to Haiti while Carolyn Doty watched their house. They toured the island as Anne listened with a writer's ear to the blacks who spoke the French patois. She learned what she was able of the plantation economy and the way the blacks had risen and massacred the whites. Characters began to form in her mind. At a bar she expressed her doubts about whether she should write such a book to a black American, and he urged her quite vehemently to do it.

On the way back, the Rices stopped in New Orleans to take photographs for the settings. In the French Quarter, the Hermann-Grima house, built in 1831 at 820 St. Louis Street, inspired the descriptions of the home of her prosperous fictional family, the Lermontants. Anne took the tours, noting fine details, the kitchen in the back, the slave quarters. She made the Lermontants undertakers, recalling from her childhood how kind such people had been.

Back in Berkeley, Anne wrote a letter to a history professor at Loyola about her novel, and he advised her not to pursue it unless she had been born in New Orleans. She understood what he meant. It takes a native to comprehend the complex conditions in Louisiana that had allowed such a group of people to flourish.

She had read about the voodoo queen Marie Leveau, who was also a free person of color, and thought perhaps she'd use the enigmatic woman as a central character. Then she realized that too much was already known about her and it would be difficult to work with her fictionally. Abandoning that plot, she got interested in characters in her own imagination, children who were growing up. The free people of color populated her new world, layered with a focus on the frustrations of adolescence.

Anne was enamored of the idea that living outside the accepted order could have its own rewards. She carefully laid out her story and its themes. While she appreciated how a community can offer protection and the preservation of a heritage, she wanted to point out the tenuousness and shortsightedness of communities rooted in a specific time and place, and how their insularity can become stifling to individual spirit: "The world is filled with varying standards of beauty and civilization," she wrote, "so that the edicts of one small time and place must never be accepted as supreme."

Anne wanted her next novel to emerge naturally from the characters so that historical facts would be unintrusive. Looking to Tolstoy's *Anna Karenina* as a model, Anne appreciated in his work the care with which he developed his women, the multilayered detail, and the complexity of relationships. She was also impressed by his ideas on freedom and spirituality—a theme that would grow into a literary obsession for her. Inspired, she set to work, hiring her sister-in-law Cynthia to do any further library research necessary.

In the spring of 1977, the Rices took another trip, this time spending almost two months in Europe and in the land of Anne's dreams: Egypt—up the Nile as far as Aswan. In England, she visited the home of her longest-standing literary inspiration, Charles Dickens. They went to Paris, Rome, Cairo, and Athens, taking a cruise on the Mediterranean to the island of Santorini, where Linda Gregg and Jack Gilbert had once lived. Although they started off in expensive hotels, they soon found that they preferred inexpensive lodgings, like the twelve-dollar pensions in Italy. Having money had made little difference to their basic perspective.

In Egypt, they saw the Great Pyramids, but Anne refused to take a camel across the desert, choosing instead to walk. "I have terrible equilibrium," she explained. "I don't like to be very far off the ground." Seeing this land that had fascinated her since childhood proved to be "the highlight of my life."

Back at home, she bought an orange Vespa. She had seen women in Rome riding around on the little motor scooters, and thought it would be a good way for her to get around, since she did not drive a car. When she started the machine up, however, the noise scared her, so she left it alone.

The Rices decided to move again and found a secluded eight-bedroom Tudor in the Oakland hills. Cynthia Rice moved in with them.

Anne was still involved with writing friends and made time to go to lunch as often as possible, even when it made her uncomfortable. Carolyn Doty had now moved to southern California, but they kept in touch by phone. Anne met a new friend named Candi Ellis, whose writing she admired. She sought out Candi's company quite often and felt a compelling affection for her. Candi also admired Anne.

"She taught me what I understand," said Candi, "about effective interior monologue, about pacing, about plot development and character. She has a brilliant and subtle mind. The finest storytellers are poets, and Anne is a poet."

Anne sought Candi's response to her novels, although Candi felt she would have no real influence: Anne would follow her own vision, no matter what anyone said. Nevertheless, she did alert Anne to something that later had a major impact on her writing method: Candi introduced her to the world of word processors. To that point Anne had done everything on her typewriter, but what Candi told her about the ease of using a computer interested her enough to look into making a change. The expense, however, was astonishing. To equip herself properly would cost several thousand dollars. It seemed an enormous investment and few writers were considering it at the time. Nevertheless, she shrewdly watched and waited for a deal.

The Rices were beginning to burn out on their parties. Anne was putting enormous effort into them, sometimes working for days ahead of time to turn out fifty different dishes. She had always considered such excess to be the spiritual side of an otherwise material activity. She loved setting out truly delicious meals, but something unpleasant was creeping in.

Floyd Salas pointed out that at the small parties before Anne's success, writers and artists had been the central attraction. Now it was editors and other publishing personnel. People spent all their time kissing up to someone who might advance their career instead of sitting around talking about art. Anne considered this. She had intended to welcome everyone interested in developing a writing community, but telling one person who told others led to large crowds. After one party Stan said, "As usual, I don't know half the people here."

"Anne didn't enjoy them," Betsy Dubovsky remembered. "Afterward she would feel strangely awful."

"I didn't regard them as successful," Anne agreed. "I felt turned inside out for several days after they were over. My old friends felt weird and would hover on the periphery. I didn't like the change that happened."

Other developments also soured her on encouraging a literary community. Anne gave a few parties for young writers and invited many of her friends to help celebrate. Her good intentions were met with cold shoulders. At a party for one novelist, some of the guests went out of their way to let Anne know that this woman was not someone worth wasting time on. Others just did not show up. "It was not an easy place to be published," Anne felt about San Francisco.

She continued to be involved with groups of women, despite her unpleasant experience with feminists. Having passed through a phase in the sixties where she had professed, as was the fashion, to prefer the minds of men, she gradually had been discovering the complexities and richness of a woman's experience. She was amazed by women who said they did not know what it was like to have an orgasm—women who had husbands and children. "I always felt I was a little more passionate than some other women that I knew," Anne said, "and they would make statements I couldn't identify with at all." Having experienced sexual excitement at an early age, she began to understand the breadth of what it meant to have sexual feelings as a woman, and bristled at stereotyping and repression. "One of the keys to understanding women," she claimed, "is to understand that statements like 'women feel this' or 'women feel that' are just crap. You have women who had orgasms at eight years old and women who are mothers who have never had one."

Those relationships that she cared about, she cultivated with passion, writing long letters of affection. "It was amazing," said Cynthia Rice, "to have both a profound love for her family and to also have space for developing intense relationships." Anne loved generously but expected a lot, and was hurt easily and profoundly when a few relationships disintegrated. It took a strong woman, according to acquaintances, with confidence in herself and her talent to respond to Anne.

Excessive and dramatic, Anne intimidated some people, men and women alike. Like her mother before her, she sought to bring a measure of goodness into her life, but her manner of seeking it seemed too demanding to some who were not as strongly motivated or energetic. She craved the rewards of a female friendship between equals, like she had with Stan, but sometimes overpowered friends with her obsessions and lost them. Although she had purged much of the acute grief from Michele's death, the occasional rejection she experienced resulted in fresh sources of pain and she found an outlet for expressing it in her writing. Tears came easily and often to her characters. Feelings of being misunderstood flowed through her fingers onto the paper. She became aware of a source for achieving authenticity: go for the pain.

Then she found out she was pregnant again. She and Stan could not help but be nervous, although it had been five years since Michele died. They were happy, though, and looked forward to being a family again. Anne stopped drinking temporarily, to be on the safe side.

In the fall, Anne went to Italy with Howard, Dorothy, and her youngest sister, Karen. They toured the country from one great city to another. Anne was not aware of it then, but she would soon be writing about Venice and Rome. On the phone long distance, Stan suggested the name Christopher for the baby if they had a boy.

"I loved it," said Anne. "We both felt it was *the* name."

Although there was pressure in Berkeley to have natural childbirth, Anne wanted nothing to do with it. She refused to take classes in breathing techniques. Nevertheless, when the moment came to give birth, the labor lasted only two hours and their new son was born so quickly that Anne delivered him without anesthesia. "He practically fell out," she said. "It was rather traumatic, like giving birth in a covered wagon, but I'm glad I had the experience." Stan was with her again in the delivery room.

Their ten-pound son was born on March 11, 1978, when Anne was thirty-six, and they named him Christopher Travis. Anne asked Stan to bring a six-pack of Miller, and she celebrated the birth with several tall, cool beers.

"It was just an absolutely joyful occasion," she said. "He was from the beginning a wonderful, sensitive little guy."

Cynthia had moved out, and Stan took a year off to attend to the baby so Anne could write. He found the responsibility a great joy, taking over once again as he had done with Michele.

In the meantime, Anne had delivered a portion of *The Feast of All Saints*. She had structured the contract to receive half of the advance upon delivery of the first half of the novel, explaining the rest of the story in outline. No one was convinced. Knopf passed on it, to her great astonishment, but Lynn Nesbit looked around and found another buyer. Anne was picked up by Simon & Schuster, with Joni Evans and John Dodds as her editors. Joni Evans had a reputation for making careers, and Anne was excited to work with her.

Evans had already read *Interview With the Vampire* and had been very impressed: "It had the biggest effect on me. I think, in that entire decade, *Interview* was the most important book for me. I was delighted to have my chance at Anne."

She liked what she saw of Anne's new novel. "She's a spectacular writer," she said, "and I've always been fascinated by New Orleans. I did not know about this entire world that she had created. What fascinated me was her strength in painting mood and atmosphere that was a blend of fiction and fact. It was so delicious and so erotic and so steamy and so special, and I relished it!"

Anne was also fond of John Dodds. He lived in San Francisco, commuting several times a month to New York. She captured his image later in *Belinda* in the character Alex, including the pink sweater he'd tie over his shoulder when he'd picked her up for lunch at the Café San Marco. John Dodds threw parties for area writers, and Anne loved his house in Belvedere for its splendid view of the San Francisco skyline. They developed an easy friendship.

2

Anne's second novel, *The Feast of All Saints,* was another novel of characters moving from innocence to wisdom. She received a $150,000 advance, which indicated the confidence of her publisher that the novel would become a best-seller, and dedicated it to Stan, her parents, and Carolyn Doty.

Anne chose the title for its metaphorical significance. The Feast of All Saints is a Catholic holy day when people remember the dead and celebrate forgotten saints. She had given a description in her first novel:

> It is the day in New Orleans when all the faithful go to the cemeteries to care for the graves of their loved ones. They whitewash the plaster walls of the vaults, clean the names cut into the marble slabs. And finally they deck the tombs with flowers. In the St. Louis Cemetery . . . there were even little iron benches set before the graves where the families might sit to receive the other families who had come to the cemetery for the same purpose.

Anne wrote the book as a tribute to the free people of color in New Orleans, symbolically placing flowers on their graves and cleaning off the dusty memories of their rich heritage so their contributions would not be forgotten. It was a complex and labyrinthine plot.

The novel is set in the 1840s in New Orleans. The free people of color, eighteen thousand strong, were feared and ignored by whites. As one of Anne's characters, a sculptor, says, "My work is admired, but I will never be admired." Some pass for white and others are distinctly negroid, living out tensions of ambiguity that both strengthen and threaten them. Stability in the community is based on family lines over generations, but beneath the surface it is an illusion "sustained day in and day out by a collective act of faith." Those who pass for white often leave the community, diminishing the race. The people do what they can to fortify themselves against encroaching forces, banding together with the understanding that "when you let a white man humiliate you, we are all humiliated." The white population seeks to suppress them, and the black slaves detest them, knowing it is *their* backs that bear the burden of the social hierarchy that allows the *gens* their tentative status. Individuals within this community are faced with either contributing to its waning strength or looking out for themselves. The community offers a sense of identity, but with that comes the threat of becoming subsumed into the group and being defined and controlled by something outside themselves, eventually lost in anonymity.

The principal protagonist is Marcel, the fourteen-year-old quadroon son of a white planter, Philippe Ferronaire, and a free woman of color, Cecile Ste. Marie. He has a sister, Marie, and two close friends, Richard and Anna Bella, also dealing with the intrusive transitions of adolescence and the threat of absorption into the adult world. Marcel shares a number of characteristics with Anne: a European mentality, a love of wandering the city, a fear of horses, a yearning for a teacher with passion, and a sense of being overwhelmed by adolescence to the point of feeling almost criminal because he is so out of tune with what people expect of him. He will never be a fast reader because, as Anne does, he thinks as he reads. He likes to draw as well, but Anne made him into a person with no real creative outlets, although he yearns for them. He also feels estranged in his environment, as she does. Despite all her years in California, Anne was feeling increasingly like an outsider, both socially and artistically, and she captures the feeling in her protagonist.

Marcel's family mirrors the stressful ambiguity of the position of his people. His mother, the daughter of a slave, keeps slaves in her house. His sister is so light-skinned that she passes for white, while Marcel, blond and blue-eyed, has kinky hair and negroid features. Their father is white and rich and moves about freely in white society.

Thirteen-year-old Marie is placed by her cold and distant mother in a position subordinate to Marcel. Her development into a young woman amplifies her lesser status. She is also plagued by her maturing body, having sexual fantasies to the point of orgasm that make her feel sinful against the backdrop of a strict Catholicism. Like Anne, Marie experienced as a girl the serenity of surrendering to church doctrines: "That Christ was with her, inside of her, had been the only thought in her mind as she walked down the aisle. The magic of the splendid painted church had merely resonated with her prayers." Also like Anne, she rebels after her first kiss at the teaching that "she might go to hell for what she'd done, just as a man who had murdered another man."

Like the mixed-blood races, adolescence is a metaphor of ambiguity: half child, half adult. They don't quite fit into either world and thus become outsiders. Anne's own experience of the burdens of the limbo between childhood and maturity has a universal quality. "All this has happened too soon," Marcel exclaims. "It's happened at the wrong time. I haven't come into my own!" Sleeping with an older woman, he best portrays the ironic clash of spirituality and libido that simultaneously assails many adolescents. It is a hint of the spiritual/material theme that was engaging Anne's attention.

The plot begins when Marcel hears that his hero, Christophe Mercier, is returning to New Orleans. Christophe is a famous novelist, educated in Paris and well traveled. He is a free man of color, a role model to boys Marcel's age, despite dark rumors of a homosexual liaison. He is purportedly returning to open a school for his people, and Marcel intends to present himself as a worthy student.

Marcel has been promised by his rich white father an education in Paris when he comes of age, and he sees Christophe's instruction as a step toward that goal. He struggles with the filmy boundaries between the spiritual and the abstract, viewing the development of his mind as his salvation. He tried to teach himself philosophy and soon realized that he needed a real teacher—an experience echoing Anne's.

Christophe is a mix of motivations that Anne both appreciated and disliked. His feelings of rootlessness and his urge to come home to New Orleans echoed her own: "I wanted to touch the oak branches, the magnolias, I wanted to wander through the streets, caressing the old bricks." His adolescence followed a route similar to that of Jean, from *Katherine and Jean,* one of Anne's favorite character types. Yet he has also turned his back on Paris and its opportunities because of his self-doubt. "He was not a character I understood," Anne said in the midst of a period of self-confidence. "I didn't sympathize with him. I had known people like him who sabotaged their own success, distrusted people who praised them, and rebelled against people who loved them. His view is cynical and dark."

Christophe witnesses Marcel's passion for ideas and accepts him into his school. The classroom setting provides an opportunity for Anne to introduce a powerful thematic metaphor when Christophe displays a rug that dazzles the students with its vibrant colors. He uses the rug to show that "the key to understanding this world was to realize it was made of a thousand varying cultures, many so alien to others that no one code of brotherhood or standard of art would ever be accepted by all men." It is part of

Anne's own philosophical agenda and central to an appreciation of the novel. She is concerned not only with the relatively unknown culture of the *gens* but also with her unique expression of it—worthy, she felt, of attention whether it fit standard literary categories or not.

Marcel gets a taste of class distinctions when Christophe introduces a black slave into the classroom. The parents pull their sons out of the school to let Christophe know the *gens* rely on slavery to maintain their status. It is a concrete expression of an ironic hierarchy in which one class oppresses another while working toward freedom from oppression from the class above them.

The class hierarchy also cuts into relationships. Marcel's friend Richard Lermontant is from an old family, the son of a prosperous undertaker who is proud of his status. Even whites respect him. Richard falls in love with Marie, but is warned by his father that the light-skinned girl is fated for the Quadroon Balls, where beautiful women of color are paraded before white men. Richard courts Marie and she falls in love with him. He decides to marry her and forgo an education in Paris. Unlike Marcel, he is enough at home with himself to be able to make something of his situation in New Orleans.

Marie's mother resists his intentions, and Marie confides in the family slave, Lisette, who listens resentfully. Lisette is also Philippe's child, but her mother is a slave. She must watch while her half-sister is lavished with luxury. Placing Lisette and Marie in the same household magnifies the divisiveness of the distinctions among the blacks created by the white culture.

Marcel's other childhood friend, Anna Bella, becomes the mistress of Vincent Dazincourt, a white planter and brother-in-law to Marcel's father. For Anne, Vincent is the ideal planter, and she based his character on what she had read of a real man from St. James Parish. She wanted a noble person of conscience who believed in slavery in order to work out a potentially contradictory point of view that does not *appear* contradictory to Vincent. Anna Bella loves him but pines for Marcel.

Marcel secretly becomes the lover of Christophe's mother, Juliet, although he is also drawn to Christophe. He ponders how activities that bring so much pleasure can be so intolerable to the community at large. His confusion is an expression of Anne's own questions over why simple pleasures for individuals are condemned by various groups.

One hot summer night, Marcel encounters Christophe in a scene that demonstrates Anne's talent for lingering with details similar to the style of the Russian writers that she loved. They engage in a discussion about life. The moment is still and quiet, making even more jarring the shattering articulation of truths that pass between them, reminiscent of Anne's bout with marijuana. As they talk, Marcel realizes that there "is no real order to things! There's nothing, is there?" He echoes the sentiment of Dostoevsky—who wrote that if there is no God, anything is permissible—when he says, "If it's really true that there's no order, then anything can happen to us. Anything at all. There's no real natural law, no right and wrong that's immutable, and the world is suddenly a savage place where any number of things can go wrong. . . . There wouldn't be any justice, and suffering ultimately would have no meaning, no meaning at all." He is horrified, but in the spirit of Sartre, Christophe points out that the real significance of what he is saying is that personal decisions bear more responsibility, "because you are creating the good and evil yourself."

For Anne the loss of absolutes was a stark realization, one that is resisted by characters in each of her novels. Many accept it only through resignation. Later in the novel, she indicated the cosmic implications of this philosophical insight when Marcel's Aunt Josette tells him, "It's an accident any of us being here or anywhere. . . . We don't care to realize that because it confuses us, overwhelms us, we couldn't live our lives day to day if we did not tell ourselves lies about cause and effect." Such statements remove all buffers between oneself and the world, implying that nothing is necessarily meant to be.

"I do believe," Anne said, "that life is based on accident. I think it's important to recognize that and not build false systems around things that happen. Our tendency is to think that things might have meaning and inevitability, and usually they don't." It is people, she felt, who make things what they are, by an effort of will. Christophe later tells Marcel that he is free to do with any experience as he likes. The message for each of the characters in its existential implications is that they own their own souls, and whether that responsibility is a burden or a source of freedom—whether they are victims or heroes—is up to each person. Even the slaves find ways to create some semblance of freedom in their confined worlds, indicating the degree to which personal freedom and responsibility are issues for Anne. It is important, she felt, to make your own world when authority figures fade.

It is such moments as those between Christophe and Marcel, or Marcel and his aunt, that make demands on readers. They must tarry with the material, think it through, feel the stillness, the shock, the evolution of character and perspective. There is much being said between the lines, and the story that evolves often turns on these epiphanies.

Marcel is soon summoned by his father's notary and told that he is to learn the undertaker's trade to support himself. He rebels, getting drunk and walking to his father's plantation. His long walk is one of Anne's favorite parts, for its dreamlike quality and complexity. "It was a stylistic adventure to write that chapter," she said. "I've always wanted to hear it read out loud by four people because he's hearing all these voices and he gets drunker and drunker and it ends with sudden violence."

Philippe beats Marcel into unconsciousness. He recuperates at Christophe's house, where they confront the sexual feelings they have for each other that have built as background tension. Anne had originally planned to make them lovers, but the editors wanted Marcel to stay straight. She agreed, deciding it was better to keep this novel wholesome.

However, she did use the scene to articulate her belief that everyone is searching for a mother and a father, but parents are just not adequate, because of their own needs, for the task of protecting their children. Marcel's mother is a cold, loveless, and selfish woman who thinks that being a white man's mistress is the best she is capable of. She represented to Anne everything in a parent that is loathsome and inadequate. Marcel has no real father, so he seeks direction from Christophe. Yet Christophe cannot deliver because he has sought in vain for direction from Michael. Each looks to another, but that other person is as human, with the same needs and seeking the same thing. The theme would come up again in later novels.

When Marcel is well enough, he is sent to the country to live with his aunt. He comes in contact with more of his people and begins to appreciate them, but he cannot bring himself to blend into a community so buffered against the white world. He does not know yet where he fits, although he does realize that his childhood is definitely over and he must take his life into his own hands. Christophe lectures him that he was not educated for Paris but for himself, "to fortify your soul."

Philippe drinks himself to death in Cecile's house. Cecile tells Marie that it is within her power to get her brother to Paris by making a good match at the balls. Marie is repulsed, and in her vulnerability, is tricked by Lisette and gang-raped by five white men. She believes she deserved it because of her sinful thoughts—a tragic victim of religious doctrines. She flees to Dolly Rose's whorehouse. Dolly Rose is a whore who reaps riches in her alternate life-style. She is an outsider among outsiders, viewed by the *gens* as a tragic figure but satisfied with what she is doing. She is the voice of the sensual individual who refuses to feel guilty about it. Dolly understands Marie's feelings and gently teaches her about sex, demonstrating the beauty of a tenderness that transcends gender. "They take the pen in hand," Dolly says, "they write the play for us . . . but we can take the pen from their hand. We are free really, free to live as we want to live."

Richard breaks into Marie's room and begs her to go to a convent. She refuses. She is willing to come to him if he wants her, but will not go somewhere just to ease his discomfort, a veiled expression of Anne's feelings about pressures from other people to write according to *their* tastes because hers makes them too uncomfortable. Richard decides to stand up to his family and to take Marie as his wife.

In the end, Marcel wonders what to make of himself. Richard is married, Juliet has a new lover, Christophe has new boys in his classes. He proposes to Anna Bella, now free of Vincent, but she refuses him. She wants him to pursue his dreams first, reminding him that he has an eye for beauty and should do something with that talent. He resists being victimized by his despair and confusion, seeing hope; his tenuous faith is a step forward for Anne from the emotional emptiness in which she had left Louis. He had been a victim of himself, and now Anne was writing about people who could be victims if they gave in, but who can also emerge as heroes of their own lives, resisting fate. Knowing one's limits, she felt, can become a means to freedom—a concept she had learned in a class on Goethe. Anne later described the novel as a "celebration of the inability to cope," although Marcel has gone past Louis in at least seeing possibilities for his future.

3

The novel moved slowly and required a careful, attentive reader. Anne had delivered a great deal of information in the process of developing characters and relationships. Impressed by Hemingway's goal of writing novels that people would understand, she worked toward creating a story so clear and compelling that even if readers cared nothing about New Orleans or race relations, they would still understand the book. She utilized a free, indirect style in which the narrator's presence blended with the voices, thoughts, and motivations of the characters.

Anne worked individually on each chapter until she had polished it. Unlike *Interview With the Vampire,* which had moved along in an almost unconscious manner, she stood back from this novel and evaluated it for textural completeness. She was conscious of the need to capture in fine detail the responses of the body to the overall situation. It had not occurred to her to put overt symbols into the novel, but when she was finished, she noticed that symbolism was evident, like the perpetual presence of insects associated with sexual fear. It worked as a subliminal signal to feelings. There was also a metaphorical quality to the setting that paralleled the story, which pleased her.

"I think that kind of stuff works," she explained, "if you are drawing on your full brain when you write, if you give everything to it in the most intense way."

The novel was set in the South, but living in California, Anne did not feel she could call herself a southern writer like McCullers, Faulkner, or Eudora Welty. Nevertheless, she was drawn to issues that typically captured the attention of such authors: the institution of slavery, extended family and its heritage, standing up to apparent defeat, having a place in society, and recognizing the fragility of social hierarchies. Like Faulkner, she used violence to react against life's general lack of control. Nevertheless it seemed to her that, having left the South at the age of fifteen, she was not really part of it any longer, not as an artist. Yet it clearly had left a lasting impression on her that beckoned to her and guided her voice. A New Orleans childhood among storytellers of the southern tradition influenced her voluptuous writing style, her romantic settings, and her impetus toward weaving with language—lots of it.

Anne believed it was the fiction writer's duty to not only entertain but to comment on human experience. She saw her task as an attempt to achieve the depth of the nineteenth-century novels for a twentieth-century audience, so she kept her eye on plot, spectacle, and character.

The Feast of All Saints was finished after two years of writing. Anne had intended to develop the lives of these characters all the way to the Civil War, but the task proved to be beyond her skill. "It peaked for me," she said, "and I really didn't know how to deal with chunks of time at that point. I just wasn't prepared. Those characters were alive for me at that time, and I didn't know how to develop it further." She still had a great deal of material left over, like the stories from the character Juliet's Haitian background, so she decided she would write a sequel, as she also planned to do with her first novel.

Anne was convinced that *The Feast of All Saints* was going to be a huge success. She had worked very hard to get the details right, and to make the characters sympathetic and interesting—even the ones she did not like or respect. She had written each chapter over and over, page by page, paragraph by paragraph, never moving on until she got it right. Finally she was satisfied, although a bit nervous. Toward the end of the book, she had been reading Flaubert's *Madame Bovary* and thought reviewers would pick up on its influence and call her work unoriginal. "I was really afraid that I had imitated the cadences of that book to such a point that someone was going to say something about it."

She had a few go-arounds with her editors. "I don't like anyone changing my words," she said. "I don't think an editor should go over a manuscript and change things any more than I think a gallery owner should heat up the paint on a canvas and go around smudging it. If I change something for an editor, that means I've failed. I'm admitting that it wasn't perfect. It's the writer's obligation to protect the integrity of the manuscript from everyone." The result was that Joni Evans respected her. "She said I had the best reasons of any author she knew for sticking to my guns."

"She was a total professional," said Evans, "and such an easy, understanding author. She was a very quick study. There was no ego there, but there was integrity—there's a big difference.''

Showing the finished novel to her father, Anne received high praise. He was delighted. ''I told her it could be a textbook,'' he said. ''She did for the free people of color what Margaret Mitchell had done for the antebellum South.''

A writing friend, Shirley Stuart, told her that her writing was like someone whispering secrets in a darkened room.

Expectations were high for this second novel, following the success of *Interview With the Vampire*. The ingredients were there, the publishers felt, for a repeat performance. The novel came out after Christmas in 1979.

Reviews were mixed once again and only about half as numerous as with Anne's first novel. Some reviewers found the story difficult to understand or categorize, which frustrated Anne. Not only did they miss details that she feared they would attack, but many of them failed, she felt, to see what she was doing. Was it a southern plantation saga? they asked. If so, where was the romance? Who were these people? What was she trying to accomplish? They were looking for trash, Anne believed, and came up against serious, reflective writing, so they called it boring. Others described her style as clichéd, quoting places where she had attempted to blend her narrative voice into the vernacular of the time. When she used the voice of the character, critics took it out of context and made it sound ridiculous, she felt. To her chagrin, *The New York Times Book Review* allowed the novel only a paragraph and gave it a thumbs-down.

Anne's editors were disappointed. ''I remember being very hurt by an early review,'' said Joni Evans. ''It was very harsh. People said it was dense. The world just wasn't ready for someone that free.''

A few reviews, however, were long and thoughtful, seeing unexpected literary quality. Andy Brumer, a friend of the Rices, tried out a new approach, calling his piece an ''inter-view,'' for the *Bay Guardian*. He noted such qualities as ''long, smooth philosophical paragraphs that roll and flow with the rhythm of poetry,'' and found it full of ''interesting structural and stylistic devices.'' He enjoyed the way Anne seemed to enter emotionally into the story. ''Anne Rice's novel,'' he wrote, ''leads us behind the accepted and approved of and allows us to see that in being human, all people (and perhaps especially the oppressed and forgotten) have within them the qualities of the saints. And this basic quality is the unifying will to survive and to overcome the adversities that continually challenge us.''

Anne responded to the review in the same article. She criticized what she thought had become routine in fiction, and hence what hindered critical acceptance of her work: "We live in an age where it is very popular to despise one's characters and it is popular not to entertain." She felt that her novel "cries to be taken seriously in spite of its historical setting and in spite of the author's love for the characters." She also indicated that she was more prepared for rejection and more savvy about the literary world than she had been with her first novel.

In another review, Ken Holditch, an English professor at Loyola in New Orleans, wrote: "What distinguishes this novel from hundreds of romances ground out every year by lady authors with poetic names is that the plot and characters make a significant social commentary, and that the protagonist undergoes a series of excruciatingly painful experiences that strip away the illusions and leave him, initiated by reality, a mature man."

The novel sold less than 20,000 copies—nowhere near expectations. The poor performance boded ill for the sale of paperback rights, which eventually came to $35,000, a major step back from the $700,000 of her first paperback sale. Everyone associated with it was shocked and Anne was devastated. "That was one of the worst disappointments of my career," she recalled. "The book was so tragically misunderstood. It was passed over. The reception was so abysmal that it just didn't get the wide audience. I don't think people wanted it. If I had come up with another supernatural book, it probably would have done better. That would have been logical to people. But I didn't do that. I did this very dramatic departure and it ran into apathy." She lost the audience she had counted on.

Anne wondered whether she had it in her to write another novel so widely received as *Interview*. Heavily disappointed, she experienced some doubt about her abilities. Listening to the responses of friends and family, she concluded that this second novel was "a heavy read" with its long paragraphs and dense information. People at Simon & Schuster had told her it was like chocolate mousse; it took them all day to read part of it. Anne had thought the response a compliment. She herself was an attentive reader. She loved "chocolate mousse" for her literary diet and had looked to the classics while she wrote it. "I was sort of trying to make it like a Tolstoy novel in the sense that I wanted it to be a novel translated from the interior of a culture, feeding information slowly and naturally. I was aiming for that, rather than the upfront, outsider statements of a historical novel." However, the publishing personnel had meant that its density might *hinder* its success. Anne made up her mind to avoid that style in the future.

"I realized," she said, "that to take the historical milieu and write a serious novel in America was just asking for trouble. There was no framework for it." Her agent told her that it fell between the literary and the popular, and people just did not know what to do with it.

Nevertheless, there was a bright side: "I did get two of the best reviews I've ever gotten—the only reviews I've ever received that said the book should win awards."

She also discovered that her books were reaching their audience in the way she had intended. At a book signing, which drew a limited but interested number of people, Anne listened as readers told her how they felt about her first novel. One woman had made a velvet jacket for it and read to Anne the sentence that she loved best. It woke Anne up to the idea that the critics were not necessarily the best interpreters of her work, and gave her a renewed sense of confidence. Perhaps she *could* one day affect people the way Dickens had.

There was nothing to do for such a self-willed writer but keep going. She already had other ideas. Eventually *The Feast of All Saints* caught on and went through several printings, but not for several years. From Anne's perspective at the time, it had failed and she had to learn from that failure or go under.

In the wake of finishing *The Feast of All Saints,* she went to a writers' conference in Lafayette, Louisiana, and went for a ride with Stan in the Cane River country. It was the anniversary of Michele's death and she was thinking about her daughter. They passed by a stand set up by descendants of the free people of color and noticed they were selling dolls. Anne wanted to go back. The type of doll they made was a rag doll called a Maman doll. Anne bought it. When she got back to Lafayette, she bought another, this time a porcelain doll that looked like a little girl. She had always loved dolls, even though she thought they were spooky, and had been disappointed that Michele had never taken to them. Now she had a baby son, Christopher, who was not going to play with dolls, either. But there was no reason why *she* couldn't have them. She became suddenly obsessed with collecting them.

"There's something about them," she said. "They combine an innocence and a beauty with a sinister quality." Over the next few months she bought more—mostly replicas of antique German dolls. Like Madeleine the doll-maker, Anne seemed to be retrieving Michele's image over and over from the grave. Sometimes she bought a woman doll and sometimes a baby doll, but most were little girls.

Soon Anne realized she was getting burned out from drinking. She had attempted to quit by herself several times, but then realized how difficult it was to do it by herself while Stan still drank. She told Stan her concerns. They were functioning fine, she knew, but she felt that Christopher should not grow up with parents who drank all the time. Stan agreed. Neither believed themselves alcoholics, but Anne knew her family history; if they went on, there was a very real possibility that she might become one. She drank a couple of six-packs of beer each day, sometimes three, and had experienced periods of blacking out over the course of their ten years of hard partying. It was time to consider her responsibilities. "I felt I had gotten from booze everything it was going to give me," she said. "I had thought it was relaxing, that it was helping me to access the subconscious. I gradually realized it wasn't doing that at all. I was sitting around dreaming about what I would do if I wasn't drunk."

"It became difficult to continue doing what we thought was valuable," Stan agreed. "We had to stop. I was tired of being sick."

On May 31, 1979, they took the step. No more booze, not even social drinking. Used to going to extremes, it did not make sense to drink a little. All or nothing. That was the way they did things. They pledged complete abstinence.

A few friends pulled away, not having much in common with Anne other than drinking together. She began to realize that when she had been drinking, those acquaintances had felt superior to her, as if she were sick. They had said things to her that she felt they would not have said to a sober person. These relationships gradually fell away. Anne found new strength in her writing.

4

Playboy magazine asked Anne to write a story. They would provide photographs and they wanted a short vampire piece to go with them. Anne agreed. The photographs she received showed a succession of shots, starting with a scene in which a man in a romantic, eighteenth-century shirt bends over a naked woman on a bed. He carries her through a dark passage to another naked woman and they engage in sexual contact while he watches.

The story Anne wrote was a spin-off from *Interview With the Vampire*. The idea was that there had been more tapes of the interview than had been published, and that there was extra material from a conversation between Armand and Louis. The pictures corresponded to Armand's description of seduction—"the art of the vampire at its peak in the year 1876." Some vampires love the struggle of their victims, he says, because it bears witness to the enduring human spirit. But he, Armand, has no taste for it. He prefers gentle seduction. He explains that he is seduced by a female victim through her dreams—her desire for death. She seeks an extraordinary love and is not afraid when she sees him. There is no need for overpowering her. She understands the ecstasy of surrender. He uses the intimate embrace to regain a memory of his mortal life, while his victim dreams as a vampire. He brings her to another woman and they cleave together.

While he tells the story it appears that he is in control and the victims are vulnerable. That appearance slides away as it is revealed that the repeated entreaty "Do you love me?" originates not with the women but with him. The story demonstrates the extreme loneliness and intense need central to the vampire's existence. It was published in 1979.

Money was running out and with no foreseeable major success in the wake of Anne's last novel, she and Stan decided to sell the big house in Oakland and find something more manageable. They put an offer on a house on five acres; but it fell through, so they moved back to San Francisco, to the Castro district, into a three-story, narrow Victorian at 3887 Seventeenth Street.

They had attended *Gone With the Wind* at the Castro Theater and had noticed a Victorian house for sale. Anne was impressed with the vitality in the area, and had no qualms about the fact that it was a center of gay culture. "I was absolutely swept up with the neighborhood, the shops open late, the people in the street. The significant thing to me about a gay neighborhood is that the gays were terrific urban pioneers. They went in and saved the Victorians. I wanted to live in the midst of that. Also, I loved gay people. I respected their courage as outsiders, and I feel a great deal in common with their aesthetic. I love gorgeous colors and a high component of quality and style. The Castro district at that time seemed like heaven. Not as green and beautiful as Berkeley or Oakland, of course, but it was a wonderful, exciting, bustling place. After being isolated on a hill in Oakland, we were right in the middle of things. Within two blocks one could get a computer disk, the best Brie on earth, any book you wanted, new or used, great Chinese food, or go to the Castro Theater. It was wonderful."

Later she set a novel, *Belinda,* there and wrote, "There is a mellowness in the Castro, a sense of people looking out for one another." Living there, they now had easy access to San Francisco State University, where Stan was destined shortly to become department chair. They subscribed to the ballet, the opera, and the symphony.

Anne set up her office on the second floor and filled it with an odd assortment of things, from a life-size cardboard vampire cutout to miniature statues of the saints, including St. Thérèse, the Little Flower. It was crowded with bookshelves to the ceiling. Anne hoped one day to have a house where she could set up a library—a dream since childhood from her observations of the grand houses in New Orleans.

She was asked to write reviews for the *San Francisco Chronicle,* which she agreed to do despite the difficulty she had reading quickly. She considered the job a great responsibility. From her own experience, she knew that people worked hard on novels and that reviewers were sometimes careless. She took up her pen with a fair mind.

Reviewing became a way for Anne to express her ideas while she worked on her next novel. In a collection of short stories, she found a resonating chord: "And we understand that if there is anything absurd or horrifying in this world it is perhaps the inability to remember what is and what is not eternal."

Almost a year later she found Jack Abbott's *In the Belly of the Beast* to be a moving expression of the struggle to become educated—one of her favorite themes. She was impressed with the development of the intellectual mind in such a brutal setting as a prison, but hoped that Abbott would eventually develop a suspicion of abstract political ideas, "especially those that draw away from the blood-and-bones reality of individual human life." It would be another eight years before she brought this idea to fruition for herself in a novel, but it clearly had been on her mind as early as her first one.

She used a review six months later to make a significant point. Delighting in Bette Bao Lord's first novel, she wrote, "Bridging the gap between the commercial and literary, *Spring Moon* proves that the split between the serious writers and the entertainers need not exist."

Settled now in a new house, Anne realized it was time to get to work on another novel. When she had finished *The Feast of All Saints* and turned it in, she had not known what to do next. She wanted to write something she knew would sell. The publishing world was going through a change. Hardcover publishers could no longer rely on paperback sales to carry expenses, and they were less willing to take risks. Anne decided to write some quick romances under a pseudonym.

She bought a series of Harlequin Romances and found she could not tolerate the writing, so she paid a girl who baby-sat Christopher five dollars an hour to read them and tell her the plots. "Then," said Anne, "I sat down and thought, I can't do this. I cannot write anything that does not have the chance to be great." She also realized that the editor would substantially rewrite it, and that sort of thing did not sit well with her.

She made a study of the work of Jacqueline Susann—a symbol of trash writing during her unpublished years—and Ian Fleming to determine whether they were writing about subjects they thought were marketable or whether they were writing what they knew. She concluded they were writing what they knew, and that insight came as a revelation. One could not really write toward "the market."

Anne also had an idea to write a novel about a rock star but never developed it. Years later, she expressed a desire to pen with a rock star an autobiography that would show the effects of rock music on the culture to someone reading about it one hundred years later. Rock stars embodied, she thought, the romantic concept of the artist as outlaw. Looking around for other ideas, however, she dipped back into history, with which she felt more comfortable. A historical framework put a wall between herself and her contemporary experience and provided an easier vantage point for making sweeping statements about culture.

"I had to write something I enjoyed," she said, "and I was looking to write something about the French Revolution and a violinist. I started reading up on music to see when the violin had first been played as a virtuoso instrument." She had studied this history as a child when she had been obsessed with being a great violinist, and she remembered some of the stories. She checked violin music out of the library and began to form an idea for a book. In the midst of her research, she encountered a description about the conservatory in Naples and the famous castrated singers.

"It was like a thunderbolt," she said. "All the lights flashed, everything went off!"

She read more about the young boys who were taken from their families and castrated as early as the age of six, then sent to the conservatories, where they were treated with great cruelty. Anne checked out every book she could find on this unusual group, reading about teaching methods of the maestros, about the opera, and about eighteenth-century Italian art and music. She listened to operas from the period and even located an ancient, scratchy rendition of the only eunuch ever recorded. She read about the lives of the most famous of the castrati, fascinated with how the singers had to improvise on stage like modern-day rock singers. There was a great deal of room for creativity in their performances, which implied a great deal of room for Anne to develop details and plot. She loved the rivalries and the way the castrati were admired throughout Europe. She also loved the notion of achieving greater and greater performance through voice control: using the human instrument for perfection. More important, she loved how they symbolized androgyny, the neutral zone between gender divisions.

As was her pattern, she became obsessed. She had gone in search of a subject, but the subject had found her. There was something intensely exciting about men who had been neutered. "I drenched myself in it and the novel took shape," she said. "I got ferociously excited and abandoned all question of writing romances for money. I dropped the violinist and everything else. The novel took over and the characters came to life." The connection she made with the castrati was more intense than what she had felt with her first two novels. They sang to her of freedom, of unrestricted sexual energy. She was going to tell the story of people considered by society to be monsters, freaks, victims, and sexual anomalies, and how they transcend the situation. She was leaving behind brooding novels about passive despair. It was time for a real hero who could make a social statement.

Across the street lived a doctor named Robert Owen, who worked at the Veterans Administration Hospital. Having lived in New Orleans and being a computer buff, he and Anne often talked together "over the fence." Anne asked him if he knew anything about the physical aspects of the castrati. Did castration block these men from sexual activity, or could they, as it was rumored, have had affairs?

Dr. Owen got interested in the subject and found information for her from the medical-history libraries in San Francisco and New York. He located a twelve-volume, unpublished manuscript of a medical study of the palace eunuchs in the Turkish empire, and was able to report that there was indeed a physiological basis to the rumors. "The castrati would have been like male children," he said, "having orgasms and erections. It is a neurophysiological event, and it is feasible to think that they were sexual beings." He confirmed for Anne what she had hoped was the case and, armed with science against the inevitable incredulous reviews, she got to work on the plot.

To write *Cry to Heaven,* Anne knew she would have to avoid the approach that had tripped up the success of *The Feast of All Saints.* She had to spell things out in the typical format of a historical novel. American readers were more used to that. She needed to cut her paragraphs in half, get things moving right away, and tell everything readers needed to know to understand the context, but not to compromise on her elaborate style. Drawing a parallel between what she had to do and what her fictional singers had to do, she wrote:

> He must know when to swell a note, how long to hold it, whether to break a passage into notes of unequal time or those of equal time, and how far he might go into ascending and descending intricacies. And he must at all times articulate the words of a cantata or aria so that in spite of all this exquisite ornamentation, the meaning of the words was clear to everyone.

"It was a fairly difficult novel to write," Anne said. "It was a dare of sorts. I was trying to construct a story that was fundamentally extremely implausible, because no Venetian aristocrat had ever been made into a castrato. To accomplish it, I had to develop a detective-novel plot. Fitting all the pieces together was a very tough job." She borrowed a few ideas from her early novella, *Nicholas and Jean,* notably the illusion of a man playing the part of a woman.

Creating the historical atmosphere was not difficult. Anne had a good memory for detail. She had been to Venice and Rome, and was able to retrieve from her experience sensory impressions to animate her imagination. For Naples, she leaned heavily on Goethe's diary of his visit to the city. There were many memoirs available, but little on the conservatories, so she made up what she needed for a setting, basing it as much as possible on fact. She was limited by her inability to read Italian, but what came clear to her was the rapid pace of the memoirs, as well as the lightness of much of the baroque music. She set about to match that tone with her writing style, listening to recordings of arias while she wrote to keep her sensibilities fresh to the glory and richness of the music. She finished two thirds of the story before she was able to sell it.

Simon & Schuster did not want this novel, but Vicky Wilson did, and Anne was back at Knopf for a $75,000 advance. It was another step back, but still considered a good advance for a hardcover novel. The expectations were not high, given the subject matter, the market conditions, and the performance of her second novel, but Anne accepted that.

5

The novel is set in eighteenth-century Italy. It traces the parallel stories of two men castrated for the sake of preserving their perfect soprano voices. Both are flung into a community of mutilated half men, simultaneously admired and scorned by the society that made them what they are. Castrati are set apart by the very nature of their appearance. As one character explains to another:

> Your arms and legs will increase in length . . . and it is this flexibility of bone which gives you such power with your voice. Every day that you practice, you increase the size of your lungs; and the elastic bones let those lungs grow. . . . But your hands will hang low on your body, and your feet will flatten out. . . . You will not have the natural muscularity of a man.

The "cry to heaven" is that of "children mutilated to make a choir of seraphim, their song a cry to heaven that heaven did not hear." The perfection of their voices, developed for religious purposes, is such that even heaven should take notice, but at an expense that no benevolent God should allow to happen. Yet God seems oblivious.

Guido Maffeo is cut at the age of six. Born into an overburdened, lower-class family, he is willingly delivered to the Conservatorio, where he has a chance for stardom. He succeeds until he loses his voice, then becomes a maestro of singing, always searching for a boy who vicariously can give back what he lost. His search takes him to Venice, where another boy's story is unfolding.

Anne was aware of the metaphorical qualities of her setting. Venice is the city of canals, built over water, the universal symbol of the unconscious. In the story, many scenes are set to rain. It is the place where the identity of Tonio Treshi, the pampered son of a Venetian nobleman, is molded. Tonio loves to sing, but when he speaks about a future as a singer, his family laughs: that is for the castrati, not for him.

Once again Anne identified with the principal male character, Tonio. She plotted out his family lineage and posted it on her bulletin board. He expresses a deep concern for his doomed, alcoholic mother, Marianna, who keeps to her room the way Anne's mother did. " 'Why can't I protect her?' he whispered. 'Why can't I save her!' " Once again, it is the child who is the parent to a parent incapable of caring for either of them: "She was much more the child than he. . . . She was helpless in her darker moods; the world collapsed upon her, and when he had clung to her, crying and afraid, he had terrified her."

The mother, Marianna, is a lost soul, full of unpredictable anger and fear. She cries a lot, is afraid of the dark, and has no outlet for self-expression. "If I hold her," Tonio thinks, "that other creature won't come out of her to hurt me." When she is not crippled by alcohol, she sings and dances like a girl, and tells stories about ghosts and witches, but is helpless to her darker moods. Her plaintive "Do you love me?" shows a clear need. She is powerless to help herself. Anne admitted in an interview that Marianna shares some of her mother's characteristics. Although Anne had a better relationship with her mother than many children of alcoholics do, she must have felt what Tonio expresses within the limitations of his young perspective.

Tonio has a brother, Carlo, who is banned from his inheritance for seducing a girl with no family name. Among the Venetian aristocracy, lineage is the image of immortality ("the name Treshi had been in the Golden Book for a millennium"). Once again Anne reveals her obsession with the fact of death and the human attempts to defy it. She would return to this theme again and again, expressing her desire for a sense of stability.

One day Carlo returns, "and then the meeting took place which was to change the very color of the sky, the aspect of the snow white clouds, and make the day take on a dark resonance." Carlo is bitter, seeing Tonio as a way to earn back his place. Tonio learns that his mother was the girl that Carlo seduced, and that he is Carlo's son. The man he had thought was his father is his grandfather, who had taken the ruined Marianna as his wife. In this complex series of relationships, no one is quite what they seem—a theme for the novel—and fourteen-year-old Tonio is hurt and confused, finding solace only in exercising his beautiful voice with the street singers.

Carlo hears that Guido Maffeo is looking for boys with promising voices. His henchmen castrate Tonio and deliver him to Guido. Tonio is stunned, but must, to preserve his life, act as if it were his choice.

Knowing Carlo is the last of the Treshi men who can have children, Tonio decides to put off his revenge until Carlo has fathered children. He goes to the Conservatorio but refuses to sing. He does not want to be one of the castrati, monstrous as they are. He stares in horror at Guido's long limbs and realizes he is looking at his own future.

Still a child at fourteen, Tonio has been forced to emotional maturity by the very act that negates him physically as a man. He must also find another means besides family to achieve immortality. All he has is his voice; a metaphor of eternity, it would never change. One of the many ambiguous symbols in the novel, he can allow his talent to mock him or to provide him with power, "a human instrument so powerfully and perfectly tuned that it rendered all else feeble in comparison."

Guido is haunted by Tonio's voice, now silenced. It is his completion—held away from him, tormenting him. The head maestro suggests that Tonio use his voice to get back at the "whole men" by revealing true perfection. Then *they* become monsters in their imperfection. This concept of transposition foreshadows things to come.

Tonio has no notion, however, of what can lie ahead. He is stubborn and afraid, grieving over what he has lost and resistant to change. Having experienced throughout his childhood the unpredictability of his mother's shifts between cruelty and affection, Tonio is familiar with the anxiety engendered by the loss of control. Cast abruptly into irreversible circumstances, he sees himself without power or choice. Like Anne, he has always feared the threat of chaos and vulnerability to forces outside himself. Seeing Mt. Vesuvius in Naples, ever threatening to erupt, he fixes on it and seeks to merge with it, to find a way to absorb its hidden violence.

He leaves the Conservatorio, but realizes the utter isolation of being part of no community. He goes up the mountain to feel the intensity of the heat of the lava, seeking to understand what he should do. "He became part of the mountain and the roaring caldron within it." It is his personal hell, the internal regions where pain and passion have no limits and darkness threatens annihilation. Surrendering to it can mean ultimate terror or ultimate transformation.

The dormant volcano is the central metaphor, representing both sexual tension and the illusion of surface appearance. It becomes Tonio's symbol of restrained power, emphasized by the deceptively light writing style that hides a theme of force. He eventually returns to Guido and agrees to sing, but still harbors a plan for revenge. Appearing to be one person committed to his new life, he is actually "a pair of twins in the same body." Carlo represents his dark side—the victim, Guido, his good side—heroic transcendence. When one side gains strength in Tonio's life, the other recedes. Throughout the novel his passion harbors as much violence as creative energy. In a parallel image he quickly develops his voice, astonishing everyone with its beauty, while his appearance becomes more monstrous.

To emphasize this theme, the people throughout Tonio's life are as divided as he is, despite what they appear to be. As at the carnivals in Venice and Rome, they all seem to be wearing masks. Christina, a contessa who attracts him, wants the freedom of a man; the Cardinal, a man of religious purity, exhibits brutally carnal desires; Marianna is both cruel and caring, with beauty that hides her ugliness; Carlo appears innocent of malice; Guido seems to hate Tonio when he actually longs for him; men dress as women, women as men. Even Venice, at times glorious and mysterious, has a whorish and seedy interior.

The tension of this incongruity between surface and inner reality is reinforced with double imagery in the background: two recurring nightmares, two contessas, two men killed by Tonio, a duet between two castrati, and repeated attention called to mirror images. In addition, there are doubles of opposition: devils and angels, calm and violence, power and vulnerability, male and female. The continuous references to doubles provide a symbolic layering, intensifying the confrontations and the feeling of restrained violence that reverberates throughout the book, from sexual liaisons to musical duets.

Tonio and Guido become lovers, but Guido encourages Tonio to take every opportunity to have sex, because he may lose his power to perform at any moment. Tonio feels betrayed by Guido's promiscuity. He continues to strengthen himself for his eventual revenge, although his attraction to Guido and the new life—his good side—weakens his resolve.

Tonio is swept off to his singing debut in Rome, with Guido as his composer. He is invited to be a guest of Cardinal Calvino, who, intrigued with his feminine beauty, approaches him sexually. Tonio is repulsed. Guido tells him he is neither man nor woman, but enviably free to be either. "You are not bound by the rules of men," he insists. "You can do these things."

Their debate touched on Tonio's resistance to taking a female role on stage. It is a role expected of a superb soprano—the prima donna. A man must do it, since women are not allowed on stage. Tonio, however, wants to retain his masculine identity, which allows him a sense of clear boundaries, an anchor in something that he knows from his past.

Nevertheless, he returns to the Cardinal and becomes his lover, although he experiences the "sense of something being destroyed, something that had been guarded desperately for so long," even though he has also gained what Guido calls freedom. For Tonio such sexual freedom touches too closely to chaos, the loss of boundaries and control. There is too much ambiguity for him. However, having surrendered to what he feels is vulnerability, he is ready the next day to don a woman's dress and present himself to Guido for his prima donna role. He is surprised at the power he exerts over others in his female garb, and the discovery opens a door that fear has kept closed. His appearance in a dress is an image that Anne found greatly arousing.

Soon Tonio slides into greedy promiscuity, taking male lovers from the meanest streets of the city, wallowing in the chaos. By stages he has moved from a male on the brink of puberty and conquering women to a female-like receptacle for other males. To this point, it has meant disintegration and he gives in as a drowning man who cannot swim.

Suddenly the Cardinal, feeling sinful, cuts him off, and Tonio voices his despair over his inability to feel as a man or a woman. "Oh, if only I understood either of you, what either of you feels . . . if I were part of one or the other, or even part of both!" He sees only love and not guilt or sin. The Cardinal's decision expresses the impossibility of joining the religious and sensual realms of Anne's experience: "He could not unite two worlds: the one infinitely powerful and bound to revelation as well as tradition; the other inevitable and irrepressible, holding sway in every shadowy corner of the earth." Tonio felt cut off from the Cardinal as Anne had felt cut off from God, "as though they'd known each other intimately a long, long time ago." However, the Cardinal's decision foreshadows a similar healing of ambivalence in Tonio.

The next step in his sexual education arrives when he falls in love with a female artist named Christina, who prides herself on having the boldness of a man in her work. Even her name is a form of the androgynous *Chris,* and indicates a new beginning. She paints turbulent seas and nude men, confusing Tonio because of the way she exercises a self-willed freedom. He is not ready for the further descent into chaos that she represents.

When he appears on stage for his debut, dressed as a woman, he gives an incredible performance and is met with enthusiastic acceptance, reminding him of the power he can exercise over others with his voice. Guido, too, triumphs.

It is a moment in the novel when Anne displays an artist's sensitivity to detail. She animates the description of the performance with chilling clarity, making the reader almost hear the dueling voices as the castrati strive to outperform each other. With language she brings both the music and the competition to life. It reveals her talent for capturing another artistic realm and drawing it into literature, as well as for filling a scene with power.

The victory has an edge of bitterness for Tonio: he achieved it as a castrato. His pain is an indictment against a fashion based solely on the horror of the church over allowing women to perform on stage. Since the perfect soprano of a young boy could only be preserved by castration, men were mutilated for the sake of social conventions. "It was taste that kept such a shape as his fashionable, it was taste that made women send him tributes and confessions of adoration, when all he ever saw in the mirror was the ghastly ruin of God's work." Not all of the castrati had successful careers, yet they could not just drop back into society to raise a family. A percentage of them were ruined for life. They were outsiders, monsters. They found acceptance only with others like them, who mirrored what had been done in the name of a fashion that would one day make even the most successful performer passé.

There is nothing inherently wrong with an outsider, save that they cannot conform to the tyranny of taste. They are people who love and grieve and need acceptance, but under the judgmental gaze of others, they are made socially powerless. Anne had covered this theme in her first novel, but here she gives it a new twist. The very conditions that threaten to defeat these outsiders allow them a different kind of power: the ability to define the community from the perspective of the individual who is not constrained by fashion. The victims are allowed some degree of freedom and dominance. To the castrati, the *community* looks ugly, like the "gilded maggots feeding on the corpse of the Venetian State." The power struggle mirrors that of Louis and Lestat as two sides of the inner self, except that the victim is gaining strength, finding a way to emerge on top. This theme would increase in significance in Anne's writing, as it increased in prominence in her own psychological development.

The situation of the castrati provides a perfect forum for Anne in her own feeling of not fitting social fashion. She had been made powerless in this way by the church, by censorship, by friends, and by the literary establishment. Her answer is to give to abnormal lives a richness that defies social judgments. Tonio was a freak, but he understood that his abnormality was a symptom not of his own lack but of a social disease among those who thought themselves normal. For him and for them, the surface, like a mask, deceives.

Tonio's reputation grows in Rome, and he and Guido are invited to tour Italy. However, Tonio falls in love with Christina. She embodies to him the peace of mind of simplicity, of an undivided will and heart. She knows what she wants. "Purity of heart," Kierkegaard said, "is to will one thing," and Christina exercises a single-minded obsession. She represents a centeredness that Tonio lacks, that gives her great creative power. His voice is dazzling, but he cannot exercise pure creativity while he is so ambivalent. The reversal between them of sexual personas, in a scene where Christina garbed in a man's clothing sits on Tonio's lap while he is dressed as a woman, is a metaphor of artistic balance—of the ideal of androgyny so meaningful to Anne.

In the simplicity of childhood as Anne had known it, she had not been restrained by sexual identity but was instead encouraged to tap her full range of creative energy. Only in adolescence and maturity did she feel the social forces of entrapment into sexual roles—she and everyone she knew. In this novel she sets up the perfect opportunity for gender-busting to create characters who are neither male nor female, and who can thus take on either role, sexually and socially.

Tonio resists this freedom, but his resistance, which seems to him a form of power, is revealed as powerlessness. Moving toward the holistic center that he fears rather than toward the fragmentation of roles to which he clings is true freedom. His fear is what hinders him, although he views it as his ally. Socially defined roles appear to offer security, but they are in fact a hindrance.

The scenes of sexual androgyny, coupled with artistic expressions, make concrete an idea that may otherwise get lost in abstract discussions. Even the thrill of Tonio's artistic talent is described in sexual terms. Understanding the message of Christina's gender freedom as a parallel to her artistic success offers Tonio the motivation he needs to engulf himself completely in his androgynous sexual identity—one that can fully release the power of his voice. He has moved through stages, beginning with his bold confrontation of chaos on the night he climbed to the volcano. Little by little he has dropped his resistance and has discovered freedom where he feared chaos, parallel to the way an artist taps the creative force. Within him the volcano is churning, getting ready to erupt.

Within each person is a similar caldron of confusing images, an overwhelming source of conflicting energies that can potentially crush someone too weak to withstand the wealth of multiple sensations. The artist can withstand it, viewing places of terror as sources of new realities which social norms have suppressed but not destroyed. The primitive resources are not neatly categorized or restrained, and can yield new perspectives and a broader range of expression to those who have the courage to lay themselves open to the experience. For Tonio that freedom was initially avoided. He clung to norms that no longer applied to him, unable to face the anarchy of a disordered existence. Flinging himself in, he was engulfed. Seeing Christina's strength coupled with the same freedom showed him the way out; he could impose an order of his own making using inner resources of discipline and choice, strengthened, paradoxically, by their tenuousness. He moved gradually from victim to hero, and the eruption he feared was more awesome than his terror had allowed him to envision. Yet it was also more empowering.

Tonio hears that his mother has died, and he realizes he can take his revenge on Carlo, but he hesitates. He is happy with Christina, with his new life, his success. However, when there is an attempt on his life, he knows that Carlo is behind it, probably frightened that Tonio is coming for him. There must be a confrontation for his own survival.

He enters Venice—his subconscious—in his stage guise as a woman—having conquered his internal chaos to the point of channeling the inner bisexual power. Going to Carlo, he moves in on his negative side—the debilitating hate of a victim. He seduces Carlo into a vulnerable position, then reveals himself. Tonio gives Carlo the chance to vow never to kill him, then releases him from his bonds and gives him a knife. Throughout the novel, the knife has symbolized irreversible change: castration, death—"the cutting edge that awaits us all." In the final scene, the knife is again the instrument of loss. Carlo lunges for Tonio and is impaled on his sword, held up in self-defense. Tonio is now free of his father and his hate. He returns to the opera, leaving the name of Treshi to Carlo's sons.

Anne had a difficult time with the ending. She was not sure how she wanted the scene with Tonio and his father to be played out. She spoke to Vicky Wilson, who wanted it to end before Tonio ever got to Venice. Anne decided it should end when Tonio stuck the sword through Carlo, but neither she nor Vicky thought that would work. She showed the draft to Stan and listened to his suggestions. Finally she wrote a concluding scene that satisfied her.

Tonio journeys to Florence, where Guido and Christina await him: Guido his positive side and Christina his sexual complement. He watches the town from a hill and it reminds him of painted scenes of Bethlehem, the town of rebirth, symbolizing a new beginning for him of unity within himself.

"It was the weirdest novel I ever wrote," Anne said, "the most otherworldly. When I reread it, I'm always shocked by its tone. It seems like something I wrote in a dream."

6

She handed in a draft, then made changes like strengthening the Cardinal's character, but balked at advice to cut down on the sex. Those scenes, she felt, had a distinct progression, and all of them were necessary to Tonio's development. Overall, however, Anne was pleased. The novel was easier to read than *The Feast of All Saints,* yet she had inserted discussions about things that were important to her. It was a book about gender, showing that the real sin is not sex but violence and cruelty. Anne had wanted to write about a good and noble character and believed she had succeeded with Tonio. Despite his sexual practices, which might prove distasteful to some readers, his soul remained pure.

Michael Riley told Anne that *Cry to Heaven* was the most audacious and intellectually daring statement he'd ever read about art and sex. "Without a misstep," he said, "she found her way to a profound statement of her conviction that in art and sexuality we have the most at stake and can find absolute and liberating fulfillment of the self."

"I think that's what the novel is saying," she agreed. "There is sexuality in art. Tonio got liberated but his mother was denied both and died as a consequence." Similarly, Anne was liberated, while her own mother possibly had been crippled from a lack of outlets for self-expression.

While she waited for *Cry to Heaven* to get published, Anne started research on another historical novel, set in England at the time of Oscar Wilde. She had read about his trial and the enormous impact it had had on the gay community there, and became interested in the artists who had lived in that society. She started to plot out a story called *The Education of Richard Lockhardt.*

It was about a fourteen-year-old boy growing up in Victorian England who is kidnapped by a man who takes him to Egypt and molests him until puberty. Anne did not physically write it, but she envisioned graphic scenes, moving Richard around in her imagination, having him kill his mother and brother and leave Egypt for London. There he falls in love with a boy, and they go to a cathedral where babies are dropped off. Richard wants to take a baby to raise, to teach it everything right. His lover persuades him that it's a repetition of being kidnapped by an older man. He opens Richard's eyes by advising him to develop a relationship with an equal, someone his own age.

Still a novel of education in which a naive boy is instructed by an experienced man; Anne was moving more solidly toward relationships between equals. She would carry it through in a new direction that was beckoning from within.

One day she was reading an interview with Mikhail Baryshnikov and was struck by his description of how his normal life had ended at the age of twelve, when his abnormal life began. She saw the theme she had expressed through vampires, free people of color, and castrati being lived out in a contemporary form and thought to herself: this will be the direction of my next book. It was very much in tune with her obsessions, and she was feeling an urge to write in a contemporary setting. She began to attend the ballet frequently and to comb bookstores for books on the subject. What she noted was how the dedication of these dancers to perfection prevented them from having a normal human existence, yet their abnormal life was as rich or richer than the people from whom their peculiar life-style cut them off. She was especially fascinated with the male dancers, against whom there was a prejudice in society similar to that of the castrati.

Her interest, however, diminished. "I burned out on it very quickly," she admitted. She had immersed herself, but the subject did not find root in her imagination.

She also had a son to attend to. Christopher was growing. Almost three, he was fascinated with color and began to work with big blotches of maroon and purple paint. Anne and Stan read to him but did not shove preschool exercise books at him. Like Katherine, they wanted him to develop freely. As with Michele, his world was filled with adults, primarily artists and writers. Anne watched him carefully, but he seemed perfectly healthy and happy.

7

Cry to Heaven was published in October 1982, dedicated to Stan and to Vicky Wilson.

Then the reviews came out. Anne read them with dismay. She felt that once again she had been misunderstood by many critics, and some were quite vicious. Few critics seemed to notice the qualities that she thought made the novel stand out, and no one understood the sexual progression as an evolution of freedom. However, *The New York Times* surprised her with a rave review, calling it "dazzling in its darkness." Her happiness was soon eclipsed, however, when the *San Francisco Chronicle* was published. Very prominently placed, complete with a photograph of her, was a review that so devastated Anne that she no longer saw San Francisco with the same eyes. She felt as if the literary community were telling her to leave the city.

"All the ingredients," said the reviewer, "of a grand and deliciously trashy historical novel are available with the premise," but the novel failed to deliver. It was "endless and repetitive," "Anne Rice at her worst," "a succession of witless sex scenes and plot convulsions," "bloated."

Anne felt betrayed and humiliated. The review had been so prominent, as if intentionally to ridicule and embarrass her. To her mind, neither the reviewer nor the editor had been responsible to her, not the way she had been as a reviewer, and it hurt her deeply. "It was one of the worst reviews I've ever seen in the *Chronicle,*" she said. "I had read the *Chronicle* for twenty years and had never seen an attack like that on any writer, let alone a local author. That review was the beginning of the end of my life in San Francisco."

Shirley Stuart and Candi Ellis, Anne's writing friends, wrote letters chastising the paper for using poor judgment. It suggested to Shirley "that someone at your paper has a grudge against her and did not want her book to do well." She pointed out how easy it is to make serious fiction appear ridiculous and that a responsible reviewer would not resort to such tactics.

Anne appreciated the support, but no longer wanted to go out. She could not pick up the *Chronicle* without pain and refused to do more reviews for them. "I never appeared at another literary function, nor went anywhere where I might see someone associated with the *Chronicle*. I withdrew completely."

Yet the bitterness had accumulated. Three novels and all of them misunderstood by the literary establishment. "I was so angry during the first three or four years of being a published writer," she said. "I was angry at the shallowness of the reviews. What was so bad is that no matter how much you know intellectually, they still hurt your confidence. I really worried about whether my work had any merit at all." There were days she did not want to get out of bed and go downstairs.

She abandoned the Richard Lockhardt novel. She was not going to do another historical, not with the way the last two had been reviewed. She realized, in addition, that she herself did not really care to read historical novels and perhaps had no business writing them. She read Mary Renault, whom she loved for the richness of her language and for the relationships of her male characters, but as a rule, historicals did not interest her. "I resolved," she said, "that I would never again write a book that I wouldn't grab off the shelf myself."

Gradually, however, she was catching on with readers. *Interview With the Vampire* had developed a cult following, and even *The Feast of All Saints* was going into another paperback printing. The readers that she heard from continued to prove to her that they knew what her books were about. She began to relax.

She thought about starting on a sequel to the vampire novel. She wanted a character of action and decided to tell the story from Lestat's point of view. He seemed to be growing as a character on the edge of her vision, and what she saw in her imagination interested her. Maybe another vampire novel would get her back on the best-seller list. She sat down to write, but the novel did not flow the way she wanted it to. She had no clear impression of Lestat's voice or how best to begin. Every time she managed to write something, it seemed too distant.

At the same time, something else was pressing, another story—*more* than that, another *voice!* Her three novels had been written under European influence, in dark tones and moods. One had channeled her grief, the others her need to fight against forces that threatened to make her helpless. She had descended into dark areas of her soul, retrieving painful experiences to fashion into literature. In the process she had evolved a means to express her erotic impulses as well.

CHAPTER EIGHT

THE DIVIDED SELF

1

Between 1982, with the publication of *Cry to Heaven,* and 1985, Anne was engaged in several overlapping projects that confirmed her acceptance in the literary world, then placed her at its borders—if not altogether outside them. She wrote for *Redbook* and *Vogue,* adopted two pseudonyms under which she published four books with sexual themes, and took a few more stabs at her vampire sequel. She was also attending to her son.

Christopher was growing up. Like Michele, he was precocious and inquisitive. The philosophy of parenting adopted by both Anne and Stan was one of freedom and enlightenment—not the truncated freedom of her parents' Catholicism, but a genuine openness to life. If he was curious about the human body, they brought home *Playboy* magazine or allowed him to watch the *Playboy* channel on television. "I definitely believe," said Anne, "in no censorship of any kind."

When Chris wanted to paint, they gave him his own materials. He loved to dab the paint on thickly, having moved away from blotches of color to distinct subjects like bodies of water and electrocuted women. A few times he peddled his paintings in front of the house to earn money. Then he gave up painting to draw. Being exposed to a wide assortment of movies, several subjects fired his imagination. "I was obsessed," he said, "with sharks and piranhas and airplane disasters, so I drew those."

Anne's fear was that he might be overwhelmed by Stan's and her accomplishments, but he seemed strong and resilient. "What pleases me about Chris," said Anne, "is to see his tremendous strength and stamina and rebelliousness. He refuses to be subsumed by other people's personalities."

Surrounded by adults, he never talked like a child and he was comfortable in adult company. "He was a precocious talker," said Anne. "At school one year, he was described as having the biggest vocabulary in the smallest body." She enrolled him in a progressive school called Synergy, where he came into contact with children his age. Anne finally had some time free to focus on her writing.

Prior to *Interview With the Vampire,* Anne had been writing pornography, none of which had been fleshed out fully to consider for publication. She had enjoyed writing those stories and had shared them with close friends, but had not thought of herself as a writer of pornography. When her first novel had been stolen, she had not put much effort into recapturing it. However, those themes were once again crowding in.

Anne's published novels had a strong European flavor and were predominantly historical. She felt pressured by the somber tone and wanted to try out new textures and make a change to something contemporary, so she came up with an idea for a novel which she called *Triana Walker*. She let it unfold in her imagination and tried to get some of it on paper.

It was about a Berkeley artist named Jeremy, who had done a series of nude females which he titled "My Life as a Woman," playing off Anne's obsession with transgender identities. He hears about a six-year-old girl, Triana, who is the victim of hippie parents. The father is a drug addict who in a crazed moment attempts to put her in the oven. The mother is passive and drugged, a woman taken advantage of by everyone. Jeremy kidnaps Triana to save her and falls in love with her. In one scene, as he gives her a bath, she seduces him, too young not to realize it's not a game. He has a guilt-ridden, long-term affair with her and eventually wants to die because of it, but she will not allow it.

Anne's protagonist was still much like Louis, experiencing remorse for feelings and deeds. However, Triana exhibits a wisdom that indicates that Anne's female side is coming to the surface, growing up and accepting sensuality.

"I wanted to write it," said Anne, "but never did. The idea was that by the time she was seventeen, she was an educated girl who knew four languages and was a tremendously healthy person. Strictly speaking, she was a victim of molestation, but she would probably have died if she had stayed with her parents. I felt it very strongly and I understood what it was about—the idea that abnormal life can be as rich and wonderful as a seemingly normal life."

Anne experienced difficulty making the scenes of Jeremy's child molestation sympathetic, although they were very clear in her imagination. Yet what blocked her even more was the rage she felt against attitudes and behaviors she had witnessed among the hippies, especially their drug-induced indifference and reluctance to help someone. "When the men would begin their brutal talk and their abuse of the children in the book," she said, "I could not write it. I didn't really know people who had done those things, and yet the writing kept turning to that extreme viciousness, as if what I had seen had meant that to me, symbolically. I had heard their rhetoric and their lies, and I'd get so consumed with rage that I couldn't write it."

She eventually put the partially finished novel aside. Looking back, she said, "I think it would have gone nowhere. It would have aroused such strong negative feelings that it would never have been reviewed or Knopf would not have published it. It was the only truly shocking thing I think I've ever written."

Even so, it was not such a radical change from her previous publications as it seemed, especially *Interview With the Vampire*. Anne was seeing connections between horror and the erotic. "There's something about the excitement of ghost stories that's like sexual excitement," she said. She had noticed in stories by M. R. James how victims of unspeakable horrors were laid waste, as though sexually molested. The violence, or suggested violence, in horror seemed to her to share similar qualities with forms of violence in pornography, although she was not really sure how to explain the connection. "I just know that's what turns me on," she said, "and I can't define it. I'm a writer who is obsessed with horror and with the erotic, so perhaps they do work together. I just know I love the stuff. It strikes some deep, deep chord in me."

She understood well the excitement induced by fear and violence. "There's this tremendous capacity for violence in me," she told an interviewer. "I've always enjoyed violent movies with a lot of action, like reruns of 'The Untouchables.' I enjoy seeing people in complicated conflict. I find it almost soothing to watch that kind of violence. I love to see one person against the odds. I think all the violence I enjoy is pretty much wrapped up with the idea of heroism." She liked the idea of consenting to forms of "safe" violence for sexual pleasure, but did not, however, want to see violence as a *punishment* for sex.

Having once visited a sex shop with Stan, Anne had been horrified by what was available in pornography. The writers, whom she thought mere hacks, seemed to be writing purely toward what they believed the market to be rather than expressing a genuinely erotic fantasy. Such poor writing, she believed, reinforced the myth that sex was sleazy and that excitement only resulted from gratuitous violence. "S&M to me," said Anne, "means games between two consenting adults. It doesn't have a thing to do with literal sadism. I don't think most people understand that. What has always interested me is the fantasies—not the acting out. I'm not even sure the acting out to any extent is a good idea. I'm not sure that's an area of one's mind that is meant to become concrete and to surround one like that. I don't know."

Anne felt there was a real misunderstanding in these books of what S&M devotees really wanted. The fact that there was little else available seemed also to deter serious writers from writing porn. It was also clear to her that the writers and publishers did not seem to realize that men had masochistic fantasies—that *they* enjoyed being victims—and that women were searching for literary sexual expression. She wanted to change that. She envisioned writing a book that she felt both men and women would enjoy: elegant sadomasochism, where the desire to be dominated could be entertained in a safe environment, where punishment enhanced rather than restricted sexual freedom. Women could still be victims, but only if that was what they wanted, and men could be victims, too.

For too long, she believed, women's erotic energy had been feared, suppressed, or manipulated, as if women needed to be protected against what they wanted—or punished for it. Anne understood that. In an interview with the *Village Voice,* she insisted, "If you grow up as a passionate child, particularly a passionate woman child, you grow up being told that you're not in some way feminine." Yet her own intense sexual energy would not tolerate the inhibition and repression demanded of women growing up in the fifties. The liberal, sensual climate of the sixties and seventies had given her the courage to try her hand at expressing the demands and desires of her body. To her, the sexual revolution had been the greatest revolution of our time.

Having herself a masochistic tendency, she figured that what aroused her would arouse other women as well. "I believe that most people have some masochism in them," Anne said. "I think very few are sadists. The ultimate form of masochism is to service someone else. People want to be passive, they want to be ordered about, they want to be in the focus of that intense devotion and attention and control. And, of course, they want to control all that. It's the fantasy of attention, of an eroticized authority figure totally devoting everything to them."

She wanted tactile pornography rather than visual, and a context in which a woman could be sexually dominated by a man without fearing for her life. She also desired a balance between cruelty and tenderness rather than mere vulgarity. There seemed to her to be a real market for it, evident in the great popularity among women of what she called "bodice-rippers," in which women were dominated by all manner of men from pirates to aristocrats. These women took what they could get, Anne believed, but were not really satisfied. They were looking for something that was not being adequately expressed in the books available to them. The writing of pornography for her became a moral cause. Not enough had been done to give women what they wanted—to affirm their own sexuality and free them from social and religious superstition.

Besides political and moral motives, Anne also just wanted to express her own elaborate fantasies. She looked over what was available in paperback pornography, then educated herself in the history of sexual customs. Other than that, she relied on her imagination for plots and images. It was time, she felt, to come out from behind the mask of a man and write about a female protagonist. Rage and self-consciousness about her own femininity had thus far prevented that, but she wanted to try it now. The decision would take her further into her own psyche than she had anticipated.

2

She wrote the first book, *The Claiming of Sleeping Beauty,* in three weeks, describing it as "an erotic novel of discipline, love and surrender, for the enjoyment of men and women." She intended it to be delicate and elegant but realistic, pacing the scenes with her natural feelings. "When I'm before that computer," she said, "I'm aroused."

There was no particular reason, Anne claimed, for choosing this fairy tale over any other, although she associated it with her mother and it had been a favorite of Michele's. "I have no idea why the Sleeping Beauty myth inspired me," she said. "I just wanted to take those fantasies and put them into some sort of form that could be written down, being true to what they were and making the least possible concession to literary form or the market." It was her intent to write something so eccentric and powerful that it would defy a rewrite by editors.

The novel utilized the hierarchy of royalty and peasants, which provided a concrete setting for sexual dominance and submission. Important to such scenarios is the master–slave relationship, and in a setting with castles and villages, a slave was really a slave.

The privacy and freedom of a pseudonym seemed to her practical and would allow the full rush of sexual energy restrained in other novels. "I had long toyed with the idea of having that freedom," she said. Pornography could not be well done, she felt, if she had to be careful about what people might think, including reviewers who scrutinized her work for a return to her first novel. She did not want her father to read these books, or to alienate fans of her mainstream persona. People who understood the fantasy would be interested, but others might be shocked. Lynn Nesbit agreed that a pseudonym was a good idea.

Anne chose the name A. N. Roquelaure. She had been reading the story, "Mr. Justice Harbottle," by Sheridan Le Fanu, about a cruel judge captured by ghosts and hanged. She came across the word *roquelaure.* Looking it up, she discovered that it meant a particular kind of cloak created by a Count Roquelaure and worn in the eighteenth century. It seemed perfect: Anne under the cloak. It also had a sexy French sound, desirable for writing pornography.

"I felt it was an experiment," Anne said of her new persona, "a way of dealing with a range of things that I wanted to do."

The opening of *The Claiming of Sleeping Beauty* begins toward the end of the original fairy tale. Beauty has been sleeping for one hundred years and many princes have stormed the walls of her castle. Thick vines full of poisonous thorns have killed them all. One prince, however, gets through by cutting the roots. He wakes Beauty with a kiss, symbolizing her sexual awakening.

According to psychiatrist Bruno Bettelheim, fairy tales serve a distinct psychological purpose. They help us to transcend social confinements to achieve greater self-understanding. Characters in the fairy tales represent facts of male and female experience, and the metaphorical messages deliver unconscious content dredged up from areas hidden from the tyranny of propriety. Fairy tales teach us about our repressed fantasies, helping us to work through fear to gain emotional security.

This is consistent with Anne's approach, since childhood, to her fears. She sometimes surrendered, but was more inclined to attack, spurred on by her physical energy. She eventually developed a love for the thrill of moving through territory like "forbidden" pornography that was fraught with emotional and psychological perils. She had no idea how it would turn out or if she could publish it, but she wanted to let loose her sexual impulses. Her aim was to break down resistances within herself created by society, family, and the church. She explored the inner process of her mental life so that she could take on socially disapproved feelings and unite the male and female within herself. By utilizing a fairy tale, she achieved within a fun and safe form of fiction a degree of bisexual integration, and took the first steps toward unifying the self-fragmentation that had occurred as a response to grief, loss, and change.

Sleeping Beauty is seemingly lost in the abyss of subconscious territory. Awakened, she is claimed by a prince who intends to show her the way to true enlightenment. They do not get married and live happily ever after. Instead, Beauty becomes his slave, returning with him to the castle of his parents. "Pleasing me," he tells her, "that is your life now. How many of those in the world can know such clarity, such simplicity?"

The story is about the psychological process of surrender, to which Anne is deeply attracted. Later in *The Witching Hour,* she would write: "He's so gentle and when he touches her, she yields to him utterly. . . . All the world would like to be this woman." Viewing surrender as something to fear blocks the inner transformation that it can offer when freely experienced.

To Beauty's great shock, the prince parades her naked through a village until she is thoroughly humiliated and confused. "To be commanded by one so very young," she muses, "is to feel one's helplessness." Yet even in her vulnerability she detects a sense of power. She can provoke in the prince the pain of desire. It is the first hint that the one who seems most vulnerable and subservient has in fact a degree of control, and a device to show that these seemingly opposite traits are not mutually exclusive but seem to blend together as a dull nickel that shines in a certain light. It was Nietzsche who spoke of the master and slave impulses originating within a single soul, and Anne gives this concept concrete application.

Beauty is taken to the castle, where she notes an atmosphere of authority among the royalty not unlike the air of priests seeking to punish disobedience: they watch in amusement as she struggles with her willfulness, they forbid her to touch her private parts, and they tell Beauty the highest thing she can do is to please her masters, especially the queen. They loathe the slightest imperfection.

She is to serve among other naked princes and princesses, and she witnesses harmless but effective sexual tortures in the Hall of Punishments and on the Bridal Path that terrify and attract her. Fear and vulnerability heighten her passion; the breathing deepens, the adrenaline races, and there is urgent need for release, but release is not allowed. The parallel between fear and sex is utilized throughout the Roquelaure series, with care to retain trust that the masters will not really harm their slaves. Without trust, fear turns to paralyzing terror, freezing the blood rather than pumping it hotter.

In this novel, Anne explored elaborate sexual games, but ironically, she employed conservative descriptions, as if not quite free of socialized decorum. She referred to genital areas as his or her *sex,* and equates masochistic desire with repetitive spankings. Although she occasionally broke out of this conservative vision, it was not until she wrote a second book that her style and images revealed an unconstrained physicality.

Beauty notices that the male slaves, kept in a constant state of erection, are quite helplessly exposed. The penis, a traditional symbol of power, is transformed into one of vulnerability. She also notices how the slaves delight in their punishments just as she does, reveling in the attention and sensuality. She represents the ambiguity of the masochistic figure as one who might be pitied, all the while being the sly aggressor, feeding off and provoking the tormentor's rage.

Unlike the other princesses, "who are too frightened the first few days," Beauty is quite passionate, and with her depth and mystery "will always suffer more than" others. She quickly becomes a favorite and learns that the slaves who serve at the castle are better off for it: "When a slave's been used, really well worked, the body is enhanced in some way." This concept hints at the process of Transubstantiation, one of the many religious images used as a mirror throughout the Beauty series. The slaves also gain in wisdom, patience, and self-discipline.

Nevertheless, Beauty feels that to give in is to lose something of herself. She is like Tonio in *Cry to Heaven,* who interpreted resistance as a way to retain free will when in fact it hindered him from finding true freedom. Surrender is the path to truth, but Beauty will only learn this by stages.

A slave named Alexi explains how he had been beaten through boredom out of his rebellion and into a passion to please. Anything is better than being bored, he insists, and punishment is easier to bear when aroused. He demonstrates to Beauty the intimacy of the master–slave relationship. Surrendering, he is favored by the queen. "The only way I could triumph was through perfect obedience." Like the religious penitent, perfection and obedience brought him closer to the godlike queen, and his seemingly weak subservience was actually his strength. It was a scene that Anne felt was quite daring, and when she eventually lost her pseudonymous cover, she felt she had lost the freedom to create other scenes quite like what she had done with Alexis.

One day Beauty witnesses disobedient slaves being carted off to the village and grows excited by the thought of the humiliation of yet harsher discipline. She sees beautiful Prince Tristan in the cart and disobeys in order to be sent with him. The book ends while they are in the cart, clearly set up for a sequel. Anne polished it and sent it to Lynn Nesbit.

3

Stan was a bit apprehensive about Anne's new direction. "I had trepidations that it would be dangerous for her reputation," he admitted. "Those were little fears, more to do with family than anything else. I wondered, is she going to put a black mark on her life and make her life more difficult? But I was supportive of the freedom."

As Anne waited for a response from her agent, she woke one night in a mental sweat. There are, she conceded, people who have no desire for either part of the S&M scenario, who would not respond to her book.

They might not realize that it was all a game of temporarily giving up responsibility and becoming self-centered without guilt. She felt she had really exposed herself by revealing her desire to express these fantasies. Perhaps they said something about her that even she did not see—that masochism might be a form of self-doubt, of the inability to cope or even of that ever present passivity that threatened to drain her of spirit. Would anyone be horrified? "If you think S&M is sexy," she said, "it needs no explanation. And if you don't, you wouldn't have the faintest idea why anyone else does." But soon she was pleased that the writing had aroused in her that sort of tension and uncertainty. It made her feel alive to her work, and that feeling was worth any editor's reaction. She trusted her imagination and believed in her direction.

"When someone writes an authentic book like that," she said, "whether it's Henry Miller or *My Secret Life,* when elements of the fantasy cohere according to real feeling, you have a window into a psyche. There's almost no literary dilution, no distortion. It's really close to the true fantasy. I believe someone could pick up the Roquelaure books two hundred years from now and learn what one kind of S&M mind is all about."

Anne realized she was going against the grain, not just of a male-dominated world but also of feminists like Andrea Dworkin and Catharine MacKinnon, who stressed that pornography exploits women and should be legislated. According to them, sexual representations are a form of discrimination. They thought that women were being socialized to view themselves as submissive sex objects and that something had to be done to counter this influence. Anne found such a point of view fascist. *She* was a woman and she did not object to pornography. It was just an expression of fantasy, something that all women had the right to do. The feminists, she felt, were no better than the repressive men they were battling: they were telling women what they should feel. Not only that, they were stripping women of free will and responsibility for their thoughts and actions.

Cultures in which sin is emphasized and punishment central, Anne believed, inevitably produce people who find punishment to be a sexual turn-on. "They can't sanitize or legislate our sexuality out of us," she later put into the mouth of a character in *Exit to Eden.* "It's got to be understood and contained." Censorship was no more the answer now than it had been in the church when she was growing up.

In an interview she said, "Women as women haven't been out of the closet for more than about twenty years. What I see now is the closet door being slammed back in our face by an alliance of feminists, Moral Majority conservatives, and old-guard liberals who seek more to protect women as victims of male sexuality than to argue for equal rights or the rights of women to express themselves sexually." For Anne such lobbying was disturbing. She wanted to hear from women what they really felt, but forces conspired to intimidate them. It was not only unfair, it was counterproductive. Repression could only block or destroy potentially positive energy. That pornography had not been done well for women was no reason to move for its restriction. Rather, go out and find out what women want.

Anne believed feminists were wrong to draw a distinction between pornography and erotica, as if one were evil and the other acceptable. Her pornography emphasized physical sensation, yes, but as the source for powerful feelings of fear and love—both of which put people more fully in touch with themselves. Domination forced people to feel things that they wanted to feel and perhaps could feel no other way because they did not allow themselves to do so. Getting involved with the sensations of the body entailed awareness of the deepest rhythms of the impulse toward life. The continuum of pain and pleasure presented the question of how fully and acutely people *can* feel. None of Anne's characters would be maimed or killed, nor would they commit suicide over sexual gratification. They would simply be allowed to work out their fantasies in harmless S&M rituals. She was interested in the heightened experience, in the potential spirituality that accompanied arousal.

"I believe the sexual side of our nature is powerfully mysterious," she said. "There are moments in my books when the most powerful feelings about exposure and sexual revelation are being examined. Some of that stuff parallels mystical writing. You get out of yourself, you become the thing that is happening to you. Part and parcel of the sexual revolution was the knowledge that it was spiritual."

According to the psychology of ritual, she was clearly on target.

Ritual, as a consciously proscribed symbolic event, speaks to the subconscious and channels free-flowing energy sources within the body to intensify the experience. The goal of ritual is to contact higher elements of the self, usually thought of as the spirit, but the lower elements must first be purified to be worthy. The discipline of ritual provides the means by emphasizing a repetition of actions toward perfection. The more you do it, the better you get. The bodily positions physically anchor the ideas by working the senses—the source of the erotic—toward more powerful acuity, providing a path to enlightenment and release.

Anne had learned this at a subconscious level in church before she had ever thought of sex, but she rejected the idea that her Catholicism was the root of her sexual fantasies, and would say as much in the soon to be written erotic novel, *Exit to Eden*: "People say S&M is all about childhood experiences," notes one character, Elliott, "the battles of dominance and submission we fought when we were little that we are doomed to reenact. I don't think it's that simple." No child, he goes on to say, ever saw the paraphernalia evident in S&M fantasies.

> These things don't come from childhood. They come from our historic past. They come from our racial past. The whole bloody lineage that embraces violence since time immemorial. They are the seductive and terrifying symbols of cruelties that were routine right up through the eighteenth century. . . . We're working with our most primitive desires to achieve intimacy through violation, our deepest attractions to suffering and inflicting pain, to *possessing* others.

The argument is provocative but does not dismiss the notion that childhood struggles provide the arena in which any given individual taps into those primitive, archetypal urges in a manner influenced by their specific milieu of choices.

It cannot be denied that Anne learned at a very young age—in part, through unconscious imitation—the notion of surrender to mystery and inner perfection through sensory stimuli set up in a ritualized manner. Day after day she knelt in unison with others, closed her eyes, folded her hands, imagined Christ's pain and humiliation, took care not to bite the communion host, and learned of the excitingly dangerous poison of original sin. She smelled the incense and candles, attended to the colors of priests' robes and stained glass, listened to chanting and music, tasted the wine, felt the fear of being under the gaze of every vigilant authority, and experienced the chill of anticipation of uniting with the divine spirit of God. The intersensory rituals were meant to be transformative, to bring supplicants closer to perfection through the death of the individual will with its sinful urges. Ordinary consciousness was thought to become extraordinary by focusing on limitless power and truth. Certainly Anne was impressed enough to throw herself wholeheartedly into the idea of becoming a nun and to pray intently in a tiny oratory for transcendence. Whether sexual fantasies emerge from struggles originating in childhood, whether they express an archetypal force of the collective human unconscious, or whether, as Anne suggests, they're a racial trait, her own exercise of those fears and desires was inevitably permeated with Catholic impressions. Certainly the notion of yielding totally to God is not unlike the experience of sexual orgasm. To love God passionately, one must be a passionate person. That sexuality and spirituality blend together in Anne's writing is no surprise in light of her childhood experiences.

Her masochists are concerned with being the center of attention, and what better way to get attention from the priests (the masters)—if perfect goodness was impossible—than to act out, be "bad"? It brings down the wrath and displeasure from the ultimate Dominant—God—but also places the punished one squarely in the light of God's attention. Anne handles ritualized sex through the more general psychology of ritual, and utilizes many religious images to express the power of the S&M

scenario. As with religion, in which God is construed as a higher consciousness and the worshiper the lower consciousness, so the master can represent the higher self and the slave the lower self. The punishments are meant to purify and perfect, to urge the energy of the lower self toward the higher self, as the worshiper moves toward spiritual illumination. The goal is a purified love.

To surrender to the sensations of the body is to find a power that makes one less willing to accept powerlessness. Learning not to fear by being forced to confront those fears is a source not of madness but of replenishment. The sexual adventurer seeks jeopardy in order to discover powerful inner truths. It was similar, Anne felt, to Catholic saints who used physical excess like self-flagellation to transcend their bodies for union with God. Happy endings were in store for all of Anne's pornography. Finding sexual integrity, according to her, is finding freedom: "I'm convinced that the work has a wholesome overview and a gentle approach."

She hoped that John Dodds from Simon & Schuster would buy the novel. He had created for her an atmosphere of warmth that made living in San Francisco since the *Chronicle* review of *Cry to Heaven* more tolerable. However, he declined to make an offer. The book did not interest him.

Vicky Wilson was also not interested, finding pornography claustrophobic, but she suggested the editor-in-chief at E.P. Dutton, Bill Whitehead, known as a pioneer in literary trade paperbacks. Bill was a witty man with a sense of style who lived in a penthouse in the Chelsea Hotel. Anne met him in San Francisco at the Café San Marco and gave him her manuscript. He took it on the plane with him and was unable to put it down. He told her it had passed the "tumescence test" and made an offer that became a three-book contract.

Anne felt that Bill really understood her novels and would see that they were tastefully published. She got to work on the next one while *The Claiming of Sleeping Beauty* was going through the publication process. She was interrupted when Bill sent her the copy-edited manuscript and insisted that she look at it. She was furious that some copy editor presumed to point out deficiencies in her writing and hotly objected.

"I felt," said Anne, "that I didn't even know who these people were. I couldn't help them with their own writing if they came to me, and I'm supposed to read their changes on my sentences? When all that crap is all over the manuscript, you can't really do the real copy editing. You miss the mistakes because you're too busy reading some amateurish rewriting of your work."

She and Bill argued about the changes, and when the dust settled, the novel came out in 1983, dedicated to Stan. Anne was pleased with the elegant cover art and soon finished the sequel.

4

Beauty's Punishment begins with Beauty and Tristan on the way to the village. The style is consistent with the first book for the first half, told in an informal third-person narrative, and then Anne suddenly breaks the frame and begins a series of chapters in first person, speaking from the point of view of Tristan. Once again she takes a male perspective. He graphically describes his experiences of humiliation and his sense of need for punishment, repeating themes from the first book. At no time does Anne deliver Beauty's point of view in first person.

There is no obvious significance to this change of format until the novel is placed in the perspective of Anne's feelings about herself. Although she viewed herself as having a bisexual mind, originating in a universally bisexual imagination, she seemed to have more trouble identifying herself other than physically as a woman. "I'd be a man in a minute," she admitted. "I would cheerfully be a six-foot, blond-haired man wearing a size thirty-eight."

Although in *Katherine and Jean,* Katherine told her story in first person, the emotions and experiences were not nearly as fleshed out or compelling as those described through Louis, Tonio, or Marcel. It may be that in *The Sufferings of Charlotte* or *The Tales of Rhoda,* the female perspective had been more developed, but neither manuscript is available, nor was either compelling enough to Anne to do much with them.

In the novel, Beauty and Tristan are auctioned to different masters, for whom they each become favorites—another theme that obsesses Anne. She enjoyed the feeling of being conquered by an attraction to her characters, which meant they had to be special. They witness public humiliations, understanding the cycle: "Their passions are roused, fed, roused again and fed again so they can no longer tell punishment from pleasure."

In this second book, the scenarios are more homosexual. There is more equality, especially among the men. Observing the courage of the life-styles of the gay couples around her in the Castro district, Anne saw what she described as pure, angelic love based on a balance of strength and weakness, of equals learning from equals. Certainly her own relationship with Stan was giving her more of a taste for that as he tolerated her "masculine" traits and found her fantasies a sincere expression of the inner psyche.

Tristan and his new master, Nicolas, become deeply involved, allowing love to permeate their S&M rituals, and Tristan realizes that love is a higher quality of attention than sadism. When Nicolas asks Tristan why he obeys, he explains the slave psychology, which Nicolas summarizes: "There is something undeniable in the true slave who worships those of unquestioned power. He or she longs for perfection even in the slave state, and perfection for a naked pleasure slave must be yielding to the most extreme punishments. The slave spiritualizes these ordeals."

With his master's love and also because of his strength, Tristan is satisfied in a way that life in the castle had never satisfied him. "It is the Master who creates the order, the Master who lifts the slave out of the engulfing chaos of abuse and . . . drives him further in ways that random punishments might never provide. It is the Master, not the punishments, who perfects him." Without the master, the slaves are lost. The description echoes how religious devotees feel about God.

Nicolas understands this. He is aware that Tristan was once a prince. "The best slaves," he says, "sometimes make the best masters." After all, he reasons, "who understands power, worships it, more than those who have had it?" People who take dominant roles in life, Anne believed, often yearn to be the masochists, and their desire expresses the concept that power and vulnerability are flip sides of the same coin.

The village is raided, and Tristan and Beauty are carried off. They find themselves in golden cages on board a ship along with other slaves. One of them, Laurent, has already caught Beauty's eye in the village for his extraordinary endowments and his ability to glory in his punishments. He is the image of the man Anne wants to be. He becomes her new hero, giving impetus to the third book in the series.

Beauty and the others soon learn that they are on their way to a sultan's palace, where "you will no longer be treated as beings with high reason. On the contrary, you will be trained as valuable animals . . . you are no more than the most abject little bundles of ever-demonstrable passion." They are about to take a step down, it seems, into the further degradation of the savage physical body. Yet, as with power and vulnerability, appearances are deceiving. At the cliff-hanger ending, they await their next adventure with great anticipation.

The book was published a year after the first one, in 1984.

Anne had not yet revealed that she was the author behind the pseudonyms, although she did not hide the fact from close friends. Allowing even a few people to know, however, inhibited her freedom with the second book and she knew it would happen again with the third one.

She gave out copies to a limited number of relatives and friends. Cathy Colman was enthused. "I thought it was fabulous! I was all for the idea of having women express their sexuality in writing."

Not everyone, however, believed that Anne was doing the right thing, and some friends were quite taken aback. Her career had seemed so secure, they felt, if only she wouldn't sabotage it. Her fans were looking for more Rice books, and here she was spending her time on books of no substance. Was she really so blind to how she was hurting herself?

Shirley Stuart defended Anne's right to work out her talent however she chose: "If she wanted to do it and was writing it well, why shouldn't she do it? She wouldn't be the first serious writer to write erotica." She told Anne that the novels were a dazzling work of imagination, although she was a bit shocked to realize these books were Anne's *fantasies.*

Other people were surprised as well. "She confused me," said Larry Rice. "She could write novels that would sear your ears, then turn around and cook a dinner for twenty-five without blinking an eye. She was brutally honest. She merely revealed to us all what lurks within."

Stan became more enthused. "I thought it was powerful stuff, honest, unique, and very sexy. It met all my expectations of something that was really successful in its mode." Anne had even included some of his fantasies.

Anne felt that the books were perfectly legitimate and she was proud of them, although she knew they would be targeted to a specialized audience. She had set out with the same intent as she had with her other books, to create an illusion with the power to affect readers and to take them into emotional experiences where they had never been. Why should she draw the line at provoking sexual feelings just because some people were uncomfortable? She considered the books to be quality writing and was only sorry that other serious writers were spending their talent on what she called "Connecticut bedroom stories" instead of exploring these "forbidden" realms of the imagination. Perhaps then pornography would be granted a more serious status. From her own experience, she had discovered what she had already believed: pornography as a form of literature could succeed as emotionally powerful writing and could touch on important human themes. It could become a mainstream form of entertainment. Those who did not like such books did not need to read them, but sexually explicit literature should be available for the people who did, without making them frequent sleazy shops.

5

When she was not writing or defending her pornography, Anne searched for a way to make her next vampire book about Lestat into a novel of action. Neither of the Roquelaure books had taken much time, and she knew she needed to get back to her sequel. She read true-crime books as well as Raymond Chandler and James M. Cain, believing their authentic style would help to loosen up the tone and make the voice she was seeking for Lestat more intimate. There was also some peripheral influence from Jack Kerouac. "I really wanted to draw in close to the character," she said.

At the same time, she started another novel which called for a new pseudonym. It had been planned as a pornographic novel with a contemporary tone, but it soon broke away as it channeled psychological energies that turned the novel into a confrontation for Anne with hidden parts of herself.

In a tribute to Charlotte Rampling, whom Anne loved in the movie *The Night Porter,* and who exemplified for her a perfectly poised woman of substance and beauty, she chose the pseudonym Anne Rampling—her "California voice."

"It's writing a novel that sounds spoken," she explained about her new style, "with an informality. I associate the California style of literature with the kind of freedom of a narrator who just steps in at any moment and talks about the characters. There's a lot of use of vernacular. I think it makes a book much hotter when you break the frame in that way."

She was beginning to feel as if she had three distinct personalities, or as if she were an actress playing out three different roles. Later she referred to her body of work as "the divided self." She had immersed herself in the historical past and in total fantasy, similar to the way she had avoided full exposure to the present when her mother died. Now she wanted to try something different. The tone of the new novel was closer to the erotica she had been writing in the sixties and early seventies, and the people were more realistic, not princes and princesses. She was coming closer to herself, to themes about her inner life not yet fully realized but pressing for expression. "I felt I was totally there in every voice. I felt a terrific rush of energy with the Rampling books."

The novel was called *Exit to Eden* and was dedicated to Stan. The two main characters, Elliott and Lisa, take turns telling their stories in the first person. Their lives are intertwined on a Caribbean island where Lisa has masterminded a pleasure resort for the wealthy. The Club has three thousand members who pay a fee as high as $250,000 to have a "slave" wait on them hand and foot, satisfying their every sexual fantasy in an atmosphere of complete safety.

The slaves are beautiful young men and women who elect to lose their identities for a limited period of time to indenture themselves. Elliott is one such person, having signed up to subject himself symbolically to his fear of being conquered. Like the Roquelaure books, a principal task for the slaves is to keep themselves under control while they maintain an aroused state at all times. In this way they subject their will to another in the most demanding and extreme manner, being for their masters and mistresses whatever they are commanded to be.

The novel is more than just a story about people romping around, playing sex games. There is both a psychological and philosophical element that ties it into more serious literary traditions. The setup of the Club is the very picture of the philosopher Jean-Paul Sartre's concept of relationships. (One of Lisa's sexual mentors is named Jean-Paul.) As humans, according to Sartre, we are free to define ourselves, which gives us our unique identity as individuals, but such freedom is frightening because it carries a heavy responsibility for the choices we make. It is easier to allow someone else to make those choices for us.

The masters' freedom curtails the slaves'. They define the scenarios and control the slaves as if they were objects. If the masters want to become objects, then they must yield their freedom to the slaves. The relationship only works if one person exercises his or her freedom and the other agrees to surrender their will and be defined.

The Club, then, is a microcosm of society, a theme evident in each of Anne's novels: to be accepted is to be defined within a role. "The ultimate degradation is that you consent and grow to like it." Individuality is limited and even submerged. The slaves exercise one choice: to choose to have no choices.

Pushing this theme further, the novel becomes a picture of the self attempting to balance opposing impulses. For Anne those impulses were the attractions to both power and surrender. As Louis and Lestat represented two sides of her, so also do Elliott and Lisa.

It is not surprising, then, that the Club is also a religious metaphor. Anne once again employs the power associated with the Catholic hierarchy to create vivid subliminal impressions. Lisa flies to Rome, the location of the autonomous Vatican, to speak with the financier, *Mr. Cross,* about creating an "autonomous country." The parallels begin almost at once, although the mirror imagery is that of people aiming toward the same goal, perfection, through apparently opposite means. The operators—one of whom is the Master of Postulants—are referred to as the "unholy Trinity," and they wear black to designate their elevated status. Lisa is granted a godlike position as the mastermind and the granter of mercy, not necessarily subject to the rules she makes. Religious imagery surrounds her: she has the "hands of a saint" and looks like the Virgin Mary in her cotton slip. The staff go about as priests or nuns, punishing fault among the slaves. The Club is referred to as both heaven and hell, and operates by ritual. Lisa refers to it as a "religious order" and her "nunnery," referring to the irony in *Hamlet* that a nunnery is a whorehouse. Her own sexual mentor has the voice of a Catholic priest, and she utilizes him in the end for confession and absolution. The relationship among the masters and slaves is one of intimacy, like a spiritual union.

Everything about the Club breathes contrast, ambiguity, and paradox to emphasize the ironic metaphor. It is the reality of fantasy, making of the outside "real" world an illusion. It is a prison of freedom, where slaves and masters can exercise their most outrageous desires but the slaves are locked in for a set period of time. Punishment means pleasure and attention or the humiliation of failure—the former being desired and the latter feared. The members join as masters, but many want to command the *slaves* to be the masters, so slaves must be prepared for either role: as slaves they must obey and become masters. The concept is not unlike the words of Dostoevsky's Grand Inquisitor, who insists that slavery *is* freedom.

The most salient ambiguity is the question that Lisa asks herself over and over: Is the Club good or bad? Is it bad because the members commit "sin" by reveling in dark, ostracized desires, or is it good because it gives an outlet to symbolic violence that might otherwise become true violence? Lisa herself embodies the multiple ambiguities that she projects onto the Club: "It's just like everything else you've said and done," Elliott says. "It could mean at least two different things."

Ambiguity creates ambivalence because it requires decision and commitment in the face of choice to a definite perspective that precludes choice. Commitment involves choosing one thing and excluding alternatives. Lisa is too unsure of herself and can make no such commitment. The Club's essence reverberates with her double-mindedness: the power of simultaneous fear and attraction, what Kierkegaard calls dread.

"The Club is what it is," says Lisa, "because it believes in itself. And its glamour and its terror evolve from that."

Writing the novel was an exciting experience for Anne. She wanted to be true to her own "weirdness," so she resisted what she might have to do to make the book commercial. A reviewer of *Cry to Heaven* had pointed out that the novel lacked humor, and Anne realized she could utilize her natural wit. She decided to put more humor into the characters in this and future books. The most important thing, however, was the sexual tone: to maintain a delicate balance between the masochists' agreement to be forced to perform in a way they pretend they don't want, and actually being violently forced to do something from which they genuinely seek release.

Digging within herself, Anne realized she was moving closer to an elusive, sometimes terrifying clarity that she referred to as "It"—something just beyond her reach that tugged at her and motivated her to surround it with language and make it reveal itself. She had been pursuing this elusive feeling since the sixties with her early stories. Her favorite scenes occurred when she felt her language was coming close to an intimacy with the characters, giving her a "buzz," as she called it. "It's the most intense moments in the book," she said. "The absolutely quintessentially interesting things. It's a feeling that what is happening on the page really, really matters—it's the most important thing you can say about our struggle in this world. I try to boil it down and get right to a moment of truth that makes your hair stand on end." In *Cry to Heaven,* Anne believed, there had been too many building blocks between such scenes. In this novel she wanted to try for more scenes that gave her the "It" feeling, with less "just stuff" between them.

In the course of writing, Elliott and Lisa came alive for her. "I fell in love with the characters right away," she said. "Something started to happen for me and it ceased to be just porn—or it became a heightened form of porn because it involved not only the same kinds of infantile sex scenes that are in the *Beauty* books, but it involved real people doing them who had a great deal more personality and history. It just got sexier and sexier, and when I finished, I felt terrific."

Anne put traits of herself into both characters, reinforcing the image that they are two sides of herself. Lisa, known as The Perfectionist, was raised Catholic and has an authoritative, intelligent father similar to Anne's own father. Many of Lisa's memories of her father have an authentic ring, as if she felt the same things that Anne had felt when she broke from the church to pursue her own ideas. Lisa respects her father, yet feels unaccepted. "He is . . . truly a spiritual man," she says. "I have not met too many people who really live by what they believe as he does. And the funny thing is, I live by what I believe . . . I would like to tell him that I too am a sort of nun, because I am saturated in what I believe." Lisa feels like a criminal for her childhood sensuality; she loves sexual outsiders for the risk they take; she is confused about her sexuality, yearns to be good, is color-sensitive, loves the Mississippi and the Nile, has lived in Dallas and Berkeley, has long brown hair, and has toyed with being a writer—all qualities shared with Anne. She is told by a master that she was born a masochist and would be one the rest of her life, similar to Anne being told by a priest that she would be a Catholic the rest of her life. Unlike Anne, however, Lisa shows no sense of humor, drives cars, and has not read Kerouac.

Elliott makes up for that by reading Kerouac to her. He, too, lives in Berkeley, has masochistic fantasies that have a religious element, and loves violence and New Orleans. He shares with Lisa (and Anne) a feeling of being "more physically there" than most people, and he is Anne's ideal masculine figure, influenced by the initial fleshing out of Prince Laurent. "Elliott is the supreme male voice for me," said Anne.

Elliott expresses many of Anne's frustrations. He has lived among Berkeley liberals and recognizes their discussions as empty chatter, just as Anne felt about the people around her. "Some people think serious conversation is a game," said Anne. "I don't feel that way about my ideas. Berkeley liberals think that talking about Nicaragua is doing something. They have a system that makes them feel good and liberal and alive if they're just talking. The liberal of the moment is the one who screams the loudest at the table while he drinks his expensive wine with his expensive meal, bought with Daddy's money. They were incredibly fascist. They didn't believe in anyone's rights, ultimately. They just believed in a slate of things they were for as opposed to what someone else was for. They had betrayed every liberal value I had ever held sacred. I felt very much enraged."

She allowed Elliott and Lisa to grow, writing in an almost unconscious manner the way she had written her first book, *Interview With the Vampire*. "The whole feeling was the same," she claimed. "It was just an outpouring of something that was subconsciously profound enough to be tremendously exciting for me. There was no attempt to control it except in the tight way of controlling for authenticity."

She used Lisa, who had felt engulfed by the masochistic role and had become a dominatrix, to understand Elliott's need to be a slave. To her he was completely exposed and could really be himself. Anne used Elliott to show Lisa how dominance was a sacrifice of part of herself similar to the surrender of masochism. Both of them were true types in that both were complex blends rather than simplistic stereotypes. They are less divided by their differences than were Louis and Lestat, and they often trade positions as if they are interchangeable.

"That's a very revealing book," said Stan. "I think that's Anne's androgynous quality in there—the male and female in her."

Anne wrote the book in four weeks, then sent it to Bill Whitehead, sure that if he liked the *Beauty* books, he would surely love this one. To her surprise he was not enthused and suggested a major revision. She was shocked. She was not about to change it, especially for someone who had not understood it. She had expected better from Bill.

"This happens to me over and over again," said Anne. "Editors who like one book won't like the next, but I wanted to do a variety of different books."

Lynn Nesbit sent the manuscript to John Dodds, now at Arbor House, who got very excited about it and made an offer of $35,000 for the hardcover rights. It was not a terrific sum in light of her earlier contracts, but it was generous for erotica written under a pseudonym which would not alert fans to the publication by Anne Rice of a new book. Nevertheless, Anne was pleased. It was her favorite book to date, and John seemed to appreciate it.

"Reading Anne," he told an interviewer, "is like getting in the saddle of a horse and saying, 'We're on our way.' "

6

Lisa begins the story as a woman frustrated at feeling torn between her family's values and her own sexual ventures. She has just been on vacation to see them, going home to a place that is alien now that she is living out her secret life. However, returning to the womb-like atmosphere of the Club is not as welcome as it once had been.

Her ambivalence has a universal quality. She dislikes having to hide what she does for fear of being rejected, and yet the secrets that she hides reveal her true self at its deepest level. The intimacy of the family should be the place where we can be ourselves, yet can often be the arena of greatest rejection. Lisa's dilemma is about her sexual desires, but her sense of being an outsider is applicable to almost any secret desire that makes a person feel unacceptable. Although her parents are Catholic, their need to control their children has wider applications.

After six years running the Club, the exotic environment has become routine for Lisa. She needs more than just a vacation. She has been fantasizing lately about a slave who would stand out as a challenge. She spots Elliott's picture and senses "the kind of man who submits to no one and nothing in the real world." Lisa singles him out for herself.

Elliott is a photojournalist who has narrowly escaped being shot in El Salvador. He has signed up to test the limits of his courage, but he wants to avoid women. His greatest fear is to be dominated by someone weaker than himself. When he realizes that Lisa has chosen him, he resists.

Their first encounter is electric and both are equally confused by it. They switch gender roles, Lisa taking the aggressive stance and Elliott submitting and experiencing a woman's perspective. Lisa fears she may not be master enough for him. "What a laugh it would be," she says, "if he knew how scared I was of disappointing him."

Her anxiety captures the paradoxical quality of sadomasochism that makes Anne's depiction of it more than mere descriptions of sexual activity. She exposes the psychology involved and gives a philosophical quality to the concept of dominance. On the surface the master is in control, yet at another level the punishments are being evaluated by the slave, who loves best the master who best punishes. That puts the slave in control as the master seeks to please. "The masochists really could take over," said Anne. "The dominatrix is a creation of male masochism. These men want someone to order them around." Lisa is a dominatrix motivated by masochism. "She allowed herself," said Anne, "to be a dominatrix to serve others." So freedom and surrender issue from the same source, and one person can move in and out of apparently opposite states.

The symbiosis of control and surrender, need and satisfaction, on the part of both participants sets up an ironical twist similar to that in the *Beauty* books, in which symbols of power are transformed into symbols of vulnerability, and vice versa. Both slave and master want something they fear: the process of perfection toward the end of attaining greater resources of power. The slave submits to pain and humiliation in order to feel things more acutely, while the master submits to the slave's perceptions in order to measure up. Each participant is a master and a slave simultaneously. They represent the self struggling within itself to exercise dominance and surrender as a *recovery* of self—the return to pre-gender wholeness.

Elliott begins to forget his original purpose in his growing desire to love and be loved by Lisa. He wants to be an equal in a relationship. Now it is Lisa's turn to resist.

Her true face has been hidden behind the masks of ritual, the way the slaves hide their identities in nakedness. Only by being loved for herself can she come out from behind the mask, but the idea frightens her. She fears intimacy and its companion, rejection. "Each of us has within him," Anne writes, "a dark chamber where real desires flower; and the horror of it is that they never see the light of another's understanding." Such a step entails both persons exercising their freedom and both taking responsibility together.

Lisa is not ready. As her mentor points out, "That's where you are, stuck between that dismal, repressive Catholic morality you came from and the vision of a world in which no form of love is a sin." For Anne this conflict touched close to home as she sought to resist habits drummed into her before she possessed the self-awareness to choose. Her new ideals of freeing sex and pleasure of superstition battled with subliminal pressures to be "good" according to how she had been taught.

Club officials begin to worry about Lisa's strange behavior, but she rebuffs them. Nevertheless, she *is* acting strangely. Against her own rules she searches Elliott's personal effects, then sends for him and tells him to get dressed. With clothing on, he seems different and it frightens her. She wants him to join her on a trip to New Orleans. He believes he is obeying his "mistress" when he agrees.

The theme of nakedness and clothing plays off a transposed ambiguity similar to that set up by the concept of the Club, where pleasure and pain form a continuum of heaven and hell. Ordinarily, nakedness is understood as a symbol of exposure, but it also works as a disguise, which Lisa realizes only when she examines Elliott's clothing. He can hide his identity in the anonymity of his nakedness, while Lisa's own clothing works like a series of masks. She changes frequently from black to white, an activity that echoes her confused state of mind. Is she bad or good, devil or angel?

Elliott realizes that Lisa is no longer in control. They are becoming equals in a spontaneous relationship, although to his chagrin, Lisa seems to be in it for the sex and fun, while he seeks from her a commitment—another gender switch. They explore New Orleans together, doing "normal" things like dancing, walking through the city, and discussing their personal lives.

The emptiness of liberal chatter, Elliott reveals, had sent him to El Salvador and Nicaragua, which had given him a clearer perspective on his desire for violence: "I was riding these experiences, like they were the roller coaster . . . I was glad the war and the violence and the suffering were there so that I could experience them. . . . I was a pretty destructive guy." His discussion with Lisa is the philosophical heart of the novel, expressing Anne's most urgent concerns about sexuality.

"There is nothing obscene," Elliott claims, comparing ritualized violence with real violence, "about two people in a bedroom trying to find in sadomasochistic sex the symbolic solution to their sexual aggressions. . . . The origins of that play are deep, deep inside us in a tangle of chemical and cerebral components that defy competent analysis. . . . So are the origins of the human impulse to make war . . . the same mystery, the same urgency, the same complexity that underlies sexual aggression."

Lisa agrees but is surprised by his belief that places like the Club could mean the world's salvation.

"There isn't any other way to save the world now," he insists, "except to create arenas to work out symbolically the urges that we've taken literally in the past. . . . Sex isn't going to go away and neither are the destructive urges wound up in it."

Lisa finds in Elliott's ideas a mirror to her own thoughts, although she still has trouble accepting the "goodness" of what she does. She has little time to muse over it, however, as she realizes that Club officials are looking for them.

She meets with them, then asks Elliott to return to the Club. He is shocked and angered at her apparent dismissal, but he obeys. Lisa goes to Bourbon Street, one of Anne's favorite places, to find solace among the transsexuals. She views them as sexual outsiders like herself who put themselves on the line to be labeled as freaks in order to live out their fantasies.

In desperation she contacts a sexual mentor, Martin, and he assures her that she is in love—a love that was "born in the very fulcrum of your secret life." In other words, resolving the conflict within herself over her incompatible sexuality and religious upbringing shows her that she need no longer fear being herself. Martin reminds her that "very few of us anymore get through life without a dramatic bid for freedom. That dramatic bid is the hallmark of our times. But most of us never really reach our goal. We get stuck halfway between the morass of myth and morality we left behind and the utopia on which we've set our sights." Lisa has scored some victories in this respect, even if she is ambivalent. She has "gone through the door" to the Island of the Innermost Self, represented by the Club—a wonderful, frightening, paradoxical place, and she has tapped the primitive elements within to free herself to stop playing the games.

Lisa returns to the Club to get Elliott, but he has gone to Berkeley. She follows him in the traditional move a woman might make, showing her acceptance of the side of herself that she has denied, and tells him she loves him. He wants her to marry him, admitting that he, too, is frightened, but that marriage is not necessarily a trap or a return to the safe, the normal, or the secure. They have been dominated by love and they should submit. Lisa agrees to marry him.

"I think what *Exit to Eden* is saying," Anne claimed, "is that to really love, you have to outgrow those games. That was a little offensive to some of the S&M community. They thought Elliott and Lisa would have worked out their scenarios, not abandoned them. But that's just the way the book went."

The gender turnabouts utilized by Anne and mirrored in the slave–master reversals result in an exchange of power. People who try to see through the eyes of either sex, as Stan and Anne had done within their marriage, gain understanding and bring to a relationship more flexibility and tolerance than if they restrict themselves to traditional sexual roles. Breaking down social taboos may expose people to frightening inner desires, but it also promotes self-growth, self-knowledge, and the ability to develop intimacy with another person. Self-expansion then creates psychological intensity that in turn yields the possibility for spiritual experience without the hindrance of social propriety.

Recognizing the urge within oneself toward dominance or submission, or both, Anne indicated, develops the "secret self" as a counterbalance to the masks worn by the "normal self." Surrender is not a *loss* of self but a renewal. If only men are allowed to be dominant, aggressive, assertive, confident, and direct, women will lose the opportunity to know and employ that side of themselves. Concomitantly, men will lose touch with the part of themselves that seeks to surrender and be dominated in love. They will feel only guilt for such desires, while women will be made to feel alienated for their urge to command and initiate. The role reversals represented in Elliott and Lisa broaden their characters, and reveal the power and intimacy available to the person who can achieve similar flexibility. True exposure, Anne felt, was knowing a person who shares our most savage desires. Elliott and Lisa, honest and aware, are able to achieve a deeper, non-gender-based affection and trust.

Through Elliott and Lisa, who are "real people" instead of fantasy creatures, Anne had taken tentative steps back into New Orleans, covering a small area of her childhood landscape. It was a psychological event that had opened her up to allowing Elliott and Lisa to take her toward self-renewal, just as they moved toward it in the book. She gave a speech later about it at the Clift Hotel in San Francisco, when there was no longer mystery surrounding her pseudonym. It was one of the few speeches she has made: "I talked about this landscape and how my work was divided—that for me, romance was the reality because I'd walked through the Garden District and had lived on the edge of it. I said that in my Rampling novels, I had at last been able to bring my characters to walk through there."

Parallel to this, *Exit to Eden* is also, significantly, the first book in which Anne took on the first-person perspective as a female. Her feminine side seemed to have taken on the darker aspects of New Orleans—a womb as well as a place of suppression and annihilation, associated with her mother's death. It had also, however, been a place of peace, joy, and clarity, and still invited her to return. New Orleans was a symbol of an inner chaos, but also of wholeness, a single source housing opposites.

Although Anne developed Lisa, she did not like her as much as she liked Elliott, indicating that it was a passage in her life and in her writing for which she was not entirely ready. "I've always felt very uncomfortable in the role of being a woman," she said. "I feel like my intellect is masculine, or androgynous." Lisa was for her too humorless. "I don't know why the tendency is to make the female characters dark. It could be that the feminine side of me is suffering and the masculine side is always the one with the sense of humor. The women invariably turn out like Claudia or Marianna or Marie." She had opened up a side of herself which thus far in her writing had been weighted toward the negative, and she did not want to become trapped in an identity that might subtract something from her.

Ironically, others observed about her a femininity that seemed profound yet unconscious. Her sister-in-law Cynthia had noticed it while living with them in Oakland.

"When I think of Anne," she said, "I see her as an extremely sensual woman. She has this depth of something that is very womanly. She would come out of the bathroom at night in a long flannel nightgown after washing her hair, and she'd smell like cream rinse and perfume. She was always fresh. I remember the warmth and the fragrance coming from her. She has a great depth of feeling and love. She's not passive or nurturing, but she's sexy because she's bright and powerful and self-driven."

With a masculine intellect housed in a female body, writing *Exit to Eden* was an important step in developing an inner unity and wholeness. Anne would eventually develop female characters with more strength and dimension, but it would require resolving further conflict within herself and finding a way to penetrate the feminine darkness into a new source of light. What she had accomplished with the Rampling voice would spill over into her next book as Anne Rice.

7

John Dodds suggested a few changes. Some of the early pages were too similar to the Roquelaure novels, where Elliott's voice sounded like the prince. There were scenes Anne felt were hot, like putting Elliott through a few more games, but John found them too outrageous, so she took them out. She also tightened up the plot to make the book move.

Exit to Eden was published in June 1985, when Anne was forty-three, and dedicated to Stan. Dell paid $150,000 for the paperback rights, targetting it toward housewives and expecting sales to be high.

It did not do well in hardcover and was essentially ignored or dismissed by most mainstream reviewers, although the review in the *San Francisco Chronicle* was positive and a scattering of other reviewers recognized its quality as erotic writing. *Publisher's Weekly* called it "pornography, plain and simple," which frustrated Anne. She thought such an evaluation was superficial and missed the point.

Then the mail came in. Anne heard from women who insisted it did nothing for them, as if she had failed. She also heard from women who responded exactly as she'd hoped. "If people have no acquaintance with sadomasochism, they're not going to understand it," she insisted, "but to people who share the fantasy, it is very luscious."

She realized what a bold act it had been to have published the novel in the first place. "I think getting *Exit to Eden* published in hardcover is one of the most daring things that happened. Sometimes I'll open it and read some of the scenes and say, 'We published that between hardcover in America! What an accomplishment!' "

She planned other Rampling novels, one featuring Elliott Slater, but she also wanted to do more with submissive female characters, discussing the difficulties for them of pursuing their fantasies. She hoped to develop the profile of sexual outcasts because she felt that S&M was still evolving and she wanted to be part of that evolution. Such projects, however, had to wait. She still had one more Roquelaure book to write and she was getting requests to contribute to magazines, something she was eager to do.

8

In February 1984, *Redbook* published a short story that Anne wrote for them called "The Master of Rampling Gate."

The story opens inauspiciously with the date of Spring 1888, the year of Jack the Ripper, although no mention is made of the notorious killer. It begins in London, told in the first person by a young woman, Julie, who wants to be a writer. Her family owns a four-hundred-year-old, uninhabited mansion in the village of Rampling, but her father seems to be afraid of some sinister creature that has driven him away to London. One day Julie sees a pale man with black eyes who embodies for her the ideal of masculine beauty. The man glances out the window of a train, and her father cries out, "Unspeakable horror!" The scene demonstrates Anne's talent for creating impressionable images from fleeting glimpses and dark hints.

After their father's death, Julie and her brother, Richard, visit Rampling and see the house "rising like a fairy-tale castle out of its own dark wood." It was their father's wish that it be destroyed. After several serene days in which Julie and Richard question their father's decree, Julie awakens one night to find the man from the train in the house. The next night, she confronts him. He reveals that he is a vampire. She experiences the sensation of floating, of knowing an ancient secret. "To see as a god sees," she thinks, quoting Keats.

The vampire gives her visions of the two of them together and of how he became a vampire. She watches as time devours a village and expresses the sentiment that Anne calls up over and over: "And it seemed the horror beyond all horrors that no one should know anymore of those who had lived and died in that small and insignificant village." The mark of disloyalty to a loved one is to forget them when they are gone. It haunted Anne in its implications—that she was not immortal and would one day die and be forgotten. Julie's horror is the instinctive revulsion Anne felt over how human indifference can diminish a life.

Julie becomes a vampire and talks Richard into giving Rampling Gate to her. She and her vampire companion go to London to hunt for victims, presumably to set off the outrage and fear that took the form of a maniac called Red Jack. The story was a simple, romantic vampire tale, carried by the wealth of detail and voluptuous writing for which Anne was becoming famous, but without the complexity of imagery and metaphor. The published version cut out a few plot twists that Anne had developed, and she soon made a decision to avoid writing short stories. The extended form of the novel seemed more fitting to her imagination.

Anne also wrote an article for *Vogue* magazine about David Bowie, whom she considered the ideal androgynous man. As a rock singer he embodied gender renunciation, romance, and freedom. He provided the springboard for Anne's ideas on the subject.

The power of androgyny, she felt, hearkened back to childhood, "a wise innocence that embraces the power of both sexes and uses it effortlessly." Children represented a wealth of energy and creative potential. It was the wave of the future, she claimed, with both men and women becoming more androgynous to meet the complex demands of everyday life.

Anne was enthusiastic about writing the article, but she discovered that nonfiction was more difficult than it had seemed. "I didn't know how frustrating it would be or how long it would take and how unrewarding it would be. I could have written a Roquelaure book in the time it took me to write that article."

9

About this time, a writer named John Preston was preparing to fly out to San Francisco. He mentioned the trip to Bill Whitehead, and Bill encouraged him to meet the author of the Roquelaure books. They had something in common since John, a gay activist and founder of the first gay community center in the country, wrote S&M pornography and gay adventure novels. Bill gave John Anne's number, and John called and arranged to meet her.

Anne suggested they meet at a small café near her home. When John arrived, she had already eaten, as if she had no intention of staying long. He had no idea how uncomfortable it was for her to meet new people. He sat down and started to talk.

"We just clicked," John said. Anne had read one of his books, and she had brought with her the galleys for *Exit to Eden* to show him. As they talked, they found they had more in common than just the desire to be taken seriously as writers of pornography: they both loved talking about computers, they both retained emotional ties to the regions where they had grown up (Maine for John), and they both had suffered from painful rejection by writing friends who begrudged them their success. They had also both had alcoholic parents. They understood each other: the forced imaginary life of escape, the need for attention, the ambivalent feelings. Anne loved the fact that John was familiar with the leather-bar scene. She had once thought about placing an ad to meet such a person, intrigued with the kind of life they led, but had never had the courage to do it. Now the opportunity was at hand.

"Establishing a friendship with me," John said, "was a big deal for her. There were lots of trust issues." They corresponded for two years before Anne went to phone calls. For Anne it became an important friendship; to her mind, aside from Stan, John was her best friend. He provided for her an outlet to express herself without reservation, yet living in Maine, he did not demand much from her, or invade her space. "Everything is passionate with her," John said. "I think it's one of the reasons she has few friends, because to be involved with her is to be *involved!* It's remarkable the amount of energy and imagination she has. It comes out in a very organic way in her life. Of all the people I know, she is the person most swept up by art in all its forms. She has nearly sexual experiences with music and visual art."

He was impressed with the Roquelaure series. "They are utterly and historically unique," he commented. "There are elements of the sexual which she's written about which simply were never seen before, or at least hadn't been seen and written about outside of gay male culture. She simply turned the feminist perception of what a cock was upside down, from the symbol of power to a deep, deep vulnerability."

Since John knew many people in the publishing world, Anne saw him as a witness to her career. "I can talk figures with her," he said, "and not be jealous. We can discuss the importance of various covers, and I can gossip relentlessly about the people she deals with in Hollywood and New York." John eventually received from Anne the chapters she had cut from *Exit to Eden,* and he has included them in a collection of pornography for gay men, called *Flesh and the Word.*

10

There was one more *Beauty* book on the burner. Anne had left her characters on a ship, headed for the unknown punishments of a foreign people, and now she returned to them to finish the story. Called *Beauty's Release,* it took Beauty and her friends to yet a deeper level in the psychology of S&M relationships, breaking down the isolation of mind from body and providing transcendence through humiliation and reverence for bodily sensations.

The captives are ornamented and forced toward greater self-discipline and restraint. Laurent explains his attraction to the punishments: "I would feel all that they could make me feel, completely." Although their "grooms" view them as animals, Lexius, the sultan's steward, is aware of their powers of reason. He explains that they are to make themselves stand out to the sultan so that *he* can win recognition. "We are lost, you see, unless they notice us." The females are taken to the sultan's wives while the males are thoroughly cleansed and examined.

Beauty discovers that the sultan's wives have been genitally mutilated so that they cannot derive physical pleasure. One woman named

Inanna shows Beauty her scars. Beauty is revolted. "And her hatred of the Sultan and all the Lords of the palace became something dark and full of anguish." She works on Inanna until she finds a way to give her an orgasm. The scene is a symbolic expression of Anne's own rage against anyone who truncates a woman's pleasure. Beauty's activity with Inanna is Anne's offering of her pornography as a means of freeing women who have too long been told what they should feel. Beauty succeeds in the way that Anne hopes her own work will succeed.

Laurent discerns that Lexius desires to be a slave and becomes a secret master to him. "It was merely the completion of a cycle," says Laurent, although he has mixed feelings, expressing the psychological complexity of the experience: "I felt terrified and sad; and half in love with him; and I hated him because he had shown all this to me; and I felt triumphant—all at the same time." Laurent most strongly embodies the androgynous balance of any of the characters Anne has yet created. "It has never been one or the other for me," he says. "In my dreams I liked both parts of the drama. . . . Moving back and forth only sharpens the whole experience somewhat." Yet the power simultaneously energizes and intimidates him.

Tristan and Laurent are forced to compete against each other. It seems unfair to Laurent, as if he and Tristan are two halves of a person—one dominant, the other submissive—but only one of them can win. The scene shows Anne's feelings about social divisions that prohibit balance. Later the roles are joined when Laurent uses Lexius to teach Tristan to be a master. "Now I have two slaves . . . or you have two masters, Lexius. It's difficult to judge the situation one way or the other."

In the most revealing moment, Tristan describes for Laurent his feeling of delight in the sultan's palace.

> The atmosphere is charged with a different sense of things . . . I am a part of a finer, more sacrosanct order. . . . We are merely part of an immense world in which our suffering is offered up to our Lord and his Court. . . . It is as if I have advanced to another stage of understanding. . . . In this place we are *nothing* but our bodies, *nothing* but our capacity for evinced feeling. . . . Since we are nothing here we are all connected to each other. In the village and the castle, we were divided by shame. . . . Here we are joined in the indifference of the Master.

The sultan is no mere master but a true sovereign. It is as if Tristan believes he is now in the presence of God. The appearance that they were becoming less by being taken to the sultan has resulted in the awareness that they are really becoming more, a religiously flavored concept.

Lexius warns them that they will be strapped to the Punishment

Cross for the night, in case the sultan (God) wanders into the garden. They must be seen as true penitents. Laurent fears the cross: "I suppose that's why I love it." He expresses the coupling of love and fear of the true mystic who comes before the presence of the most divine and frightening of beings.

In this third novel Anne took her pornography to the heights of spirituality, but then had no further sense of direction. "I kind of got locked in with the sultan's palace," she said. "I think it had really run its course. I was sick of trysting by that time." She had taken a purely physical situation, deepened it psychologically, and then made it spiritual by exploring the rhythms of the body linked with strong emotion. Perhaps for her, *striving* for perfection was more interesting than *arriving.* Or perhaps, like Laurent, she feared what the presence of the sultan might mean. She decided that the village offered more opportunity for variety, so she rescues her characters out of the palace. Beauty is clothed and told that her parents want her to return home. She rebels at having her freedom snatched away. Laurent and Tristan are sent to the stables and sentenced to be ponies—the lowest form of degradation in the village. They are secretly pleased. "I felt," says Laurent, "as I always did at the core of punishment: the coming of a tranquility, a quiet place in the very center of frenzy, in which I could surrender all the parts of my being."

At home, Beauty refuses all suitors, then tries one out as a slave, but "was too jealous of the suffering she inflicted, too eager for subjugation." She yearns for Laurent, who would understand what she desires, but he is having a great time pulling carts. It was the character of Laurent that kept the book alive for Anne. "He was my hero—he was Elliott and Lestat. He saved the book for me." Still, all good things must end.

Laurent's father dies and he returns to his castle. Having been exposed to the extremes of vulnerability, he is ready to take charge. "Maybe it would always be so with me. The moments in which my soul yielded, in which everything formed a complete pattern, were moments when I was in command." He hears that Beauty is available and goes and commands her to be his wife and secret slave. Their reunion frightens and thrills them—like Elliott and Lisa: the idea of the "worst and most hopeless captivity of all." They go to live happily ever after, completing the story, as in *Exit to Eden,* with a joining of the dominant and submissive, the male and female.

"To me," Anne said, "those books were a great and wonderful experience to write." She adopted a label for the style in which she was now writing, flowing but more controlled, calling it *the essential dream.*

"That was a term I had for accessing the subconscious and just moving along as if it were a dream, but I use the word *essential* because of the writing process—it wasn't just a stream of consciousness, just going in and having it all. It was taking the intensity of the dream and trusting it, but making it tighter. It's edited, but at the same time it's only a dream." As with her characters, surrendering yielded new perspectives: "When I write, I trust that the meaning will be there."

11

Anne's trinity of voices seemed to her to mark divisions in what she was writing. As A. N. Roquelaure, she had given expression to her masochistic fantasies, and as Anne Rampling, she had escaped the darkness of characters drawn by Rice. However, she still had novels to write as Anne Rice, and they would be affected by her growth in her other voices. Despite her diverse directions, the work to date—including the historical novels—had been unified by her effort to balance aspects of her personality: the dominant/submissive, the masculine/feminine. She had burrowed into elusive psychological spaces by following her personal obsessions as a guide to what she would write next, and the progression revealed distinct patterns.

The protagonists Louis, Marcel, and Tonio were young men trapped or manipulated by circumstances. Beauty was a young woman similarly caught. Initially she was acted upon; things happen *to* her. Then Tristan emerged, loving his enslavement but acting to make it better for himself. Each of these characters since Louis showed increasingly clear signs that they could take charge, despite their circumstances. They could be heroes, expressed most strongly in Tonio. Strength of will emerged, but it was will that understood vulnerability, paralleled by a diminishing need for a teacher. Even the tone of the novels became more active, less contemplative.

Then, in *Exit to Eden,* Anne emerged in the first person as both Elliott and Lisa. She put her male and female sides on equal footing, allowing both to escape gender and to experience a mix of dominant and submissive qualities; they merged in the third Roquelaure book, which gave birth to the high-spirited Laurent. He taught the masochistic Tristan how to become as good at being a master as being a slave, and he wed the masochist Beauty to live "happily ever after." For Anne the freedom of using the pseudonyms produced in her, as the author, qualitative changes of perspective. Still, although she had developed female protagonists, she had returned to the male perspective and would do so again in the future. The female would emerge slowly.

Written during the same time period as *Exit to Eden* and taking the themes of that book to an extreme, the *Beauty* books helped Anne to work out some of her sexual alienation. She was not yet aware of it, but she had brought the Roquelaure voice to a cathartic completion. "I'm not really interested in that world anymore," she said years later. "It was there. It was something I really wanted to do. I wanted to create the books I couldn't find." Her characters evolved, as promised, into people of greater patience, wisdom, and self-control.

Anne thought about doing a more shocking Roquelaure novel but Bill Whitehead did not pick up on it. He did, however, get excited about another suggestion. She described for him a novel that she wanted to call "Catholic Girls." The girls were to be sexual maniacs who adopt an Italian priest named Santino and seduce him in the rectory until his faith in religious dogmas is utterly confounded. It was to be presented from Santino's point of view as a heterosexual romp, except for some activities among the girls. She wanted to explore a sophisticated religious mind when confronted with blatant sensuality, tracing Santino's evolution into becoming a slave. The book was her answer to *Candy,* but she never wrote it.

In New York, people were trying to figure out who the real author was behind the Roquelaure books. It seemed strange and even objectionable to some columnists that the books were being treated as if they had literary quality. The *Village Voice* hinted that it was Joyce Carol Oates, since she was a Dutton author. She denied it in print. Although there was some hype, it was not really that difficult to find out. Dutton kept the secret out of print, but Arbor House included the information in a press release and Anne herself told people who asked.

John Preston encouraged Anne to confess on a larger scale. He thought she was unrealistic to think she could tell just a few people. She was an outlaw, so she might as well go all the way.

She called her father and told him not to read them, then allowed the publicity to spread. No one seemed shocked or horrified, and it was not long before Anne was expressing her desire in print to become one of the most famous female pornographers in America. The books acquired an immediate cult following among S&M practitioners.

An anthropologist who read Anne's books and participated in an S&M group invited Anne to her apartment. "She graciously showed me her entire collection of whips and handcuffs," said Anne, "and told me all kinds of safety things. She also invited me to the groups." The invitation involved going with the group from dungeon to dungeon to see what innovative creations each member had done, but Anne balked. "I just couldn't do it," she admitted. "I didn't want to know them that well."

She was also invited to the S&M Janus society but never went. "I had no interest in getting involved." She found them to be too organization-oriented, like an S&M Tupperware party.

"I'm really a writer and that's it," she insisted. "I think meeting those people resulted in closing down the series with three books. I might have kept going if that had not happened."

One thing she requested was to meet a real dominatrix. She was willing to pay the hourly rate, whatever it took, just to talk to the woman. She was told she would have to take the hygiene class offered by the dominatrix, but she declined. "I wasn't interested in doing such a thing just to go meet her."

She did, however, attempt to order a pair of leather handcuffs to hang on her office wall, but ran into resistance from the woman taking her order. "She kept asking me what size, and I said it didn't matter, and she kept insisting that I give her a size, like she was making me admit to something personal. So I never got them because I refused to give her the size." Nevertheless, Anne did finally acquire an S&M memento. A fan sent her a red and black cat-o'-nine-tails, which she hung in her office.

While Anne was writing about sexual freedom, something was happening to threaten the potential effect of her books: AIDS. People in the Castro district were growing seriously ill and dying as a result of their sexual activities. Anne was immediately supportive of efforts to assist. She gave out her books to use as fund-raisers and decided not to write more pornography. The disease saddened her. Several years later, when John Preston learned he was HIV positive, Anne was instantly concerned, calling him whenever test results were due to find out how he was. "Anne's support for me," John said, "took our relationship to new levels." She wanted him to feel no compunction about using her name in the context of AIDS.

In interviews Anne was pressed repeatedly for the source of her fantasies: what went on behind bedroom doors? The questions annoyed her, but her good-natured response was that she wanted to retain some mystery.

"She's no more sadomasochistic than she's a vampire," said Stan. "But she has the capacity to empathize with and imagine a whole range of things that are so intense in her mind that they don't require the experience. No one could have that many experiences. She has to be making it up, and she is."

Her books were less about her sexual practices than about the psychology of a woman of trans-gender perspectives who was still "a divided self." Here was someone alternately shy and aggressive, vulnerable and assertive. She thought of her mind as masculine, yet heterosexual scenes described throughout her novels are clearly the fantasies of a woman. Like many artists, her imagination was a complex array of ideas, desires, and images. She had the courage and ability to articulate a wide range of them and to allow them to facilitate an evolution in her own perspective in the process. The divisions would merge as she plunged again and again into the subconscious.

For three years Anne had been on a sexual odyssey. It was time, finally, to get back to the vampires. She had broken off the sequel for a year because it had not come together in the way she envisioned. Now, however, she had momentum. She had found in the development of Elliott Slater and Laurent the perfect male voice for her protagonist, the vampire Lestat.

CHAPTER NINE

LESTAT

1

Lestat had been hovering, as if waiting for his chance, and now he came alive for Anne, giving her the physically charged experience that she needed to write a compelling story. She utilized the freedom of the Rampling voice to develop her new vampire antihero. "I think Elliott and Lestat are the same character," she said. "Like they're played by the same actor. When I got back to *The Vampire Lestat* I was loosened up to make him the intimate, warm-blooded man. Elliott was for me what Lestat was for his mother."

Lestat's mother had said to him, "You are the man in me," and Lestat quickly became the "man" in Anne, as Elliott had been. He had the physical appearance she desired for herself, his characteristics were motivated by repressed assertive impulses that she expressed best in fictional form, and she made him do things that she longed to do. She empowered him with erotic energy that coursed through her as she wrote. What Lestat says of his mother was true of Anne: "She spoke . . . of my being . . . the organ for her which women do not really have." He was a reflection of a new growth and independence, of a new edge to her sensuous imagination, with a fierce, mischievous rebelliousness.

"I've gone through several significant changes in the last ten years," Anne admitted. This new novel would reveal the differences. No longer under the paralysis of grief and regret, Anne looked back on Louis's passive introspection with a degree of scorn. "At the time I loved him," she admitted. "I don't now." Through Lestat's perspective, she described Louis as "the sum of his flaws," and was eager to get "into" Lestat.

In earlier novels her characters had been trapped by their own lack of knowledge and experience, but there would be none of that for Lestat, a man of action. Although Louis and Lestat share an intense desire for answers about their vampire identity, their approaches differ considerably. Lestat is a rule-breaker, an anti-god, a creature who wants to *affect* things. "What fascinates me," said Anne, "is the fact that he knows right from wrong and he still does what he has to do. He's determined to be good at being bad." Weary of novels about young people struggling to realize themselves and become something, Anne wanted to write about a person who already *was* something, with more humor, less darkness. She wanted to create "someone who had never had a teacher and never really bemoaned the lack of one," determined to express the freedom she felt within herself through a character of excessive emotion and audacity. Although the supernatural would become an increasingly attractive medium for her through which to tell a story, the dark themes of suffering, loss, and the suppression of sexuality did not weigh as heavily as they once had. Lestat and his spirit of adventure would remain a feature of Anne's imagination over the years, representing to her an image of her "male energy."

As she wrote, she looked at the world through Lestat's eyes. It was a favorite device, putting herself centrally into a character and bringing that character into her own reality. It was a way to tap a full range of resources. To create a good fantasy it is necessary to become fully involved in vivid detail to make the characters three-dimensional. Anne was putting Lestat into the twentieth century, and he presented greater flexibility than had her historical characters. He seemed almost physically present, provoking a wide range of decisions about how to form and present him. What would he want? How would he perceive this situation or that? Should she give him a more expensive car? Dress him extravagantly? If he donned a coat, it was the color she would have chosen for herself. Immersing herself with Lestat, Anne inevitably nourished him with subconscious influences, and he emerged, naturally, as a character who was in many ways like herself.

As a boy Lestat was a loner with a degree of feisty independence. About him, his mother observes, "You're such a fighter, my son. You never *accept*"—something Anne's mother might have said about her. Lestat had been fiercely enthralled with the priesthood, much like Anne's determination to be a nun, and his motivation was due in part to his attraction to the orderliness of the monastery compared to the chaotic conditions at home. He also "knew an intense happiness because someone for the first time in my life was trying to make me into a good person, one who could learn things." He fell in love with the notion of being good. He also developed an excessive sensitivity, laughing hysterically or given to bouts of crying, not unlike Anne's tendency to feel things deeply. And as she did, he loved his mother fiercely, but "mingled with my love was a powerful resentment of her"—something children feel when parents become unpredictable. Even so, Lestat was terrified of separation from her, as if they were "two parts of the same thing." Also, like Anne, he had nightmares about fire, and he struggled with the notion that he could not be good and still defy his family. And he loved the exotic sound of the violin.

One of the most powerful experiences of Lestat's life was his sudden encounter with the "dark moment" of mortal dread, a description of Anne's experience of smoking dope. While she had given this dread to other characters, for none was it more fully developed or more pervasive than for Lestat. Perhaps the strongest primal link between Anne and Lestat was this dread of ultimate meaninglessness that erodes substance into nothingness, a concept that still confused and frightened Anne. As Lestat's best friend, Nicki, observes, his goodness has not prepared him for the darkness and it hit him harder than it did most people. "You have a light in you that's almost blinding," Nicolas says.

Anne, too, seemed to be a victim at times of her urge toward goodness. She shared Lestat's philosophy: "I do not think I could go on if I did not believe in the possibility of goodness." Friends as far back as grade school had commented on her moral integrity, and one person even described this trait as a beacon. Her struggle to believe in goodness, despite renouncing the structure and guarantees of her faith and despite her bouts with suffering, can be attributed to her strong will and her need to believe in something to resist the void. Like Lestat, she was a fighter and in moments of crisis had taken hold of her life and pushed forth. The way Lestat sums up his existence echoes Anne: "Sheer will had shaped my experience more than any other human characteristic." Anne firmly believed in her will as the power to be free.

Another connection to Anne's inner life is Lestat's mother, Gabrielle. The physical model for her was Stan's sister Cynthia, but the prototype, Anne admitted, was Katherine. Certainly Gabrielle shares some of Katherine's characteristics: she "never said anything ordinary," "she read all the time," and she did not like to be called Mother, paying little attention to her socially dictated female duties. She also knew she was dying, although Anne was not aware that Katherine had predicted her own death. Gabrielle gives support when it is needed and she spots in

Lestat, just as Anne's mother had spotted in her, qualities that she cherishes. Nevertheless, there is more to Gabrielle than being an idealized projection of Katherine. She is developed during and after Anne's breakthrough with Lisa into a female point of view. Lestat says of women, "For the first time in history, perhaps, they were as strong and as interesting as men," and this observation may say as much about Anne as it does about contemporary culture. Gabrielle was destined to break the pattern of tragedy given to other mother figures in Anne's darker novels, and to provide for Anne another form of freedom.

2

Although Anne had shied away from being labeled a horror writer after her first novel, she had since read other writers in the genre that she admired, like Stephen King, Whitley Streiber, and Peter Straub. She especially liked in *The Hunger* the idea that the vampires could not die, although she had already hinted as much in *Interview* with Lestat's mysterious resurrection. "One of the things that's very painful for me to face," Anne admitted, "is that they influence me if I read them, but you can't be overscrupulous about this. Black-and-white movies influenced *Interview With the Vampire.*"

Unlike Streiber, she did not think aging vampires should wither but should instead grow stronger and more resilient. From a fleeting inspiration she strengthened an important part of her vampire mythos. What she gained from these writers, however, was the conviction that good writing could be done in the supernatural genre and that there was not necessarily any stigma attached. Fans, she felt, were astute and perceptive, allowing writers of fantasy the greatest amount of freedom with their visions that could still be philosophically compelling. "I don't think there's any moral, aesthetic, or psychological limit to supernatural fiction," she said. "We forget that *Hamlet* has a ghost and *Macbeth* has witches."

Her books, she believed, were essentially mainstream, asking strong questions about the human condition, and she rejected mainstream realism and middle-class values of conformity and mediocrity, which was guarded, she felt, and failed to take significant risks. "The only way to write anything great," she believed, "is to take the risk of making a fool of yourself." She was more comfortable now with the genre label than she had been in 1976, although it would continue to invite what she felt was misunderstanding from critics.

Anne was back at Knopf, with Vicky Wilson and a $100,000 advance—which indicated a careful but optimistic show of confidence in her resilience in the marketplace. It had been almost a decade since *In-*

terview With the Vampire had been published, and the much heralded movie had not yet been made. Anne was not sure anyone would even remember Lestat, let alone want to read another vampire story from her. Many things had changed in the culture. Was there still a spiritual thirst? Would anyone like Lestat as much as she did? She had heard from fans that they wanted a sequel, but would they accept Lestat as she now saw him?

Under the same name she had written two novels that had failed to keep readers, and then had gone off and published four books under different names. Using pseudonyms had satisfied her with the freedom of expression they had provided and with taking her back to undeveloped themes within her psyche, but the results of such a practice were mixed. People who liked her mainstream books who might also like the pornography might not know she had written them; yet there was always the possibility that fans who had discovered them had been alienated. To add to her dismay, the critics had been mixed on everything she had written, perhaps cutting her off further from her potential audience. Also the sexual revolution and the free spirit of the seventies had worn off, and censorship had reared its head. She had cause to be discouraged by the downward trend of her career and by changes in the book market. Perhaps Anne Rice had fallen out of favor with the reading public just as she was preparing to reenter the scene. She had no idea what to expect, or how to view her future. Yet she hoped that the way Lestat had caught her attention might also capture others.

3

Looking over *Interview,* Anne discovered a line that hindered what she had planned for *Lestat.* Louis had told the boy reporter that he had seen Lestat earlier that year, which made it tough, since Anne wanted Lestat to awaken after Louis's account had been published. She decided to fall back on the foibles of point of view. Louis had lied, it was that simple, just as Armand had done when he said two other vampires had been made with Lestat. "Their versions were different," said Anne, "because they were each serving their own needs. When my family gets together to tell stories, they're that different."

There was also the question of Lestat's character, seemingly quite different in the new novel. For Anne, however, Lestat was the same in both books, just seen from different perspectives. Louis was bitter and his version would be uncharitable. "He told the tale," Lestat explains, "as he believed it."

The novel opens as Lestat is awakened in 1985 by a rock band after decades of lying dormant in the ground. Originally, it had taken Anne two hundred fifty pages to bring Lestat into the twentieth century, but she had found that approach unmanageable and had abandoned it. Instead she woke him right up, and after a short period of adapting him to contemporary life, she made him a rock star—an image that still enthralled her. The rock-star angle, however, impeded the book's initial reception. According to a clerk at a New York bookstore, readers expressed dismay with the image. Louis, after all, had retained many of the trappings of the nineteenth-century vampire literature. It was not long, however, before Lestat's musical antics were accepted with enthusiasm, and his popularity surpassed Louis's.

To Anne, rock stars epitomized the romantic artist in their independence, willingness to be outrageous, and in their employment of surprise. "Rock stars are symbolic outsiders," she said on National Public Radio, "just as vampires are symbolic outsiders. You can imagine a vampire becoming a rock star with everyone just totally accepting it. They can get on the stage and do anything they want, and everyone would think it was just special effects." She explained in another interview that rock stars take on "the burden of all our irrational drives" and help us act them out. In the novel, she refers to them as "biblical angels," and notes that both actors and musicians are on the level of saints because they would not accept living a lie. They are images of beauty in the horror of meaninglessness, driving back nihilism by using art to make meaning. Rock stars play with illusion to turn ordinary props into magic. Like Lestat, they are "good at being bad." It was a natural move to make Lestat into a rock star.

So he jumps right into 1985. He rides a Harley, listens to Bach on a Sony Walkman, and dresses in current fashions—with a predilection for velvet. Watching videos, he discovers movies like *Apocalypse Now,* and his thoughts on the subject set up the theme for the rest of the novel.

Apocalypse Now is a contemporary reworking of Conrad's novel *Heart of Darkness,* and is set during the Vietnam War. The protagonist is sent after a renegade American named Kurtz who has set up a kingdom in the jungle based on his own inner emptiness, an indifferent and essentially violent philosophy. He thinks nothing of cutting off someone's head, and as a self-justified god to the natives, he is allowed free license to do it. The American soldiers are horrified at the lack of standards against which to judge his actions as evil.

"I felt that movie was exactly what I was trying to write about," said Anne, "that there's no easy accommodation of evil. Kurtz had found the Eastern way when he told the story of the little kids getting their arms chopped off. He said it was brilliant and beautiful. It's the Eastern solution. But we can't do that. The corruption of that war was the fact that we never really give evil its due. We're always struggling to clean it up and make it good. I think most evil comes from a lack of imagination and the inability to empathize with people, subjecting people to ideas. Almost anytime someone is killed for symbolic reasons, evil is done. I don't think the Eastern way is good, I think it's evil. They are really anti-life and into oppression and keeping millions of people quiet and suffering and believing it's just fine to have their heads chopped off by the emperor." We can't be a friend to horror, Anne felt.

"Horror and moral terror can never be exonerated," says Lestat. "They have no real value." The vampire *nature* is ruthlessly destructive and Lestat finds that he must deal somehow with the inevitable urge to kill night after night. He knows it is evil but he finds life too beautiful to give up. His blood thirst is tempered only by his ties to his former humanity. His attitudes about life are essentially Western attitudes. He wants to be good despite his dark nature. Thus, when he realizes that as literal evil, he has no place in the twentieth century (thanks to vampire fiction that makes his existence unreal), he feels he can still do good by portraying evil symbolically, in "art that repudiates evil . . . in the roaring chants of the rock stars who dramatize the battles against evil that each mortal fights within himself." Thus, he can ensure that humans do not make a friend of horror but keep it in its place, as something to be resisted.

"The challenge," said Anne, "of writing a vampire novel in the twentieth century is to write a novel that's fun about creatures of the night, yet to bring them into some sort of philosophical context that satisfies me. That's why Lestat has to face the fact that there's no place for him in the twentieth century. There's no way that evil can be enthroned in a good way except as a symbol of something to be wiped out. That's what he seeks to do as a rock star." To her chagrin, no reviewer seemed to understand what she was trying to do.

Lestat soon discovers Louis's confessions, published as *Interview With the Vampire*. He is shocked by what he views as blatant lies and contradictions, and decides to set the record straight by writing his autobiography.

4

His story begins in eighteenth-century, prerevolutionary France, where as a young man of twenty-one, the seventh son of an impoverished marquis, he sets out one day to hunt a pack of wolves on his father's land. It was the device Anne needed to get him right into action, to show his strength against impossible odds. He kills eight wolves in a fierce battle, then collapses at home. In the intimacy of his suffering, he learns that his mother—his only ally in the large family—is dying. He is forced to find inner strength, as Anne had done with her own mother's physical deterioration, to endure the shock.

Lestat befriends Nicolas, a merchant's son and masterly violinist. They create in their drunken discussions the "Golden Moment," in which they fantasize about going to Paris, as Anne and Ginny did in Texas about going where something was "happening." Finally they do it. Lestat becomes an actor in a small theater and Nicki plays the violin.

Through Nicolas, Anne recalls her childhood obsession with this exotic, human-sounding instrument. She feeds into the novel its history and hypnotic power. Lestat is often overcome by Nicki's playing, and it is partly due to his talent that Lestat is attracted to him. Nicolas was not a character Anne liked, although she allowed Lestat to love him. He was too much like Louis in his darkness and dependence, and his philosophy of life was a cynical Nietzschean idea: "As I see it," he said, "there's weakness and there's strength. And there is good art and bad art. And that is what I believe in."

As Lestat's acting fame spreads, he is snatched from his bed by a three-hundred-year-old vampire named Magnus, who passes the Dark Gift of vampirism on to him, then destroys himself. Lestat is suddenly transformed from a young man obsessed with moral goodness to a monster who kills to survive.

Magnus leaves behind an impenetrable tower and a room full of riches. Lestat distributes the wealth to friends and family through a lawyer, unable to tear himself so abruptly from his humanity. In a brief appearance at the theater, however, his powers frighten those he loves, and the implications of isolation are too great to bear. It is a metaphor similar to Lisa from *Exit to Eden* of Anne's feeling of being a monster to people from whom she most wanted acceptance. Lestat's despair is enlarged by her own need, fear, and anger.

Gabrielle comes to Paris to see her son before she dies. Lestat offers her immortality and she accepts. Not like Marianna was she, à la Hemingway, going to be killed off. In an erotically symbolic perversion of the Catholic ceremony of the last communion before death and salvation, Lestat bends to take her blood and replace it with his own.

> I leant forward and kissed the blood on her open lips. . . . My arms slipped around her light little form and I lifted her up and up. . . . And jetting up into the current came the thirst, not obliterating but heating every concept of her, until she was flesh and blood and mother and lover. . . . I drove my teeth into her, feeling her stiffen and gasp, and I felt my mouth grow wide to catch the hot flood when it came.

The mother figure who went mad in *The Feast of All Saints* and died a tragic alcoholic in *Cry to Heaven* was going to be saved and transformed, a moment of breakthrough.

"Gabrielle was a real turning point for me," Anne admitted. "I decided that the mother was not going to die again. She was going to escape. I was definitely thinking of my own mother and her death." To her thinking, Lestat demonstrated great maturity in offering the Dark Gift to his own mother. It meant he was treating her as an equal.

Her friend Andy Brumer was incredulous. "Isn't that kind of bonding," he asked, "paid for with a loss of the self?"

"When you have eternity," Anne replied, "you can work out anything, even an Oedipal complex."

Gabrielle's transformation worked on two levels for Anne. Gabrielle and Lestat are two sides of a single soul, as he describes it, just as Anne had felt about her mother. Not only did she save her mother symbolically, but also what her mother represented to her—her own female identity. She envies the male body, gravitates toward the masculine, and has not fully integrated her feminine side, but Gabrielle's development is a step in this direction. Making Gabrielle into a vampire was more intense for her than making Claudia one. "The writing is much, much closer to the character." The breakthrough was made possible by dealing with the feminine darkness in Lisa, and it would later issue in even stronger female characters as Anne grew more interested in exploring her feminine experience through her fiction.

Gabrielle, however, will not be defined by gender roles. She changes from burdensome female garb into men's clothing, because as a vampire taking on a gender-free form of sexuality, she neither wants nor needs symbols of vulnerability. She once said to Lestat, "You are the man in me," and she easily adopts a masculine appearance. Lestat finds her extremely seductive, strengthening bisexual tendencies in him hinted at with Nicolas. However, when Gabrielle tries to cut her hair, it grows back, and she realizes that she has little control over her gender-specific appearance. Unable to avoid social expectations altogether, she moves away from society. She recedes somewhat from the story and merges with an inner darkness represented in the earth and trees with which she becomes obsessed.

One night Lestat and Gabrielle are attacked by a band of vampires who have captured Nicolas. They encounter the leader, Armand, from *Interview With the Vampire*, and learn that these vampires use the dogmas of satanism to give their existence meaning. Lestat announces that he is the vampire for a new age—the new evil. He takes Nicolas and leaves with Gabrielle.

Nicolas demands that Lestat give him the Dark Gift. In an erotic scene that employed the sexual quality of Anne's imagination whenever she dealt with physical relations between men, Lestat succumbs. Soon, however, he regrets what he has done. Nicolas becomes sullen and Lestat realizes that the darkness of his soul will be magnified as a vampire.

"Lestat couldn't save him," Anne said. "His view was too dark. The idea was that when that character was made into a vampire, whatever that darkness was, it just erupted. So much of his life was based on rebelling against authoritarian principles and these crazy bourgeois delusions that he just didn't have strength. Once he had maximum possibility and maximum nihilism, he couldn't handle it. Lestat was always infinitely stronger than him and tried to protect him. He loved Nicolas, but Nicolas was doomed."

Four vampires from the coven claim that Armand is destroying them. Lestat gives them the theater, puts Nicolas in their care, and tells them to become actors. Thus is born the Theater of the Vampires.

Armand warns Lestat about the vampire's isolation and seeks intimacy with him, but he resists. Armand tells his story.

Although each of Anne's novels contains storytelling as part of the fictional frame, none up to that point develops the intricacies of stories within stories, called a boxed narrative, which give the impression of going deeper within. This she developed in *The Vampire Lestat.* Lestat is telling a story about Armand telling his story, which involves other immortals who will tell their stories.

Armand explains how he was made by a vampire named Marius, who possessed secrets, and how he was abducted by a coven of satanic vampires whose dark rituals had given him meaning through the passing centuries. Now that Lestat and Gabrielle have destroyed things, he wants to join them. They reject him and leave Paris.

This is the point at which the novel had bogged down for Anne for over a year. The chapter called "The Devil's Road" was rewritten more than any other section. "It was an utterly defeating chapter," she said. "It just drove me crazy."

Lestat searches the world over for Marius, believing he holds the key to primal truths about the vampire existence. In his determination he echoes Louis, who also sought other vampires for enlightenment. Although Anne had intended to develop a character who had no need of a teacher, Lestat's search reveals the presence of a strong appreciation for the perspective of the student seeking expansion. Lestat also seems to falter a bit in fulfilling Anne's impulse toward creating a man of action, as he sets out with the purpose of "sitting at the feet" of another. He is not as passive as Louis, but he is not altogether independent, either. Since Anne allowed her characters to emerge from within herself, her intentions were prone to being thwarted when her vision failed to parallel her psychological development.

Lestat hears about the French Revolution, the death of his brothers, and his father's escape to New Orleans. To capture his feeling for family, Anne broke the action to write a segment that she felt was vivid and compelling because it got close to Lestat's soul. "I dreamed a dream of family," says Lestat. "We were all embracing one another." In the dream Lestat saves his family by making them into vampires, granting them immortality and giving his blind father sight. It was a metaphor for what Anne wished she could do for her own family. The dream indicates that the vampires represent to her a family of likemindedness in which bonding is more intimate than in families in which there are fundamental differences—and thus blindness—among members. It was an ideal for which she strove, a dream from her own childhood.

Gabrielle parts from Lestat, impatient with his attachment to humans. They had become as incompatible as lovers, intense in their affection but divided in what obsessed them. Her disappearance from the story indicates that Anne is still more obsessed with her male side and not yet ready to deal with what Gabrielle offers. Lestat sinks into the earth, withering away, as if the loss of his mother demands a deep grief.

However, the male side is revived and expanded when Marius arrives. He is aware of Lestat's persistent search, and feeds him his magical blood. They go to Greece, where Marius shows Lestat "Those Who Must Be Kept." They are the vampire progenitors Enkil and Akasha, who sit as living statues, preserving the immortality of all vampires. Lestat is overwhelmed at the connectedness. He is a leaf on a vine, the way Anne thinks of family. Marius tells his story.

He had been a scholar in the Roman empire when he was kidnapped by a blond man named Mael, imprisoned in an ancient Celtic fortress and told that he was to become a god to ensure a successful harvest. The old god has met with calamity.

Anne drew on druidic legends described by Caesar. Druids sacrificed condemned criminals in a huge ceremony every five years to ensure the fertility of the crops. The more they killed, they believed, the greater the crop. The criminals were burned in colossal structures of wicker and grass to appease the god of vegetation. Anne had also researched Stonehenge in England but forgot to include it.

Marius discovers that the old god, a vampire, is burned to a blackened husk yet is still alive. The description came from Anne's childhood exposure to a shriveled mummy on display, still vivid to her. The god urges Marius to discover why vampires everywhere have suffered his fate. He makes Marius a vampire. Marius then escapes the druids and travels to Egypt, the land that symbolizes timelessness to Anne, and meets other vampires. It is within Marius's story that Anne weaves her vampire mythology.

He is told by an elder about Enkil and Akasha, who had been placed in the sun to end the vampire race. "Cut them and you cut us. Burn them and you burn us." The great age of the royal couple had preserved them but the exposure had damaged or destroyed their "children." Marius is appalled at the loss of control over his fate. "I could not live with the thought that I could die at any moment on account of some alchemy I could neither control nor understand."

He learns that vampirism began as an accident when a demon who wanted a body entered the bodies of the king and queen, and that vampires should not exist. This theme of accident provides for the vampires the same tenuous sense of existence as it had for the free people of color in Anne's second novel, and would give Anne supernatural license in novels to come. Marius ponders what to do and Akasha rises to beg his help. He takes her and Enkil away.

Marius was like Lestat in his desire to preserve the values of Western culture. Through art he had kept in touch with his ties to humanity. As such he is also a voice for Anne. Like her, he fears chaos and its concomitant meaninglessness, taking solace in the notion of a continuous and stable awareness:

> The idea was simply that there was somebody who knew everything, somebody who had seen everything. I did not mean by this that a Supreme Being existed, but rather that there was on earth a continual intelligence, a continual awareness. And I thought of it in practical terms that excited me and soothed me simultaneously. There was an awareness somewhere of all things I had seen on my travels . . . someone or something knew what the peasants said to each other in their little farmhouse outside Athens right before the Spartans brought down the walls. . . . I was comforted by the notion that nothing spiritual was lost to us. That there was this continuous knowing.

In previous work Anne had revealed her horror at the thought that whole towns could prosper, then disappear, forgotten. It meant such a thing could happen to her, that the lack of someone being aware of her, as a witness to her, robbed her of substance. "I've always found the idea of the continuous awareness to be very seductive," she said. "It was an idea I had as a child that I took for granted. I saw it as a sense of God and Christ at the final judgment, that there would be a moment when everyone gathered together and the truth of every moment would be told. There's a great promise of recognition; of order and justice and harmony; of all the suffering and pain and confusion being redeemed in a moment of great illumination and understanding. I'm afraid there really is no continuous awareness; there is no one who knows everything that's happened."

She had felt this horror deeply, at an early age, with the loss of a caring mother. Marius gives vivid expression to her desire to believe that things would not be so easily forgotten and that caring upheld the universe. As an immortal who takes great interest in the human community, he stands as the consciousness that Anne longs to believe could exist. Yet there would be other characters in novels not yet written who would surpass even Marius in age, caring, and wisdom, as if with each book she is reaching for an image that would adequately replace the god she has rejected.

Anne also got much more involved in developing the powers of her vampires. She emphasized their increasing strength, preserved by confidence. She gave them powers of mimicry and immunity to everything save sun and fire. Armand was no longer the "oldest vampire." Anne had, since *Interview,* read through mythological accounts like Frazier's *The Golden Bough* and books by Joseph Campbell. She was astonished at the similarities between vampires and the ancient vegetation gods like Osiris. She had already seen them as dark angels, and the imagery of a god appealed to her. Enamored of Egypt, the mythos was a natural for her, and it made sense that vampires could be much older. The thought excited her. Such a vampire could be powerful, indeed.

As the legend goes, Osiris and his sister, Isis (who later became his wife), were born of a union between the deities of earth and sky. He became the king of Egypt and turned the people away from cannibalism toward the consumption of grains. A jealous brother, Typhon (Set), tricked him into putting himself in a coffin into which he was sealed, then threw him into the Nile. Isis eventually recovered the body, but Typhon found it and cut it into fourteen pieces, scattering it. She found all of the parts but his genitals (the part, Lestat wisely noted, that was not needed by a vampire) and wrapped him in linen wrappings—the first mummy. He was resurrected as the King of the Dead and the Lord of the Underworld. Egyptians saw in him the power of eternal life beyond the grave (a typical appeal of the vampire). They set up funeral rituals to reenact the divine mystery of death and resurrection, believing that the whole body was resurrected. Their fertility ceremonies likewise imitated the legends. Only human sacrifice prevented the failure of the crop. Using a red-haired man for his resemblance to ripened corn, they slew him on the harvest field and, mourning his death, burned him and scattered the ashes to ensure a good harvest.

"I was swept up," said Anne, "with how the Osirian myth seemed to have to do with vampires. I mean, Osiris becoming the King of the Night and coming back from the dead. And how they would sacrifice blood at the festivals. They would kill all red-haired people and sprinkle their blood all over the fields. Things like that just sort of knocked me out. Once I got on the trail of the vampire being a sort of an image of a vegetation god, I took it back to the earliest vegetation god that we know of, which is Osiris. It was a natural progression."

In earlier novels Anne had looked to themes from the classics, like Dickens and Tolstoy, but with the second of the Vampire Chronicles she sought out the legends which articulated in a more primitive and immediate fashion feelings and intuitions arising from the human condition. She had not abandoned her desire to write her novels as serious literature, but was moving in a direction that she felt might give a satisfactory account of vampires and still retain thematic threads that could make her writing transcend genre. It was but a short step from Osiris to Dionysus, the god with whom Lestat later identifies, capturing a philosophical theme more subtle, sophisticated, and complex than she had tried with Louis.

The Greek god Dionysus, half human as the vampires are, was also a vegetation god. His was a transient glory. He represented the dynamic exhilaration of frenzy and excess, and he appealed to the Greek love of mystery and savagery. He was the expression of a universe filled with a ceaseless and spontaneous flow of energy as he bound together the forces of violence and excitement. He was violently destroyed and cut into pieces, but returned from the dead. He quickly became the most popular god, worshiped in wild dancing. The celebrations of his life and death cycles were passionate, centering on the manner in which Dionysus transmuted from one form of energy to another. They tore sacrificial animals apart with their teeth, as if stripping from the god his animal nature. Freed of the animal and also paradoxically represented by the animal, Dionysus eats—via the worshipers filled with his spirit—his own flesh. The legend foreshadows the Eucharist—the Transubstantiation and the consumption of the flesh and blood of a resurrected god.

Dionysus was used by the philosopher Nietzsche as a model for human nature. Nietzsche called for a renunciation of Christianity and a recognition of the body, restrained by enlightened self-discipline. He envisioned a set of values based on instinct, which he called the will to power. The new values were put into place by an *overman*—a being of moral courage who could face the total collapse of meaning required to replace it and could shoulder the burdensome responsibility of creating new standards of right and wrong. This cycle of rising and falling, of old meaning replaced by new, would be repeated endlessly in an eternal recurrence, mirroring continuous resurrections throughout history. Nietzsche had a far-ranging and profound impact on Western literature, and although Anne was barely familiar with his ideas, the parallels expressed through Lestat tie her firmly into this literary tradition.

Dionysus was also, not coincidentally, the patron god of the theater (and thus of rock stars), which plays off illusion similar to the hypnotic vampire. Dionysus is an innocent and a god. The actors are like saints. Lestat, the vampire, puts it all together: "This god Osiris was the god of wine to the Egyptians, the one later called Dionysus by the Greeks. And Dionysus was the 'dark god' of the theater. . . . And now we had the theater full of vampires in Paris. Oh, it was too rich."

Lestat can be thus construed as a noble innocent following his animal nature. He moves through the world as Dionysus, transcending traditional religious notations of good and evil, utilizing the physical immediacy and excesses of rock music, and making himself vulnerable to be torn limb from limb as he prepares later in the novel to go on stage as a rock star. He is a Nietzschean overman, creating a new meaning for a new age of good and evil, and he has the courage to see it through. He does this by showing the emptiness of the old moral concepts. It is an ingenious device to deliver through metaphor Anne's feeling of betrayal by a church that clings to empty dogma.

Another device deepens the metaphor into paradox. Lestat is not seeking to make clear the nature of good and evil as Louis was. Instead he plays with the concepts for his own purposes. Gabrielle remarks about Lestat that he had once held so tenaciously to the Christian concept of goodness that it seems contradictory that he can so readily be a vampire. But it is the very ambiguity in the word *good* that makes the paradox of Dionysus work. Lestat slides from Gabrielle's moral concept of good into the notion of good as excellence of skill. "I was a good marksman when I was a young man," Lestat tells her, "a good actor on the stage. And now I am a good vampire. So much for our understanding of the word *good.*" The advent of a new vampire for a new age relies on this kind of slipperiness. The concepts of good and evil must be malleable, meaning different things in different contexts but seemingly linked by a thread of continuity. "You must know," Lestat tells Armand, "that the forms of goodness change with the ages, that there are saints for all times under heaven . . . and so it is with evil, obviously. It changes its form." Lestat foreshadows this malleability early: "My eyes are gray but they absorb the colors blue or violet easily from surfaces around them."

To strengthen the feeling of molten standards, the novel is filled with opposites that become interchangeable. Absolutes slide into relativism, similar to but more substantial and fluid than those that had been employed in *Interview With the Vampire:* vampires as gods, death as life; the coffin as the womb; solidity as fragility; female as male; fiends as actors pretending to be fiends. Lestat's logic defies standard formulas because it ignores accepted canons of logic. Unlike Louis, however, he is not confused or betrayed by this loss of absolutes, but sees the power of nihilism and chaos as a means of transition from one set of values into another. He believes he is setting people free to subtract from their lives a false god and to find good within themselves. Further imagery emphasizes this connection.

When Lestat was dismembered by Claudia in the first novel, he claims that his thoughts had traveled to "the dimly envisioned groves of mythical lands where the old Dionysian god of the wood had felt again and again his flesh torn, his blood spilled. If there was not meaning, at least there was the luster of the congruence, the stunning repetition of the *same old theme.* And the god dies. And the god arises. But this time no one is redeemed.'' He says later, ''So let us take on a new meaning.''

5

It would be a long time, however, before Lestat sees the implications of what Marius has revealed. Marius warns Lestat about the burden of immortality and of mistakes that can be made. The next night when Marius leaves, Lestat enters the chamber where the royal couple sit. He plays a violin in an audacious attempt to make them move and wakes Akasha, who offers her blood. He drinks, but Enkil intervenes and almost crushes his skull before Marius arrives to drive him back. Lestat is forced to leave.

He goes to New Orleans to find his father and spots the desperate young man, Louis, from *Interview With the Vampire.* Ignoring Marius's advice, he creates companions for himself in Louis and Claudia. When they later rise against him, Akasha's blood saves him. Louis's abandonment and a betrayal from Armand drains him of his will to continue. He experiences the real horror of immortality, according to Anne's conception of it—that he can be tortured past all endurance with emotional and physical pain, yet be unable to escape through death, like a living soul trapped in its own grave. In 1929 he goes into the ground for the second time.

Anne's inclusion of this section was questioned by her publishers. ''They didn't want me to put in the chapter called ''Interview With the Vampire,'' she said. ''I said no, it had to be in there. He has to deal with his version of what happened.''

The novel draws to an end as Lestat reiterates how he came out in 1985, formed the rock group, and used the music and his autobiography to make the vampire legends known around the world—breaking more rules. Ironically, his ''new meaning'' is really the old meaning presented in a unique way: the vampire is evil and should be destroyed. ''Drive out the vampires and the devils,'' he sings, ''with the gods you no longer adore.'' He seeks to bring out the wrath of the vampire hordes, to start a war. He is getting set to take them on when Louis approaches him.

The reunion is highly charged, like a long anticipated meeting between lovers, especially when Lestat first spots Louis walking toward him in the darkness. Parallels in the gay experience arise as they embrace as equals. It exemplifies Anne's ability to create with excessive language and measured atmosphere erotic tension with no explicit mention of sex. They settle their differences and renew the bond as Lestat gets ready for his concert debut.

To prepare to write about Lestat's rock concert, Anne booked seats for herself at the Cow Palace. She sat through a group that traveled with Iron Maiden, and on another occasion she saw the BeeGees. The experience of watching the lights go down and the Bic lighters illuminate the darkness all around provided details about the feel of that arena, the roaring of the crowds, and the general setup of a rock concert. She based Lestat's voice on the clear voice of Jim Morrison, playing repeatedly for herself his recording of "L.A. Woman." "I wanted that engine-heating-up noise," she said. "That's the voice Lestat would have."

Louis goes with Lestat to the Cow Palace. The scene is set for a wild Dionysian frenzy. "Now I knew," Lestat says in retrospect, "all that had been left out of the pages I had read about rock singers—this mad marriage of the primitive and the scientific, this religious frenzy. We were in the ancient grove all right. We were all with the gods."

He sings about the twentieth century's form of evil, circling back to his remarks about *Apocalypse Now:* "All your Demons are visible/All your Demons are material/Call them Pain/Call them Hunger/Call them War/ Mythic evil you don't need anymore." With Nietzsche he urges his audience to give up the superstitions of old religions. There is a new innocence available through the absence of the need for illusion: "a love of and respect for what is right before your eyes."

When the concert is over, enraged vampires close in, although they burst inexplicably into flame. Lestat thinks Marius must be near. To his great delight, Gabrielle shows up for another emotional reunion. She takes Louis and Lestat to Carmel Valley.

Lestat calls to Marius. He receives a broken message of danger and realizes that Akasha has risen. But it is dawn and he must sleep. As he loses consciousness, he feels a cold hand.

6

It was a cliff-hanger ending, but there was no way to wrap up the story quickly. Anne had already written one thousand pages, twice as much as she had with *Interview,* and there was more to tell. She broke off with the promise, written on the last page, that "the Vampire Chronicles will continue."

Delivering the manuscript, she braced herself for editorial suggestions. She was not altogether happy with what she had sent.

"I think *Lestat* is a very badly structured book," she admitted. "What makes it work for me is the language and what happens. It takes too long to get him to Paris. The book doesn't really begin until he gets there. I just got caught up in that other world. I thought it was necessary. I kept trying to compress it. I was horrified that it took this many pages before he got on the road to Paris. I never could beat that problem. It wasn't tightly done."

To Anne, *Lestat* was something of a failure. "I never was satisfied with descriptions of the village and his life there," she said, "or of his life in Paris before he became a vampire. Or even of Magnus and the tower."

What had hurt the structuring of the novel, she thought, was the length of time it had taken to write it, spread across several years. Anne felt she wrote better when she wrote fast. "The part where Marius wakes up Lestat until the end took eleven days to write," she said. "It was three hundred pages, and then I revised it in another four or five days. That's why it all hangs together. The worst sections of the book are the ones that took years."

She also viewed the ending as flawed, and when fans eventually expressed their disappointment at the lack of closure, Anne thought they were right to feel outraged.

Nevertheless, she believed she had created a good read. A teacher in college had once said about a short story she had written that it was a failure but more interesting than most successes. "That's the way I feel about *Lestat*. I think it's a very interesting failure, and it's more valuable than many successes—I hope. I'm proud of the book. What makes it succeed is his personality and his character."

Anne felt she was taking a risk. She had been beaten down by the lack of reception of her historical novels to the point where her confidence had been shaken. *Interview With the Vampire* had done well and was still in print with a large cult following and impressive financial rewards, but would readers respond to another book like that? Like other writers with one major success, Anne wondered at times if she'd had hers. She had almost a year to wait to find out.

7

In January 1985, Tommy Tune asked Anne to write the script for a Broadway musical called *Desert Song*. Having read *Interview With the Vampire* and being impressed enough to consider adapting it to the stage, he felt that Anne could really tell a story and he wanted a plot with pieces that kept people guessing. Anne agreed to discuss it with him. They met in New York several times and got very excited about the project. The idea was to take the existing music by Sigmund Romberg and write a fresh plot. Anne liked Tommy Tune, although she was vaguely uncomfortable with the star quality surrounding him. While in New York, she spent time backstage at *My One and Only*. Waiting in

Tommy Tune's dressing room gave her the detail she needed for the character Ollie Boon in the next novel she was planning—a story that would recapture something from *Katherine and Jean* yet with a new sophistication.

Anne put aside her other projects to spend several months on the libretto. "I wrote a conventional story with a conventional plot," she said. She sent it off to New York, but it was received with less enthusiasm than she had hoped.

"It didn't work out," she said. "He decided not to do it and he was probably right. To be the director of a musical like that, you have to believe in it totally. He didn't."

The piece had not taken long to write, so she shrugged off the rejection. "I remember when the letter came," she said. "I thought, 'Am I going to have a big emotional reaction to this?' Then I thought, 'No.' " She had actually been nervous about the idea of going to New York to do the work required. "I never did see how it was going to come together for me. I'm not a collaborative writer. I don't bend well. I think it was probably better that it folded at that point than later." It was with some relief that she called her friend John Preston and told him the project had been canceled.

John visited her that summer in San Francisco when he was at the American Booksellers Association convention. They sat together in her kitchen talking about his activities. Anne proposed that they write a book together. *Exit to Eden* was already out. *Beauty's Release* was imminent, and *The Vampire Lestat* was scheduled for publication later that year. She was feeling a bit blocked and was unsure what the market could bear. She was not yet ready to dive back into her vampire world.

After finishing *Lestat,* she had created a few new supernatural characters to put into the sequel and had toyed with them in the computer. She'd thought about having a spirit named Lasher come to Armand, but then he'd become involved with a family of witches and the characters had seemed to invite her away from vampires. She had decided to write a separate novel about them that she called *The Witching Hour,* but was not ready to launch into it. For that she'd need to return to New Orleans for an extended stay. She could not adequately describe the textures of the city, she felt, without being there. So she turned to John with an idea.

John responded to her suggestion. They would write a book as a set of letters back and forth between a brother and sister. "I was to write one set of letters in the correspondence," John explained, "and she the other. The brother had just come out of the monastery and was going to explore the sexual world. Unbeknownst to him, his sister was a high-class madam. She was to instruct him on sexual adventure and he was to report back about his experiences, on the level of the eroticism of *Exit to Eden."* They would goad each other into productivity with "dueling word processors," Anne excitedly said. Could they really do it? How would it work to compose a book through letters? Could she maintain the integrity of her writing? She encouraged John to find out what his contacts back at the convention would think of such a project.

John told Anne that the idea had been received with great enthusiasm. "I walked onto the floor of the convention and started to mention that Anne and I were thinking of a collaboration. They *flocked* to me. People were talking hard–soft deals and the whole bonanza." When he went home to Maine, he sat down to compose a few chapters, writing letters about learning how to buy a sexual identity. He sent them to Anne.

She withdrew apologetically. She just was not much of a collaborator, she said. The situation was too confusing for her, and she did not want to get blocked on another idea that was already engaging her attention.

John was disappointed but not surprised. He understood how she felt about absolute control over her work.

8

The movie of *Interview With the Vampire* had not yet been made. Paramount was dragging its feet. "It languished there," said Anne. She had made suggestions for the development of a script in 1977, which had gone nowhere. Someone had suggested to Anne that the problem had to do with a story that centered on two men and a female child caught up in an erotic relationship. She had tried to rewrite the story, staying true to the plot but making Claudia older; however, she found that it did not really work. "What happens to the material," she said, "is that it gets dirty. You think you're saving it from something that's like child molestation and it gets prurient. When she's a child, the scenes have a luminescent symbolism–they mean something about procreation and eternity. When she's twelve, it's just groping."

Anne had heard rumors that the project had been thrown into a deal with John Travolta, but was told nothing concrete. It had gone on the back burner as a low priority for several years while Paramount made a new rendition of *Dracula* with Frank Langella. In the eighties, however, interest picked up again.

The original contract had included a clause that stated that if the producers had not begun principal photography within ten years, the rights reverted back to Anne. She would have to pay them $150,000 to sell the rights again, but they could lose it. The script was given to the television division at NBC, commissioned from Bill Bast and Paul Husen, writers for "The Colbys." The two writers set about creating a bible for a television movie. Now decisions had to be made about who should play the parts.

At the same time, *The Vampire Lestat,* not yet released, was creating interest in Hollywood. Producer Julia Phillips, who had worked on *The Sting* and *Close Encounters of the Third Kind,* wanted it. She had read *Interview With the Vampire* with great interest and had already envisioned what it could be like as a film. She approached Paramount about the rights, but they would not give her a reasonable price. Anne liked Julia and they developed a close relationship.

While Anne waited to see if Paramount would beat the January deadline, seventy-five thousand copies of *The Vampire Lestat* hit the bookstores in October 1985 and showed up on *The New York Times* bestseller list within two weeks. It remained on the list for seven weeks, and Anne was on her way to a thirteen-city promotional tour.

9

It was her first shot at a major hardcover book tour. She had never liked the idea of being under scrutiny and was concerned with how she looked and what people would think of her at press parties. She lost weight and changed her style of dress to blazers, white blouses, and gray or khaki skirts that Stan helped her to select. "It was a very comfortable uniform for me," she said.

Still, she was nervous. To Stan and John Preston, she worried about upcoming events and what people would think of her. Her anxiety levels ran high, fueled by her intense energy, yet when she finally made her appearance, she was collected and professional, working the room with charm and grace as if she were born to it. Even those working closest with her were unable to see how the effort exhausted her. Afterward, she continued to wonder about the impressions she left behind.

"Some authors don't care what they say," said Pam Henstell, who helped Anne promote the book. "Anne is very careful. She's suspicious of a lot of motivations behind questions. She reads a great deal into what's said to her in conversation. She dwells on the dark things."

Much as she loved the idea of the attention paid to her and its function in furthering her fame, she was horrified by the experience of it. It further developed the gap between her private persona, who shyly wanted to go about invisibly in the world, and her public persona, who desired—even expected—the trappings of recognition. When she was involved, she was in control, but when she thought about what fame demanded of her, she was dominated by it and vulnerable to it.

Still, she loved her fans and was amazed and gratified by the long lines of people waiting to have her sign her books—not just the Vampire Chronicles but her other novels as well. Michael Riley went with her to a signing in San Francisco because she thought there would be "dead periods" when they could talk. "The place was packed the entire three hours!" he exclaimed. "People told her that her books had changed their lives forever." They seemed to come from all walks of life, from teenagers to scholars. Professional couples came together, and some people dressed up as vampires or wore Egyptian jewelry. Many fans gave Anne gifts. One group in Chicago told Anne they were vampires, but they seemed to her like wholesome kids. Another group of adolescents claimed they were waiting for Lestat to come and save them, as if he were a hero. They were convinced that he would be good to them. She was glad that her work had not been connected with satanic groups. She had captured the popular imagination with well-drawn characters and resonating mythology rather than with a figure generally thought of as evil. People wanted Lestat to walk out of the pages and be real. Some fans cried when they discovered he did not exist, and Anne realized she had achieved another goal: to affect her readers as Dickens had.

Many people also commented on how they were caught up with the voluptuous language and erotic imagery. Lestat's sexual appeal had gone beyond Louis's. He was a vampire for the eighties, with his materialistic tastes and his emphasis on special effects and video-music. Wild and carefree, making even his mother a vampire, he exhibited a vitality that caught audiences by surprise and gained an impressively large and loyal following. Lestat also proved to be popular among gay men.

"The passages about initiation," John Preston explained, "and the concepts of being separate from society—perhaps even above it, but always estranged by it—fit most gay men's self-images. Many gay men find the descriptions about becoming a vampire to be parallel to coming out, especially involving the welcome seduction by a being who holds the secret to the future. Gay men also relate to the voluptuousness of the descriptions and the heavy sensuality. Also, Anne has never turned away from gay society—something very important to a group which perceives itself as stigmatized. There's also the veracity of her point of view. Her take on how it feels to be in a gay relationship is very strong and accurate. It reads . . . *right* to a gay man."

With the new novel's success, Anne was back in the limelight of the critics. Once again there was little consensus. In *Vogue,* Mary Cantwell was unenthused. She found the prose "hot and humid," and thought the book dizzying. In contrast, Eric Johnson reviewed it in *Library Journal* as "a rich and unforgettable tale of dazzling scenes and vivid personalities. This extraordinary book outclasses most contemporary horror fiction and is a novel to be savored." Yet *People Weekly*'s Ralph Novak disagreed. "If these fiends don't get you by biting you in the neck," he insisted, "they bore you to death with prattle about the 'Dark Gift'. . . . Reading this novel is like playing a slot machine; you keep giving it one more page, and you never get a payoff." The *San Francisco Chronicle* ran two reviews side by side, one faintly praising it but the other panning *Lestat* as one of the worst books ever written.

Anne waited to hear the verdict from *The New York Times Book Review*. Reviewer Nina Auerbach had a mixed reaction. "Anne Rice," she said, "brings a fresh and powerful imagination to the staples of vampire lore; she makes well-worn coffins and crucifixes tell new tales that compose a chillingly original myth." She felt the book was more ambitious than the first one, but also a bit sillier at times and "chokes on its own excesses." Nevertheless, "it is a brilliant work, funny, wild and disturbing, with characters that are clearly alive for the reader."

Some critics spotted the literary appeal of the vampires as metaphors, others did not, although Anne had attempted to show how these characters had a vantage point of human existence that could have an impact on how readers think of themselves and society. Her heroes face inner hurdles in the struggle between good and evil, and emerge with moral integrity to provide an expanded vision for the human race. Using mythical themes, Anne had pursued her own passion for clarity on human existence.

At times in the novel she shows a combination of amusement and scorn over the human capacity for self-deception and even self-destruction: "And this lesson about mortal peace of mind I never forgot. Even if a ghost is ripping a house to pieces . . . mortals will accept almost any 'natural explanation' offered, no matter how absurd, rather than the obvious supernatural one, for what is going on." The transparency of religious concepts is expressed by Gabrielle: "Satanic is merely the name they give to the behavior of those who would disrupt the orderly way in which men want to live." Marius is even more disillusioned: "Very few beings really seek knowledge in this world. . . . On the contrary, they try to wring from the unknown the answers they have already shaped in their own minds—justifications, confirmations, forms of consolation without which they can't go on." He hints that without gods, mankind will crumble. "The mind of each man is a Savage Garden . . . in which all manner of creatures rise and fall." Lestat, too, is aware of a dark side:

> Maybe I was not the exotic outcast I imagined, but merely the dim magnification of every human soul. . . . We dream of that long ago time when we sat upon our mother's knee and each kiss was the perfect consummation of desire. What can we do but reach for the embrace that must now contain both heaven and hell: our doom again and again and again.

Still, there is optimism, the capacity for self-transcendence that can push a culture in positive directions. Lestat notices the modern day sinless, secular morality, "where the value of human life has only increased." If there were no religion, no one would ever again be tortured or killed in the name of it. Marius, who has seen the centuries pass, acknowledges the brighter horizon on the human landscape: "But maybe something more wonderful will take place: the world will truly move forward, past all gods and goddesses, past all devils and angels." Without illusions to cling to, there may be hope. This is Anne's vision for the human race, a secular humanism that involves inevitable moral progress. It is not necessarily a new idea, but the vampire story was a unique medium, especially since the ideas made the characters themselves more complex than the stereotype allowed.

Few critics mentioned these themes or noticed how she had woven mythology into her plot. "It's amazing the degree to which the theme of *Lestat* did not get across to reviewers," Anne said. "People wrote flippant things like 'Apparently the twentieth century is something only a vampire could love.' They ignored things Lestat was trying to say. People who don't read speculative fiction don't understand that it's often philosophical and that readers are responsive to style, atmosphere, and to the poetry and metaphor. That's just not known by the straight reviewing press, so when they pick up a novel in which all the characters are vampires, they expect it to be trash."

Nevertheless, she started to gain attention on college campuses, receiving calls from students who told her they were writing papers on her books. She was buoyed up by her fans.

10

Paramount was still trying to make their deadline with the movie. They called and asked Anne what actors she would like to see in the roles of Louis and Lestat. She named one person and they said they would be unable to get him by the deadline. Would she consider extending it? She said she might. She was not sure she really wanted it on television. Julia Phillips urged her to turn down the extension. Then a friend in Los Angeles sent Anne a copy of the script. She was stunned at the changes.

What she remembered about it was that the boy reporter was a woman and Louis was a millionaire who drank from a blood bank he owned. There was no moral dilemma for him to struggle with. Armand was a woman and Claudia was a girl of eighteen, still incongruently dependent on Louis and Lestat. She was rescued by Lestat and he took Louis into the 1920s to locate her. She committed suicide by riding a gondola into the sunlight.

"They had removed everything I had done which was original," Anne moaned, "and replaced it with a stock device. For example, Lestat was killed by a stake through the heart. It had been reduced to an uninteresting love story. The immortals cared only about their girlfriends and boyfriends. It was slick and smooth and eviscerated."

She was also upset with the blood bank idea. "I was furious at that imagery, with people dying of AIDS."

She refused to extend the deadline. Nevertheless, the producers went ahead, trying to beat it. They planned for Richard Chamberlain to play Louis, but were unable to shoot the principal photography in time. The rights came back to Anne.

Julia Phillips and Michael Levy had already purchased *The Vampire Lestat* for CBS Theatricals. When CBS moved away from theatricals, the option for both novels was picked up by Taft Barish with the idea of making *Interview* into a Broadway musical. Julia Phillips consulted Sting about writing it. Eventually Taft gave up the option, and Lorimar purchased the rights along with the third vampire novel after Anne wrote a fifty-page synopsis of what she had in mind. She was hired to write the bible for the project, with an emphasis on the second and third books, but her work was delayed by a writers' strike.

Anne was distressed and joked that the project was cursed. She noticed that other vampire movies seemed suspiciously familiar, as if her ideas were being cannibalized. Finally she was able to write the bible. "In an effort to save the story from *Interview* and to save Claudia," she said, "I suggested we make Louis a woman. It works. It's all the same passivity, the same philosophical ideas, the same inability to fight Lestat's domination. It's fine for Louis to be a woman because he is a woman—he's really me."

With Cher or Meryl Streep in mind, she set about creating a transvestite, trans-gender female, whose husband and daughter had died on the way to Louisiana from the Islands. Since women could not inherit plantations, the character steps on shore in her husband's clothes and challenges anyone to say she's not a man. Everyone knows she's a woman and she gets into brawls. "She was a good swordsman," said Anne, "and a good gunfighter, and she kept her plantation, which everybody wanted, by fighting people off. So it was an interesting story. And there were very famous transvestites in that era. It was a common motif."

Lestat sees her resemblance to Gabrielle, and he falls under her spell.

"When he makes her a vampire," said Anne, "and when he presents Claudia to her, he's appealing to this maternal instinct that she'd never really wanted to deal with, since she's lost her daughter. Moments like that have enormous strength."

Anne was pleased with the story, and so were the people at Lorimar. They sent her flowers and prepared to turn her bible into a script. Anne had been impressed with Ridley Scott, who had directed *Blade Runner*. She wanted him for the vampire movies. "He's far and away the greatest director to do it," she said. She also had spotted the perfect man to be Lestat: Dutch actor Rutger Hauer. She'd seen him in *Blade Runner* and was instantly struck by how he embodied her character. Timothy Dalton appealed to her as a candidate for Louis, with his darkly handsome looks.

Then there was talk again of Broadway. "Elton John wanted to make a musical based on this," said Anne, "and he wouldn't proceed until he knew I was willing." She and Julia Phillips met with him and lyricist Bernie Taupin, and Anne went to one of his concerts. "When he came backstage all glittering with adoration," she said, "I grabbed him and hugged him." She gave them the green light on their ideas, but Lorimar owned the stage rights, so the project was put on hold. Then Lorimar was bought by Warner, delaying it yet again. David Geffen got involved and decided that Anne's bible leaned too heavily on Lestat's story and the Egyptian mythology, while he preferred the story from *Interview*.

Anne was also hearing from shocked readers who loved Louis to leave him just as he was. She tried to convince the producers not to use her script, and as it turned out, they had already decided to seek another writer. Julia Phillips fought to keep her attached to the project but no agreement could be reached. The experience frustrated Anne and she washed her hands of it. "They couldn't pay me enough to write a script now."

At the same time she had pitched her vampire novels to Lorimar, she and Julia Phillips had met with Howard Rosenman to toss around another idea, called "The Voice." Anne had agreed to write the treatment and the three of them had become partners. Intended as a musical, "The Voice" utilized the theme of immortality in a Faustian manner, covering a span of three centuries. Anne had kept the literary rights in case she decided to write the book.

Around that time, Anne invited her sister Karen to move in. Karen set about typing novels that their sister Alice was writing by hand, checked by their father for technical errors. It seemed that the whole family was involved in literary pursuits, including eight-year-old Christopher. Influenced by disaster movies, he wrote a story about the burning of the Golden Gate Bridge. Stan was busy as chairperson of the creative writing department at the university.

In the meantime, Anne was at work on another book. She had put the vampire story aside, despite the demand for a sequel, because she felt the urge to pursue another Rampling novel.

CHAPTER TEN

LIBERATION

1

Anne proposed to Vicky Wilson a book about a painter named Jeremy who falls in love with a young girl and is destroyed by it. He paints her in the nude but never shows the paintings, for her sake. When he meets her years later, she tells him he should have shown them.

It was an attempt to rescue ideas she had worked on before that had never come through in novels already published. She was not aware when she proposed the plot that she was embarking on a book that would be a psychological breakthrough as significant as *Exit to Eden*.

The new novel, dedicated by Anne to herself, hearkened back to *Nicholas and Jean, Katherine and Jean,* and *Triana Walker*. An older man is sexually attracted to a beautiful adolescent, and the adolescent moves easily into the relationship, having no qualms about sex—even eager for it. The man acts as a protector, while simultaneously experiencing guilt over the illicit affair. He is torn between secret desires that most fully express his inner self—embodied in the adolescent—and his awareness of how those desires make him a social pariah. There is a doomed beauty about the two of them.

After eight novels Anne was still grappling with the impact on a person, vampire or otherwise, of nurturance. Having had a mother whose ideals demanded rich and involved mothering that could guarantee superior children, Anne had been influenced to view the parental bond as an intellectual and spiritual placenta. She had been cheated when Katherine had fallen short of that ideal, then died, and Anne had yearned all the more to become educated and sophisticated. That her own child had died when there had been so much promise deepened the sense of children truncated in their development. Anne's obsession with nurturing shows up in the way her characters search for, then bond with mentors, and how the mentors influence innocent, malleable souls primarily in a sexual direction—the most strongly repressed aspect of Anne's personality. She wanted more from this relationship than she had gained in life, and thus the nurturing process in her novels gradually fulfills its idealistic promise. This time, however, she added a twist.

The adolescent, matured by early development and the confusions of adult society, would now be the teacher. This development indicates Anne's own reversal from a person seeking someone who can help her to learn into someone taking charge of her life. With the success of her eighth book on the heels of brashly publishing pornography, and free of excessive drinking, she was more in control than she had ever been. *Belinda* would be a statement of the inner power that Armand had urged Louis to discover and tap and that Lestat had utilized.

Although the adolescent character still resists social forces that turn a sexually aware child into a virtual criminal, it is the way her struggle parallels the artist's bid for freedom that makes this novel go further than previous books. Both forms of erotic self-expression are equally taboo in the public eye. Although Anne had meant to work on a sexual theme, it also worked on her, drawing her into both characters and helping her to confront inner truths. It would become Anne's clearest and strongest expression yet of a personal bid for freedom.

Anne used a poem of Stan's to open the novel. Called "Excess Is Ease," it prompts the reader to concentrate on what is at hand. "It is an argument," Stan explained, "for the solace of the immediate, which is referred to as excess because it's the excess of being right *there* when you are where you are or who you are." It involved the idea of the uselessness of running blindly from pain toward a future that, for all one knew, might hold something even worse. The best thing is to burn cleanly, right now, like a star. "Don't let dread make you afraid, so that you'll be less tomorrow, and then even less the next day." The only solace is what is at hand.

It was the first time Anne had ever used his work. "I felt the poem was perfect," she said. "That book *[Belinda]* really was the first one that I felt was about art and life even more immediately than *Cry to Heaven,* about being liberated through art and sex." Stan was calling for an all-out immersion into the immediate, and Anne was ready to unravel that message in narrative fiction.

She used real settings, like a hotel suite in which she had stayed, restaurants she knew, the Castro Theater, and John Dodds's Belvedere house. Jeremy's house is modeled on Anne's in the Castro, although she added an attic for his studio. It is filled with Victorian dollhouses and the dolls from Anne's own burgeoning collection. "That was such a liberation for me," she said, "to be able to use what was around me instead of eighteenth-century Paris." Like her protagonist, Jeremy, she was moving away from dream images to the hard surfaces of reality.

2

The novel begins as Beat-influenced, forty-four-year-old children's book artist Jeremy Walker spots blond, voluptuous, sixteen-year-old Belinda in a bookstore. She seems imaginary to him, though, prophetically, she was "more real perhaps than I ever was." Her blond hair and blue eyes are like a ray of sunshine in his otherwise dark and shadowed life—what Lestat was intended to be for Louis.

"The blond and the blue had a great significance to me," said Anne. "They meant the sun and the summer skies of the Mediterranean."

As the novel opens, Jeremy is signing a thousand copies of his latest best-seller, one of his many books about little girls named Charlotte or Bettina or Angelica. Anne was a collector of illustrated children's books and had researched the careers of several best-selling children's authors. Confirmed in her directions, she went ahead with her development of Walker.

Jeremy muses over the long lines, thinking about how he both loves and hates the exposure. Anne, true to her style, had "gotten into the skin" of her protagonist. She, too, was around forty-four and felt similar ambivalence. "This is an ego-booster all right," Jeremy says. "Every book signing is. But it's also purgatory. . . . I took all these people home with me in my head . . . I loved them. But to meet them face to face was always excruciating. Rather read the letters that came from New York in two packets every week, rather tap out the answers carefully in solitude."

There are other similarities between Anne and Jeremy. Obsessed with painting little girls, Jeremy's description of his artistic development reads as if Anne utilized her own background to fill in his character: "I was able to draw what I saw when I was eight years old. By sixteen I could do a good oil portrait of a friend in an afternoon. . . . I believe in the eloquence of the accurately rendered image. . . . And in my case weirdness is inevitable."

What he says about his method describes Anne's method of writing: "Representing something exactly as it looks—that is automatic with me. . . . I work best when I work fast, on every conceivable level. If I stop to think . . . I might get blocked. . . . One of the surest signs that I am doing something bad, that I am on the wrong track creatively, is that something takes too long to finish." From her own experience she felt that "the best writing comes when it is done extremely rapidly, in long, uninterrupted periods."

She also fills in from her own reviews the comments Jeremy has heard about his talent: "No one has ever called me dull or static. On the contrary, I've been labeled grotesque, baroque, romantic, surreal, excessive, inflated, overblown, insane . . . sinister and erotic. . . . The lushness of New Orleans is in everything I do."

Besides his paintings of little girls, he also does dark paintings of moldering New Orleans mansions with gardens that are jungles, filled with giant roaches and rats—Anne's childhood terrors. "All of Jeremy's paintings are what I would paint if I were painting," she admitted. "I put myself into that character." He keeps them locked in his attic—a hidden part of his psyche—unsure what to make of them. The meaning is fragmented for him. They seem to have no moral theme, something on which he prides himself with his books of little girls depicted in dream images. Although Anne did not do such paintings, they represent secret urges and dark ideas that she stored away in the attic of her own psyche.

Jeremy has nothing new to say to interviewers, a feeling Anne had experienced in the crush of publicity over *Lestat*. He even snaps at them from fear that they might press the issue that he is merely writing now for commercial ends rather than creating art. *"Looking for Bettina,* what did it mean?" he asks about one of his books. "I couldn't find her myself anymore."

Anne had felt that way about getting pushed back into writing about vampires. Although she'd had a sequel in mind for her first novel, friends who knew her claimed she strongly resisted the pressure to write it, wondering why everyone wanted another book about vampires. Was she writing for herself when she sat down to do Lestat, or, as Jeremy said, doing it because "it was what my audience wanted"?—and a way to make money. Impossible to know for sure, since, as Jeremy puts it, "A serious writer, artist, whatever the hell I was, has to be smart enough not to say things like that." Nevertheless, the novel *is* about freedom of expression, and Anne had fought for nine years against getting boxed in with her writing; she'd even gone in directions that could have ruined her career. Then, returning to Lestat, she'd changed the themes and tone to something that had interested *her,* even though it meant further risk. *Belinda* expresses what she wanted as an author. It contains many parallels with Anne's inner life.

The blond girl, Belinda, seduces Jeremy, then leaves. Confused and ashamed, he becomes obsessed with capturing her likeness on canvas. He works fast, at night, the way he did the dark paintings—and the way Anne wrote *Interview With the Vampire* and *Exit to Eden,* her novels of inner exploration. Yet he cannot get it right. Something eludes him, just as something had seemed to be eluding Anne—what she referred to as It. The answers would take Jeremy back to New Orleans, just as they would Anne, although she did not yet realize it.

Belinda comes to his house and he wants to take care of her. She tells him his books about little girls in dark houses are erotic. He resists the idea that he is sublimating into his work a sexual attraction to little girls. His words echo Anne's reaction to pat reviews: "I work six months on a book. I live in it, dream in it. I don't question it. . . . Then somebody wants to explain it all in five hundred words or five minutes."

"Then what's the threat?" Belinda asks. He does not answer, admitting later that it is his character to be evasive—an important foreshadowing. By the time Anne wrote *Belinda,* she had become more skilled at structuring a book, and the scenes involve more complex symbolism and less explanation than did earlier novels.

Belinda wants Jeremy to fall in love with her, answering the question Anne had been asking over and over in her work through various characters: "Do you love me?"

"If we were in love," Belinda explains, "I wouldn't be drifting. I wouldn't be nobody."

The source for the constant, fretful question comes clear as Anne's fear of the anonymity of lost lives—of the absence of a caring, continuous awareness that preserves the identity of the least person beyond death. Love offers substance to the loved one, especially the love of an artist who can render the loved one's image in some lasting piece of work.

Jeremy asks about her parents and she resists his probing, telling him that if he asks again, she will leave. He photographs her, then sleeps with her. Again she disappears.

Jeremy meets with a friend, Alex Clementine, loosely inspired by John Dodds. "It was a tribute," said Anne, "to his tremendous vivacity and storytelling ability, and his humor and charm." John had opened the door for Anne with his acceptance of the Rampling novels, just as Alex opens the door for Jeremy to come to California from his childhood in New Orleans. However, Jeremy's emigration allows him to escape something in New Orleans that he has not yet confronted, something involved with his deceased mother. Anne, too, feels the tug of something about herself back in the "Big Easy"—something dark and mysterious that she is confronting in gradual stages.

Alex has starred in pictures made from the novels of Jeremy's late mother, inspired in part by southern writer Frances Parkinson Keyes, and they became friends, with a brief homosexual fling. He has just written an autobiography which left out the juicy stories he knows. The theme for the novel is set up in their conversation when Jeremy insists that people want to be told the truth, that a little scandal won't kill a career.

"It's got to be the right dirt in the right measure," Alex responds. "It's just a new set of illusions. . . . Sex, yes, as long as death and suffering comes with it, gives them the moral overtone they've still got to have." He accuses Jeremy of writing his children's books because they sell rather than because it's what he really wants to do as an artist.

"People love us more for the truth," Jeremy insists.

Alex is not persuaded. "You've got it made with those kids, and if and when you write your life, you'll lie for them and you know it." He knows that Jeremy wrote the last two novels for his mother while she was dying and that the story was covered up. The issue for Jeremy is left open with this uncomfortable contradiction, another example of his self-blindedness.

The conversation contains the arguments Anne had over revealing her authorship of the Roquelaure and Rampling books. Friends and associates insisted it could harm her career. She wanted to acknowledge them because to her the books were not just pornography but had artistic and political significance. She placed the message in *Belinda*.

3

Jeremy searches for Belinda and finds her in the Haight. She is wearing a "horrid leopardskin coat," one of Anne's possessions from high school. Taking her back home, he shows her two paintings he has finished of her in the nude but assures her they will never be shown. She is upset by this and leaves, but later that night calls for help. Jeremy poses as her father to extricate her from a police investigation and is recognized. The incident excites him and he later tells Belinda his secret desire: "I wish something violent would happen, something unplanned and crazy. . . . If I were a writer, I'd invent a pen name. I'd get out." This is a feeling not unlike what Anne went through when she wrote and sent off her pornography. She was frightened. It was a major change in her focus, in her life. If things worked out, she might become a famous pornographer.

Jeremy feels that his career has made evasion into art. He knows it is a failure of sorts, though a failure with power to affect a wide audience. He has been trapped into a fraud similar to the fraud perpetrated when he wrote his mother's novels. He is tired of his little girls and wants something new.

That he is growing becomes clear at an art show for his friend Andy Blatky, modeled on the Rices' sculptor friend, Joe Slusky. Andy is a modern sculptor who works with enameled metal shapes, with "bulbous arms almost tenderly embracing each other." On impulse Jeremy buys one of the sculptures. The act parallels the breakthrough he is making in his own art, as he tells Andy that he is doing "some really wild new things." He puts the sculpture in the backyard, symbolic of putting it in the back of his mind the way he puts Belinda's paintings in the attic with the rat and roach paintings. The sculpture seems to recede from the novel. Yet it does not really recede. It is a subliminal symbol that shows up again at an important moment.

Jeremy does not understand the piece but buys it anyway. Similarly he does not understand what is happening within himself. He paints little girls in haunted houses that resemble his mother's New Orleans mansion—just as it was when she died twenty-five years before—and little girls in the house of a deceased mother. Anne seems to be connecting Michele with her earlier loss, as if put together with New Orleans, they represent something significant to her. Jeremy has never been back, and he returns to the house only in paintings that represent his evasion.

Belinda, the voice of a new impulse emerging in Anne's life, is almost Jeremy's opposite in the way she confronts life. She is educated, fluent in several languages, and understands art—the sophisticated, gorgeous blond adolescent that Anne had longed to be. She is self-aware, recognizes her sexual maturity, and is incensed that Jeremy wants to hide his depiction of it. She already feels like a criminal, existing in a legal limbo until society recognizes her at the arbitrary age of twenty-one.

"I had my first period when I was nine," she tells him. "I was wearing a C-cut bra by the time I was thirteen. The first boy I ever slept with was shaving every day at fifteen, we could have made babies together. . . . But what is a kid here? . . . You can't legally smoke, drink, start a career, get married . . . all this for years and years after you're a physical adult. All you can do is play till you're twenty-one. . . . We're all criminals . . . to be an American kid, you have to be a bad person. . . . Everybody's an outcast. Everybody's a faker." She wants to be allowed to be exactly who she is.

Jeremy convinces Belinda to stay with him and promises not to probe, but behind her back he gets his lawyer, Dan, to find out about her. His exposure to Belinda presses subconscious buttons as her apparent innocence taps deeply moving religious memories of his childhood: "Then a lot of forgotten things came back, those long, lush church ceremonies I'd witnessed a thousand times when I was a little boy in New Orleans." Vivid but suppressed impressions suddenly return, especially images of little girls in white processional dresses and the distinct light in the church during Holy Communion. It is as if Anne's stronger side—her male voice—is connecting her to her childhood, the roots of her secret self. The original purity had become entangled with a sensuality that Anne now understood. The connections feel "dangerous."

On a whim Jeremy dresses Belinda in a white veil and dress, and gives her a prayer book and rosary so that she looks like a little girl, pure but sensual, at her First Communion. He is indulging in what is forbidden by all his childhood teachings, reaching into himself more boldly than he ever had before. He even pours wine into her vagina during sex and drinks it out. "This is my body. This is my blood," says Belinda, echoing the priest administering the ceremony of Transubstantiation—turning bread and wine into the flesh and blood of Christ. Anne becomes her own priest as she depicts this "Holy Communion" of physical love. Jeremy and Belinda make each other more real in the flesh than either has been before.

Once more Anne blends religious images with sex to turn the meaning of both around. The ultimate union of person with person is made akin to the ecstatic union of a person with God. On the one hand, it is blasphemy to a church that views sex as dirty—the ultimate degradation of holy concepts. On the other hand, to someone who views sex as the ultimate human life force—the full expression of the erotic—equating it with Holy Communion means exploring and expressing its depth and power.

When Jeremy paints *Holy Communion,* he feels that it calls on his most profound skill to blend illusion with reality. He is an artist-priest. "If this isn't the breakthrough of my career," he says, "then I don't have one. Everything I know about reality and illusion is there." The problem is, the illusion at this point is that Jeremy believes he knows the difference.

Much of the thematic complexity centers on Jeremy's artistic development. Anne uses illusion paradoxically to cancel itself, which simultaneously validates it: things are not what they seem—not even that statement of their illusion. It is a tricky and subtle device to emphasize the elusiveness of self. Jeremy does not yet understand the implications. As with his first impression of Belinda, what he believes to be illusion is reality and vice versa. The true point of breakthrough happens when these opposites are reversed. Jeremy, however, does not realize what that reversal means.

Belinda is suspicious and warns Jeremy not to betray her. It is Jeremy's warning to himself—and perhaps Anne's warning to herself—because, as it turns out, they are two sides of the same person, the way characters in Anne's other novels had been, although they would eventually blend together rather than develop contrasts. He decides that sneaking around behind her back is not really betraying her. Lying to himself in this manner sets him up for self-betrayal.

In one scene at the house, Belinda reveals her kinship to Anne's subconscious life. She and Jeremy fight over the amount of liquor she consumes, and she blurts out that she knows all about drunks. Jeremy asks her if she's drinking out of loyalty to someone. It is a telling point. Many children of alcoholics frequently fall into the drinking patterns of their parents, despite denying that they would ever do such a thing. Some psychologists believe it is a form of imitation that binds them closer to the parent, reinforced by a genetic tendency. The argument represents Anne's look back at her own period of drinking, as if she has come to understand what it was about as a way of holding on to her mother while mourning a similar grief. It also parallels Jeremy's symbolic intoxication with his little girls as loyalty to his own mother. It is another strong clue that Belinda and Jeremy have parallel stories, that they are the same person, and that they are both Anne, with Belinda becoming Anne's inner self. Whatever Belinda and Jeremy do to each other, they do to themselves.

Jeremy continues to paint Belinda in various poses until he has a dozen large canvases. The props he finds erotic, like riding clothes, communion dresses, Victorian gowns, and schoolgirl pleated skirts, are erotic to Anne, depicting romantically historical periods. She liked the classic trappings of sexuality rather than contemporary images of cops and military personnel that she discovered in some pornographic circles. She preferred mystery over representations of overt violence, and Jeremy follows her preferences in his growth as an artist. "The pictures were cleaner, harsher and utterly free of the Jeremy Walker clichés that had encrusted everything before this. . . . Yet never had I painted anything as dark and frightening as these pictures of her."

What he says about his paintings is what Anne felt about her Rampling books, that they were cleaner in language, an attempt to do something different. "I want the freedom of the primitive painters," he insists, "to focus with love on what I find inherently beautiful. I want it to be hot, disturbing. Yet gorgeous always."

In the paintings Jeremy notices how Belinda seems to reproach with her frankness, pushing him deeper within himself to places that frighten him. She is the part of him that is rising to the surface as he explores his new talent. Her father, G.G., had referred to her laughingly as Rumpelstiltskin and that is what she is: a mysterious being able to spin gold out of straw. She is the part of Anne that fights the guilt and conservative nature of her religious socialization, moving toward something she believes is good. Belinda is honesty and freedom, the will creating the self, a light shining in the dark, illuminating places that have been sealed off by fear.

Jeremy decides to let go of his little girls; he is painting a woman now. Anne, too, is coming to grips with her mature feminine side. Belinda is an extension of that, allowing her a female adolescence without guilt that results in the sophisticated woman she desired to be. "But it has gone on too long," Jeremy thinks to himself, "my soul wandering through these dark rooms. It has become a pattern that is a dark room in itself." The old houses in the books have to fall down, he explains. He has to get outside to contemporary life.

4

"Jeremy's paintings," Anne admitted, "are the vampire novels in a sense." The fans had shown her, through success and failure, just which books would sell, but she had resisted, feeling that the darker books demanded too much pain and restricted her range of expression. She had returned to the vampires after trying out her other two voices, yet wanted to write another Rampling novel. All the while she struggled with many of the things that hound Jeremy, wondering about her directions as a serious writer. Is she doing what she really wanted or just playing to the audience? She had not been entirely satisfied with *The Vampire Lestat.* She had loved *Exit to Eden.* What was her true direction? There were no easy answers, although she could work out Jeremy's life for him.

He is definitely on the road to self-honesty with his paintings of Belinda and he will continue, no matter what the price, even if his audience feels betrayed. He is going to use the lies he has told in his art as a platform for the truth. "It doesn't make a damn bit of difference whether or not the truth sells," he insists. "The truth is just the truth, that's all, even if it brings you right down to the bottom."

Psychoanalyst Otto Rank discussed how the artist gives the greatest expression to the creative life force. For children, he explained, the first experience of the will is that of parents and social institutions. As children develop a sense of self, their wills counter authority and they feel guilty. If parents value independence, as Anne's mother did (within a Catholic framework), children gain courage to exercise their wills. The most creative people turn out to be those who exert their own will to the greatest degree in seeking unique directions. This is represented at one level in the story of Jeremy and his struggle, and at another in Anne as the novelist, struggling to say something with her work. The creation of art is like the creation of a self.

The dilemma of the artist, however, is that individuals are born into a group culture and they can only become individuals within the culture. Their success depends, ironically, on the group's recognition. Transcending the group means making personal sense of the world in a godlike vacuum, looking to themselves as the sole authority. Individuals (and artists) want to use the full force of their passion to assert their individuality, but they can only be judged as successful by critics who utilize the very validation they resist. Thus, there is no true resolution of these opposing forces, and the creative urge utilizes the tension to express the dynamism of life.

Jeremy has stifled his creative force for a long time, and it comes out in dark paintings of rats and roaches and in the preservation of the house where his mother died. Anne's artistic expression is equally connected with dark areas of her past. With Belinda, Jeremy is propelled toward becoming the artist he wants to be, and his constant repetition of erotic paintings of her reinforces his tentative steps. The impulse sends him striving toward more complex levels of integration that will reduce the traumas and guilt of his childhood, along with the conflict over morality represented in his paralyzed loyalty to his mother. Anne, as the writer making these choices for her character, would achieve similar benefits.

The direction of the book had changed from the original proposal of an artist brought down by his sexual involvement with a young girl. "I don't really write things like that," said Anne. "As soon as the characters get into their sexuality, they get released instead of going downhill. That's what always happens in my work." Refusing to link death with sexuality had become for her a political agenda, empowered by her own emerging urge toward sexual expression. Naturally an optimist, she had been crushed by life events, then had re-emerged; the light within was beginning to shine more brightly.

As the pieces of the mystery fall together, Jeremy learns that Belinda is the daughter of a famous movie star, Bonnie. He discovers a cover-up and learns that private detectives are searching for the girl. Jeremy connects Belinda to film producer Susan Jeremiah, who made an acclaimed erotic picture called *Final Score,* in which Belinda, as a fourteen-year-old, appears in a lesbian scene. Watching it, he understands her desire to be perceived as a woman, not a child.

Belinda discovers that Jeremy is on to her and she leaves. Jeremy realizes in a moment that rings with autobiographical tones that his feelings are like the extremes he knew in his youth, "before success and loneliness became routine. I had not known how much I missed them."

Bonnie arrives at Jeremy's house and tries to blackmail Jeremy with the nude photographs that he took of her daughter. He resists and Bonnie gives back the negatives. He wonders how she got them, since there is no evidence that her detectives broke in. She warns him not to show the paintings.

Bonnie has much in common with Jeremy's mother in the way in which they try to squelch their children. Both women saw their children as mere extensions of themselves. Jeremy's mother, Cynthia, assumed he would continue her name by writing books, to ensure her immortality. Similarly, Bonnie—made helpless by her own mother's death—wants Belinda to take care of her, and in the process crushes her with her own selfish concerns. They both are the internalized voice of repression: don't be who you are, be who I want you to be. Bonnie now steps in as Jeremy's mother: don't continue in the direction in which you're going in order to achieve your individuality, i.e., don't show the paintings.

In Anne's own life, this was like the teachings of the church, channeled through parental restrictions. Be who you are but don't veer away from what you should be. Although Anne's mother had encouraged individuality on one level, she had seen her children as an extension of herself, had wanted them to be the genius she had not become, and had asked of them a perfection she had not achieved. Be who you are/be who I want you to be: the contradiction fed into Anne's subconscious, where paradox is more easily tolerated. Anne did not see her mother as the oppressive figure she wrote about in her books, and yet over and over, the mother figures (even Louis and Lestat in the first novel) exert strong pressure on their children to live up to a vision that they possess for them. Katherine believed she was encouraging freedom, but she unintentionally restricted it through her own unconscious needs. Only Gabrielle sets her son free, but Gabrielle is Katherine in an image of what she might have become, filtered through Anne's emerging feminine strength.

When Jeremy picks up Belinda and takes her to his mother's old home in New Orleans, they have a frank talk about parents. Belinda has had to take care of her mother, keeping her from suicide and cleaning up after her alcoholic illnesses, as if she were the mother and Bonnie the daughter. Anne had found herself in a similar role as her own mother declined. When she wrote the scenes in which Bonnie was outrageously incompetent as a mother, she got very involved. "It gave me a sensation like a white light flashing. When her mother said to her, 'I loved my mother so much I would have scrubbed floors just to keep her alive,' Belinda says, 'Those are things one does for one's child, not one's mother.' [Belinda does not actually say this, but Anne remembered it from an early draft.] The way her mother had everything screwed up, it gave me great delight to write that. Now, I couldn't tell you that was my mother because it wasn't. It wasn't my father, either. But it was something that causes great rage in me and I don't know what it is. I believed in that part of the novel totally, just as I believe in the part where Jeremy's mother thought it was just fine that he write her novels under her name for the rest of his life. I think his mother was only interested in herself anymore."

Although Jeremy does not face what Belinda sees clearly about his mother and her bid for immortality at his expense—"It was annihilating what she did," Belinda points out—he is more inclined than before to see how his little girls have trapped him. "We keep their secrets," Belinda says, "and we pay the price." They draw together as victims of inadequate parents.

Anne had felt the impact on her writing of the realization that parents cannot protect their children because they are still trying to protect themselves, having had parents who failed them in some manner. "Children always have to take care of parents in my novels," Anne said. Jean is abandoned by parents, then abused by older men. Katherine is betrayed by her mother's death. Lestat takes care of his father. Marcel's mother is inadequate, Tonio's helpless. Both Lisa and Elliott struggle with fitting the image that their parents have for them. Claudia is betrayed by her two "fathers."

It is no surprise that this theme would show up. From Bible stories of children like David, Joseph, and Moses who received no protection from their parents, to watching her own mother slowly deteriorate, Anne felt early this vulnerability. Later, as a parent herself, she had been helpless to keep her daughter from succumbing to leukemia.

"I think it's the same theme," said Anne, "as Dostoevsky and Dickens—that you have to become your own parent. I think the history of the nineteenth and twentieth century in literature is children coming of age in a world where parents have relinquished their responsibility almost on a cosmic level. We're concerned with the breakdown of the authoritarian family. We don't have any mothers or fathers anymore in heaven or on earth, and so we have to find out who our brothers and sisters are. Technology and warfare and science have reached a point where parents can't give you answers anymore. After the shock of the world wars and the atom bomb and the Holocaust, we live in an age where authority is suspect." She had experienced the sixties, when kids questioned the way their parents bought propaganda from Washington and religion, and felt the burden of shouldering the responsibility for honesty. "Conventional religions no longer have the answer," said Anne. "Political dreams that promised answers have not really delivered anything substantial. There are very few novels that I can recall of people who loved their parents, saw them as profound models, and followed in their footsteps."

Jeremy and Belinda both realize that she has grown up in the paintings, going through stages until Jeremy depicts her as a ripe young woman in his mother's bed. He has freed himself from his obsession with the domination of the mother whose fear of mortality was the fear of a little girl against an unseen threat. That part of his mother (a blend of Katherine and Michele, both of whom faced a powerful, invisible threat) was being relived within himself. As he broke away, the little girls grew up into Belinda, looking from the canvas now with a direct gaze, no longer innocent or afraid. His inner self, represented by Belinda, has been allowed expression in the open, not hidden away in an attic. He can grow up himself and become a man.

Jeremy is feeling closer to Belinda than he has ever felt before—closer to his own breakthrough. In one painting he no longer needs to paint her nude. The idea had found similar expression in *Exit to Eden* when Elliott and Lisa left behind their games and got dressed. He also sees more darkness around her than he had in earlier paintings, as if he is not yet ready to give in to the light that she brings, or as if her emergence brings with it the inner darkness of unresolved issues, since there is no clear division between the two within the self.

In New Orleans, Jeremy feels safe. The smell of flowers, the sound of chattering katydids and rattling streetcars fill him with a sense of ease, as if this is where he had always belonged. He and Belinda run around the city together. Anne includes a description of her favorite walks past her old church and through the Garden District, as she had done in *Exit to Eden.* She pushes her characters further in *Belinda,* however, into the more threatening Irish Channel as far as the river, getting deeper into her roots and the powerful wash of primal, inarticulate memories. Anne had always become most swept up in her books when the problems were complex, locking in and writing quickly. "To me, when they're psychologically dense and complex," she said, "they're fairly easy to write. There's an exhilarating, exciting feeling of casting into deep water." The literary exercise drew her closer to that elusive something that she was trying to grasp with her writing.

Getting close to primal roots, however, has its dark side for Jeremy. Still plagued by how Bonnie got the photos, he finally realizes that Belinda gave them to her, that she betrayed him! Stunned, then enraged, he confronts her, slapping her and demanding that she leave. He cannot listen to her say she did it for him, or face the fact that he was betraying her at the same time. He struggles to keep Belinda's honesty from overturning the status quo of his life. It is the moment of truth for him and he cannot surrender. He puts his fist through the wall, smelling a "stench of rottenness. Of rain and rats and rottenness." Resisting her drives him back to the darkness.

"You wouldn't just trust me!" Belinda cries. He forces her out, stealing the substance his love had granted her. "Her crying echoed down the long hall, like a ghost crying in a haunted house," and she sits with "the eyes of a dead person." She has no choice but to leave; she cannot survive in his darkness.

5

Five days later Jeremy receives Belinda's diary in the mail. As in *Exit to Eden,* Anne moves from first-person male point of view to first-person female to tell Belinda's story. In the diary, which includes several autobiographical revelations about Anne, she describes the ordeal of being the child of an irresponsible, vain alcoholic. She also tells how she became friends with Susan Jeremiah, who presented sex between women as something clean that could give her the freedom of a man. It was Susan who shocked her into taking hold of her life by asking her, "You want to be somebody or somebody's girl?"—a question posed years before by an O'Briens' family friend, Woody. It had created upon Anne a strong impression: act or be acted upon.

Belinda explains how she ran away after her mother turned on her and went to her father, whose life subsequently fell apart. Like Lisa, Louis, and Lestat before her, she worries about the harm she brings to those she loves. In the process she reveals to Jeremy her reservations about confiding in others, a trait she shares with him and which they both share with Anne: "I don't think I will ever be much of a confider. I don't have enough faith in talking about things." It was a complaint of some of Anne's acquaintances that she rarely revealed herself. It also sets Jeremy and Belinda up for the way they betray each other.

Each had perceived the other as innocent, themselves as guilty. Belinda, who is Jeremy's ray of light, is immersed in her own darkness and wants to be like him as she watches him find his way out. They help each other, though neither seems to perceive his or her own power in facilitating the emergence.

Like Anne before her, Belinda heads for Haight-Ashbury. Her observations are based on what Anne had seen: "And one of the things that came clear to me was that the girls on the street were very different from the boys. The girls went nowhere. They got pregnant, went on drugs, maybe even became prostitutes. They were often fools for the guys they met. They'd cook and scrub for some broke rock musician and then get thrown in the street. But the boys were a little more smart." She puzzled over it. "How did the streets wear out the girls, while boys passed through them? Why did girls lose while boys won? . . . They had a kind of freedom the women just never seemed to have." Belinda decides to adopt the facade of a gay boy, acting out a fantasy for Anne, who had viewed herself as a gay man.

Androgyny as a source of power is fully accomplished in this novel. Jeremy had expressed himself through female images, Belinda through male posturing. Jeremy lets the female inside him mature to help him become more fully a man. Belinda uses the power of the male freedom to become more fully a woman. What seems a heterosexual triumph is laced with bisexual overtones, just as it was for Lisa and Elliott and would continue to be for characters in future novels.

Belinda explains how Bonnie's husband, Marty, had discovered where she was. To allow her mother to feel that the power over the situation was in her hands, she gave Bonnie the negatives of her in the nude. It was a betrayal toward the end of achieving some good, just as Jeremy's deceit and betrayal of her had been justified by him. She even feels that she may have betrayed her mother. "And was I guilty all along of a worse betrayal of her, of never trying, for her sake and mine, to break through the games we all played?"

Belinda recognizes that lying had become a way of life with her, a common trait of children who grow up in self-protective alcoholic family systems. Anne, too, had felt some responsibility in her mother's death, as do people who go along with a status quo that, unbeknownst to them, is calculated toward disaster. It is no one's fault, but the feeling of guilt and helplessness tells a different story. Was she a perpetrator or a victim? The ambiguity can never be resolved, not for her, not for Belinda, not for Jeremy.

Belinda has observed that Jeremy is finding himself. Though she is still a shadow lost in her own "dark house" while she awaits the three-dimensionality of adulthood, he is not. He can be the power for them both, and she urges him to unlock the inner force that will win for him salvation through his art. "But if I am right about all this," she tells him, "you are out of the old house now. You have painted a figure that finally broke free." She is referring to the painting of herself as a woman.

The letter prompts Jeremy to exhibit his paintings, even though it will ruin his career as a children's book author. To him it means artistic freedom and giving Belinda the substance she seeks. "It was a moment of synchronization," says Jeremy. "My needs and her needs became the same." He hopes the exhibit will tell her he loves her and get her to return.

Alex Clementine tries to talk Jeremy out of what seems like lunacy. He wants to close up the New Orleans house—a statement symbolizing repression—but Jeremy keeps the windows open, the breezes coming through. The open window was a device Anne had used before to symbolize freedom. This discussion, carried on through Jeremy's scotch-induced haze, was one of Anne's favorite parts. "To see that move fluidly," she said, "with all those voices and all the information conveyed, that's a wonderful chorus of voices, and there are whole sections of the Vampire Chronicles that don't touch that for actual skill."

The pace of the book picks up and the energy level heightens. The exhibit is set up and people accuse Jeremy of secretly wanting to molest little girls; feminists blast the exhibit and he hears about book burnings. "My heart was thudding," Jeremy says. "It had begun!"

When Belinda fails to show up, Jeremy is suspected of murder. He is enraged. "The pictures were supposed to be a celebration," he insists. "They were supposed to be wholesome and beautiful. They were a tribute to her sexuality and to the love between us and how it saved me. . . . If you let it out that you think I killed her, then you make it all kinky and dirty . . . as if people couldn't break the rules and love each other—without there being something ugly and violent and bad!"

Alex reminds Jeremy that people in America want sexual license punished. "This link between sex and death, well, hell, it's as American as apple pie. . . . Americans make you pay that way when you break the rules. It's a formula. The cop shows do it all the time."

Meanwhile, the critics praise the paintings, and museums and collectors make exorbitant offers. Jeremy's bid for freedom is rewarded. Anne grants him success along with inner salvation through his erotic art. The choice she makes for this turn of the plot indicates what she wanted for herself and, in part, what she had experienced when she had revealed herself as the author of pornography (although not financially). "It wasn't terrible," she said. "It wasn't ruining my life at all. *Belinda* is a symbol of the pornography and of the way it meant breaking down barriers and opening doors."

Jeremy tells his lawyer to give away his dolls and get Andy's sculpture out of his backyard to where people can see it. He is growing in his awareness of what the union of life and art is about as he sheds his negative psychological baggage.

Susan Jeremiah and an eccentric furrier named Blair, symbols in the novel of quirkiness that seems pretentious but is in fact authentic, facilitate Jeremy's reunion with Belinda in a limousine chase reminiscent of the reunions in *The Vampire Lestat,* and they flee to Reno to get married. They have their picture taken and they appear "more real than real." They have more substance together than they ever had separately, symbolizing the wholeness of a person who acknowledges the inner self.

In the aftermath, Jeremy is amazed at how he had closed himself off for twenty-five years in a world full of wonderful subjects to paint. "Bend down and kiss what you see," said Stan in the opening poem, and now Jeremy can do that. He had passed through a darkness—the threat of which had scared him away from a hidden inner freedom—and into the world of light and life. For him the revelation of truth won over the concealment of lies.

6

Anne finished *Belinda* in about six months. The book was intended for Knopf, but Anne did not feel that she and Vicky Wilson reached a rapport about it. She was unhappy with the general lack of enthusiasm. To her mind, it was a significant book, yet no one else seemed to agree. Even Stan, always supportive, was put off by the California style and by what he felt was a dearth of rich metaphors found in her other books.

Anne sent a copy to Allen Daviau. He admired her attempt but chastened her about the shortcomings of her insight into the male mind. "You don't have down what he would love about a sixteen-year-old girl's body," he told her. "You should have consulted with your horny male friends to find out their fantasies." At times Jeremy was like a nurturing mother, playing with a doll, and he emphasized Belinda's sweetness, her candy lips, her pouty face. Anne needed to say more, she was told, about the feel of a young person's skin. Anne laughed and admitted that perhaps she did not want to face the difference between a young person and a person of forty-four. At any rate, the novel worked for her on a symbolic level and such shortcomings were superficial.

Belinda ended up at Arbor House with John Dodds, for a $60,000 advance, another financial step backward. *Exit to Eden* had not done as well as projected, and although she would own up to the Rampling pseudonym on the cover of *Belinda* and thus exploit the Rice appeal, no one was convinced that it would do well on the heels of *Lestat*.

John Dodds also suggested changes. Anne listened to him, to Lynn Nesbit, and to anyone else who had read a draft, then rewrote. She developed the character of Alex and deepened the psychological layering. "It became more of an Anne Rice book," she said, "whereas before it was more pure Rampling, with a very fast, breathless pace. I went back and had fun stretching things and deepening things. At the time I thought I was improving it and clearing up whatever problems people had pointed out. But I'm not sure in retrospect that it wouldn't have been fine as it originally was."

She also changed the ending. Originally she had intended Jeremy and Belinda to get away to a place in Texas owned by Susan Jeremiah, based on a house in Kemp on Cedar Creek Lake that Anne and Stan had purchased. "That was what was off about it," she said. "What I realized was that that Texas landscape was not pertinent. I felt better changing it to the Hollywood landscape." She also hammed it up by including the theater scene and the limousine chase. "I love stuff like that."

Anne felt better about this novel than she had about *Lestat.* It was her most ambitious novel to date in terms of complexity and structure. She had never before included so many detailed portraits of diverse characters, or set for herself the task of working fully in a real-life contemporary setting, which meant getting fine details right. "Those people," she said, "are very much like people I knew when I wrote it." Choosing Hollywood had involved learning about how contracts were done, what movie stars and producers were like, how films were made. "A lot of nitty-gritty research went into *Belinda.*" She'd had her own experiences to draw on, including her meetings with producers, but she also located books about the scheduling and preparation of television series. Her cousin Allen, about to be nominated for a cinematography award for *The Color Purple,* had answered many questions.

She felt the writing was better than she had done to date and that she had mastered difficult scenes. "I took great pleasure in the craft of the book," Anne remembered, "the conversations, the people moving through space, things that I think are hard to do as a writer that look easy. To me that book was about more than a lot of my stuff is. All of my books are attempts to break down some door and get through it, and each time I think I get a little further through that door. That novel was a big push through the door. Less lay between me and what I wanted to touch." While she had worked consciously on symbolic breakthroughs for Jeremy, she had experienced similar discoveries for herself.

Anne also liked the detective quality and the gradual uncovering of mystery. "It's much fresher," she claimed, "more skilled, and the illusion is better. There are whole chunks of *Belinda* that I like to read myself because the writing is so good." It puzzled her that the vampire novels seemed to affect people more intensely than did *Belinda.* "For me writing *Belinda* was incredibly intense because I was really writing about everything that mattered to me. It has the dark feeling of locking into what matters." Because it had been set in her own house, with her doll collection, it had a more immediate feel than any of her previous novels. Jeremy walked the streets she had walked, loved New Orleans the way she did, and loved the Castro. His bid for freedom was hers. "Writing that book was an obsessive, hot experience. It was layers of crackling excitement."

She expected success, but to her distress, *Belinda* was not widely reviewed. Anne saw only three, all of which were favorable. One review was in the *Los Angeles Times,* by Carolyn See, who had liked *Exit to Eden.* She was impressed with the way Anne seemed to take common fantasies and get behind them, calling the book "a sexual fantasy . . . utterly charming."

Anne received another prominent review in the *San Francisco Chronicle.* Patricia Holt called her "one of the most natural storytellers on the modern scene,'' possessing ''profound literary skill.'' She perceived *Belinda* as Anne's ''most controversial book to date,'' and commended her on making the adult–child relationship seem almost defensible, although she felt that Anne never really addressed the issue of sexually active teenagers and the responsibility of adults.

The New York Times completely ignored the book, yet asked Anne to write a review on a children's book author in the same month *Belinda* was released. Anne was chagrined but did not miss the ironic humor.

In an article in the *Village Voice,* Dorothy Allison hit on a theme that would be echoed by others, that Anne had not really called on the full capacity of her creative talent to write the Rampling books, that they were lesser works. This kind of response disturbed Anne, since she had worked very hard to make the books top-quality and had, herself, experienced them profoundly. She wanted readers to understand the message of personal perseverance against forces of betrayal—even one's own betrayal of oneself. Whether betrayal comes from parents, religion, society, peer groups, or from the very conditions of life, we each have the power within ourselves, Anne believed, to press on and take charge of our lives. People did not seem to understand the book, although she felt she had written it the way Jeremy talked: with ''chalk-stroke clarity.''

''I don't know how to effectively do something that divergent from one's own path,'' Anne said. ''I didn't conquer the problem. I have an overflow of stuff and I can't find a successful way to really do it. I'm still searching for that.''

There were predictions that *Belinda* would be made into a movie or a miniseries, and Anne had a conversation with one producer but no offers were made.

John Dodds threw a publication party for her, and John Preston toyed with the idea of surprising her by attending with a pair of handsome, near naked, leather-clad men on motorcycles. Instead he just told her what he'd had in mind. ''She howled when she heard the plan,'' he said, ''thinking it would have been wonderful, and she'd have loved me forever if I'd done it.'' As they talked, John was inspired to write a novel about entertaining a character—Anne—with the perfect S&M party. He wrote the book, *Entertainment for a Master,* and allowed Anne to decide on a name and physical description for the character. She named herself Adrienne and became a ''stately, trim'' blond smoking unfiltered cigarettes.

Belinda did not do well in hardcover, even though Anne included her own name with her Rampling pseudonym. She thought perhaps the readers were confused, although she received a few letters from fans telling her that this was just not the book that they were looking for; they wanted the sequel to *The Vampire Lestat*. *Belinda* had a big release in paperback but did not make any best-seller lists.

Anne believed the lack of success had been due to mispackaging by people who had misunderstood how seriously she had intended the novel. The paperback cover embarrassed and saddened her, targeted at the housewife audience who bought romance novels—an audience that had resisted her books. She had hoped for an artistic cover, like Balthus, but got something that did not convey the content, and to her dismay, she had to work hard to quash rumors that she was writing romances. "If anything," she said, "it was a hard, glittering Hollywood novel." No one picked up on that.

"It's just one of those unfortunate things," Anne said of the lack of response. "The Rampling books were a labor of love that were largely unrewarding in publication. It was an experiment that didn't work. I wanted the freedom of another voice to do something different, but my readers just didn't respond."

It was ironic that Anne had used this novel to express the importance of artistic freedom, only to get crushed by the lack of interest in its message—or in her expression of it. Just as her first novel may have tapped a social current that gave it a boost, this novel seemed to have encountered the opposite. It had a late sixties feel, with the artistic yearning and the sexual breakthrough. Although the novel had the potential to move readers through struggles with individuality and had enhanced Anne's own psychosexual growth and acceptance, society had swung away from concerns with the inner self and into materialistic directions. The erotic quality of Anne's writing that might have saved it had diminished as she moved away from atmosphere and male relationships; the heterosexual clichés she had wanted to avoid were present in a superficial reading, even though the sexuality was meant metaphorically. Nor did the perversion of religious symbols capture attention the way they had in the vampire novels, not even to provoke outrage the way they would within three years. Although some of her literary acquaintances thought *Belinda* was more a novel of substance than any other book Anne had written, and although English professors might acknowledge merits of structure and style, it seemed that the popular audience was not impressed. Anne looked back on the slowly building success of the vampire novels and used that to fortify her hope that *Belinda* would eventually do well.

"I really think," she said, "that *Belinda* is my unappreciated book."

The Vampire Lestat came out in a Ballantine paperback at about the same time that *Belinda* was released in hardcover. *Lestat* stayed on the best-seller list eight weeks. Anne agreed to another tour, and while on it, in Philadelphia, she received a terrible blow. John Dodds had died of cancer at the age of sixty-four. She knew he had been ill while they worked together on *Belinda* but had not expected that she would never see him again.

"This was a terrible loss," said Anne. "I loved this man greatly. He was a real inspiration to me. And his courage in publishing *Exit to Eden* meant an enormous amount." Subsequent printings of *Belinda* carried a memorial in his honor.

San Francisco was even less inviting now. "It seemed," said Anne, "the last bit of love I had for San Francisco went out of me after John died."

She had been reviewing books again since the appearance of *The Vampire Lestat,* writing for the *Washington Post* before she concentrated on reviewing for *The New York Times Book Review.* Sensitivity to negative comments of her own work prompted her to find something positive before she criticized. She preferred true-crime novels, although she did a short review of a children's book by Chris Van Allsburg, appreciating the seduction of everyday life for a supernatural being. In the crime books she emphasized narrative quality, drama, and detail—distinctive features important to southern writers. She also noted the moral tone even as she bemoaned the pettiness of non-mysterious criminals. One book that caught her eye, Scott Turow's *Presumed Innocent,* seemed to be succeeding at her own ambitions of blending serious work with popular elements, but she thought he marred the book with a slick genre ending. He lost his authority for her as a serious storyteller at that point, as well as losing the trust of the reader.

The year 1987 brought another unexpected blow. Bill Whitehead died of AIDS in his Chelsea Hotel apartment. The bad news too closely on the heels of Anne's loss of John Dodds, and both deaths reminded her too much of her daughter's death. She had never had the chance to thank Bill for introducing her to John Preston, or for his wonderful courage and taste in publishing the Roquelaure books, and now he was gone.

In the aftermath of the disappointing release of *Belinda,* Anne was not sure what to do next. She was getting depressed in San Francisco. "The city just became in my mind associated with pain and death and disappointment." John Dodds was gone, Dennis Percy had died, memories of Michele's illness and death pervaded the place, some friendships had been lost, and every time Anne looked at the *Chronicle,* she felt the sting of humiliation. She loved her friends in the Castro and those over in Berkeley, but she was feeling restless.

About that time she was on a flight, watching *The Empire Strikes Back.* She listened to the dialogue between Darth Vader and Luke Skywalker, wondering why evil was always portrayed in stereotypically dark figures. Suddenly the theme for the third vampire novel struck her.

CHAPTER ELEVEN

THE GUISE OF EVIL

1

While Anne thought through her next novel, she and Stan looked into buying a second home away from the city. They found a small house on five acres of redwoods in Sonoma County, east of Santa Rosa. It was at the edge of Mark West Creek, shaded by huge trees through which sun rays filtered as if through a cathedral window. Anne was enchanted enough to include it as a significant setting in her vampire sequel.

"What was beautiful about it," she said, "was the primal quality of the creek and the steepness of the banks and the untouched quality. It was a blessed place. You could sit in one spot and hear three different musics coming from the creek as the waters rushed over the stones."

Christopher was not so easily won over. "It was a place where Jason would dwell," he said, referring to a popular teen slasher movie. His curtainless window looked into the forest. "At night it was pitch black: no moon, no lights, nothing." The things he imagined *out there* paralyzed him at times.

Nevertheless, Anne spent time at the house developing new characters, themes, and scenes.

Although she had crystallized for herself the basic plot, she complained to John Preston that she couldn't get started. She was nervous. This was not like either of the first two novels in the vampire series. It was much more ambitious—the book of her dreams that would span a depth and breadth that she had never before allowed herself to explore in writing. In the past she had imagined such tomes, but the execution had seemed always beyond her skill. Now she was ready. She wanted to capture the enormous vision, really work it out. But would it be accepted? Could she actually do what she wanted?

John finally told her, "Woman, just go write the damn thing!" She did, and for his part in motivating her, he earned a dedication, along with Stan and Chris.

Having purchased a Tandy 2000 computer to replace an Osborn, bought when it had first been unveiled, Anne employed the freedom it yielded to create a vast spectacle, to move back and forth between scenes and chapters, sometimes writing the first chapter last. For the first time she felt she was using the computer as it was meant to be used, as a tool to raise standards and allow fine nuances essential to the quality of intense artistic creation in language. "You're no longer making the mechanical compromises," she said in an interview, "that move it away from poetry."

As she had with *Belinda,* she wanted to use one of Stan's poems to introduce the theme. Glancing through his books, she was surprised how much of his work echoed hers. "It was almost like I'd written a chapter with his poems or he'd written a poem to go with the chapters, so I used all of these different quotes. I was knocked out by the fact that we seemed obsessed by the same themes and the same images." She selected them for similarities, like the belief in substance. "One of the major themes in *The Queen of the Damned,*" Anne explained, "is that the flesh teaches all wisdom and when we become too unanchored and get into abstract thinking that betrays compassion for the individual, that's where the real danger lies."

2

Lestat is back to finish the story begun in his autobiography. However, he is just a player this time. It is not his actions that move the plot, but those of two strong female vampires, both six thousand years old. Like the Jungian archetype of the feminine, one represents life and wisdom and the other destruction, although not as Darth Vader had been depicted. The novel would be more philosophically involved than anything Anne had written to date, more reflective and more far-reaching in the implications of the vampire as metaphor.

Lestat has changed. He has become more cynical, "a little meaner," but a little more conscientious of the struggle of good and evil "in the private hell of body and soul." He has moved closer to his vampire nature, but the human in him is also closer to the surface. Of his own story, he does not know whether he is the hero or victim, since events swept him up despite his belief that he caused them. The tale involves many characters who each contribute to the central event that changes them all, so Lestat steps out of first person to present the individual stories that join at his rock concert.

1. Marius comes to San Francisco and enters a vampire bar, Dracula's Daughter, where he hears how vampires are plotting against Lestat. The bar is a composite based on several gay bars in the Castro district near Anne's house. He is aware of Lestat's deeds, and in his new fortress, in a "snow-covered waste," he plays for Akasha and Enkil Lestat's music. He returns to find Enkil destroyed, and realizes that the source for the existence of all the vampires is in Akasha. She is the Great Mother—the dark side of the feminine, an image of ancient goddesses who demanded blood sacrifices. Akasha destroys the hiding place, trapping Marius under ice from which he sends a message of danger.

2. Vampires all over the world dream of red-haired twins being raped and mutilated. Many vampires are caught in a blaze of fire and annihilated. One such story is told through the eyes of a motorcycle chick named Baby Jenks, which brings the vampire mythos down from the aristocracy to include even the most ordinary people.

3. The vampire Pandora, first mentioned by Marius in *The Vampire Lestat,* emerges as a character and learns that Marius is trapped. She induces the vampire Santino to help her find him.

4. Daniel, the boy reporter from *Interview With the Vampire,* has become Armand's human companion, in response to readers who had asked what had become of him. Daniel begs for immortality. Armand sadistically plays with him in a segment that Anne thought almost as daring as her erotica. The debate between them exposes the human ambivalence at the heart of the matter: Is eternal life all it seems, or is there a price that makes mortality worth its own price? Armand reluctantly makes his first "child," and together they go to San Francisco. He teaches Daniel how to call forth "those who wanted to die," a reference to the story Anne had written years before for *Playboy.*

Anne originally had planned to make Armand central to the events that form the plot, but his development in the twentieth century improved him as a person and he was no longer the nihilistic vampire she needed. "I loved all that," said Anne, "like his experiences with the microwave and the telephone. They make it a rich kind of book. It was a theme of exploration."

5. The vampire Khayman is introduced as an ancient vampire with great strength and power. He can travel without his body to distant lands and can follow up an impulse to destroy other vampires just by thinking it. He is harder of substance, smoother and colder, "after centuries of the blood working, drying out his cells, making them thin and white and strong like the chambers of a wasps' nest." Khayman is lonely and moves with love toward other blood drinkers, but the ones he sees are destroyed. He realizes that Akasha is responsible as she aims for him, but he is invulnerable to her attack. He is drawn toward San Francisco.

6. Another human character, thirty-five-year-old Jesse, figures in the story by virtue of her lineage. She is descended from a red-haired woman, Maharet, who bore a child before she became a vampire in the time of Queen Akasha. Associated with Maharet is the vampire Eric, and also Mael, who became a vampire after Marius fled the druidic ceremony. Jesse is invited to spend the summer at Maharet's compound in Sonoma County, deep in the redwood forest—based on the setting around Anne's house. Anne sat for hours by the creek to plan these scenes, just as she had Jesse do in the novel.

Jesse does not realize Maharet and Mael are vampires, although she is puzzled by their strange behavior and by the fact that "Maharet's body felt like stone that could breathe." At the compound is a tapestry, woven with rich colors, that serves as a metaphor for the complexity and vividness of the story. Jesse is also shown Maharet's records of the historical lineage through six centuries of the family, traced all over the world. It reads like something out of the Old Testament and reinforces Anne's concept of family as profound interconnectedness. "It's horrible that most families disappear into chaos within a few generations," said Anne. "I thought, how wonderful if you knew your family all the way back. The Great Family was born from that idea." This careful documentation is symbolic of the continual awareness about which Marius spoke in *The Vampire Lestat* and provides another dimension to the bid for immortality. "It was the Great Family that mattered . . . the vitality in each generation, and the knowledge and love of one's kin."

To a lesser degree the theme had appeared before in the way family lineage gave substance and status to the free people of color and to the aristocracy of eighteenth-century Venice. It would show up again in *The Witching Hour,* and it is both a psychological and literary metaphor of bonding and continuity.

Jesse has psychic abilities and is contacted by an organization in London called the Talamasca, which has collected evidence of paranormal events since the year 758. The name was an ancient designation for a witch or shaman which Anne had run across in a book called *Witchcraft in the Middle Ages,* by Jeffrey Burton Russell.

"I saw the word Talamasca," Anne said, "and it inspired the whole idea of the organization. I thought the word was so beautiful."

Jesse is trained as a researcher, documenting reported hauntings and noting the research on witch families being watched by the Talamasca. These families would be the subject of Anne's next major literary effort, but the focus for Jesse would be on vampires.

She is sent on to New Orleans to document locations from Louis's book, wanting to prove that the book is just disturbing fiction. "There is something obscene about this novel," she says, echoing reviewers of *Interview.* "It makes the lives of these beings seem attractive. You don't realize it at first; it's a nightmare and you can't get out of it. Then all of a sudden you're comfortable there." She discovers properties around the city owned by a Lestat de Lioncourt, then sees Claudia's ghost. Breaking with the Talamasca, she attends Lestat's rock concert, suspecting Aunt Maharet is really a vampire.

3

At the concert, real vampires, including Daniel and Armand, mix with kids dressed as vampires. Mael is there to protect Jesse, and Khayman to observe. Backstage, Louis waits nervously, unaware that Akasha is passing over, destroying all the vampires except those protected by Lestat's love, as if they have been marked with the blood of the sacrificial lamb, which Lestat, as a Christ figure, represents.

To strengthen the symbolic parallels, he is described as having blood running like rivulets as if from a crown of thorns, as being unkillable, and as emerging stronger from the suffering forced upon him. "To join with him was to live forever." He offers to his audience the Transubstantiation, "This is my body. This is my blood." He is Christ echoing Dionysus—"Kill the god. Tear him limb from limb." The concert is full of energy and sensual descriptions which heighten the sinister atmosphere.

Jesse rushes onstage and touches Lestat to confirm her suspicions. She is then thrown against a wall by another vampire and has her neck broken. As she feels herself dying, she expresses fears personal to Anne: "When I was little," says Jesse, "I used to think it would be like this, death. You'd be trapped in your head in the grave, with no eyes to see and no mouth to scream. And years and years would pass. Or you roamed the twilight realm with the pale ghosts; thinking you were alive when you were really dead." Maharet saves her by making her a vampire, adding details that give the experience the erotic sensations of ultimate surrender, gleaned from writing pornography: "She felt it all being taken back, drawn out. Like the whistling wind, the sensation of being emptied, of being devoured; of being nothing!"

After the concert, the hostile vampires explode into flame. Lestat leaves with Gabrielle and Louis, as recounted in *The Vampire Lestat,* then is abducted by Akasha.

The book then divides between what Akasha wants of Lestat and what the surviving vampires do about it, and much of the format involves philosophical discussions about free will, nihilism, and moral responsibility. On a subliminal level, Anne completes the theme of paradox begun in the other two Chronicles, with implications for idealistic abstractions as part of any plan, political, religious, or social, for how to live. Although she creates atmosphere, it is not the tension of forbidden relationships but of something genuinely sinister now confronting the force of moral goodness.

Lestat learns that Akasha wants him to help her actualize a plan for bringing an era of peace to the world by creating a new world order. "The Children of Darkness are no more," she tells him. "And we shall have only angels now." Just as Dionysus had been taught by women, so Akasha teaches Lestat his powers and reminds him of how he once had prayed so hard to be good. "You said you would suffer martyrdom . . . if only you were to be someone who was good." She explains that goodness exists "because we put it there," and that he and she are destined to be the gods sung about in the world's religions. Akasha understands that to be a god is to possess all truth. She decides that truth is what she makes it, and if it originates with her, then she *is* a god.

As the oldest vampire, she has surrendered to and been "perfected" by demonic blood until she is like marble. Her body hardened and her human empathies diminished. Lestat describes her as "a dead and perfect thing . . . the icy skin seemed absolutely impenetrable." Similarly, her thoughts and visions have a rigid quality. She is the least human of the vampires, a condition with metaphorical implications.

A human being is open to future possibilities, striving to transcend limitations through choice. The vampire is trapped in its situation and is closer to an animated corpse. Vampires like Lestat, however, who retain human memories and sympathy, symbolize ambivalence, with a foot in both worlds—the picture of a dualistic concept of human consciousness linked with the philosophy of Sartre. Although Anne did not consciously develop her story according to this philosophy, the parallels clearly emerge, indicating how she is attempting and accomplishing more than merely telling a vampire story.

According to Sartre, we freely choose what we are and through that choice we possess the power to transcend our situations. However, it also means taking responsibility for what we do or become. Since we have a limited perspective on the future and the capacity to make mistakes—even to fail—we would rather relinquish this responsibility. We look around and see objects that simply are what they are, without choice or responsibility. That kind of existence is attractive, despite the fact that giving up our humanity and becoming a thing is accomplished only at death, when we become corpses. Nevertheless, we mimic objects by defining ourselves in ways that diminish our personal responsibility, as with rigid social roles which, like vampires, can drain us of human essence.

This is like the pure concept of the vampire, an animated corpse, a *thing,* with no way to transcend what it is. The older vampires grow, the less vivid are their human ties. "It is the human that has become myth to us," claims Lestat. Becoming a vampire is being emptied of the blood, the essence of human life, and being filled with blood empowered by an evil spirit. Perfecting the vampire nature destroys the human part—the heart and the will, like "being dissolved as a pearl in wine." Unless vampires make a concerted effort to remain sensitive to their humanity, as Marius did through art, they grow too distant to care about what they do among the human race.

The other vampires in the novel remember what being human was like and cherish what it meant. "To be human," says Lestat, "that's what most of us long for." They don't want to die, but immortality carries the price of being trapped forever in their static essence; so they want to be human, which means death but it also means the evolution available only through free choice.

Akasha has no contact with humans that keeps alive the ambivalent bond because she is sustained by her progeny. She is finished with life. Even as a mortal woman she despised her limitations and consequently does not struggle to retain human compassion. In her centuries-long dormancy, while her body ossified, her mind fed on the concept of absolute perfection—an idea formed by what she was becoming. She wants to create a new Eden, a plan for a defined arena in which she is master and humans are her slaves. Her blueprint calls for a reign of violence to ensure her status as the divine meaning-maker. She is a combination of object and goddess, both forms of existence which cancel the possibility of being human.

Lestat is to be her witness and her tool. Akasha requires that he surrender to his power and put it to use for her purposes. She offers Lestat the world if only he will follow her, the way Satan tempted Christ. He is her mirror image, she insists: she, too, wants to do "good," and his resurrection in the twentieth century was also hers. Citing the centuries of cruelty and injustice against women, and the fact that only women can actualize peace, she tells him that he has to help her kill ninety-nine per cent of the males in the world. It is the men, she claims, who are responsible for most of the world's violence, and reducing their numbers will ensure peace. The women will worship her as the goddess of their salvation.

Akasha embodies the theme that had come to Anne as she watched the *Star Wars* movie: she has a good idea that is still evil. It is not clothed in darkness but takes the guise of enlightenment. "The real evil in the world," said Anne, "is a complex and seductive thing that sounds brilliant." Anne felt that Akasha was right in what she said—that most violence is caused by men—but wrong in viewing wanton destruction as an answer.

Akasha sets out to "spin a great and glorious religion" with the mesmerized Lestat as her chosen prince, until it becomes the "Bethlehem of the new era." She is the new Madonna, a symbol of salvation, a reversal of the Christian religion.

Although Anne thought Akasha's violence paralleled the AIDS epidemic in its focus on victimizing predominantly males, Akasha is more potently the image of Hitler in her vision of the ultimate paradise at the immediate expense of millions of lives. She seeks absolute power and absolute obedience, and in return she will provide answers to all the questions that plague humans—*her* answers. The world will be modeled on her vision. She seeks to replace the values of humans that have been hammered out through flesh-and-blood experience with those generated by abstract thought influenced by petrification. She will turn humans into things that fit her framework. Like Dostoevsky's Grand Inquisitor, Akasha's reign will relieve them of free choice. She will replace the Christian kingdom of God—wherein a faulty and chaotic system of free will undergirds human evolution—with the Kingdom of Woman, where she is in control. "I am the way," she says in echo of Christ. "The gateway to innocence." To accomplish this image, she must find a way to dissolve current value systems. The evil, blood-sucking vampire must be reframed as God.

Lestat sees his own idea taken to an extreme. He had wanted to use his evil powers to do good. He thought he could accomplish that by driving people toward the good, although he worked his scenario out through powerful religious imagery that actually made him more attractive. He exhibited himself as a Dionysian Christ figure who offered immortality, even as he emphasized, "Am I not the devil in you all!" As a god-devil, he acquiesces to Akasha's logic, albeit ambivalently. He already embodies, she points out, the vampire's questionable justification of killing in order to survive to kill again. The self-devouring cycle renders moral values for vampires inherently meaningless. Lestat vaguely acknowledges this.

He is put into action on a small island, Lykanos. As he kills one man after another in an orgy of gore, he is repulsed but also excited. "I loved it beyond all reason, loved it as men have always loved it in the absolute moral freedom of war—" Anne describes the violence in sensual terms, as if the killing were orgiastic in the way that the symbolic violence of her pornography issued in sexual release. Some reviewers later criticized the amount of violence.

"To me," said Anne, "it was not a particularly violent book. The ancient immortals would be very savage and they would tear bodies apart, but I don't think that's violent. They were so cold it would take an enormous amount to warm them up. The theme of killing runs throughout the book, so when Lestat confronted this ability to kill all kinds of people instantly, that was a progression."

Although Lestat had insisted to Gabrielle two hundred years before that he would resist such an attempt by vampires to take over the world, he is completely caught up in it, partly because it makes him most fully himself and partly because he is drugged by Akasha's beauty. "It struck me that never in all my life had I beheld anything quite as beautiful as she was. . . . It was the pure serenity, the essence that I perceived with my innermost soul. A lovely euphoria came over me as she spoke." She is his own vampire nature taking over.

Lestat serves as Akasha's masculine symbol, to perform her will. He is "perfectly what is wrong with all things male," and the men are sacrificed to the embodiment of their own violence. She takes him to other places like Sri Lanka and Nepal to continue the slaughter, and he responds once again but feels guilty and confused.

His debate with her is Anne's debate with herself. She feels a great deal of anger at the injustices women have suffered and against the mindless aggression of men. In most of her novels she takes note of the animal violence in men and the desire to cause pain that women cannot understand—evident even in her most sympathetic male characters. She had witnessed it in men she'd known and had discussed it with them. She felt that Akasha had something valid to say, and Anne was curious herself at what a world run by women would be like. Yet she resisted the idea of depriving people of their willed evolution, believing that human culture was moving in positive directions.

Akasha's plan is complicated, involving nihilism—devaluing all values to the point of meaninglessness—as its foundation. For her there is no objective standard of truth, and without that, what one person sees as true or right may be just as feasibly seen by another as false or wrong. Akasha depends on this slippery relativism to mold moral values to her own purposes. The only absolute is her own power. "In the name of *my* morality! . . . I am the reason, the justification, the right by which it is done! . . . I am the Queen of Heaven . . . I am anything that I say I am." She takes pride in the paradox of drawing her own meaning from the void of meaninglessness as if it were similar to provoking a smile on an impassive face. Hers is not the power of chaos but of pure abstraction, doomed in its very perfection.

4

In the meantime, the vampires who have been spared Akasha's fire gather at Maharet's compound in Sonoma. The house itself, "a great hidden dwelling within the mountain," is a symbol for the hidden powers and mysteries about to be revealed. It can also be understood as the hidden part within each person where the tension of good and evil makes possible the creative evolution of moral ideals.

Armand comes with Daniel; Santino and Pandora bring Marius; and Khayman comes with Louis and Gabrielle. Mael and Eric are already there. Consistent with Anne's novels, the reunions are charged with sexual feeling and bittersweet emotion, portrayed most strongly in the meeting after five hundred years of Marius and Armand. "He kissed Armand's lips, and his long, loose vagabond hair. He ran his hand covetously over Armand's shoulders." Such scenes drew out strong responses from female readers. The freely expressed affection between male figures provides a feminine element in the relationships with which women can identify enough to go a step further and experience their masculine sides in the perspectives and erotic feelings of the characters. The subliminal tension of blending experiences normally divided into male and female is exciting, almost dangerous.

Each of the vampires is aware of the significance of the others and now has a chance to scrutinize them. Through this device the reader is reunited with familiar characters and alerted to tensions among them, as if each has stepped into this novel from a larger world. Maharet holds them all in awe. She is the immortal who "had never slept, never gone silent, never been released by madness . . . who had walked with a rational mind and measured steps through all the millennia."

Maharet and Akasha are Anne's strongest female characters, made psychologically possible by her development in the earlier novels of Gabrielle and Lisa. Maharet and her descendant, Jesse, are the mother and daughter lost to Anne, now reclaimed. Maharet especially is as strong and wise as any of the male characters and clearly emerges as the leader in the crisis. She speaks with the forthright simplicity of primitive times and is the most truly immortal on several levels. She has been the ultimate "continuous awareness" for six thousand years, as well as keeping her finger to the pulse of her immense human family. She represents most fully the vampire and the human in equal measure. Maharet assures the others that Akasha will not harm Lestat "because she doesn't want to harm herself" and tells them how Akasha became the first vampire.

5

Anne knew she had a difficult task ahead as she set out to write the ancient tale. She had read a great deal in archaeology and anthropology, but the trick was expressing it through the consciousness of Maharet. "It was a very important challenge to create Maharet," she said, "to take people who were supposed to be thousands of years old and imbue them with wisdom and try to imagine what their shortcomings would be. I wanted a concept of a really wise person who had flaws that came from the time she was made into a vampire."

Maharet had a twin sister, Mekare, and they were powerful seers, known as witches, in a time when Egyptians practiced cannibalism of their loved ones to imbibe their spirit and prevent the body from decaying. The use of twins emphasizes the theme of duality that occurs in the novel, a symbol of ambiguity as well as of the repeated image of two sides of a single entity.

Anne had known several pairs of twins. She had dated a twin once, and had questioned Linda Gregg about her experience with her sister, learning how they'd related, how they had developed their own language, how they'd been identical but different. Anne used the information to assist her in her fictional portraits. "I was enthralled with the idea of twins," she said. "I find it fascinating that twins are genuine clones of each other. I think when you talk about what twins do to each other and what they are, you're getting a real heightened look at us. We're all brothers and sisters of each other."

Similarly, Maharet and Mekare forged a unique bond and doubled their mother's power. They spoke to spirits, who were giant, ageless, invisible bodies of whirling energy with tiny cores of physical matter and morally inferior to humans. Anne's discussion of spirits incorporates the research of modern parapsychology with ancient beliefs, although the notion of having infinitely large shapes was her own invention. She had been inspired by a notion of Bergson's that the brain would dream endlessly if it did not have the physical imperative of the body. When they concentrated themselves, she indicated, they had the power to move the physical world. She adds a bit of polemic. "Perhaps their obsession with the erotic," says Maharet, "is merely something abstracted from the minds of men and women who have always felt guilty about such things." Some spirits, like Amel, were jealous of human bodies, but were impotent to obtain flesh, though Amel kept trying.

In another land, King Enkil marries Akasha. They hear about the witches and send for them. Maharet and Mekare refuse to come, sensing "a mixture of good and evil that seemed more dangerous than evil itself." Their mother sickens and dies. They prepare to eat her brain, the seat of the human spirit, and the heart, where feeling resided.

The soldiers of the king and queen crush the feast, kill the tribe, and abduct the twins. They come before the royal couple and perceive that Akasha is a woman of spiritual emptiness, who deceives herself about her motives and actions.

> A moral cloak had been thrown over the Queen's purpose, a cloak through which she could not see . . . and even deeper beyond her deception, we beheld the mind that made such contradictions possible. This Queen had no true morality, no true system of ethics to govern the things that she did . . . for always in her there was a dark place full of despair. And a great driving force to make meaning because there was none. . . . It was a youthful belief that she could make the light shine if she tried; that she could shape the world to comfort herself.

Akasha is impressed with their tales. "It was the spiritual question which fascinated her . . . the abstract idea was everything." She is afraid, but also bitterly disillusioned when the supernatural does not measure up to the myths. Her psychological development feasibly parallels what had happened to Anne. Taught to believe in a great and wondrous religious system that failed to deliver when she most needed it, she fell away from it into a dark skepticism that did not satisfy her as much as her childhood beliefs. There is great pain associated with breaking away. Her descriptions seem authentic:

> The dark secret place inside her was becoming larger; it was threatening to consume her from within; she could not let such a thing happen; she had to go on. . . . On the other hand, she was angry and the rage she felt was against her parents and against her teachers, and against the priests and priestesses of her childhood, and against the gods she had worshiped and against anyone who had ever comforted her, or told her that life was good.

In an interview in 1988, Anne acknowledged that she still felt anger against church dogmas. She and her character Akasha enter the same inner abyss, with its primitive and malleable elements, but for Anne this pain eventually took the direction of psychological liberation, while Akasha sank deeper into a self-fed cycle of spiritual and moral disintegration.

Akasha declares that the spirits of the witches are demons. To prove they have no power, Khayman, the king's steward, is ordered to rape them. They are set free, and Maharet has a baby.

A year later, Khayman comes after them and tells them that an evil spirit has entered the bodies of the king and queen and that they are afraid of light and are ravenous for blood. Their very substance has been changed, transubstantiated.

The twins return and witness the change, understanding that the event is an accident of circumstances. What seems a transformation into gods is in fact the possession of demons. Enraged, the queen condemns them to die. Mekare declares that she will stop the queen in her hour of greatest menace. She loses her tongue while Maharet loses her eyes.

The queen turns Khayman into a vampire. Furious, he gives the "gift" to Mekare so that she will have the power to fulfill her prophecy. She makes Maharet into a vampire, but they are sealed in separate stone coffins, taken to opposite oceans, and set adrift, losing track of each other. Maharet retains her bond with her family through the lineage of her child, but she never gives up her search for Mekare, who she fears has lost her mind.

Maharet shows the other vampires the immense family tree—"an endless ink-drawn vine"—traced through the matrilineal heritage. She understands that the essence of humanity is the ability to transcend the present toward the future through will and choice. As such, there is always hope for something better. She cites the trend away from the supernatural toward a life of reason and universal vision as evidence of a move toward something positive. It is clear that she is the feminine side of Anne that believes in something good, that is trying to free herself of the grim qualities of the feminine that have plagued her in her writings: Lisa was humorless, Marianna hit her child, Gabrielle was a loner who detested her family, Akasha embodied nihilism and violence, killing her children, while Maharet preserves hers with great care. In this novel Anne does not move back and forth between the male and female. Instead the female has emerged and divided into two perspectives: one associated with pain and death and the other with life. Each seeks to annihilate the other because it is difficult to have hope weighed down by skepticism. One or the other must yield.

Lestat asks to see his friends. Akasha decides to allow it, believing she may have to destroy them to force him to join her. The vampires with Maharet are aware of what Akasha has been doing and tell her that they are prepared to stop her even if it means they will all die with her. Maharet and Marius attempt to convince Akasha that she is wrong. "It is not man who is the enemy of the human species. It is the irrational; it is the spiritual when it is divorced from the material."

Akasha's separation from experience as she lay dormant for centuries has blinded her; she is as Maharet described, the "thing that has no flesh." She represents "the idea"—abstractions that leave no room for humanity. Maharet confronts Akasha with the fact that it is she "who has not changed in six thousand years," while mortals have continued to evolve beyond primitive violence toward attitudes that hold promise for the future. Marius agrees. "Men and women are learning animals . . ." he says. "They are creatures ever changing, ever improving, ever expanding their vision and the capacity of their hearts." Lestat joins in to plead for Akasha to see that her vision is false. "It is the very simplicity and elegance that make it so wrong! . . . Through complexity men struggle toward fairness; simplicity demands too great a sacrifice." She cannot truly be a god because all she can do is kill.

Anne tended toward the view that this century had demonstrated that religion, and even the concept of evil, was not essential to ethical behavior and that love among people who recognize their kindred bonds can have a positive impact on the world. In fact, to her mind Akasha represented the destructive power of religion on a massive scale. Anne believed that humanity should keep moving toward enlightenment free of religious tyranny, and her sympathies were with Maharet and Marius.

Akasha is not persuaded by the arguments. She demands that Lestat come to her side, but he does not yield. Without him, she is weakened. She needs him as her mirror, to justify her plan.

Then Mekare, the lost sister, rushes in and pushes Akasha through a glass wall, cutting off her head. The scene is surprisingly quick for such a long buildup. "Sometimes one of the reasons I don't protract a scene," said Anne, "is that I can't with words protract a violent scene like that much longer than I did." For Anne it was not really the climax.

Akasha reaches for her severed head as the other vampires black out. Maharet moves faster and grabs the exposed brain; she gets Mekare to consume it along with Akasha's heart—the body parts of their mother destroyed by Akasha's soldiers. The act saves the vampires from destruction and they all recognize the image from their dreams. It is the ultimate reunion, replacing Akasha as the negative side of the feminine with Mekare, the true completion of the self. The story has come full circle.

"That part of the book felt dreamlike," Anne said. "Like the dream of seeing the white figure walking down the sidewalk and hearing that it was my Regis grandmother. To write it was the most heightened, wonderful experience, and it was the biggest dare that I had ever tried to pull off in a book, to have that moment come when everyone understood the funeral feast and the message of the dreams. There were times when I thought, 'You can't pull this off.' "

6

What brings Akasha down is her own system. It is based on paradox, but paradox is realizable only in thought. It cannot be lived. For example, to say of the phrase, "This sentence is false," that it is true is to become involved in something like a snake eating its own tail. Saying, "Yes, it's true," makes it false. Saying, "No, it is false," makes it true. And if true, then false! Such a sentence has no real meaning. It can be played with on a conceptual level, but it can never have concrete impact in the physical world. It mirrors on a mental level the fluctuating primitive energies within the self that must be stabilized in thought and behavior to be expressed. The "new order" Akasha has set up is based on the fact that "this sentence is meaningless" has meaning. She declares the world to be devoid of meaning and uses that declaration to be *her* meaning. Like other paradoxes, it threatens to cancel itself and thus cannot really dictate the practical actions of human beings.

Added to that, her system is reinforced by sleight-of-hand with the concept of symmetry—an exact balance of properties, mirrored in each other. She first recognized the perfection of symmetry in the red-haired twins, viewing it as the source of their mystical power. Through what they abstractly represented to her as mirror images, she worked out a logic of symmetry to assist her bid for the status of godhood. Make the world in *her* own image. Lestat fits into the system as her male completion—the symmetry of opposites, the male/female. Her logic involves three steps:

> 1. With pairs of opposites, one is defined against the other, as with good and evil. If one is rendered null, the other collapses; i.e., if good has no meaning, neither does evil because its context for definition is erased. Nihilism renders all moral concepts null: they are thus mirror images in their meaninglessness.
>
> 2. If they are the same, they are no longer opposite: if nothing is true, then everything is true, because if nothing is true, then nothing is false. Hence, everything is also false.
>
> 3. Being the same, the concepts are interchangeable in the way synonyms are.

Thus, Akasha has the framework she needs. She dissolves meaning so that opposite values reflect each other as meaningless, then reverses them and breathes new life into them via her status as God. What had been evil is now good. Women can take the place of men. Myth becomes reality. Darkness replaces light. Murdering men becomes an act of benevolence rather than malice. Akasha, the vampire queen, becomes a goddess. The other vampires can become her angels. "My head swam from the paradox," says Lestat.

Her reliance on this sleight-of-hand, however, is also her stumbling block. Power becomes vulnerability. It is her insecurity that finally betrays her. She needs a mirror image for herself that will remain a mirror image—a companion apart from her who reinforces her vision. However, this companion must also retain his individuality in order to provide external justification. If she collapses opposites into a unity, then her companion is herself and she is alone—something she cannot endure. "Not in all the long centuries of stillness had she ever been alone, had she ever suffered the ultimate isolation." Her own existence becomes a paradox as she seeks to impose her image on the world and make it so like herself—a thing, trapped by its nature—that she actually loses what she most wants: beings outside her that will worship her. True worship is based in love and love entails choice. Her logic of *deep* or absolute symmetry conflicts with her desire for only *apparent* symmetry and the confusion weakens her resolve.

Lestat recognizes her vulnerability. "I had found the key . . . it was her need of me; the need of one ally in all the great realm; one kindred soul made of the same stuff that she was made of. And she believed she could make me like herself." She denies it, but her denial reveals that the source of her momentum lies not in the concept of symmetry but in self-deception.

Akasha can transform values through paradox and symmetry only by ignoring contradictions. For example, she cannot have an enduring human race without men to assist in procreation, but rather than admit the deficiency in her militantly feminist system, she reframes, as simple graciousness, the blemish of keeping some men alive: "But for the conceptual framework to be changed, the males must be gone. . . . It may not even be necessary to keep the one in a hundred. But it would be generous to do so." She tries to establish an abstract system and fails to see how it clashes with the concreteness of life itself. Thus her foundation for a new world order becomes the vehicle for its own disintegration.

In perfect symmetry, fundamental elements are identical and therefore indistinguishable. But like paradox, symmetry can be grasped only in thought. It is an aesthetic principle of simplicity that is imposed on the world by those who seek perfection. But it represents the absence of dynamic; there is no opposition, no diversity. What Akasha saw in the symmetry of the red-haired twins was not true symmetry at all. Their spiritual power resulted from a blend of different but complementary traits. Maharet was cautious, Mekare assertive. Each had her own unique access to the spirit world. Life itself arises from interactions among pairs of true opposites that coexist in creative tension, as with androgyny. It is a man with a woman that begets a child, not a woman with a woman. She thus misconstrues symmetry as a generative power rather than the leveling force it really is.

Dissolving the dynamic of opposites through symmetry eventually results in a regularity that revolves, according to physicists, toward repose, austerity, and even death. Thus, the "vital link" in Akasha's logic for transforming values is also the greatest obstacle to her plan. Akasha cannot think otherwise, however, since her vampire nature dictates an evolution toward "thingness" rather than toward the dynamic of life. A world order molded by her thinking must, like her, slip into the dark, lifeless nothingness of the mummified corpse.

Lestat perceives the "chaos, the total loss of all moral equilibrium." There was "no way for her to have value and be the thing that she was." He saw the contradiction clearly: "She was absolutely right and absolutely wrong!" He fears what she represents and resists her, clinging to the human, as represented in a hand-wrought iron gate that stood as something solid and man-made in the chaos. "I loved her but I couldn't stand with her," he realizes. He is stung into seeing how self-deceptive his own ambitions have been. Akasha represents the place within himself where he wrestles with his contrary nature. Admitting his hypocrisy, he gains the strength of honesty to find his resolve. "We're not angels, Akasha; we are not gods." He smashes the symmetry when he stands with the others on the side of traditional moral values.

In the end, all symmetry breaks down. The twins are further divided with Mekare's new status as the source of the vampire power and the "goddess" is brought down "with a human gesture." Freedom is saved so that humans can continue to wrestle with the agonizing but life-enhancing questions of good and evil. The dialogue of human evolution is salvaged from the raging effects of nihilism.

The metaphorical struggle in the story is on a global level, depicting dictators who strip people of freedom and even of life. However, it also applies on an individual level as the struggle that lies within every person between having existence fully defined, like objects, and having the power to choose, even though it entails responsibility. It is the struggle between relinquishing our lives to someone else's dictates and being alive to our continuous evolution: being "somebody or somebody's girl," victim or hero. It is, ironically, the vampires who teach us what it means to be human, just as Anne had intended from the first book, by going to the heart of our moral dilemmas.

The place where an ending might seem natural is not the place where Anne stopped. Her characters are too real to her to leave their fates up in the air.

7

The surviving vampires recover together, and Lestat concentrates on writing down the whole story. He follows Louis to New Orleans, and here Anne moves him through reveries of the loss of mother and daughter—Akasha and Claudia. He was the prince that had brought to life both "sleeping beauties." Deeply involved in their fates, as Anne was with her mother and daughter, he feels a sense of loss and responsibility. "Real hauntings have nothing to do with ghosts finally; they have to do with the menace of memory."

His soul still aches for something that he cannot put his finger on. To Louis he asks the question ever present in Anne's novels: "Do you love me?" Although *Belinda* brought Anne close to what she sought as she cut through layers with her work, this novel seems to have brought back the sting of something lost and seemingly inaccessible. "Blessed darkness has come again," Lestat says to Louis. The feeling of being enveloped in darkness still quickened something in Anne, especially in a New Orleans setting.

Lestat takes Louis with him to the headquarters of the Talamasca in London, where he breaks rules that the vampires have agreed on. He delights in feeling good about being bad. A note at the end assures readers that there will be yet a fourth installment to the Vampire Chronicles.

8

Anne turned in the finished draft of *The Queen of the Damned* at Christmas, feeling exhilarated that she had written the novel she wanted without compromising. *"The Queen of the Damned,"* she said, "was the only book I ever wrote exactly the way I wanted to write it. It was the first totally realized vision that I'd ever created, and it was a very pleasant experience." The vision was all there in a complex weaving of multiple plot lines and characters. "I think it has more meaning in it than anything I've ever written, about the truth in substance and what that sacred cannibalism meant. The part that was most exciting to me was when Jesse was made into a vampire and she says that it anchored her to substance forever."

She thought perhaps it should have been longer. There had been a lot of talking back and forth among the vampires, and she felt she needed more detail with Lestat and Louis in the final chapter, or with Daniel or Jesse. She believed she should have taken up each of the characters in full to balance the form, but it would have meant many more pages, so she decided to wait until the fourth novel. As it was, she had taken a big step forward in accomplishing something as a writer.

"It is a much more demanding book than *Lestat,*" she said, "because the form is good and tight. You have to concentrate on what's going on." She felt the writing was better than even *Belinda,* and she attributed her artistic growth to writing the Rampling novels.

Vicky Wilson suggested Anne shorten the last chapter. She rewrote it and made it longer. She had to restrain herself from cutting out things that seemed to her to bear similarities to other novels. She had read Stephen King's *The Stand* and wondered at the possible influence but realized she was being overscrupulous, that this was an original work and not really anything like *The Stand.*

Before *The Queen of the Damned* was even in galleys, Anne went to work on another project. Independent producers Larry Sanitzky and Frank Konigsberg visited her in San Francisco to invite her to write the bible for a miniseries for Richard Chamberlain—hopefully for CBS. Anne had been toying with the idea of writing a mummy story with a romantic twist—she described the concept: the mummy would be a beautiful man. To her delight, they were interested. She developed a plot and started to write.

In the midst of her project, the house in the woods was sold, to Christopher's great relief. Anne felt that she had gotten her money's worth for the value of its inspiration. The house had been a substitute for her for the big oak trees of the South, but the redwood forest just did not fill the empty space. The Rices realized they could afford a second home in New Orleans so Anne could continue with *The Witching Hour.* In July 1988, Stan took a leave of absence for one semester and they headed for the Crescent City.

Anne wanted a house near to where she grew up. Her own childhood home on Philip and St. Charles was almost in ruins due to the negligence of an absentee landlord. Their real estate agent found a house on the other side of the Garden District, in the Irish Channel, at 1020 Philip Street, right around the corner from her cousin Billy, living now in the house of his parents.

"The move to New Orleans," said Anne, "has been the culmination of long-time dreams. At times, things worked out so well, they seemed aided by some preternatural element."

The house was one hundred and thirty years old, pink-hued on the outside with hardwood floors throughout. The Rices filled it with antiques. It was just a block out of the Garden District, across Magazine Street, and only a few blocks from St. Alphonsus and Redemptorist School. More important, it was only two blocks from the imaginary setting of *The Witching Hour,* just down Philip Street. Christopher was resistant, wanting to go back to the place that *he* knew as home.

Although they had made frequent trips to New Orleans, they were not at all sure they would like taking up permanent residence. Anne wondered if the city would pale against her rich memories. She knew that she needed to be there to get the right atmosphere for *The Witching Hour,* but she was not at all sure that living there would be the best inspiration. For all she knew, it was being away that worked best for her, the grief and the longing to be back. So they kept their house in San Francisco just in case.

Coming back, Anne realized that the southern Gothic ambience of New Orleans was just as intense as she had remembered, and she described her experience of coming home through the character of Michael in *The Witching Hour.* She wrote to the sound of rain falling on an immense growth of plants and trees, and felt that the atmosphere made her descriptions richer and deeper. She loved the smell of flowers and river breezes, and seeing the violet skies again.

Stan now had the freedom he had always wanted—and the space—to try his hand at painting large canvases. He needed a break from teaching poetry and had always longed to see what would develop in another artistic direction. He set up a studio in the carriage house out back and experimented with a wide variety of styles, interspersing his newfound leisure with bicycle trips with Chris to explore the city that he was liking better all the time. Chris adapted to his surroundings and became a regular companion to his Uncle Billy but watched the settling in with a suspicious eye.

Anne readjusted herself to her hometown. She set up her computer on a table in the bedroom, from which she could see the steeples of St. Alphonsus and St. Mary's Assumption. She wanted to get back to *The Witching Hour,* to really immerse herself in the landscape of her childhood. Wandering the Garden District, she relived the awe and trepidation, letting the sensations and images brew in her mind along with literary ideas.

"It was very important for me to come back to New Orleans," she said, "and the older I got, the more bitter I became and almost panic-stricken about not being here because I couldn't establish any kind of rooted feeling in California. I needed to be near the landscape and incidents of my childhood. It means a great deal to me to pass the church where I made my First Communion and to see the church where my parents got married. I consider them valuable to the continuity in one place of several generations growing up. These people share a genetic history with you and there are things they can tell you, things that happen with them just don't happen with anyone else. I wanted to be around the colors, textures, shapes, and smells that I had experienced as a child. I experience a day-to-day happiness and contentment here that is extraordinary."

9

Anne finished the script of *The Mummy* and sent it to Hollywood. She was stunned at the treatment her work received. The bible she had written was torn apart. The producers wanted to change almost every part of her story. In a conference call, she listened as they suggested new ideas.

Finally she walked out and sent the bible over to Bob Wyatt at Ballantine with the idea of turning the story into a trade paperback. Anne had retained the rights to her characters, and she wanted them to talk and behave according to her own visions. She wrote the novel along the lines of the original bible, without substantial change, and sent the manuscript to Wyatt just before she was scheduled to begin her tour for the publication of *The Queen of the Damned*. The experience, excruciating as it was, reminded her that she was not good as a collaborator, and it gave her a sour taste for the people in Hollywood. She felt as if they had no respect for her as a writer, that she was nothing more to them than a painter who comes in to change the color of the walls. She was not going through that again.

In October, *The Queen of the Damned* outsold *The Vampire Lestat* by four to one in hardcover. Anne was amazed. The book went to the top of *The New York Times* bestseller list the week it was released and stayed on the list for seventeen weeks. It eventually sold almost four hundred thousand copies and was number seven in sales for fiction that year.

Anne went on another publicity tour, and people waited in line for hours to get her to sign their books. She could hardly believe how her novels had picked up in popularity. People even asked her to sign the pornography.

The novel was widely reviewed.

In *The New York Times,* novelist Eric Kraft found Baby Jenks "the liveliest voice in the book" and noted the "lush imagery," but seemed disturbed by the way the "book wallows in gore while preaching peace." He acknowledged Anne's "enormous ability" but felt her gifts were "wasted on vampires."

Other reviewers agreed. In the *Wall Street Journal,* Donna Rifkind yearned for the "grand passion" of the old Dracula image. She found Anne's vampires "juiceless," "vain," "demanding," "quarrelsome," "insecure," and "materialistic." They were "cardboard monsters." Rifkind found the writing pseudo-Gothic and dull, although she thought the novel was "inventive." In *People Weekly,* Ralph Novak perceived no metaphorical value and felt the story lacked internal consistency. In a review comparing Anne to previous vampire authors, Jewelle Gomez wrote in *Belles Lettres* that Anne had lost the tension of her earlier books and that this one was too cluttered and rambling.

However, in *Library Journal,* Michael Rogers pronounced it "quality fiction written with care and intelligence. There are no false steps or wasted words in the multilayered plot and the many characters each have a distinct voice."

In Tennessee now, Andy Brumer pointed out the metaphorical nature of the novels. He saw within the work explicit archetypal images of the divided soul and the Great Mother, and viewed the novel as a philosophical treatment of the aesthetic and chemical highs during the Vietnam War period. "These vampires . . . are highly tuned to life's rhythms and patterns, and are constantly in awe of the physical world as it is revealed to them through their senses." He perceived the contradictions as essential to the style.

Ironically, now that Anne was in New Orleans, a good review appeared in the *San Francisco Chronicle.*

Again, the variety of reactions was confusing to her. One reviewer saw no metaphorical value, while another praised the richness of metaphor. One thought it rambled while another found it tightly woven. Although bad reviews still hurt, Anne now perceived how "arbitrary and irresponsible" reviewing could be. "With my books," she said, "I always get a bunch of vicious reviews and a bunch of good ones. There's no critical consensus. The gulf between the way my books are received by the readers and the way they're received by reviewers is larger than with most American writers. They don't expect vampires to have subtlety or nuance. As I get older, I realize that this is just a total crap shoot. It's very embittering. You have people writing awful stuff about books they don't understand, but that's the nature of book reviewing. Nobody holds anyone to account. In opera reviewing, in drama, in music, you must know what you are talking about. In book reviewing, the level of responsibility is very low."

To her delight, her work was being taken seriously by some academics. Her books were assigned in courses, and at Carnegie-Mellon in Pittsburgh, students started a newsletter discussing the vampire characters. A woman sent a master's thesis that she had written on Anne's novels, and in New Orleans a national fan club formed and quickly grew. She received letters from psychologists and scholars along with her regular fan mail. Anne was also invited by a group of scholars to speak at their annual conference. It had been her dream to reach a popular audience and still be taken seriously, which seemed to be happening.

Anne had adjusted herself to reviews that called her style excessive and florid. Although they were negatively intended, she was beginning to understand that it was a regional response and typical of reviews for southern writers. To her delight, she had heard that many people in New Orleans considered *The Feast of All Saints* their book. In California she had not felt entitled to perceive herself as part of the southern tradition of writing, but being in New Orleans, coupled with a deeper grasp of how the city had affected her perceptions and her style, she felt more at home with the label.

"I feel that I am a southern writer," she said, "not only by virtue of being here now but by virtue of having written so many books set here. The people, the geography, the cadences, and the language are a basic backdrop for a southern writer's fiction. The tradition of southern writing to me is a tradition of very lush descriptive writing with a great deal of romance thrown in—I'm referring to the romantic view of life that has to do with describing the life of the mind and the imagination and primarily the emotions, as opposed to, say, pedestrian realism—writing about the problems of the middle class in stripped-down language. To be a southern writer is to grow up here and to have this storytelling of the southerners in your head, to be drenched in this sensuous environment, to be affected by this pace, and to be profoundly influenced by other southern writers. The language of the story shapes the story. It involves a belief that language is the shaping element of consciousness."

In October, during a book signing, Anne was officially welcomed back to New Orleans. Representatives of the city came with the news media from a local station to present her with a fake honorary deed to a burial plot in St. Louis Cemetery. She also received a wreath of garlic that she hung near her typewriter until the smell drove her to move it. A group of writers and poets threw a party, and she was gratified by how friendly everyone was. She felt more at home here than she had in the literary community back in California. "We met all these people," she said, "and they laid their books out on the coffee table and wanted to introduce us to the community of writers. They're warm and open and not horribly competitive. They were much more accepting."

The city was experiencing an artistic revival, and Anne was excited to be a part of it. Stan extended his one-semester leave so they could stay in New Orleans for the next nine months. They celebrated their first Christmas in New Orleans, basking in the glow of Anne's recent success.

For her Christmas had always been a special time, a time of renewal, like New Year's Eve to other people. She loved Dickens's *A Christmas Carol* for its theme of rebirth. It seemed that everything was working out and she felt deeply happy. The sense of wholeness, of piecing together lost fragments of her life, would be expressed in her next major hardcover book, *The Witching Hour*.

CHAPTER TWELVE

THE GREAT FAMILY

1

In the spring Anne and Stan agreed that they wanted to stay in New Orleans. He officially quit his job as chairperson of the creative writing department at San Francisco State after twenty-five years of service. He was forty-six years old. He was approached to teach in New Orleans, but he declined, completely taken up with exploring his new talents as a painter. Anne encouraged him. Her success had ensured that they could pursue what they had dreamed about and discussed for hours early in their marriage: freedom to follow their artistic visions. It was an exciting and rewarding time, although Christopher was unhappy and wanted to return to San Francisco. He did not grasp the beauty in which his mother was totally enveloped.

Anne sympathized but felt that she had lived many years away from her home, and she wanted a chance to immerse herself in the atmosphere. Christopher eventually accepted the fact that they were there to stay and tried out his hand at painting, although his ambition was to become an actor. He spent hours with his parents watching movies. Just as Michele had been like Stan, Christopher seemed like his mother.

"She and I are a lot alike," Christopher said. "She's very sensitive and doesn't miss a beat. She knows what's going on around her and what other people feel, and she worries a lot. If she didn't worry like that, she couldn't put herself in other people's points of view as well as people think she does."

Walking around the Garden District, Anne spotted the Brevard-Clapp house on First Street, and it "called" to her to buy it. Architecturally the house was an amalgam of Greek Revival and Italianate styles. In the front, the eight columns on two stories represented the three classical styles: Ionic, Doric, and Corinthian. Cast iron lace lined the double porches, or "galleries," threaded with motifs of iron roses which inspired for the property the name Rosegate. The brick walls, inside and out, were twenty inches thick. Designed by James Calrow, then built by Charles Pride in 1857, the mansion was surrounded by lush gardens and huge, buttress-rooted oak trees. Scattered throughout the yard were Anne's beloved banana trees and crepe myrtles. She wondered if her grandmother had ever done domestic work in that house.

Inside, fourteen-foot ceilings with ornate medallions and crown moldings graced the rooms of the lower floors, which included a double parlor or ballroom and the floor-to-ceiling library that Anne had always wanted. The modern kitchen and breakfast room looked out onto a pool into which flowed a dozen tiny jets of water.

The house was reputed to be haunted. Although there were stories about a man who committed suicide by shooting himself on the twenty-seven-step staircase, the ghost was thought to be that of a previous owner, Pamela Starr, who had lived there from age seventeen until she died in the thirties at the age of ninety-two. Her initials were carved into the frames of the large smoked mirrors in the ballroom and she had left behind a basket.

The house was like the mansions that had haunted Anne's dreams. She had walked by it many times, wishing that someday she could own one like it. She had continued to dream of such houses even when she settled in California, never imagining that she would one day return to New Orleans as a citizen. Conferring with Stan, Anne decided that if they bought this house, it would be their ultimate house, the home in which they would settle.

Anne checked on the price, in the million-dollar range. Tired of mortgages, she wanted to pay in cash, but the five hundred thousand dollar advance from *The Queen of the Damned* would not cover it. She urged her agent to structure her next advance in such a way that she could purchase the house as soon as possible. The power of her success was evident when Lynn Nesbit sold a two-book package to Knopf: *The Witching Hour* and the fourth Vampire Chronicle for five million dollars.

2

The manuscript of *The Mummy* was sent to Chatto & Windus in England, and the editors provided feedback about details of London only a resident would know. Anne made minor changes, but the second half was almost verbatim to the script. "It has more dialogue," she said, "than anything I'd ever written because it was a script."

Editor Bob Wyatt was enthusiastic. "Working with Anne was a total joy. I'd always wanted to work with her. It was an opportunity to work with one of my favorite writers." Anne had sent him part of the manuscript, and he worked quickly to ensure a spring release.

"I really wanted to do *The Mummy* in paperback," said Anne. "I'm delighted that Ballantine was willing to do this. I have a chemical in my brain that just keeps making plots and characters, and it overflows hardcover publication. I'd like to do a whole series in paperback where I go back to the themes of the B-movies I loved as a child. It was fun evoking that atmosphere and doing outrageous things that I wouldn't do in other books. I felt that my voice was there just as much as in the Vampire Chronicles and I was able to get into my characters and love them, and talk about their hearts and souls and philosophies."

Anne wrote a full-page dedication to let readers know her intention. She noted old mummy movies and hoped readers would pick up on the fact that this story was a fast-paced adventure. She wanted the tale to be fun but structured with a clear logic that made sense in light of contemporary scientific discoveries. It was meant as a deviation from her typical style, like a famous actor who does a small stage show just for fun.

Nevertheless, she wanted the book taken seriously for what it was—a romp in the style of the Indiana Jones movies. Although it was light reading, Anne insisted that it was "important to make a distinction between a light book and a shallow book." It was light because no one had to kill to be immortal and the story had none of the conscience-stricken darkness suffered by Louis. Nevertheless, she believed it had character development and philosophical implications.

Her idea was to bring an immortal to life who is not crippled by the vast changes in the world around him. She had always planned a mummy novel, wanting the man to be unwrapped as a beautiful, brilliant person rather than a leather-faced monster. As determined as she had always been to face down her fears, she did not let this mummy go shambling around like the mummies who had so frightened her in the movie theaters. She was terrified of the image of an unstoppable force.

Anne had first seen a real mummy when an exhibit came through New Orleans. "It was the mummy of a child," she recalled, "and it was unwrapped, and I remember its black, burnt appearance and the buckling skin. It had a powerful influence on me."

The story opens with a typical setting: an archaeologist discovering the tomb of an Egyptian king, Ramses II. On the door is a curse on anyone who opens the tomb. Inside is a shriveled, linen-wrapped mummy. "Was there a mummy that did not arouse in one some deep, cold fear of death? You could believe life lingered there somehow; that the soul was trapped in the wrappings." A scroll identifies the mummy as Ramses, who claimed to have been immortal and to have been a lover of Cleopatra's some one thousand years after he died.

The archaeologist is killed and journalists spread the rumor that he was a victim of the mummy's curse. The discoveries are shipped to the archaeologist's daughter, Julie, in England, where the mummy comes to life as a perfect man.

Ramses had first been mentioned in *The Vampire Lestat* as an immortal who was not a vampire. Later, in a draft of *The Queen of the Damned,* Anne had written Ramses into the book, having him come to the Sonoma compound, but then changed it. "I didn't feel that Ramses was part of the canon," she explained.

Julie falls in love with him and introduces him to London museums. He grows angry over how Cleopatra has been vilified in modern society: "She had become a symbol of licentiousness when in fact she had possessed a multitude of amazing talents. They had punished her for her one flaw by forgetting everything else." Anne admired Cleopatra and felt she had become a victim of historians. Through Ramses she redresses this injustice.

Ramses wants to go to Egypt to take leave of his past. Julie makes plans and her ex-fiancé, Alex, and his father, Elliott, insist on going with her. Elliott perceives that "Ramses" is the mummy and he is curious about the immortality elixir. He is old, with painful arthritis and a bad heart. He became a hero figure for Anne as a bisexual man who, she felt, really deserved immortality. Elliott is the most self-reflective character in the novel, and through him Anne examines the notion of the impact on an aging person of the idea of immortality, both of which were important revelations in her own life.

Julie and Ramses grow closer as they explore Egypt, following paths Anne had taken on her own trip. The party arrives in Cairo and Ramses visits a museum to see mummies on display. He is disturbed at how the sacred remains have been trivialized for tourists. He sees an "unknown woman" mummified by the mud of the Nile and he recognizes Cleopatra. Returning that night, he sprinkles the elixir on her.

This scene greatly excited Anne. She had seen people sneak into Cairo museums over and over in the movies, and now it was her turn to create that scene. Originally, Ramses's former love was going to be a princess named Bianca, but then Anne changed it to Cleopatra. She had some trouble getting the character going but soon got deeply involved. "It was fun to bring Cleopatra back to life," she said. "It was such a great moment for me when I realized that the queen should be Cleopatra." To her, Cleopatra represented a woman of great strength and resourcefulness.

Cleopatra comes to life, however, as a monster. Her mind is disoriented and much of her flesh is gone. Ramses abandons her but Elliott rescues her. She kills indiscriminately and one victim winds up in a factory that produces "authentic" mummies for rich tourists.

"The mummy factories were an original idea of mine," said Anne. "I don't know if there were any, but I do know that there was a great deal of faking of antiquities. The British people did have unwrapping parties early in the century, before people began to care about what happened to the mummies."

At this point in the novel, Anne was moving away from developing Julie and Ramses. She got involved with Elliott and Cleopatra, especially as Cleopatra began to remember things. "I love to do things like that," she said, "just go layer after layer into a character and find out what's ticking in the brain."

Elliott bargains with Ramses for the elixir for Cleopatra. Ramses follows him and saves his life when she tries to kill him. Ramses attempts to reason with her, but she is hurt by his rejection. She takes up with two tourists, killing them both.

Anne did not feel that Cleopatra was particularly violent, only disoriented, in pain, and unsure of her strength. Hers was the reaction of a woman of primitive times, and her behavior was part, Anne believed, of an authentic portrait.

Cleopatra sees Julie with Ramses and decides to hurt him. She moves to kill Julie, but then pulls back. Her decision was Anne's way of redeeming her. Ramses sees her and she flees, gets struck by a train, and goes up in flames.

Julie drinks the elixir, as does Elliott. Cleopatra recovers, allowing her revenge to simmer. The ending is left open with the promise of a sequel.

3

In this novel there is little discussion of the ramifications of being immortal, apart from the problems of allowing the secret into the hands of those who would abuse it. "I don't think there are too many people on earth," said Anne, "who could pass up immortality if it was offered to them. It wouldn't take *me* long. Characters who won't take it are boring."

Anne inserted feelings of her own and gave passing attention to such concepts as androgyny, bisexuality, and moral progress, but she spent little time developing themes in depth. The goal had been to make the characters real and to develop her own version of a mummy scenario. She eventually wanted to write a full-scale Egyptian horror novel, but that was in the future.

The Mummy was released at the end of May for summer reading and jumped immediately onto the paperback best-seller lists.

Anne had a sequel in mind because she wanted to continue to work with Ramses and Cleopatra, but CBS had picked up interest in the wake of the novel's success. They ordered another script. Exasperated, Anne told the producers the story was the one they had rejected. Still, they assigned a writer to the project.

The reviews were mixed once again.

Michael Rogers, writing for *Library Journal,* thought the beginning was slow and the characters boring. He advised Anne to stick to vampires. Other disappointed reviewers echoed these sentiments. In *The New York Times Book Review,* Frank J. Prial found the prose dead, and indicated that there was no point in reading any of Anne's works if *The Mummy* failed to touch readers, although he admitted, "If you liked her vampires, you're going to love her mummies." The *San Francisco Chronicle* got its digs in. "Reads as if she wrote it in a week," they said.

Reviewers who understood the novel's intentions praised it, and most reviews across the country were positive. Clifford Brooks found the book evocative, and Alida Becker, writing in the *Philadelphia Inquirer,* recognized "enough twists and surprises to bring smiles of delight to the beach and bubblebath brigades."

4

By the time *The Mummy* was released, Anne was at work on another project, an idea for a television series for Fox Network. It was about a police officer named Rusty who moves into a house haunted by an evil female ghost. The cop tries to get the spirit to help him do good. Anne wrote a treatment, but when a scriptwriter approached her, she dropped out of the project.

"The same thing happened that had happened with *Katherine and Jean,*" she explained. "He wanted to make my characters 'more real.' " Where the writer suggested the characters be more vulnerable, Anne felt they should show strength. Why should a ghost bother to fall in love with an ordinary man? "People respond to my characters because they are of mythic proportions."

She decided to just accept her fee as the creator of the series. She had long realized she was not a collaborator and hated the feeling that her treatments were a blueprint for someone else's art. Eventually she got the rights back and toyed with turning it into a novel.

The success of *The Mummy,* following *The Queen of the Damned* and occurring simultaneously with moving into the Garden District, gave Anne a sense of security. She and Stan made arrangements to rent their house in San Francisco and flew back to pack up their belongings. As she left her house, where items for a yard sale sat on the street, she saw the colorful long dresses from the early sixties fluttering in the wind and felt a pang of sadness.

5

Anne was chafing to get back to *The Witching Hour.* The story had taken shape so vividly in her imagination that she felt if she could just sit down at the computer, the words would flow like automatic writing. This would be a book about coming home, and the anticipation charged her with excitement. However, with workmen everywhere in her new house, decisions to be made about a family reunion, and visitors one after another, she had been unable to give the novel the attention it needed. By September, the reunion was over, eleven-year-old Christopher was in school, and Anne was free at last. She was not aware at the outset just how deeply this novel would reach into her.

In preparation, she had gone back to Nathaniel Hawthorne to capture his dark mood and use of language, reading "Young Goodman Brown" and part of *House of the Seven Gables.* She also read Henry James's *The Turn of the Screw* to get the effect of a haunting done well in literary form and to re-establish the connection she felt to these authors. It was her intention to capture the feeling of a house that seems alive, that one is holding some force at bay.

In the meantime, the movie rights to the vampire series were renewed with scriptwriter Michael Cristofer, who had written the script for *The Witches of Eastwick.* Anne also learned that her sister, Alice Borchardt, had sold a novel. Katherine's and Howard's literary influence had paid off again.

This novel was Anne's longest one yet. She finished it in February on the night of the Comus parade, the last parade of Mardi Gras, which had frightened her as a child. She went out to watch, then rewrote the last three chapters to include her experience of the parade—a turning point for her protagonist and symbolic of how she had faced down her own childhood fears.

6

The novel opens provocatively with a psychiatrist haunted by a dream. He tells the dream to Aaron Lightner of the Talamasca, the organization from *The Queen of the Damned* that documents paranormal activity. Their motto, along the lines of the Pinkerton agency's "We never sleep," is "We watch. And we are always there." It is the essence of the notion threading through Anne's novels of a continuous awareness, and the sense of omniscience is most striking in this novel, more detailed and concrete than with Maharet. Aaron is the ultimate father confessor, gently and authoritatively inviting the people he encounters to bare their souls and be free, although he refrains from offering "the consolations of the church." His primary concern is with a family in New Orleans who inhabit a Greek Revival house in the Garden District—Anne's house.

Although she had originally set the novel one block away in a house on Philip Street, she made adjustments in order to "haunt" her own house. She dirtied it up in the novel, since it was supposed to be deteriorating, and added a pool full of scum. As she wrote, she would go into various rooms to absorb the atmosphere and envision what would happen by a fireplace or in the library, then return to the keyboard. One of the significant features of the house—an Egyptian keyhole doorway—became a symbol in the central mystery of the plot.

Everyone in the novel, it seems, is closely involved with death, as if being in New Orleans again has confronted Anne with this aspect of her experience there. She describes how awareness of death has been practically erased in California, in contrast to the funeral rituals prevalent in her childhood. In New Orleans the coffin was open, flowers were sent in abundance, and people spent the entire day in services or conversations about the deceased. As one character says: "In New Orleans, we never really leave them out." Anne's description of a funeral presents a vivid picture of what such ceremonies are like, and she places in the coffin a dark-haired woman dead at forty-eight. She even utilizes to some degree the same funeral home on Magazine Street so central to the customs of her family—a composite of Leitz-Egan and another funeral home that had once been on Jackson Avenue. The cemetery she chose for some of the action is Lafayette, the deteriorating Garden District graveyard of her childhood wanderings.

The fictional family is comprised of generations of witches, male and female, who attract and manipulate invisible forces. The Mayfair lineage includes plantation owners in Haiti, giving Anne a chance to use research on Haiti's history that she had left out of her second novel. The women retain control of the family fortune and the Mayfair name.

Once again the concept of family is prominent, and in the Mayfair clan the connections are almost supernatural. "There is a saying that all the Mayfairs 'feel it' when the beneficiary of the legacy dies." They take care of each other and consider blood relations a priority. The blood itself seems more than symbolic: "In most families . . . when a person dies, all that the person knows dies with that person. Not so with the Mayfairs. Her blood [a deceased matriarch] is in us, and all she knew is passed into us and we are stronger." Connection, substance, and preservation are all evident in the way Anne thinks of this family, similar to the vampires, which indicates what the concept means to her, strengthened in her hometown.

Descriptions of the family called up images from Anne's childhood, surrounded as she was by a huge family clan. She also utilized her memories of Catholicism to depict how central to the life of the New Orleans families were the church and the parochial schools.

The Mayfair witches are designated, one per generation, as the beneficiaries not only of the legacy but also of the powers of "the man."

The Talamasca know him as Lasher, a bisexual spirit who gives the witches gifts, excites them sexually, and protects them. Exactly who or what he is provides the central mystery of the novel. At times he is associated with imagery of death and darkness through subliminal symbols of shadows and insects. At other times he has qualities of a god, and thus combines concepts of opposition. He is a romantic figure from another era, something out of Dickens impressed into Anne's fantasies. He is not ugly as the devil is supposed to be, but possesses a face "bland as the face of Christ" and the power to muddle perception, break glass, and create storms. Metaphorically, he is the child's sex demon—the feelings of excitement experienced by some children and certainly by Anne, which are forbidden by the church. Later Anne remarked that the novel could be read as a metaphor for masturbation and of people's terror of it. Lasher offers the lure of immortality and the embrace of the womb, a warm, protected place of unqualified acceptance, but he is also a vampiric figure, gaining strength from attention and substance through sexual desire. He is the strongest archetypal image in the novel.

Lasher represents the force within ourselves empowered by self-deception, which Carl Jung named the Trickster. It is the human potential for destruction at its most seductive, promising the fulfillment of our deepest longings—union with the infinite. Uncertainty about what is true and what is false allows us to move toward evil in the name of good, a point of ambiguity between God and the devil, a void that is the source for both. This image shifts its shape to accommodate us and, step by deceptive step, leads us down when we believe we are going up. This part of ourselves goes back to the primitive frenzies of Dionysus—the god of excess and orgy that takes us paradoxically into pleasure that becomes potential destruction, robbing us of reason and control along the way. This capacity can be a thief of the soul, stealing our best traits to feed its own frenzy. Jung spoke about it as an archetype hidden in the shadow. If we ignore it, we may be destroyed. If we face it, we may experience real transcendence.

Lasher has attached himself to Deirdre, the most recent witch, who sits catatonic from shock treatments intended to cure her of her delusions. Deirdre's daughter, Rowan, was adopted at birth by California cousins in order to break "the chain of evil." Rowan is one of the principal protagonists, named for a tree thought by the Irish to have the power to ward off evil. She becomes a neurosurgeon with a special diagnostic vision reminiscent of Dr. King, Michele's attending physician. Sensing that not all doctors possessed this talent, Anne gave it to Rowan, who also shared with Anne the ability to discern intent behind people's mannerisms.

"I've been told," Anne acknowledged, "that I have an uncanny ability to know what people are thinking and feeling so I can tell when I have an enemy. I don't think that's psychic. Some people are more focused."

Rowan also possesses the power to change cellular matter. It helps her to save lives but is also destructive—another blending of opposites. She feels she has been responsible for several deaths. Like everything else in the novel, her power is a knife that cuts both ways, a source from which both good and evil can spring.

Rowan is lonely, a product of California attitudes of commitments without sacrifice that Anne found potentially destructive. Through her Anne expressed her own dark views.

> All that was ever meant was loneliness, hard work, striving to make a difference when no difference could possibly be made. . . . It was like dipping a stick into the ocean and trying to write something—all the little people in the world spinning out little patterns that lasted no more than a few years, and meant nothing at all.

Keeping to the androgynous vision of her writing, Anne gives Rowan masculine characteristics: she is strong, determined, decisive, has a husky voice, and wears masculine clothing. An admission of need is unthinkable. Her gray eyes, as with Lestat, suggest ambiguity, and her blond hair is symbolic, as it was for Belinda and Lestat, of a light in the dark. Like most of Anne's women since Lisa, Rowan drives cars in a frantic, determined manner—the way she performs surgery. She is a person of action, believing she can effect positive change. One of her secret desires is to experience herself as a man being made love to by another man.

Rowan expresses Anne's developing attraction to the masculine men of her childhood—firefighters and policemen, who save lives. "She's an educated girl who likes old-fashioned men." For Anne that meant reaching for her roots, although she wanted her "old-fashioned man" to have a literary mind. She was inspired by an actual person who embodied this ideal when she discovered the firefighter novels of Dennis Swift at Walgreen's drugstore.

"I went nuts," she said. "It gave me a sexual turn-on to get involved with that stuff because it made me think of my roots and the people in my family who were firefighters and cops. It was a side of the proletarian life that I'd turned my back on and was craving to know again. I read all his novels about people being trapped in fire and burned, and I found it captivating."

Anne's descriptions of male characters consequently had evolved. What had once excited her in the feminized male had lost some of its appeal, replaced by a masculinized woman that freed her to give her male characters a stronger masculinity. "There's been a gradual increase in my work," she admitted, "of more macho men. Maybe I had to get to this age to appreciate them. They exist now for my pleasure as I look around the city on construction sites and wherever. They're very much a turn-on to me. Elliott and Lestat were the first two who started to be like that. Jean and Louis were androgynous, but now I'm moving toward this other kind of guy."

Focusing on her female experiences and working with them in her characters had allowed her to pull apart the blend of genders in her early males, although even apart, both male and female are a mix of traits. Yet the men are more manly as defined by social customs. Her writing had assisted her in working through gender concerns, in confronting the female, in developing her sensuality, and in becoming more involved with attractions of heterosexual relationships. The other protagonist is a well-built, "old-fashioned" man.

7

His name is Michael—the name of the angel who "drove the devils into hell." He owns a construction and restoration company called Great Expectations, named after his favorite book.

Dickens's novel is a subliminal clue to the theme of *The Witching Hour.* Dickens wrote about the struggle between good and evil through characters who were a complicated mixture of both. There is promise in the idea of great expectations of better things to come, emerging from a goodness based on inner worth. For Dickens things were not as they appeared, and he relied on strong moral feeling to move the book along, creating an infinite variety of characters. The same is true of Anne, with special emphasis on Rowan and Michael.

Michael is the ideal for Anne. He is the priest from the novel about the Catholic schoolgirls that never got written. He is the fireman with a literary mind. "Out of the caldron of your own mind," Anne writes, "will come the truth," and Michael's character is evolved from Anne's life: "Michael is more like me than the other characters," said Anne, "except that I didn't grow up in the Irish Channel and I didn't have his father. Everything in these novels comes from my life, and there's more of it in Michael than in anything I've written so far, and it feels so alive in the book." He fits in with other children more than she did—perhaps an expression of her desire to have been more accepted—but he is also a person in his own right.

He has the Curry name from Anne's father's side and had a German grandmother. Like Anne, his relatives were firefighters and policemen. His thoughts and attitudes reflect hers when he talks about family gatherings, Catholic ceremonies, architecture, friendships, his relationship with his movie-hungry and unhappy mother, his love of long walks in the Garden District, his obsession for knowledge, his fear of humiliation, and his love of books, especially Dickens. "My description of Michael in the library," said Anne, "is really a description of me discovering I could learn from books." For that she thanked her father, although she gives Michael a father who resists his literary inclinations. Michael learns chess from a book the way Anne did, and he longs to be a great violinist after seeing a performance by Isaac Stern.

Although Anne had not intended to use her own mother as a model, when she looked over what she had written, she was surprised. "It was very strange to realize how much of my mother was in Michael's mother."

Michael went to Redemptorist, where events are described—like the boy forced by nuns to stand in a trash can—that actually occurred when Anne was a student. Michael also went to San Francisco, where he applied himself with passion to college (majoring in history for the same reasons that Anne majored in political science), hated the cold, shook his head over the arguments of his Marxist friends, and lost his mother to alcoholism. He loved the city but felt like an outcast there, just as Anne did. "Were there not moments when he felt empty? When he felt as if he were waiting for something, something of extreme importance, and he did not know what that was?" He even felt he did not belong in the twentieth century. "Different from the start, that's what he'd been." Anne was forty-eight when she wrote the novel, and Michael is forty-eight as the story is told. He has softened toward the people he left behind in New Orleans, "the only paradise he had ever known."

Michael is saved from drowning and claims to have seen dead people who gave him a mission to return to New Orleans, although he has forgotten the details. He has also developed a new power to sense images by touching objects. He shuts himself away from people who want to use his "visionary services," wanting to see only the woman who rescued him and indulging in a long drunk similar to Anne's after the death of her daughter.

He decides he must return to New Orleans just as Rowan, his rescuer, contacts him. They fall in love, but Michael insists he must leave. For him the world has been made of fragments that seem to be falling into place as he thinks about returning home from his long "exile." It is the way Anne described her own experience, part of the impetus for writing—to gain clarity and wholeness.

Rowan gives him a new perspective on his vision that introduces ambiguity: perhaps he is a pawn in the hands of the "people" he saw and his memory loss is part of an evil plan. The idea irritates him because he wants to believe that he has a choice. It is this tension between free will and destiny that provides much of the literary thrust, and is another expression for the conflict between heroes who initiate action and victims who are acted upon. It also underlines the conflict between the natural and the unnatural that becomes an issue in the book.

In New Orleans, Michael's experience of coming home is a direct expression of the way Anne felt when she arrived. An entire chapter is devoted to the smell and feel of the city, especially the Garden District. "Was there any place in the world where the air was such a living presence, where the breeze kissed you and stroked you, where the sky was pulsing and alive?"

The return trip for Anne decreased her fear of death. "Now that I'm back here, all my fears about death, old age, and the passage of time are much less because I'm where I want to be. I'm home. I don't have that feeling of being rootless and anchorless, and I also have derived much satisfaction from being here, that feeling of a dream fulfilled. When you feel that, you're not panicky about dying." This increased sense of security would mold Michael's character and his own claim late in the novel: "If I were to die right now, I wouldn't be afraid. Because I can't believe that horror or chaos awaits us."

Michael arrives drunk at the house on First Street, where he has been "sent," sees "the man," and meets Aaron Lightner, who followed him. He tells Aaron about his vision. The number thirteen comes clear and he learns that Aaron knows about Rowan.

Aaron is afraid of her power. She is the first of the Mayfair women who can kill without Lasher's assistance and seems to have inherited the strongest traits of the genetic line—traits passed down from witches and men of science who could alternately destroy or heal. He feels that if she knows her history, she will be able to resist the power. Michael reads the file on the Mayfair witches, dating back to 1689.

In the files are letters written by Talamasca member Petyr Van Abel, in which he describes his acquaintance with the first of the Mayfair witches. He tells how he rescued Deborah from Donnelaith, Scotland, where her mother had been burned as a witch. It was her mother who had first called up the spirit Lasher, named for the winds he created.

"One of the problems I had with *The Witching Hour,*" said Anne, "and one of the reasons I put off writing it, is that the scenes of torture and burning at the stake and what happened to witches are so awful that I didn't want to write them. Yet to write a witchcraft novel in which someone's ancestor was burned at the stake, you have to deliver something."

She had researched the Knights Templar and read every scholarly book on witch persecutions she could find in order to capture historical authenticity.

"At night before I went to bed, I had to put those scenes out of my mind. I would be a real ripe candidate for someone to say, 'Well, you were reincarnated. At some point you were there, that's why you over and over again imagine this is happening to you.' Fear of fire is not an active fear in my life anymore, but when I was little, I felt unprotected."

Deborah is a merry-begot, a child conceived during village festivals. Such children are thought to be "of the gods." Anne once again uses reverse imagery to depict as holy something traditionally considered tainted, and throughout the novel the holy and the demonic are linked. Petyr speaks of how the beauty of the witches makes them appear as angels, similar to the way Anne described the vampires. A portrait of Deborah painted by Rembrandt reveals a fragile light in the midst of darkness, a metaphor for the possibility of redemption *through* the darkness.

Deborah seduces Petyr, searching for a kindred soul. They are outsiders together, a witch and a seer, and it is a brief nod by Anne to a theme that has threaded throughout her corpus. Significantly, she does little to explore the outsider psychology that occupied her in earlier novels, and perhaps that is because she felt at home, accepted. She insisted that she would continue to write about outsiders, but the force of that inner conflict is missing in this novel.

Deborah is burned as a witch. Her daughter, Charlotte, flees to Haiti. Petyr seeks Charlotte to see if she is his daughter and is seduced by her to produce another witch. She keeps him in a prison on a cliff overlooking the sea—the symbol of the unconscious. The torment he goes through is that of a person who has descended into what Carl Jung had called the Abyss, the inner primal source. He becomes confused by the vague, undefined form of it to the point of moral surrender. Petyr then bares his soul: "I believe nothing, and therefore like many who believe nothing, I must make something and that something is the meaning which I give to my life." Through the Abyss he finds strength, a foreshadowing for other characters.

Events proceed toward a culmination that appears to have been planned by some greater force, with successive generations of witches surrendering to it. However, apparent flaws in the "plan" subject to doubt the idea that humans can be so easily engineered; in addition, the fact that Lasher "learns" and strengthens his purpose also hints at the notion that things could have been different. One character claims that the future is not predetermined but simply predictable, based on weaknesses in human nature. The actual force operating is never fully clear.

Anne uses imagery to emphasize this ambiguity, reinforcing the theme through symbols: (1) scenes in which grayness or shadow dominates; (2) the use made by spirits of natural phenomena like storms, mental illness, and heart disease to mask their apparent intervention; and (3) drinking, dreams, and overactive imaginations by means of which odd visions can be dismissed. The lack of clarity in interpreting events is a subliminal device. It is a condition of life that obscures insight and decision, and is brought into the story not only as a way to heighten mystery but also to employ the tensions of opposition inherent in ambiguity for stronger visceral qualities in character conflicts.

Petyr is intrigued with Lasher, despite the danger, as is everyone in the novel. It is the vision of the Romantic of wanting union with the infinite, mingled with dread of how total surrender may spell annihilation. Lasher is a spirit called out of chaos who advances himself in the physical world by learning first how to make himself dense enough to transport objects, then to kill and to possess a human body. His attempts to take on the form of flesh have been of limited success.

Lasher serves another function for Anne. She points out that he may be no more than a collection of physical elements ("The same cells that make up your body or mine"), and that beliefs about him are related to historical cycles of how the god images of conquered people become demons. What Anne seeks is confirmation of substance. Her treatment of all supernatural phenomena in her novels is to find a physical explanation for their existence. She goes to great lengths to indicate how modern discoveries can be used to understand entities once thought of as otherworldly to show the role of nature in supposedly supernatural events. She was fascinated by research by credible sources on near-death experiences and on past-life regressions because she wanted evidence of the continuity of that energy. Having left a church in which the mysteries of the spirit were emphasized, Anne adopts a framework by means of which such beliefs can be reinterpreted. If things heretofore unknown can be anchored in natural process, then they will one day be understood. Calling them demonic only retards the process.

Nevertheless, she still appreciates the mystery, perhaps another expression of male/female duality: "The fact is," says one character, "for all we learn about ourselves, for all we codify and classify and define, the mystery remains immense."

Anne's characteristics poke through in each generation of the lengthy chronicle. Mary Beth and Deirdre, both relatively contemporary witches, are closest to Anne, sometimes as an expression of her dearest fantasies and sometimes as a fictional enactment of events in her own life.

Mary Beth is a cross-dresser, with the appetites of a man. She has been thought of as unfeminine for her brusque, forward manner, as well as in her lack of preoccupation with femininity. She loves gadgets, is quiet, strong, and has definite financial goals. People think she is self-centered when she is generous. She is the last of the really powerful Mayfair witches.

Mary Beth's brother, Cortland, fathers Stella, her daughter, keeping the line "pure." With Stella, he fathers Antha. Stella shares with Anne the desire to give the family continuity.

Antha runs away to New York, where she lives with an artist and becomes a writer. "Only writing can save you," she says. People thought that she could be a good writer, if only she would write about the experience she knows, there in New York, rather than about morbid, high-pitched fantasies set in New Orleans. The same was said of Anne in California. Antha believed that only writing could save her, as it did with Anne. "I'll write about my past . . ." she says, "but I won't talk about it . . . won't give it life here, outside of art." Although she is speaking about Lasher, it is similar to the pain of Anne's past that still haunts her.

Antha's daughter is Deirdre, who resembles Anne, although she also exhibits traits of other people. Her tendency to climb trees echoes Anne's sister Alice, but when she wears unmatching shoes, she is Anne. She ends up at a boarding school off the French Quarter based on St. Joseph's Academy. Ironically, she comforts a friend there who cries every night, a picture of Anne comforting herself. She also loves swinging in the pecan trees at twilight, as Anne did. Deirdre goes to college to Texas Woman's University, where her secret spot is Anne's secret spot. Like her, Anne went there dressed in white. About her hangs an aura of sensuality and people say of her that she is oversexed.

Deirdre becomes pregnant by Cortland. Her baby, Rowan, is adopted by cousins. The Talamasca keep their eye on both.

The history of the family is a chronicle of every type of forbidden sexual union: incest, homosexuality, bisexuality. It also includes madness, violent deaths, and secret rituals. Anne had become more aware of how connected was the erotic with the supernatural, and she actively links the two in numerous contexts. As Lasher closes in, sensuality increases with the fear: "She could actually hear him gathering, hear the pressure building, hear the draperies rustling as he moved against them, writhing and filling the room around her, and brushing against her cheeks and her hair." The physical descriptions of the intruding force echo erotic activities. "The promise of Lasher at the end of the hallway," said Anne, "is the promise of a good orgasm. It came together much more clearly in *The Witching Hour* for me."

8

Michael finishes the file and one thing seems clear: that predestined events seemingly can be averted—although possibly even that is planned. He also has the impression that people who have died have gone into an existence in which they are wiser—an idea that intrigued Anne from studies of near-death experiences—and that the witch Deborah seems to want him to save Rowan from Lasher. If she is in fact wiser and not part of "the plan," then Michael not only can exercise his free will but represents, on an abstract level, the very essence of free will in human history. Unfortunately, he is not certain about his purpose there, which is exactly the dilemma: is it by acting *according* to a purpose that free will is expressed, or by choosing *against* it?

While Michael is reading, Rowan comes to New Orleans to attend Deirdre's funeral. As she explores the city, she notices details cherished by Anne: girls in white dresses with ribbons in their hair, cathedral-like churches, cemeteries. She walks into the arms of a huge, welcoming family—a hallmark of the South—and is overcome by the symbolic embrace. She is part of a great genetic and cultural network, and the sense of kinship for her, as for Anne, is "indescribably exotic" after the "barren, selfish world in which she'd spent her life, like a potted plant that had never seen the real sun." For Anne it was as important to come to New Orleans for her son as for herself. She felt that he should grow up knowing his cousins so that he would have the network of caring people that Anne had missed.

Rowan attends the funeral, then meets Carlotta at the house. Carlotta tells her what has happened with her mother and grandmother and explains that she had been meant for the legacy but had refused it, believing that fighting it put her on the side of goodness. Although Carlotta has trapped her own "goodness" in layers of meanness and cruelty—echoing the way authoritarian figures model "goodness" in religion—she does express one of Anne's own beliefs:

> Didn't matter if God in his heaven was a Catholic or a Protestant God, or the God of the Hindus. What mattered was something deeper and older and more powerful than any such image—it was a concept of goodness based on the affirmation of life; the turning away from destruction, from the perverse, from man using and abusing man. It was the affirmation of the human and the natural.

Carlotta tells Rowan that "the man" is Satan and he rules with "promises of servitude" that inevitably ensnare his weaker mistresses, an echo of the S&M psychology explored in Anne's pornography. Only the strongest women have made him the slave. Rowan's strength, Carlotta claims, has been bred into her, and it is she who can send the man back to hell.

Rowan is aghast at the condition of the house, especially when she is shown jars in which body parts have been preserved, and discovers the body of a Talamasca agent wrapped in a rug. Carlotta shows her a trunk full of dolls made of the hair and bone of each of the witches except Deirdre, and explains how she drove one of them to her death. Rowan sees herself in a set of mirrors, reflecting into one another endlessly as a metaphor of infinity–the infinity of the human struggle with good and evil. Carlotta tells her, "We have all . . . from time to time . . . been reflected in these mirrors."

Rowan grows more angry the more she hears of the evil done in the name of good. She uses her power to kill Carlotta and gains a feeling of satisfaction, ironically doing as Carlotta herself had done.

This spontaneous violence in Rowan is another of her androgynous features. Throughout her novels Anne has attributed bursts of violence to men. In *The Mummy* she indicated that men have a need to hurt; Maharet experiences the fact that a man can rape a woman even when it pains him; gentle Jeremy Walker senses an animal within himself when he is sexually aroused; and the vampires are killers, as is Lasher. Even Michael says that he fears the violence in men, and Akasha, a dominant woman, is ready to wage a war on men to eradicate their violence via annihilation of the male population. There is anger evident in these lines, and Anne believes that this sort of violence is evil.

Yet she is also attracted to some forms of violence that exhibit heroic qualities, and at times violent imagery seems to have a soothing effect on the perpetrators: Cleopatra's killing soothes her pain; Akasha's slaughtering is orgasmic (a feeling shared by Lestat); Carlotta takes satisfaction in "doing good" through violence; and Louis speaks for the vampires when he says, "I knew peace only when I killed." The ambivalence goes back to the struggle between dominant people capable of really hurting someone, and submissive people who make themselves vulnerable to cathartic, symbolic violence. As Elliott points out to Lisa, such relationships can be evil or good, and there is a fine line between them. For Anne, who expresses both sides of her personality, images of violence become a source of fear and anger as well as of a sense of power and security.

After killing Carlotta, Rowan puts on the jewel and sees a man. The image fades as Michael comes through the door, good penetrating evil, a light in the dark. Rowan welcomes him and explains what has happened. True to the thematic ambiguity, Carlotta's death is attributed to the woman's advanced age, and when the bodies are carted away, Michael tells Rowan about the Talamasca file.

Anne uses their relationship for the gender-switching that had become her trademark. Rowan approaches Michael as a man might a woman, and Michael is dependent on her. She thinks of him as a sex object. He wants to be loved. Through Rowan, Anne reveals another anecdote of her life when she describes a friend who told her that women do not find men's bodies attractive. Rowan, like Anne, is very much attracted to a man's body, especially bodies like Michael's. "She had always loved men for both what they did, and their bodies . . . silky and hard, that's what men were." Rowan, as the voice of Anne, describes how erotic men are to women in fine detail and thrills at the image of Michael as an archangel making love to her.

While Michael sleeps, Rowan reads the file, then meets Aaron at the house. She tells him that the Talamasca has turned on a light for her in her darkness.

Michael wakes up and walks the Irish Channel—the landscape of happy memories of his youth, as it was for Anne. "How extraordinary it felt to have money in his pocket in his old home town, to know he could buy those houses, just the way he'd dreamed of it in the long-ago hopelessness and desperation of childhood." He is grieved, as she was, at the deterioration. Like Anne's house back on St. Charles, his childhood home is boarded up and surrounded by a chain-link fence. He is shocked by the condition of his old school, Redemptorist, and the gymnasium which "he" helped to get built. As Anne did, he gives a nun twenty dollars to be allowed inside St. Mary's. He sits contemplating the statues of the saints, the Virgin on the high altar, and the echoes of holiness that had once been part of his life.

"I have great love for the churches," said Anne, "but it's a love for one's ethnic background. That description of Michael going into St. Mary's and realizing that he didn't believe in anything and that it was quite impossible to pray in that church, that would be my feeling. I'm totally agnostic."

Rowan tells Michael she has decided to stay in New Orleans. She believes that she may spell the end of Lasher's reign. In creating her as a woman of great strength, it may be that Lasher has ensured his own destruction. She reminds Michael that to focus on demons is to become passive and confused, reworking the "somebody-or-somebody's-girl" formula: "Don't be a pawn in somebody's game. . . . Find the attitude which gives you the maximum strength and the maximum dignity." They decide to reclaim the house in love. Michael opens a window to let in the light.

As they roam the house, they express more of Anne's homecoming sentiments. They discover several sets of valuable china—a feature of Anne's house, since collecting china was one of her passions. The house speaks to Michael the way it spoke to Anne: "In a way he had always lived in it, it was the place he had longed for when he went away."

In Deirdre's old room, Rowan asks Michael to use the power in his hands to determine whether Deirdre had been happy. He is immediately engulfed in a confusing array of images that urge him to the chest containing the bone dolls. It is a scene reminiscent of Marcel's drunken journey to his father's plantation in *The Feast of All Saints* and Jeremy's drunken conversation with Alex and G.G. in *Belinda.* The scene moves quickly, despite random input from a variety of sources, with short, incomplete sentences to convey the urgency and chaos in Michael's own mind. It shows Anne's skill in moving seamlessly from narrative to mental impression, which changes the pacing and the tone, and foreshadows greater confusion to come.

Michael moves to the jars and in the most gory and hideous scene of the novel, breaks them open to reveal a vast array of rotting heads, the last of which looks exactly like Lasher. He has a vision that Lasher had possessed the bodies of the preserved heads, altering matter slightly to cause a mutation, but failing to gain a body. Michael is repulsed by the intimacy established with this spirit and leaves the house with Rowan.

She meets with the Mayfair lawyers and discovers that the legacy is worth billions. It is a typical pattern in Anne's books that her principal characters have no financial insecurity, and that many are wealthy: the vampires were predominantly of the aristocracy and used their powers to get as much money as they wanted; Tonio came from a wealthy family and became financially successful in his operatic pursuits; the Roquelaure characters were all of royal blood; Lisa and Elliott both had money; Jeremy made millions on his books and paintings; Belinda was from a wealthy family; and Julie was an heiress. Only in *The Feast of All Saints* were the main characters struggling with limited resources, and only toward the end. As dark as many of Anne's images get, and despite her belief that limitation can be a source of power, she does not deal with financial insecurity. Having money of course gives these characters access to more possibilities and thus to more freedom, yet the pervasive image of wealth also indicates Anne's desire for security.

The restoration on the house begins, and many of the descriptions arise from Anne's own experience. Although her house had been renovated by a previous owner, there was still work to be done. Another autobiographical incident is the trip to Florida, where Anne and Stan purchased a condominium.

Michael and Rowan also tour the city, following in the footsteps of Elliott and Lisa, and Jeremy and Belinda, but going farther. Anne was in New Orleans now. She could take them anywhere. They explored the Irish Channel and even went uptown where the old Victorians surrounded Audubon Park, seeking to know the perimeters of their home. More than any of her "true life" characters before, Michael and Rowan represent Anne finding and holding on to her roots; she was no longer just tentatively exploring them through projected images. "To me, this means something very deep," she said. "It means a lot about battering down these doors and drawing closer and closer to something you really want to explore."

Anne had spent her life breaking down layers in her imagination, trying to get to a mysterious essence or feeling of clarity that she often called It. This time she was as close as she ever had been. Several characters had faced stark truths and had persevered. "It just delighted and thrilled me to no end," she said. "It felt very good in my brain to write it. I felt that I was in touch with *It* pretty much the whole time."

9

Yet tension still exists. Michael cannot shake the feeling that everything is "planned" and that he has a mission. Rowan thinks he has to choose for himself to break the destiny of events. What she does not understand is that her advice itself may be part of "the plan."

They learn that the mysterious number thirteen refers to thirteen witches and that the "door" is the opening through which Lasher will come from the spirit world. Michael points out to Rowan that *she* is the thirteenth witch and she is the door.

They get married and the wedding ceremony is like an invisible protective power, but soon Lasher appears to Rowan. She resolves not to tell Michael, waiting until he goes to San Francisco to close up his house before she draws the spirit into a conversation. That Michael would leave Rowan, knowing Lasher could come, seems naive. It was clear that he had to leave, but not so clear why he left her alone in the house.

Ostensibly, Rowan's intent is to learn how to destroy Lasher, but she is also powerfully attracted to him. "I don't want it, and yet it's so . . . so seductive!" She is also frightened for the baby growing inside of her, which she and Michael call Chris, named after Anne's own son.

In the conversation between Rowan and Lasher, Anne inserts her own philosophy of matter and spirit, much of it derived from *The Queen of the Damned* but expanded in its implications for modern genetic research. Lasher is an eternal entity, made self-conscious by the explicit attention of man. "You feed him when you question him. You give him oil as if he were the flame in that lamp." At times it appears that Anne intends to say that spirit issues from matter and at times that spirit exists apart from matter, without real intelligence. For the first time in any of her novels, however, when the question is asked of an immortal being about the existence of God, the being is unsure, but answers that it thinks that God may exist. The vampires had come to the opposite conclusion, seeing themselves as the new gods. Even the humans in this novel seem ambivalent, wanting to name the sense of God as simply the principle of nature and goodness. Yet Lasher indicates that he believes there is a God and that this God has caused his pain.

The conversation between Rowan and Lasher seems once again to be two halves of one person, as if Anne is arguing with herself. She wants to present the optimistic view that has been emerging in her novels since its first tentative steps in *The Feast of All Saints*. Yet she is still seduced by her own dark side, by questions and doubts created from painful episodes in her life when she loved and bitterly suffered because of that love. Her faith in God, transmuting into a faith in human goodness, has been sorely tested and betrayed. The questions still disturb her, along with religious superstitions, despite the gains she has made in breaking away from the darkness, in seeking sources of light through which she has turned inner demons into literary visions. The psychological evolution is evident but the darkness has not yet been transcended, although the conversation between the spirit and the strongest human woman yet to emerge in Anne's writing is more intimate and revealing than any before. Rowan discerns the source within herself for seeking power and control, and for turning values of goodness inside out. Anne could only settle in New Orleans when she had faced down the specter of her lost mother and of a faith that had once been a source of security. She seems less bitter as she looks at the church through Michael's eyes.

Lasher tells Rowan that he craves to feel things, to have dreams and ambitions, to become flesh. Rowan's power to change matter and her knowledge of cell regeneration—to which she is both attracted and repelled, as she is with Lasher—will make the fusion of spirit and flesh possible. He relies on her skill. Together they will produce a being of immense power.

Lasher represents the seduction of the greatest love and surrender. Rowan resists at first, believing he is tricking her. He seduces her and she begs to be raped, becoming the image of the victim of horrors unknown that had stimulated Anne's imagination as a child. The exchange between them is the symbiosis of slave and master. They struggle with the balance of surrender and control. When it is over, Rowan appears to be in control because she commands the spirit and he obeys, but in reality she is being sucked into him.

More specifically, Lasher is Rowan's inner being, the beckoning voice of the personal demon. The consequences of her decisions can issue forth as good or evil. There are no absolutes against which to measure herself, and she must choose according to her gut sense as a member of the human race.

Aaron argues with Rowan over the morality of doing Lasher's bidding. Their argument touches on the debate of modern science and religion over whether people should intervene in the natural process of evolution and create artificial mutations. Is resistance merely ignorance or is it the sole protection of humanity? Mutation takes place in nature, Rowan points out. People are part of nature. Why not use our abilities and knowledge to make changes that could be positive? She expresses the side of the Trickster archetype which reveals its gradual development into a savior, a compensatory relationship to saints.

Aaron takes the conservative side while Rowan argues for the amorality of scientific discoveries. Aaron insists that humans can transcend natural process and the ruthlessness of life by creating society and culture and by loving one another. Rowan feels he has no logical grounds. He tells her his position is the message of substance that can feel pleasure and pain. He urges her back within herself to where she will find the most strength and the right answers.

Michael returns and realizes Rowan has been lying to him, so he meets with Aaron. They talk about the meaning of Christmas, an occasion for Michael, as for Anne, of renewal and symbolic rebirth. It is also the winter solstice, a time when the forces of the earth are at their strongest. Aaron gives Michael a medal of the archangel Michael.

Lasher tells Rowan he can make her immortal. She realizes his weakness, that he is afraid to surrender lest the form in which he finds himself traps him into something he does not want. His fear is her fear, the surrender of the inner self to its own void.

At midnight of Christmas Eve, when "the Word was made Flesh" as the son of God, and on the anniversary of Rowan's discovery that her mentor was engaged in the horrors and wonders of live fetal research, Lasher is born. He takes the fetus from Rowan and fuses with its fast-growing cells to become flesh. He is now her child, the like of which has never been seen on earth.

Rowan is engulfed through Lasher in the place within herself where contradictions constitute the tensions of subconscious reality. The chaos within is the challenge of the soul, either trapping and crippling it in its own fear or freeing it through creativity. The inner darkness is a threat, the point beyond which knowledge becomes speculation, where logic, order, and control have little leverage. Rowan is the embodiment of the creative mind as she goes "down" into this being in order to come back "up" toward a higher spirituality—the vision she needs to know how to wrestle with it and utilize the powerful forces for good. Lasher represents a fertile chaos. He is a volatile, mutable mass of paradoxes. Rowan is the person strong enough to accept the ambiguities into herself with Dionysian openness in order to embrace life at its fullest—with all of its upheavals and confusion. She must go within to the fountainhead of inner forces represented in Lasher's impetus to be born into flesh so that she can discover the point at which the threat of annihilation evolves new life. She has to affirm the void—join with Lasher—and face the loss of stability in order to locate where chaos is digested by creativity.

Religious mystics understood that God was found in the darkness, that the threshold to transcendence lay at the brink of the Abyss. Only those who surrender to the risk of negation can reap potential spiritual profits, like runners who break through a pain barrier to a physical and mental high. It is the growing pain of the organic process of moving into a new stage of life. Although going with Lasher appears to be succumbing to evil, it actually presents to Rowan the greatest opportunity to turn a vital force toward good, albeit at risk of failure.

Rowan flees with Lasher, giving the house to Michael. Writing in his journal, he grapples with the meaning of it all. He believes there is goodness and wisdom in Rowan—she is the light in the dark history of the Mayfairs represented in Deborah's painting—and that he was not a pawn but only the victim of Lasher's lies. Not knowing for sure, he is forced toward faith. He contends, with the vampires, that choice and accident are the essence of what makes us human, giving meaning to goodness and to life itself.

There is a feeling that this story has not been resolved. Readers know nothing of what will happen with Rowan, other than glimpses allowed through the dark glasses of Michael's belief. Lasher's purpose and future activities are unclear, as is the Talamasca's response to the situation. Yet it is this very lack of knowledge and resolution that allows readers the visceral impact of Michael's ordeal and moral triumph.

"The reason for the ambiguity," Anne insisted, "was quite definitely my feeling that we would not know."

Michael has been to the Comus parade, facing down his childhood fear of the drums, "a sound to do with some dark and potentially destructive energy," and has emerged stronger. He believes that ultimate horror cannot be the final answer. Faith is strongest in the tension of uncertainty, and when Michael makes his commitment, readers are only allowed as far as the bounds of his belief in the forces of goodness within Rowan and potentially within us all.

10

Michael has become Anne. Through him she is expressing her own beliefs, forged in pain, resignation, and loss as well as in an optimism and faith. Michael has lost the mother and child. His suffering is akin to Anne's, yet he does not give up and sink into drunkenness. He embodies her determination to keep believing in goodness, despite random accidents that violate happiness and teach us about death.

In the closing paragraphs, Anne mentions that free will allows us to conduct ourselves as if we were the children of a "just and wise god," whether or not such a god exists. We choose to do good, even if it is not vindicated or illuminated after death. She again emphasizes the theme of communion of the human family in a beautiful world that makes possible a moral force of love that can ensure the positive evolution of the race toward a heaven on earth. We need to choose life over death and the natural over the unnatural.

One of the most revealing paragraphs is about faith and loss. "And I suppose I do believe in the final analysis that a peace of mind can be obtained in the face of the worst horrors and the worst losses. It can be obtained by faith in change and in will and in accident; and by faith in ourselves, that we will do the right thing, more often than not, in the face of adversity."

In structure and symbol, the novel comes full circle, mirroring Anne's return to New Orleans: Michael leaves and returns to New Orleans, as does Rowan; snow in the city twice announces the advent of loss; Christmas Eve symbolizes rebirth as well as the revelations of fetal research and the physical birth of Lasher; Michael is saved from drowning at the beginning and at the end, with visions both times; his childhood fear of Mardi Gras becomes his adult triumph; and in the end he realizes that he is now "the man" haunting the First Street house. With the closing of the circle comes the wisdom of faith, echoed in the progression of Anne's novels.

Guilt and despair were the most salient themes of her first novel, and darkness in one form or another pervaded successive novels, with the exception of the Roquelaure trilogy. However, there also came an increasing light of moral vision.

Parallel to this development was Anne's struggle with female identification. Anne had suppressed her feminine side—the side that was more painful, seen even in Louis, an androgynous, feminized man—until Lisa finally freed her to give that part of herself more latitude. Gabrielle, however, was cold and sought distance from the human race. It was Maharet who first expressed an optimism in the female side, just as she gives strongest expression to Anne's belief in moral progress. It seemed as if Maharet had won, yet Rowan, for all her blondness, has not yet shown the power of the feminine to bring about the force of goodness for the betterment of humankind. It is Michael, a man in the spirit of Elliott and Lestat, who expresses the faith that it will happen. The task however, is given to Rowan, and perhaps it is she who will ultimately triumph and find the source of light in the midst of her inherited darkness.

"I believe," says Michael, "that we can through our reason know what good is, and in the communion of men and women, in which the forgiveness of wrongs will always be more significant than the avenging of them, and that in the beautiful natural world that surrounds us, we represent the best and the finest of beings." His response suggests the survival of moral integrity, but does not affirm it as a certainty.

For Anne, that sense of goodness is synonymous with being where she wants to be, in New Orleans, with the breeze and the patter of rain on the banana leaves. Having settled in, having found a sense of security in her roots and in getting in touch with the innocence of her childhood, she sees the world differently. The beauty around her seems to have strengthened the optimism and beaten back the darkness, at least for a while.

Suggested throughout the book is the theme that no one is as they appear, an application of a literary tradition. The ambiguity of good and evil, of truth and lies, is pervasive. It all seems to rest on the paradox of a liar accusing others of lying, and it is not clear who really is the liar. Is Michael's vision an intervention in the name of goodness, or is it all part of Lasher's plan to make him a pawn? Is Rowan moral or immoral in her attraction to the experiments of science toward the ostensible end of improving the human race? Is Carlotta evil when she murders people to save them from evil? The impression is that Michael's apparent weakness—naivete—will be his strength, that Aaron's apparent impotence will in fact have a tremendous impact, and that Rowan's strength will be her weakness, since she seems blind to how she plays into Lasher's plans. Yet the theme turns upon itself. The *idea* that things are not as they appear is *also* not as it appears (once again), deepening the paradoxical quality of the novel. That is, by the end Michael does seem to have failed to effect the change, Aaron does in fact seem impotent, and Rowan's strength appears to have defeated everyone except Lasher. And yet even this is not clear. The story is not over. Michael's musings over the ordeal indicate that he has the strength to have faith that something good will yet happen—no mean feat—and that his love for Rowan and belief in her will manifest itself in her using her strength for good. Thus, as with all paradoxes, the idea that the theme undermines itself is, in its own turn, undermined, restoring the potential for it to hold its own. Anne, too, is a Trickster of sorts, inviting readers into the void to seek their own visions.

Anne had no plans to continue this book, although many questions remain unanswered. For her the ending was completely satisfying. After copy editing, however, she gave more thought to the possibility. "My feeling is definitely that Michael is right," she said. "Those witches are not earthbound, and Lasher made Michael's vision. He was sent there to stop Lasher. That's my theory, but I won't know until I write the sequel."

The news from New York was good. Some who read the novel proclaimed it Anne's best yet. Stan gave her the same feedback, and even Christopher read part of it, having previously read only *Belinda*. Anne was gratified. The novel was an expression of something important to her about her past and her attachment to New Orleans.

Printing was set at 375,000 copies in hardcover, then increased to over 500,000. Soon Warner Brothers paid one million dollars for the movie rights, and the Book of the Month Club bought it in a heated auction for a main selection. *The New York Times* gave her a positive review, and royalties statements from previous novels told Anne that things had never been better financially. She had achieved most of her dreams, and to her delight Knopf agreed to publish Stan's poetry.

She took a trip to Amsterdam, then went on a publicity tour, losing weight and confirming her faith in her own will and inner strength. Meeting her readers was much easier now and a source of joy and even of tears. She was featured in *The New York Times Magazine, Newsweek,* and several television programs. *The Witching Hour* went to number two on the *Times* best-seller list the first week of its release and remained on the list for five months. Most of the copies sold to make it number nine in fiction sales in 1990. Within two months Anne was at work on another book.

CHAPTER THIRTEEN

THE PRISM

We shall not cease from exploration
And the end of all our exploring
Will be to arrive where we started
And know the place for the first time.
—T. S. Eliot

1

Writers make choices, both consciously and unconsciously, about how and what they write. The subjects they choose quicken something within them, and they organize their stories according to their responses to the world. Many factors blend together in the writer's psyche, producing images that reveal, ideally, the writer's inner life, as well as a way to connect with readers who respond. Anne Rice was sensitive to those factors and wrote her first novel in such a way that she managed to define a contemporary perspective for readers while she was also unfolding her imagination and exploring the darkest areas within herself.

Anne's mother wanted to raise geniuses. According to legend, a genius is the attendant spirit presiding over a person's destiny, working as either the light or dark spirit of a polar pair. Contemporary notions of genius abound with metaphors of light—brilliant, enlightened, luminous—and no doubt Katherine had such qualities in mind. Yet the darkness, too, has much to offer. Little Howard Allen yearned for mystery and gravitated toward ghost stories. If a spirit presided over her destiny, it was apparently the dark one of the pair that exerted its force on what would later emerge in her creative directions.

In the shadow of the psyche lies primary, archaic matter inaccessible to the "searching light" of the conscious mind. It contains in mobile currents emotionally coded perceptions from an individual's life. Because it is elusive to the rational mind, it seems dark and blurred, yielding dreams and images. In the darkness, where mystery and chaos seem to reign, the images shift into one another, opposites blend together, and ambiguity dissolves certainty. The person seeking clear distinctions is threatened. Darkness is then equated with something to be avoided. It becomes a dumping ground. Whatever is frowned upon by family, friends, religion, and society, and whatever is feared, is stuffed surreptitiously into the shadows, increasing its negative charge. The more the "light" is emphasized in the conscious realm, the more the personality is polarized, and the consequent repression gives energy to the shadow.

Yet God, the essence of light, is just as elusive and indistinct to the rational mind. God may bear closer kinship to the darkness than the polarization admits. Just as the same primal matter generates opposite sexes, or black can be both the absence and full mix of color, so can gods and demons be projected from the same accumulation of emotional power. When concepts are malleable within the depths of the mind, darkness can alchemize into light. Disequilibrium threatens, but people who can withstand it can avoid becoming potential victims out of control, and instead become heroes who wield control.

Anne Rice has experienced the tug of both. Having had a mother with heroic visions who ultimately succumbed to being a victim, and having herself submitted to paralyzing fear and grief, she experienced the precarious balance between being caught in the deluge of her own pain-filled subconscious and discovering a means through writing to stay afloat without shielding herself from what the pain offered. What she expressed was the result of an unusual combination of elements.

As a little girl Anne possessed a fine sensitivity to perceptual stimulation and the capacity for a strong emotional and sensual response. Her first impressions were of a sultry, exotic world full of sounds, smells, and sights that were enhanced by fluent, imaginative parents who encouraged artistic pursuits. Even the church contributed to her developing temperament by exercising her imagination and offering the excitement of an unreachable spirituality and the wonders of the Transubstantiation—the magical change of inner realities. Anne's mother wanted perfection, the church wanted purity, and little Howard Allen developed a keen moral vision based in goodness and free will. She wanted—needed—to be extraordinary. Being the center of attention and feeling loved gave her the sense of substantiality necessary to fend off her many fears. She created a vivid and complex daydream world in which she wielded creative power and found continuous self-expression. Linked with that was an appreciation for language. As a slow reader, she developed a sensitivity to fleeting nuances in the words and style used in literature. She experienced the music of poetry and sat in rapt attention in a world of storytellers. Encouraged by educated parents and by her own inner drive to sharpen and distill her sensitivity through articulation, she began to write, using personally salient dimensions of her experience as an organizing focus.

Unfortunately, however, her models were imperfect. Church officials had human weaknesses, as did parents. The formulas presented for attaining love and for transcending mediocrity were faulty. Katherine's behavior was unpredictable, Howard was often absent and the nuns could be cruel. Anne felt like an outsider at school, yet came home to chaos. It was difficult to find a safe place, a womb in which to develop, although she cast her mother in the best possible light. She relied on her fantasies and on examples set by the saints. Katherine's death erased a buffer, erratic as it was, and the sudden loss of loving attention provoked Anne to grow up fast—to take charge, meet her fears head-on, and make a safe place within herself.

Yet she was still an adolescent, someone acted upon who had to await a legal age to become the hero she sought to be—the foundation for becoming extraordinary. Before that moment came, she faced the loss of childhood with the suppression of her natural feistiness and sensuality in preparation for becoming a woman. As she watched girls around her mature, she became aware of social standards against which she came up short and which amplified her sense of feeling different. She had identified with the "masculine" trait of intelligence, and as she developed it, a gap widened between her inner and outer worlds.

She was taken from New Orleans and exposed to a new environment that excited her but also created a further sense of lack. Her world had lost its sense of wholeness, and her strong identification with the disparate pieces made her feel the fragmentation within herself. Loss of religious faith exacerbated Anne's search for a protective space, and she fell victim to morbid fears of the humiliation, finality, and erasure of death. Believing in God had ensured that Someone was always aware, always caring, ensuring substance and omniscient consciousness that promised ultimate truth and drove back chaos. Losing that support meant finding other ways to gain it back.

Marriage provided one hedge through the attention of a loving husband, Stan. It was also a step toward reconciling some of the opposites divided by gender expectations, although it did not diminish the rage she felt against fashion that threatened to withhold social substance and approval. Family was important to Anne and now she could make a home of her own, a safe place. Through Stan's influence the physical world came into focus, offering a hard, tangible edge to reality, although Anne continued to listen to accounts of near-death experiences and haunted houses. Stan's talents eventually usurped his attention and ironically nudged Anne into the shadowy identity of being "Stan's wife." She found a secret place—the back bedroom—where she could be herself, just as she had in her childhood fantasies.

Attracted to the male physique but feeling as if she had more the sexual libido of a man than a woman, she identified with gay men. Like her, they did not fit what society expected of them, nor did they define themselves neatly by gender, but they endured ostracism with courage. They represented to Anne, through androgyny, the freedom from female restrictions and the freedom to acknowledge her sexuality. Strict standards that had stripped her of momentum and hinted she was less than perfect as a woman were dissolved. Gay men symbolized sainthood, the transcendence of gender through spirituality, a sexual demilitarized zone that was accessible to her, if only in her imagination. The perfection of the asexual mystics was beyond her, and there was no return to the bisexual innocence and energy of childhood (as the problems with developing Claudia had proven), so gay men gave her a new way to express herself. She could develop substance through her fantasies without bowing to social standards. Her early writings carried out this theme.

Eventually, Anne had a child—a person who could carry on the continual consciousness of a family line that ensured for its members perpetuation and preservation. Anne would not be lost in the void of fading memories. She would be *someone,* at least for her family.

Then Michele died and her death struck a hard blow. Along with grief and pain came the irretrievable loss of a witness. The only escape was into the false womb of alcohol, and Anne teetered at the brink of becoming a shadow of her mother.

She took her life in hand and saved herself, ensuring at least the continuity of a sustained marriage with a husband who believed in her. And she wrote, allowing the inner abyss with its montage of New Orleans, alcoholism, Irish storytelling, sensuality, strained relationships, poetry, contradiction, androgyny, excess, grief, guilt, anger, and spiritual quests to wash up through her into a metaphor about a vampire plagued by the possibility of ultimate chaos. The extreme experience of grief brought her closer to her inner darkness than she might otherwise have willingly risked.

The novel plugged into a social chemistry that was exactly right to receive it, and it gained for Anne the wide audience she sought—the special attention she desired. "Do you love me?" her characters asked, and they became what she wanted to be—extraordinary, "nonpareils of their species," the fulfillment of someone's dream. Reunions between lovers were high points in her fiction, and she developed a mythical sense of family, where parental figures became brothers and sisters to their children in a world moving toward love and tolerance.

Anne found other symbols for her urge toward individuality, specialness, and resistance of social fashion in the free people of color and the castrati. Yet she needed to express other concerns and sought freedom to write her most outrageous fantasies without offending readers. Thus she allowed her inner complexity to dissociate in fiction as she explored different paths through two pseudonyms—"secret names of power." Sexual and artistic freedom became issues for Anne, and she made psychological breakthroughs as she dipped autobiographically into her life to pull out characters who offered cathartic release. "It's not hard for me to create these various characters," she said, "because they all represent longings and aspirations within myself."

However, her new directions still expressed old themes: two sides of the self caught up in a struggle for balance: male/female, light/dark, dominance/submission, hero/victim, freedom/suppression, and mystery/enlightenment. The dualities paralleled each other without being reducible to each other, setting up a multisided perspective through which Anne could express increasingly complex images and ideas. Just as Rowan claimed that Lasher needed her to give himself purpose and bring him closer to life, so Anne needed her fictional characters. Through them, she understood total surrender as both the threat of annihilation and the path of godlike transformation.

The supernatural pressed again as readers clamored for more, so Anne left the victim, Louis, behind and deepened her mythological connections to create characters who took charge. She anchored the supernatural in the physical, although mystery still beckoned, as if Kierkegaard were right that humans are composites of finite and infinite, and that suppressing one would not erase the other. "Writing about the supernatural," she said, "is very intense for me. I'm comfortable with it, and it gives me a powerful way to write about real life. It strikes a deep moral chord in me." The characters made meaning, hoping for a better world, though they still worried about hurting those they loved. Brief glimpses of optimism from early novels evolved into full-blown moral and aesthetic philosophies as characters found inner power to commit themselves to the fullness of life. No matter what the circumstances, they did not give in. They provided for readers a medium through which to explore self-knowledge, self-mastery, self-redemption, and self-reinvention through the triumph of moral integrity.

As Anne looked to both great literature and ancient mythologies for themes and style, she expressed archetypal images that resonated for her audience deep within the psyche. The breakdown of the self toward ultimate resurrection and greater freedom was prominent, parallel with her own life. She also concentrated on developing unique ways of expanding such traditional themes as the lure of immortality, moral education, the descent into darkness for psychological enrichment, the outsider image, and the erotic as the pulse of life.

True to the sixties and seventies, Anne emphasized the power of the will, and her message was received by others who sought to keep the notion of self-empowerment alive. She presented androgynous characters who allowed identification on many levels, and she provided through outsiders new perspectives on life. All the while, she strove for greater clarity of knowledge and expression. As she saw it, what affected outsiders most strongly was an apparent absence of choice. Anne used such constriction as a force to confront them with moments of feeling most alive. When feeling and form harmonized in a direct realization of inner and outer worlds, she felt the most intense connection with her fiction, and she struggled to take her characters to new levels of experience.

Transubstantiation has been a key concept throughout the novels, used to transform images of darkness into images of light by mimicking the highest church sacrament. Change in substance was instrumental in explaining the existence of vampires, mummies, ghosts, and incubi; adolescents and castrati experienced physical changes; the bodies of masochists who submit to ritual flogging took on a special quality; and those characters who did not change physically typically went through mental transformations that produced a similar spiritual ascent.

Anne's protagonists blended dualities. Males cried readily and sought commitments; females displayed strength and decisiveness. Anne herself evolved as her characters evolved. Starting with a feminized, passive male, she moved through the bridge of adolescence, where the question of being a victim or hero of one's own life is typically decided, into the world of sexual dominance and submission. Using gender switches and equality between slaves and masters, she achieved a balance through which the female point of view emerged, then strengthened. The male receded while Anne brought together an angry female (who symbolized dogmatic religion) and a visionary female (who symbolized the freedom of inner control) to struggle for dominance. The visionary triumphed but did not release Anne from her inner darkness. She had to return to New Orleans for that, moving through emotional layers in her novels toward a clarity of perception that she called the mysterious It. She finally arrived, a multiprong plug seeking a socket, through a gentle but macho male character, Michael, who was more like her than any previous character.

New Orleans, the place of her birth and a happy and unrestricted childhood, represented a place of wholeness to Anne, entangled with images of her mother as a happy person and with God as a loving warmth. Many of her characters have come there to find self-realization. Going to the city herself meant for Anne a direct confrontation with her inner center, without the mediation of fiction. To stand up to what it meant involved becoming a hero who could confront the pain and heal the divisions.

Anne walked through her old neighborhoods and even went into the churches to meditate over her lost faith and the life that might have been. The novel she wrote while living there is the first book to acknowledge that God might exist as an essence of goodness, although the idea is fleeting and does not diminish the pain. Still, Anne saw this place as if for the first time, inspired by faith in a positive future for herself and for humankind. She had traveled into her own darkness, transforming monsters, forbidden sexuality, restrictive femininity, and the threat of eternal chaos and anonymity into images no longer frightening, more human and acceptable, and even possessing a transcendent power. She identified the outsider as having the possibility for a rich life through the freedom of individuality, and the "differences" about herself that had once caused pain and shame were no longer avoided. She felt safer there.

Anne has developed new perceptions of traditional images. She has used devices like paradox, unresolved ambiguity, and excessive language to explore artistic possibilities for forms of prose typically ignored by mainstream writers. With shifts of perception she tantalizes readers to become involved. Her writing haunts us with questions about ourselves, our society, and our world.

Analyst Mary Louise von Franz said that people who have worked with their shadow side gain an aura of substance and moral authority. Through her novels Anne used her own self as a transforming process for creating a prism through which things typically associated with the night could be refracted into various images of moral light.

2

Anne Rice still has many novels to write and has a number of ideas to pursue. Some she thought up and cast aside years ago, but claimed, "I might get to them. Who knows?" A look to the future reveals her intention to remain with her evolving visions.

One of the next novels will be *In the Frankenstein Tradition,* dealing with the making of a perfect man and possibly including mythologies from Mexico. Anne read Mary Shelley's *Frankenstein* and wondered about creating the mind of a synthetic man who is afraid he has no soul. For ideas she rode around New Orleans with a police officer and visited the morgue. She attempted to rewrite her ghost story idea for the aborted television series, "Hello, Darkness," but felt it was not working out, so she put it aside.

The next novel of the Vampire Chronicles, tentatively titled, *Once*

Out of Nature, will be told from Lestat's point of view, and it will include Louis and David Talbot. Claudia will also make an appearance. It will be about an adventure of Lestat's, bringing back Anne's hero. He feasts on serial killers and explores new contexts for evil. "Answers to questions raised in *Interview* will be resolved," Anne said. "It's the worst one in terms of pessimism and what constitutes evil. It may be the last one. That's how it feels." She may also broaden the setting. Visiting Miami for the promotion of *The Witching Hour,* she noted what she viewed as the "supernatural quality" of the city and thought perhaps Lestat should walk through it. She does not, however, rule out a fifth vampire novel. "I'll write them as I see them."

There may also be, for vampire fans, an encyclopedia of her vampire universe, à la *Silmarillion,* in which Anne would tell brief stories of all the vampires. "It would have to be something that had artistic scope."

A sequel to *The Witching Hour* may be forthcoming as well, since Anne has more ideas on that story and has begun writing it.

Anne also wants to write a series of *Mummy* novels, although she may not do it in paperback again. "It raises too many questions," she said. The next one is tentatively titled *The Mad Scientist,* which may cast a new darkness on immortality.

Staying with supernatural themes, she has worked on a treatment about the devil and immortality called "The Voice," which she may turn into a novel. She was also inspired by what she viewed as a poor interpretation of *Dr. Jekyll and Mr. Hyde* in a television movie to think about writing her own version. "The way to do it," she says, "is to make Hyde beautiful and seductive. I'll make it deliciously sadistic and masochistic."

Anne may also write more erotica. During an obsession with UFO stories, she thought about writing a horror novel along those lines. She especially loved Whitley Strieber's descriptions of sexual molestation aboard alien ships, and saw similarities between what he wrote in *Communion* and what she had written in her *Beauty* trilogy.

Anne has expressed an interest in doing something more with twins. She has an idea for a treatment to be written for Danny DeVito that would deal with twins; and she foresees a short story about a pair of doubles.

"I'll write the novels," she affirmed, "that demand to be written."

What Anne Rice desires for herself above all else is that people will take her seriously, care about her work, and be witnesses to her creativity for years to come.

"I want," she said, "to be read and valued."

NOVELS BY ANNE RICE

Interview With the Vampire (Alfred A. Knopf, 1976)
The Feast of All Saints (Simon & Schuster, 1979)
Cry to Heaven (Alfred A. Knopf, 1982)
The Vampire Lestat (Alfred A. Knopf, 1985)
The Queen of the Damned (Alfred A. Knopf, 1988)
The Mummy (Ballantine, 1989)
The Witching Hour (Alfred A. Knopf, 1990)

As Anne Rampling:

Exit to Eden (Arbor House, 1985)
Belinda (Arbor House, 1986)

As A. N. Roquelaure

The Claiming of Sleeping Beauty (Dutton, 1983)
Beauty's Punishment (Dutton, 1984)
Beauty's Release (Dutton, 1985)

CHRONOLOGY

1938 Howard O'Brien marries Katherine Allen on Thanksgiving Day, November 25, at 5:00 A.M.; they live at 2301 St. Charles Avenue with Katherine's mother.

1939 Alice born

1941 Howard Allen (Anne) born October 4 in Mercy Hospital.

1942 Howard goes into the navy for three years.

1946 Anne's first writings

1947 Tamara born
Anne changes her name from Howard Allen.

1949 Karen born
Mamma Allen dies.

1950 Anne sees 1936 film *Dracula's Daughter* and is impressed by emotional resonance; she also hears the story "The White Silk Dress," about a child vampire.

1951 Anne writes a novella about two aliens from Mars.

1953 Anne writes several plays.

1956 Katherine O'Brien dies.

1957 Anne is sent to St. Joseph Academy boarding school.

1957 Howard remarries and is transferred to Richardson, Texas.

Anne sees Stan Rice in a journalism class. They develop a casual relationship. He edits the high school newspaper; Anne writes features.

1959 Anne graduates high school. She enters Texas Woman's University. Her stepmother, Dorothy, buys Anne her first typewriter. Completes two years of college in one year.

1960 Stan arrives in Denton for college, but Anne goes to San Francisco; they correspond.

1961 Stan proposes by telegram. Anne returns to Texas to marry Stan in a civil ceremony on October 14.

1962 Anne and Stan return to San Francisco and take night courses at the University of San Francisco until they can enroll in day courses at San Francisco State University. They live in Haight-Ashbury.

1963 Anne writes *The Sufferings of Charlotte* and *Nicholas and Jean*; Stan gains reputation with his poetry.

1964 Stan and Anne graduate from San Francisco State—Anne takes a B.A. in Political Science, Stan in Creative Writing; Stan starts Ph.D. program at Berkeley but drops out and returns to SFSU.

1965 Anne publishes short story, "October 4, 1948," in *Transfer*.

1966 Move to Taraval; Anne gives birth to Michele on September 21. Stan starts teaching at San Francisco State University. Stan's poetry is getting published and he gives readings; he receives a $1000 grant.

Anne publishes first chapter of *Nicholas and Jean* in *Transfer*.

Anne is in graduate school, changing majors from Art History to German to English.

1969 Anne and Stan move to Berkeley, 1621 Dwight Way. Anne writes a short story called "Interview With the Vampire"; she writes a novella, *Katherine and Jean*, which she sends to publishers. There is some interest.

1970 Stan wins Joseph Henry Jackson Award for poetry and they use the $1500 to buy a red MG sports car.

1970 Anne enters the Ph.D. program at the University of California at Berkeley. She is dissatisfied and leaves to complete a master's in creative writing at San Francisco State University.

Stan and Anne move to an apartment in North Berkeley at 1275 Bonita Avenue; she writes *Tales of Rhoda*.

Anne is haunted by her New Orleans past; begins extensive research.

Michele is diagnosed with leukemia.

1972 Anne takes master's degree in creative writing. Master's thesis: *Katherine and Jean*; orals on Woolf, Shakespeare, and Hemingway.

Stan receives a grant from the National Endowment for the Arts for $5000; they take Michele to Disneyland.

Michele dies on August 5.

1973 Anne quits job to write full time; turns "Interview With the Vampire" into a novel in five weeks and sends it out to publishers. It is rejected.

1974 Anne enters *Interview With the Vampire* in a contest and is rejected; takes it to Squaw Valley writer's conference where Phyllis Seidel reads it and agrees to represent it; sells it to Vicky Wilson at Knopf for hardcover release and a $12,000 advance.

1975 Stan publishes *Some Lamb,* poetry about Michele, The Figures Press.

1976 *Interview With the Vampire* is published; 75 reviews; Paperback sale of $700,000; Paramount buys film rights for $150,000 for 10 year option.

Stan publishes *Whiteboy,* Mudra Press.

Anne and Stan move into a succession of houses in Berkeley and Oakland.

They visit Port au Prince and New Orleans, where Anne researches for *The Feast of All Saints*.

1977 Anne and Stan go on a grand tour of Europe and Egypt.

Stan wins Edgar Allan Poe Award for Poetry.

Anne returns later to Italy with her father, stepmother, and sister.

1978 Christopher born on March 11.

1979 Anne and Stan stop drinking on Memorial Day.

1979 *The Feast of All Saints* published by Simon & Schuster; $150,000 advance.

A short story about vampires is published in *Playboy*.

1980 Anne and Stan move to a Victorian in the Castro district, where Anne writes *Cry to Heaven*.

1982 *Cry to Heaven* published by Knopf; $75,000 advance.

"Master of Rampling Gate" appears in *Redbook*.

Anne is devastated by a terrible review in *San Francisco Chronicle* and begins to withdraw.

1983 *The Claiming of Sleeping Beauty* by "A. N. Roquelaure" published by Dutton; three-book contract.

Article on gender appears in *Vogue*.

Stan publishes *Body of Work*, Lost Roads Press.

1984 *Beauty's Punishment*, Dutton (second Roquelaure)

1985 Anne writes "Desert Song" for Tommy Tune.

Exit to Eden published by Arbor House, under "Anne Rampling"; $35,000 advance.

Beauty's Release published by Dutton (Roquelaure).

The Vampire Lestat, Knopf hardcover, $100,000 advance; makes best-seller list in hardcover.

1986 *Belinda* published (Rampling), Arbor House.

Editor John Dodds dies of cancer; Anne withdraws more from San Francisco.

Paramount's rights revert to Anne. Lorimar picks up the option. Lorimar has rights to *The Vampire Lestat* and *The Queen of the Damned*; Warner buys Lorimar.

Anne writes treatment for "The Voice."

1987 Anne and Stan buy a house in Sonoma County on seven acres where she writes parts of *The Queen of the Damned*.

Editor Bill Whitehead dies.

1988 Stan and Anne sell the Sonoma house and buy a second house, at 1020 Philip Street in New Orleans; Stan takes a leave of absence from teaching.

The Queen of the Damned, Knopf hardcover, $500,000 advance.

1989 Anne and Stan move to New Orleans permanently; Stan retires from teaching to paint; they buy a large mansion in the Garden District.

The Mummy, or Ramses the Damned, published by Ballantine.

1990 *The Witching Hour* published by Knopf as part of two-book contract for $5 million advance; Warner purchases film rights for $1 million; BOMC buys it as main selection.

1991 Anne writes fourth Vampire Chronicle: *The Witching Hour,* released in paperback.

SOURCE NOTES

This book is based primarily on interviews in 1989, 1990, and 1991 with Anne Rice and with people who know or have associated with her. Some of the interviews were conducted in person and some on the phone. All quotes attributed to Anne Rice are from these interviews or from letters, unless otherwise noted.

Chapter One

Howard O'Brien's memories of his relationship with Katherine came from phone interviews conducted in April 1989.

The incident of Anne's name change was created from the memories of several people, primarily Anne.

Impressions of Mamma Allen came from Howard O'Brien and from Anne and her sisters Alice and Tamara.

Gertrude Helwig, George Daviau, and Patt Moore supplied memories of Katherine in phone interviews.

Katherine's thoughts about her wedding came from

Page(s) Anne's memory of what her mother had told her, and from Howard O'Brien.

Chapter Two

Quotes from Howard O'Brien, Patt Moore, Gertrude Helwig, Alice O'Brien Borchardt, Billy Murphy, Allen Daviau, George Daviau, and Tamara O'Brien came from phone interviews in 1989 and 1990. I also spoke with Howard O'Brien and Billy Murphy in person.

Quotes from Lucy Provosty Harper were from letters and phone interviews in 1990.

Anne's memories of her mother and grandmother were written to me in a letter dated March 1989.

All references to short stories and plays came from the memories of the people quoted. No copies exist today.

The description of Anne's voice on a tape recorder was from the actual tape, played for me by Howard O'Brien.

Karen O'Brien shared her memories with me in person.

On poetry and children: Ellen Winner, *Invented Worlds: The Psychology of Art,* Cambridge, MA: Harvard University Press, 1982.

The conditions of genius and creativity: Silvano Arieti, *Creativity: The Magic Synthesis,* New York: Basic Books, 1976.

On alcoholism: Claudia Black, *It Will Never Happen to Me,* New York: Ballantine, 1981.

19 "There is this . . . puritanism." *Exit to Eden,* New York: Arbor House, 1985, p. 194 (Dell edition).

20 "And my mother . . . psychiatrists." *Ibid.*, p. 12.

26 "When I was . . . scream." *The Queen of the Damned,* New York: Knopf, 1988, p. 228 (Ballantine edition).

30 "I've had the feeling . . . people." *Exit to Eden,* pp. 224–225.

30–31 "I couldn't . . . fantasies." *Ibid.*, p. 193.

37 "Prayer . . . saints." *Interview With the Vampire,* New York: Knopf, 1976, p. 5 (Ballantine edition).

43–44 "I've always been . . . as well." *The Queen of the Damned,* New York: Knopf, 1988, p. 289 (Ballantine edition).

Chapter Three

Phone interviews were conducted with Judy Murphy O'Neil, Ann Bailey Johnson, Howard O'Brien, Tamara O'Brien, Stan Rice, Sister Lydia Champagne, Lynn Packard Phelps, Ann Fekety, Lucy Provosty Harper, Stanley Rice, Sr., Ginny Mathis Hiebert, Jack DeGovia, Ed Stephan, Cynthia Rice Rodgers, Nancy Rice Diamond, Allen Daviau, and Jesse Ritter in 1989 and 1990.

Michael Riley, Lee van den Daele, Lucy Provosty Harper, and Larry Rice wrote their accounts in letters to me.

Dorothy O'Brien told me in person the story of her meeting with Howard.

Letters from Anne to friends were provided by Ann Fekety and Lynn Packard Phelps.

52 "Never had . . . trousers." "Katherine and Jean," Unpublished thesis, San Francisco State University, 1972, p. 92.

52 "I could see . . . sexuality." *Ibid.*, p. 280.

52 "Some vital . . . head." *Ibid.*, p. 280.

54 "The fear . . . read." "Katherine and Jean," p. 186.

59 "Her dad . . . ideal." *Exit to Eden*, p. 193.

60 "Richard . . . gone away." *The Feast of All Saints*, New York: Simon & Schuster, 1979, p. 195 (Ballantine edition).

63 "You told me . . . remember." *Exit to Eden*, p. 279.

64 "Right near . . . drowned." "Katherine and Jean," p. 47.

65 "My father . . . soul." *Ibid.*, p. 79.

66 "Does the . . . singing?" *The Queen of the Damned*, p. 193.

Chapter Four

Phone interviews were conducted in 1989 and 1990 with Stan Rice, Jack DeGovia, Cynthia Rice Rodgers, Dr. Jesse Ritter, Allen Daviau, Casey Sonnabend, Betsy and Tony Dubovsky, Linda Gregg, Jack Gilbert, Laura Chester, Carla DeGovia, Floyd Salas, Marjorie Ford, and Joe Slusky.

I also spent time with Betsy Dubovsky, who showed me each of the houses in which Anne had lived in Berkeley and Oakland.

Michael Riley, Larry Rice, Laura Chester, and Annette Arbeit Van Slyke wrote their memories in letters to me.

Anne's letters to Lynn Packard Phelps were provided by Lynn.

Descriptions of the sixties: Todd Gitlin, *The Sixties: Years of Hope, Days of Rage*, New York: Bantam, 1987; and Geoffrey O'Brien, *Dream Time: Chapters from the Sixties*, New York: Penguin, 1988.

81 "My teacher . . . different word." *The Feast of All Saints,* p. 111.

85 "The poet . . . environment." Stan Rice to Andy Brumer in *San Francisco Review of Books,* April 1978, p. 10.

85 "I am . . . somewhere." Stan Rice to Andy Brumer, p. 10.

85–86 "Eating It," *Some Lamb,* Berkeley, CA: The Figures Press, 1975, p. 38.

90 "If you would . . . only." "Nicholas and Jean," *Transfer,* June 1966, #21, p. 9.

90–91 "One night . . . died." *Ibid.,* p. 5.

94 "Their favorite . . . car." Anne Rice, "October 14, 1948," *Transfer,* May 1965, #19, p. 17.

94 "The ivy . . . hair." *Ibid.,* p. 18.

94 "As very gently . . . to come." *Ibid.,* p. 23.

97 "It was as if . . . process." *Interview With the Vampire,* pp. 20–21.

99–100 "It was as if . . . spoke." "Katherine and Jean," pp. 208–212.

101 "I realized . . . floor." *The Vampire Lestat,* pp. 55–56.

101 "I'll tell . . . living." *The Queen of the Damned,* pp. 88–89.

101 "The world . . . hopelessness." *The Vampire Lestat,* p. 59.

101 "What caused . . . die?" *Ibid.,* p. 59.

102 "I was cold . . . screamed." "Katherine and Jean," pp. 250–251.

102 "Like all . . . goodness." *Interview With the Vampire,* p. 65.

Chapter Five

Phone interviews were conducted in 1989 and 1990 with Tamara O'Brien, Betsy Dubovsky, Floyd Salas, Stan Rice, Howard O'Brien, Carla DeGovia, Linda Gregg, Jack DeGovia, Martha Nawy, Stanley Rice, Sr., Jim Bodishbaugh, Laura Chester, Shirley Stuart, and Cathy Colman.

Michael Riley, Dr. Robin Gajdusek, Dr. William Weigand, Larry Rice, Annette Arbeit Van Slyke, Carolyn Doty, and Shirley Stuart wrote their memories in letters to me.

Anne's letter to Lynn Phelps was provided by Lynn.

117 "On hearing . . . what is." Stan Rice, *Some Lamb,* Berkeley, CA: The Figures Press, 1975, p. 23.

120 "The pictures on the wall, Mommy!" Kathy Macay, *San Francisco Chronicle,* April 4, 1976.

123 "We create . . . anymore." "Katherine and Jean," p. 284.

123 "I was sure . . . each other." *Ibid.,* p. 38.

123 "The tragedy . . . loses." *Ibid.*, p. 204.
123 "I'd spent . . . act." *Ibid.*, p. 86.
125 "Everything was . . . stranger." *Ibid.*, p. 295.
125 "I was smiling . . . dandy." *Ibid.*, p. 122.
125 "Let's go . . . dandy." *Ibid.*, p. 237.
126 "I loved . . . to open." *Interview With the Vampire*, p. 105.
126 "What does . . . chains." *Some Lamb*, p. 25.
127 "The rapid . . . die." *Interview With the Vampire*, p. 75.
128–129 "Anne in her . . . hello." *Some Lamb*, p. 30.
129 "It would do . . . turning." *Ibid.*, p. 71.
129 "Look! . . . went." *Ibid.*, p. 85.
130 "I looked . . . nothingness." *Interview With the Vampire*, p. 145.
131 "Love went . . . see." *Some Lamb*, p. 35.
131 "We lose . . . flow." *The Witching Hour*, New York: Knopf, 1990, p. 126.
132–133 "Anne drinks . . . enough." *Some Lamb*, p. 31.
133 "Every death's . . . maybes." *Ibid.*, p. 61.
134 "It's hard . . . ruined." *Ibid.*, p. 61.
134 "Fear . . . we do." *Ibid.*, p. 63.
134 "I dreamed . . . help." *Interview With the Vampire*, p. 77.
135 "I could not . . . him." *Ibid.*, p. 8.
135 "I saw myself . . . pardon." *Ibid.*, p. 17.
138 "Write what . . . else will." Interview by Stanley Wiater, *Writer's Digest*, November 1988.

Chapter Six

I conducted interviews over the telephone with Pam Henstell, Stan Rice, Howard O'Brien, Casey Sonnabend, Kathy Macay, Dr. Richard Wiseman, Cynthia Rice Rodgers, Victoria Wilson, and Allen Daviau.

I received letters from Phyllis Seidel and Carolyn Doty, who also sent me a brochure from Squaw Valley Writer's Conference.

The following quotes in this chapter are from *Interview With the Vampire* unless otherwise noted.

142 "Some things . . . grief." Stan Rice, *Body of Work*, Eureka Springs, AR; Lost Roads, p. 15.
143 "It was part . . . ever known," p. 334.
143 "A vampire . . . creatures," p. 40.
143 "I was a . . . ninety-one," p. 4.
144 "I cannot live . . . dead," p. 11.
144 "I lowered . . . itself," p. 168.

145	"A rat . . . vases," pp. 144–145.
145	"The movement . . . passion," p. 18.
147	"It was . . . first time," p. 20.
147	"When I saw the moon . . .," p. 20.
147	"Pain is . . . vampire," p. 88.
147	"Killing . . . slowly," pp. 28–29.
147	"The sucking . . . my hands," p. 29.
148	"For me the most . . . woman." *Newswest,* January 6–20, 1977.
148	"I meant to imply . . . surrender." *Chicago Tribune,* May 1977.
149	"I think I have a gender screw-up . . . thinking" *Newswest,* January 6–20, 1977.
150–151	"What I wanted . . . work." Interview with Eric Bauersveld, KPFA Radio, 1976.
151	"The vampire . . . cartoon," p. 3.
151	"Now . . . Ecstasy!" John Keats, "Ode to a Nightingale."
151–152	"It is . . . misunderstood." Kathy Macay, *San Francisco Chronicle,* April 4, 1976.
153	"And what . . . nothing," p. 30.
153	"Represented . . . life," p. 41.
153	"For vampires . . . kill," p. 256.
153	"In that instant . . . more pain," p. 74.
153	"String . . . labyrinth," p. 126.
153	"A vampire . . . now," p. 79.
154	"I knew peace . . . killed," p. 87.
154	"Yet more . . . unknowable," pp. 102–103.
155	"Which of you did it?" p. 109.
155	"If there's . . . doing." Bauersveld interview.
161–162	"I am . . . guilt," p. 287.
162	"The only power . . . ourselves," p. 255.
162	"It was as . . . hope," p. 240.
162	"Do you know . . . let you go," p. 251.
162	"To give . . . form," p. 268.
162	"Hell . . . hatred," p. 134.
163	"I'm at odds . . . have been," p. 288.
163	"It's as if . . . beyond it," p. 287.
163	"She's my . . . parent," p. 283.
163	"You feel . . . intact," p. 286.
163	"She's an era . . . burden," p. 284.
163	"I cannot . . . I die," p. 294.
163	"You see . . . do nothing," p. 284.
163	"I told . . . the lid," p. 300.
164	"A cry . . . being," p. 306.

164 "The one . . . Armand," p. 306.
164 "Powerful . . . regret," p. 340.
164 "Closeted . . . my grief," p. 310.
165 "That passivity . . . evil," p. 309.
165 "You showed me . . . to become," p. 340.
165 "I had . . . finished," p. 319.
165 "Now the . . . ashes," p. 321.
165 "It was . . . in life," p. 343.
167 "You wrestle . . . consequences." Bauersveld interview.

Information about the seventies is from *The Seventies: From Hot Pants to Hot Tubs,* Andrew J. Edelstein and Kevin McDonough, New York: Dutton, 1990.

170 "Use the power inside you," p. 257.
171 "Everyone feels . . . of a century," p. 288.
171 "You die . . . to die," p. 236.
171 "If God . . . human life," p. 238.
172 "Once fallen . . . nothing," p. 150.
172 "I'll travel . . . vampires," p. 81.
172 "Had . . . club," p. 248.
172 "Weak vampires . . . to them," p. 254.

Chapter Seven

Telephone interviews were conducted in 1989 and 1990 with Joni Evans, Lynn Nesbit, Floyd Salas, Betsy Dubovsky, Cynthia Rice Rodgers, and Howard O'Brien.

Michael Riley, Shirley Stuart, and Candi Ellis wrote their memories in letters in 1990.

The following quotes are taken from *The Feast of All Saints,* New York: Simon & Schuster, 1979 (Ballantine edition), unless otherwise identified.

179 "The world . . . supreme," p. 525.
183 "It is . . . purpose." *Interview With the Vampire,* p. 108.
184 "My work . . . admired," p. 385.
184 "Sustained . . . faith," p. 529.
184 "When you . . . humiliated," p. 506.
184–185 "That Christ . . . prayers," p. 200.
185 "She might . . . man," p. 196.
185 "All this . . . own," p. 307.
185 "I wanted . . . bricks," p. 189.
185 "The key . . . all men," p. 277.
186–187 "Is no real order . . . at all," pp. 412–413.
187 "Because you . . . yourself," p. 413.
187 "It's an accident . . . effect," p. 507.

188 "To fortify your soul," p. 477.
188 "They take . . . to live," p. 584.
194 "The art . . . 1876." *Playboy,* January 1979.
195 "There is . . . one another." *Belinda,* New York: Arbor House, 1987, p. 36 (Jove edition).
196 "And we . . . not eternal." *San Francisco Chronicle,* November 2, 1980.
196 "Especially . . . life." *San Francisco Chronicle,* August 2, 1981.
196 "Bridging . . . not exist." *San Francisco Chronicle,* January 3, 1982.

The following quotes are from *Cry to Heaven,* New York: Knopf, 1982 (Pinnacle edition), unless otherwise identified.

198 "He must . . . everyone," p. 201.
199 "Your arms . . . a man," pp. 258–259.
199 "Children . . . hear," p. 477.
200 "Why can't . . . save her?" p. 26.
200 "She was . . . terrified her," p. 23.
200 "If I . . . to hurt me," p. 9.
200 "The name . . . millennium," p. 14.
200 "And then . . . resonance," p. 39.
201 "A human . . . comparison," p. 76.
201 "He became . . . within it," p. 179.
201 "A pair of . . . same body," p. 336.
202 "You are not . . . these things," p. 355.
203 "Oh, if only . . . both," p. 401.
203 "He could not . . . the earth," p. 399.
203 "As though . . . time ago," p. 399.
203–204 "It was taste . . . God's work," p. 300.
204 "Gilded maggots . . . state," p. 173.
206 "The cutting . . . us all," p. 247.

Chapter Eight

Telephone interviews were conducted with Stan and Christopher Rice, Cathy Colman, and John Preston in 1989 and 1990.

John Preston, Shirley Stuart, and Larry Rice wrote their memories in letters in 1989 and 1990.

213 "If you grow up . . . feminine." Dorothy Allison, *Village Voice,* December 1986, No. 51, p. 25.
215 Bruno Bettelheim, *The Uses of Enchantment,* New York: Vintage, 1975.

215 ‘‘Pleasing me . . . simplicity.’’ *The Claiming of Sleeping Beauty,* New York: Dutton, 1983, p. 23.

216 ‘‘He’s so gentle . . . woman.’’ *The Witching Hour,* New York: Knopf, 1990, pp. 584–585.

216 ‘‘To be commanded . . . helplessness.’’ *The Claiming of Sleeping Beauty,* p. 12.

217 ‘‘When a slave . . . in some way.’’ *Beauty’s Release,* New York: Dutton, 1983, p. 141.

217 ‘‘The only . . . obedience.’’ *The Claiming of Sleeping Beauty,* p. 223.

218 ‘‘They can’t . . . contained.’’ *Exit to Eden,* p. 224.

218 ‘‘Women as women . . . sexually.’’ *Lear’s,* October 1989, p. 89.

219–220 ‘‘People say . . . others.’’ *Exit to Eden,* p. 223.

222 ‘‘Their passions . . . pleasure.’’ *Beauty’s Punishment,* New York: Dutton, 1984, p. 177.

222–223 ‘‘There is . . . ordeals.’’ *Ibid.,* p. 178.

223 ‘‘It is . . . perfects him.’’ *Ibid.,* p. 178.

223 ‘‘The best . . . masters.’’ *Ibid.,* p. 169.

223 ‘‘You will . . . passion.’’ *Ibid.,* pp. 224–225.

The following quotes are from *Exit to Eden,* New York: Arbor House, 1985 (Dell edition), unless otherwise identified.

227 ‘‘It’s just like . . . things,’’ p. 265.

227 ‘‘The Club is . . . that,’’ p. 2.

228 ‘‘He is . . . believe,’’ p. 194.

229 ‘‘Reading Anne . . . our way.’’ Steve Chapple, *Image,* May 18, 1986.

230 ‘‘The kind . . . real world,’’ p. 22.

230 ‘‘What a laugh . . . him,’’ p. 143.

231 ‘‘Each of us . . . understanding,’’ p. 105.

231 ‘‘That’s where . . . is a sin,’’ p. 289.

232 ‘‘I was riding . . . guy,’’ p. 219.

232 ‘‘There is nothing . . . aggression,’’ p. 221.

232 ‘‘There isn’t any . . . in it,’’ p. 222.

232–233 ‘‘Very few . . . our sights,’’ p. 289.

236 ‘‘And it seemed . . . village.’’ ‘‘The Master of Rampling Gate,’’ *Redbook,* February 1984, p. 58.

237 ‘‘A wise . . . effortlessly.’’ ‘‘Playing With Gender,’’ *Vogue,* November 1983, p. 498.

The following quotes are from *Beauty’s Release,* New York: Dutton, 1985, unless otherwise identified.

238 ‘‘I would feel . . . completely,’’ p. 13.

238 ‘‘We are lost . . . notice us,’’ p. 49.

239 ‘‘And her hatred . . . anguish,’’ p. 100.

239 "It was merely . . . cycle," p. 88.
239 "I felt . . . same time," p. 90.
239 "It has never been . . . somewhat," p. 162.
239 "Now I have . . . the other," p. 137.
239 "The atmosphere . . . Master," pp. 138–139.
240 "I suppose . . . love it," p. 145.
240 "I felt . . . my being," p. 190.
240 "Was too . . . subjugation," p. 209.
240 "Maybe . . . in command," p. 222.
240 "Worst . . . of all," p. 238.

Chapter Nine

Telephone interviews were conducted with John Preston, Christopher Rice, Andy Brumer, and Alice Borchardt in 1989 and 1990.

John Preston also wrote letters in 1989 and 1990.

The following quotes were taken from *The Vampire Lestat,* New York: Knopf, 1985 (Ballantine edition, 1986), unless otherwise identified.

245 "She spoke . . . have," p. 62.
246 "You're such . . . *accept*," p. 60.
247 "Knew . . . things," p. 31.
247 "Mingled . . . of her," p. 37.
247 "Two parts . . . thing," p. 61.
247 "You have . . . blinding," p. 72.
247 "I do not . . . goodness," p. 72.
247 "Sheer will . . . characteristic," p. 497.
248 "For the first . . . as men," p. 7.
249 "He told . . . believed it," p. 499.
250 "Rock stars . . . effects." Interview on National Public Radio, "All Things Considered," 1986, #861009.
251 "Horror and . . . value," p. 10.
251 "In art . . . himself," p. 10.
252 "As I see it . . . believe in," p. 72.
252 "I leant . . . it came," p. 157.
253 "Gabrielle was . . . her death." Interview with Stewart Kellerman, *The New York Times,* November 7, 1988.
Conversation with Andy Brumer, taped in 1985.
253 "The writing . . . character." Interview with Helen Knode, *L.A. Weekly,* October 19, 1990.
253 "You are . . . man in me," p. 62.
254–255 "I dreamed . . . one another," p. 351.
255 "Cut them . . . burn us," p. 435.

255–256 "I could not . . . understand," p. 446.
256 "The idea . . . knowing," p. 398.
Legends of Osiris and Dionysus are from Sir James Frazier, *The New Golden Bough,* edited by Theodor H. Gaster, New York: New American Library, 1964.
258 "This god . . . too rich," p. 330.
259 "I was . . . *good,*" p. 336.
259 "You must . . . its form," p. 227.
259 "My eyes . . . them," p. 3.
259–260 "The dimly . . . redeemed," pp. 501–502.
260 "So let us . . . meaning," p. 531.
260 "Drive out . . . adore," p. 541.
261 "Now I knew . . . gods," p. 539.
261 "All your demons . . . anymore," p. 541.
261 "A love . . . eyes," p. 381.
267 "And this lesson . . . going on," p. 254.
267 "Satanic . . . to live," p. 334.
267 "Very few . . . go on," p. 380.
267 "The mind . . . rise and fall," p. 465.
267 "Maybe . . . and again," p. 494.
268 "Where the value . . . increased," p. 465.
268 "But maybe . . . angels," p. 465.
Information on the vampire film projects comes from Anne Rice and from Julia Phillips, *You'll Never Eat Lunch in This Town Again,* New York: Random House, 1991.

Chapter Ten

Telephone interviews were conducted with Stan Rice, John Preston, and Allen Daviau in 1989 and 1990. John Preston also wrote his memories in letters.

The following quotes are from *Belinda,* New York: Arbor House, 1986 (Jove edition).
274 "More real . . . was." p. 4.
274 "This is . . . solitude," p. 5.
274–275 "I was able . . . inevitable," p. 37.
275 "Representing . . . periods," pp. 37–38.
275 "No one has . . . I do," pp. 38–39.
275 *"Looking for Bettina* . . . anymore," p. 21.
275 "It was . . . audience wanted?" p. 19.
275 "A serious . . . like that," p. 19.
276 "I work . . . five minutes," p. 29.
276 "If we were . . . nobody," p. 29.
277 "It's got to be . . . to have," p. 48.

277 "You've got it . . . know it," p. 50.
277 "I wish . . . I'd get out," p. 78.
278 "Bulbous . . . other," p. 79.
278 "Some really wild new things," p. 80.
278 "I had . . . faker," pp. 87–88.
278–279 "Then a lot . . . New Orleans," p. 106.
279 "If this isn't . . . is there," p. 129.
280 "The pictures . . . of her," p. 143.
280 "I want . . . gorgeous always," p. 251.
281 "But it has . . . in itself," p. 148.
281 "It doesn't . . . the bottom," p. 158.
284 "We keep . . . the price," p. 253.
285 "Stench of . . . rottenness," p. 260.
285 "Her crying . . . house," p. 258.
286 "You want . . . somebody's girl?" p. 307.
286 "I don't think . . . things," p. 334.
286 "And one of . . . smart," p. 345.
286 "How did . . . to have," pp. 345–346.
287 "And I was . . . all played?" p. 370.
287 "If I am right . . . broke free," p. 371.
287 "It was a . . . same," p. 422.
288 "The pictures . . . bad," p. 427.
288 "This link . . . the time," p. 434.

Chapter Eleven

Telephone interviews were conducted with Stan and Christopher Rice in 1989 and 1990.

John Preston wrote his memories in letters.

The following quotes were taken from *The Queen of the Damned,* New York: Knopf, 1988 (Ballantine edition), unless otherwise identified.

295 "You're no . . . poetry." Interview with Stanley Wiater, *Writer's Digest,* November 1988.
297 "After centuries . . . nest," p. 130.
297 "Maharet's . . . breathe," p. 159.
297 "It was . . . one's kin," p. 154.
298 "There is . . . there," p. 178.
298 "To join . . . forever," p. 230.
298 "This is . . . blood," p. 230.
299 "When I was . . . dead," p. 228.
299 "She felt . . . nothing," p. 241.
299 "The Children . . . angels now," p. 250.
299 "You said . . . was good," p. 262.

299 "A dead . . . impenetrable," p. 251.
300 "It is . . . to us," p. 451.
300 "Being dissolved . . . wine," p. 393.
300 "To be human . . . long for," p. 451.
301 "A great . . . religion," p. 447.
301 "I am . . . innocence," p. 369.
302 "Am I not . . . you all?" p. 230.
302 "I loved . . . war," p. 295.
302 "It struck . . . she spoke," p. 296.
302 "Perfectly . . . male;" p. 369.
303 "In the name . . . I am," pp. 299–300.
303 "He kissed . . . shoulders," p. 274.
303 "Had never . . . millennia," p. 267.
304 "Because . . . herself," p. 281.
305 "Perhaps . . . such things," p. 310.
305 "A mixture . . . itself," p. 337.
305 "A moral . . . herself," p. 330.
305 "It was the spiritual . . . everything," p. 332.
305 "The dark . . . good," p. 339.
306 In an interview in 1988 . . . *The New York Times,* Kellerman, November 7, 1988.
307 "It is not man . . . material," p. 448.
307 "Who has not . . . years," p. 447.
307 "Men and women . . . hearts," p. 442.
307 "It is the very . . . sacrifice," p. 446.
309 "My head . . . paradox," p. 376.
309 "Not in all . . . isolation," p. 397.
309 "I had found . . . like herself," p. 397.
309 "But for . . . to do so," p. 439.
310 "No way . . . that she was," p. 470.
310 "She was . . . wrong!" p. 367.
310 "I loved . . . her," p. 450.
310 "We're not angels . . . gods," p. 451.
310 "Brought down . . . gesture," p. 465.
311 "Real hauntings . . . memory," p. 478.

Chapter Twelve

Telephone interviews were conducted with Stan Rice, Christopher Rice, and Bob Wyatt in 1989 and 1990.

321 "Was there . . . wrappings." *The Mummy,* New York: Ballantine, 1988, p. 23.
321 "She had become . . . else," *Ibid.,* p. 157.

The following quotes are taken from *The Witching Hour*, New York: Knopf, 1990.

325 "In New Orleans . . . out," p. 624.
326 "There is a saying . . . dies," p. 381.
326 "In most families . . . stronger," p. 401.
327 "All that was . . . at all," p. 119.
328 "She's an educated . . . men," p. 610.
329 "Out of the caldron . . . the truth," p. 910.
329 "Were there not moments . . . that was?" pp. 60–61.
329 "Different . . . he'd been," p. 36.
330 "The only paradise . . . known," p. 36.
330 "Was there any . . . alive?" p. 203.
330 "If I were to die . . . awaits us," p. 964.
332 "I believe nothing . . . my life," p. 357.
332 "The same cells . . . mine," p. 886.
333 "The fact is . . . immense," p. 190.
333 "Only writing . . . you," p. 528.
333 "I'll write . . . outside of art," p. 529.
334 "She could actually . . . her hair," p. 900.
334 "Barren . . . sun," p. 633.
335 "Didn't matter . . . the natural," p. 648.
335 "We have all . . . mirrors," p. 653.
336 "She had always . . . men were," p. 680.
336 "How extraordinary . . . childhood," p. 771.
337 "Don't be a . . . dignity," p. 698.
337 "In a way . . . went away," p. 708.
338 "I don't want . . . seductive," p. 728.
339 "You feed . . . lamp," p. 649.
341 "A sound . . . energy," p. 733.
342 "And I suppose . . . adversity," p. 964.
343 "I believe . . . beings," p. 964.

INDEX

abnormal lives, 204, 207, 212
absolutes, 68, 100–103, 187, 259
"Absolution," 95–96
abstinence, 193–194
abstract, the, 185, 303, 305, 307, 309
abyss, 215, 306, 332, 341
accident, 187, 256, 341, 342
acute granuleucytic leukemia, 116–121
adolescence:
  and sexuality, 272–273, 351
  as a literary theme, 184, 272, 350
  as horrifying for Anne, 51–52
advances, literary, *see novels by title*
AIDS, 170, 243, 269, 293, 301
Akasha (character), 261, 299–311
  as first vampire, 255, 260, 299, 303–306
  as destroyer, 300–310, 335
  as Egyptian queen, 305–306
alcoholism, 12–13, 23, 34, 35, 41–44, 132–136
  and Anne, *see* Rice, Anne, and alcohol
  and Katherine, *see* O'Brien, Katherine, alcoholism
alienation, 100–102, 148, 162, 241
Allen, Mamma, 6, 12–13, 34–35
All Quiet on the Western Front, 81
Altamont, 107
ambiguity, 27, 91, 150, 183, 201, 216, 226–227, 231, 259, 326, 327, 332, 341, 346, 351
Amsterdam, 344
androgyny, 30, 63, 80, 106, 148, 170, 202–206, 229, 237, 287, 310, 323, 327, 335, 350
Anna Karenina, 179
Apocalypse Now, 250, 261
Arbeit, Annette, 98, 115
Arbor House, 229, 289
architecture, 25, 79, 143, 175, 179, 195, 319, 325
Arieti, Silvano, 18–19
Armand (character), 156, 161–166, 194–195, 253–254, 257, 259, 260, 273, 296–297, 298, 303
art, 86–87, 108, 140, 174, 205, 206, 274–275, 278, 281–282, 318
authenticity, 143, 145, 182, 224, 288

Bailey, Ann, 49–51
Ballantine, 170, 292, 314, 320
ballet, 207
Baryshnikov, Mikhail, 207
Bast, Bill, 264–265
Baudelaire, 156
Bauersveld, Eric, 151, 167
Beats, the, 56, 68, 78–79, 82, 83, 104, 274
Beauty (character), 215–217, 222, 223, 238–239, 240, 241
Beauty's Punishment, 222–223
  as metaphor, 223
  dominance and submission, 222–223
  homosexuality in, 222–223
  masochism in, 222–223
  publication date, 223
  theme, 222–223
Beauty's Release, 238–241, 263
  dominance and submission, 238–239, 240
  freedom of women, 239
  homosexuality in, 238–239

publication date, 263
spirituality, 239–240
Belinda, 92, 114, 183, 195, 272–293, 337
adolescence, 52
advance, 289
Anne's attitude toward, 291–292
art, 274–275, 278, 279, 281–282, 292
as metaphor, 279, 283, 285, 287, 292
autobiographical elements in, 273–274, 286
duality of self, 279–280, 286–287
freedom of expression, 275–276, 288–289
parents and children, 273, 281, 283–284, 291
reviews of, 290–291
style, 287–288, 289, 290, 292
substance, 285, 288
Belinda (character), 274–289, 327, 337, 338
as an adolescent, 272, 274, 278
as inner self, 275, 280–281, 285, 287, 288
as voice of Anne, 280
as the voice of sexual freedom, 52, 278–279, 287, 292
Belles Lettres, 315
Bergson, Henri, 69, 304–305
Berkeley:
as home to Anne, 108, 115, 175
in the sixties, 107
Bettelheim, Bruno, 215
bisexuality, 238–239, 323, 326, 333, 348. *See also* sexuality; homosexuality
Bishop, Leonard, 138
Blackwood, Algernon, 27
Blade Runner, 270
Blake, William, 151
blood, 43, 146, 298, 326
Body of Work, 142
bondage, 89, 115. *See also* dominance
Borchardt, Alice (O'Brien), 10, 13–15, 17, 18, 21, 24, 27, 31–35, 36, 37, 42–43, 59, 166, 270, 324
Borgia, Lucrezia, 39–40
Bourbon Street, 232
Bowie, David, 236–237
boxing, 109–110
"Brenner the Shape-Shifter," 88
Brumer, Andy, 159, 191, 253, 315
"Caesar's Ghost," 39–40
Cairo, 179, 321
California:
as Anne's home, *see* Berkeley; Haight Ashbury; Oakland; Castro district
in the seventies, 147, 170–171
in the sixties, 78–79, 82, 84, 104, 106–107, 126, 289
"California voice," 225, 289
Campbell, Joseph, 257
campus riots, 106–107
Camus, Albert, 69, 155, 171–172
Cardinale, Claudia, 154
cards, 14
Carmel, 124
"Carmilla," 149
Carrie, 171
Castenada, Carlos, 147
castles, 14, 89
castrati, 197–198, 207, 350
and community, 201, 204
and fashion, 199, 203–204,207
as singers, 197, 199, 202, 203–204
as symbols of androgyny, 197
physical description, 198, 199
Castro district, 195, 274, 290, 293
Candy, 242
"Catholic Girls," 242, 329
Catholicism:
censorship, 19, 51
doctrines, 26, 347
education, 19–20
rituals, 19–21, 27–28, 51–52
saints, 30, 36, 115, 221, 258, 348
uniforms, 2, 20
CBS, 312
CBS Theatricals, 269
cemeteries, 3, 25–26
censorship, 19, 51, 204, 249
Chamberlain, Richard, 269, 312
chaos, 101, 154, 201, 202, 203, 205, 223, 234, 256, 259, 303, 310, 332, 337, 340–341, 346, 351
Chatto and Windus, 320
Chaucer, 112
Cher, 269
Chester, Laura, 113, 134, 167
children and parents as literary idea, *see* parents
Christ, 19, 29, 30, 66, 220
Christmas, 29, 316–317, 340
Christmas Carol, A, 317

Christophe (character), 185–187, 188, 189
Claiming of Sleeping Beauty, The, 214–217, 221
as expression of sexual freedom, 214
as metaphor, 216, 220
as a fairy tale, 214, 215
as a pseudonymous work, 214–215
publication date, 221
clarity, 111, 227–228, 267, 290, 330, 338, 350
Claudia (character), 154–156, 161–165, 253, 259–260, 268–270, 298, 311, 348, 352
Cleopatra (character), 321–322, 335
Club, the, *see Exit to Eden*
Collins, Micki Ruth, 59
Colman, Cathy, 140–141, 160, 223
Communion, 252, 279
as literary theme, *see* Transubstantiation
Big, 28–29
Little, 28
community, 21, 116, 151, 172–173, 179, 201, 204, 256–257
computers, writing with, 180, 295
Comus parade, 29, 324–325, 341
Confirmation, 28–29
conformity, 172–173
Conrad, Joseph, 250
conservatives, 108
continuous awareness, 256, 276, 304, 347–348
contradiction, 3, 22, 150, 305, 310, 315, 340
control, 230, 265
Count of Monte Cristo, The, 17, 19
Cow Palace, 261
creativity, 18–19, 173, 204, 341, 352
"Creature Features," 173
Cristofer, Michael, 324
Cry to Heaven, 38, 92, 197–210, 221, 228, 252, 273
advance, 199
appearances, 200–202, 204
as expression of sexual freedom, 202–205, 206–207
as metaphor, 200, 201, 204
as symbol of androgyny, 202–206
community, 201, 204
difficulty in writing, 198, 206
doubles imagery, 202
publication date, 208
reviews of, 208–209, 227
style, 198, 199–200, 203
transformation, 201, 204
"Cyrano de Bergerac," 79

Dalton, Timothy, 270
Daniel (character), 142–143, 165, 296, 298, 303, 312
Dark Gift, 252
Dark Moment, the:
for Anne, 100–102, 134, 347
for Katherine, 102, 124
for Lestat, 100–102, 247
Daviau, Allen, 11, 35, 73, 82, 160, 289, 290
Daviau, George, 7, 11, 34
David Copperfield, 5, 49
death, Anne's fear of, 100–102. *See also* Rice, Anne, fears
DeGovia, Carla, 109, 119, 127
DeGovia, Jack, 69, 79, 83, 96–97, 98, 109, 120, 127, 157
Delon, Alain, 115
Denton, Texas, 65, 66, 72, 74
Desert Song, 262–263
devil, the, 125, 326, 335
Dickens, Charles, 131, 179, 257, 326
as literary inspiration, 27, 49, 86, 143, 193, 266, 284, 328–329
Katherine's love of, 8, 17
novels of, 17, 49, 317, 328–329
themes of, 328–329
Die, Die My Darling, 110
Dionysus, 258–260, 261, 327, 341
dolls, 34, 107, 154, 193
Dodds, John, 182, 183, 221, 229, 235, 274, 276, 289, 291, 292–293
dominance, 148, 151, 213–214, 219, 220, 223, 230, 233, 240, 335, 350
dominatrix, 229, 230, 243
Dostoevsky, Fyodor, 113, 160, 187, 227, 284, 301
Doty, Carolyn, 139–140, 157, 160, 168, 174–175, 178, 183
Dracula, 149, 264
Dracula's Daughter, 40–41, 149
dream worlds, *see* Rice, Anne, fantasy life
dreams, 15, 111–112
"Dress of White Silk," 40
drugs, 68, 98–99, 104
Druids, 255
duality, 152, 163, 295, 300, 339, 349, 350

Dubovsky, Betsy, 113–114, 120, 135
Dworkin, Andrea, 218

Edgar Allen Poe Award, 167
editors, *see* Dodds, John; Evans, Joni; Whitehead, Bill; Wilson, Victoria; and Wyatt, Bob
Education of Richard Lockhardt, The, 207, 209
Egypt, 179, 180, 207, 255, 257, 321–322
Egyptian art, 44
eighties, 249, 266, 292
Elliot (character), 226, 230–234, 235, 240, 241, 244, 245, 336, 337, 338, 343
  as Anne's male self, 241, 244, 245
Ellis, Candi, 180, 208
Empire Strikes Back, The, 293, 301
Entertainment for a Master, 291
E. P. Dutton, 221, 242
equality, 52, 63, 72, 139, 182, 207, 231, 232, 252
erotic, the, 212, 219, 253, 276, 305, 334, 350
erotica, 89, 209–244, 352
essence, as artistic pursuit, 98
essential dream, 240–241
European mentality, 110, 184, 186, 209, 211
European trips, 179–180, 182, 344
Evans, Joni, 182–183, 190–191
evil, 27, 125, 187, 250–251, 293, 327
  and Lasher, 326–327, 341
  and vampires, 162–163, 171, 174, 253, 259, 301, 303, 307, 310
  as abstraction, 171, 250–251
excess, 115
"Excess Is Ease," 273
Existentialism:
  as read by Anne, 65, 69
  as relevant to Anne's work, 155, 162, 172, 187, 226, 300
Exit to Eden, 19, 25, 30, 59, 63, 65, 218, 219, 225–235, 238, 240, 241, 252, 263–264, 272, 276, 281, 285, 286, 289, 290, 293
  advance, 229
  as expression of sexual freedom, 232–233
  as metaphor, 225, 227
  autobiographical elements, 228–229, 231, 233
  publication date, 235
  reviews, 235
  sexual slavery, 225–226
  the Club, 225–227, 230, 232, 233
Exorcist, The, 169, 171

fairy tales, 120, 215
family:
  as important to Anne, 26, 255, 348–349
  as literary theme, 255, 297, 306, 326
Family, the Great, 297, 306
fan club, 315–316
Faulkner, William, 189, 190
Fear of Flying, 170
Feast of All Saints, The, 60, 81, 177–194, 196, 206, 209, 252, 316, 337, 339
  accident, 187
  adolescence in, 184
  advance, 183
  ambiguity in, 184
  as metaphor, 183, 184, 189
  community, 184, 189
  expectations for, 190
  free will, 187, 188
  parents and children, 188
  paperback rights, 192
  reviews of, 191–193
  slavery, 186, 190
  style, 186–187, 189, 192
Feast of All Saints (holy day), 183
Feeling and Form, 72
Fekety, Ann, 56, 59, 61, 66
feminism, 51–52, 149, 309
  Anne's attitude toward, 64, 139, 213–214, 218–219
  in the seventies, 139, 213–214
fifties, 49, 60
Figures Press, the, 167
financial security, 337
fire, 41–42, 331
First Street, 319, 325, 330, 342
Flaubert, Gustav, 104, 190
Fleming, Ian, 196
Flesh and the Word, 238
Florescu, Radu, 149
Frankenstein, 27, 351
"Frankenstein: The True Story," 149
Frazer, Sir James, 257
freedom of expression, 179, 189, 205, 217, 231, 232, 241, 249, 280–281, 288, 290, 292

free people of color, 178–179, 183–184, 256, 297–298
free will, 187, 188, 201, 230, 247, 299, 300, 301, 310, 332, 334, 338, 341, 350
French Quarter, 4, 143, 153
Fuller, Blair, 168
Full Fathom Five, 174
funeral, mother's, 48
  daughter's, 130–131
future, 351–352

Gabrielle (character), 247–248, 252–255, 259, 261, 269, 299, 303–304, 306, 343
Gajdusek, Dr. Robin, 122
Gallier House, 153
Garden District, 2, 25, 26, 51, 175, 234, 285, 312, 313, 319, 325, 330
Geffen, David, 270
Geisinger, Dr. David, 158
gender:
  as a literary theme, 202–204, 243, 350
  as a personal issue for Anne, 64, 328, 348
  See also androgyny; bisexuality; homosexuality; sexuality; transgender
genius, 8, 15, 18, 24, 345
gens de couleur libre, see free people of color
ghost stories, 16, 27, 212, 248, 319, 348
Gilbert, Jack, 84, 88, 179
God, 220–221, 339, 346, 347, 350, 351
Goethe, 189, 198
Golden Bough, The, 257
Golden Moment, the, 113–114, 252
goodness:
  as a literary theme, 27, 171, 247, 252, 259, 301–302, 303, 334–335, 342, 343
  as significant to Anne, 29–30, 37, 171
Great Expectations, 27, 328–329
Gregg, Linda, 83–84, 120, 121, 161, 179, 304
Guillain-Barre Syndrome, 137
Haight-Ashbury, 67, 73, 78, 82, 104, 286

Haiti, 178, 326
Halloween, 27
Hamlet, 17, 18, 143, 226, 248
Hauer, Rutger, 270
Hawthorne, Nathaniel, 140, 324
"Hello, Darkness," 323–324, 351
Hemingway, Ernest, 54, 95, 115, 121–122, 138, 144, 189, 252
Henstell, Pam, 173, 265
Hermann-Grima House, 179
hero, 49, 116, 136, 189, 197, 201, 205, 241, 296, 310, 346, 350, 351
hippies, 69, 102, 104, 108, 212
Hollywood, 289–290, 292, 314
Holy Name of Jesus School, 20
homosexuality, 148, 194–195, 237, 266, 286
  Anne's interest, in 63, 70, 105–106, 115–116, 195, 348
  as literary theme, 90–91, 106, 148, 222, 253, 277, 333
horror, 175, 248, 251
  and sex, 212, 334, 339
House of Seven Gables, The, 324
Howard Allen, 1–2, 10
Hunger, The, 248
Husen, Paul, 264–265
Huxley, Aldous, 69

Idiot, The, 160
illusion, 198, 227, 279, 288, 290
imagination, freedom of, 15, 19, 46–47, 82, 96
immortality:
  and Egypt, 255
  as Catholic doctrine, 146
  as literary theme, 143, 164, 260, 270, 284, 340, 350
  elixir, 321–322
  mummies, 320
  symbolized by family, 200, 255, 297, 306
  symbolized by vampires, 146, 155, 164, 255, 300
"Impulsive Imp, The," 24
individuality, 21, 58, 139, 172–173, 292, 349
Interview With the Vampire, 97, 110, 126, 130, 134–135, 141–176, 183, 189, 191, 192, 193, 194, 209, 211, 212, 229, 248–249,

251, 257, 259, 260, 261, 262, 265, 276, 298
advances, 160, 168
bought by Knopf, 160
first version, 142–144, 152–156
movie rights, 168
movie scripts, 177, 264–265, 268–269, 324
paperback sales, 168
promotion of, 170, 173–174
rejection of, 157
reviews of, 148, 168–170
second version, 161–165
style, 144, 164
symbolism of, 147–150, 164–165
themes of, 150, 164
In the Belly of the Beast, 196
In the Frankenstein Tradition, 351
Irish:
Anne's ethnic background, 6–7
as storytellers, 16, 190, 316, 347
Irish Channel, 4, 26, 285, 329, 336
Isis, 257
It, 111, 227–228, 290, 338, 350
Italy, 182

Jack the Ripper, 236
James, Henry, 324
James, M. R., 27
Jane Eyre, 27, 53
Janus Society, 242
Jean (character), 89–91, 115, 124, 148, 185
Jeremy (character), 211, 272, 274–289, 290, 335, 337, 338
Jesse (character), 297–299, 312
John, Elton, 270
Johnson, Kay, 41, 286
Johnson, Lyndon, 82
Joseph Henry Jackson Award, 113, 140, 157
Joy of Sex, The, 170
Julius Caesar, 39
Jung, Carl, 326–327, 332

Kandel, Lenore, 126
Karloff, Boris, 33
Katherine (character), 112–113, 122–126, 273
Katherine and Jean, 52, 54, 64, 99–100, 112, 118, 122–126, 136–137, 185, 222, 263, 272, 323
autobiographical elements in, 123–125
homosexual themes, 124
thesis committee reaction to, 122, 126
Keats, John, 151, 236
Kennedy, John F., 82
Kerouac, Jack, 49, 95, 225, 228
Keyes, Francis Parkinson, 277
Khayman (character), 297, 298, 303, 306
Kierkegaard, Soren, 65, 69, 204, 227, 349
King, Stephen, 171, 248, 312
Knopf, Alfred A., 160, 182, 248, 289, 319
Konigsberg, Frank, 312

Labyrinthitis, 137
Lafayette Cemetery, 25, 325
Langer, Suzanne, 72
Lasher (character), 326–327, 330–331, 332, 334, 336–337, 338–340, 344, 349
as evil, 326, 341
as Trickster, 326–327, 338, 339–340
symbolism surrounding, 326
Laurent (character), 223, 228, 238–241, 244
"L. A. Woman," 261
Le Fanu, Sheridan, 149, 215
Lestat (character), 152–156, 209, 224–225, 229, 240, 244–270, 311, 312, 327, 343, 352
and Akasha, 300–303, 306–308, 310–311
and the Dark Moment, 100–102, 247, 298–299
as Christ figure, 257, 298–299, 301–302
as Dionysus, 257, 259–260, 261, 298–299, 301–302
as rock star, 250, 260
as vampire, 152–156, 163, 165, 249, 252, 266
Levay, Anton, 170
Leveau, Marie, 179
Levy, Michael, 269
liberals, 108, 229, 232
liberal values, 108, 179, 187
libraries, 104, 116, 178
Library Journal, 169, 266, 315, 323
Lisa (character), 30–31, 226–234,

240, 252, 306, 327, 336, 337, 338, 342–343
Lolita, 87, 89
Lorimar, 269–270
Los Angeles Times, 290
Louis (character), 222, 229, 241, 251, 254, 258, 260–261, 273, 299, 303, 311, 312, 335, 352
  Anne's attitude toward, 166–167, 246
  and Armand, 156, 161–165, 177
  and Claudia, 153–156, 162–165
  as moral figure, 153, 163, 165, 171
  as vampire, 141–144, 152–156
  as victim, 144, 145, 152, 189, 211, 252
Louisiana, 116, 143, 178, 179, 269
Louisiana Historical Quarterly, 116
love, 106, 261, 276, 286, 349
Loyola University, 179
LSD, 68, 98–99, 104, 106

Macay, Kathy, 159
Macbeth, 166, 248
Madame Bovary, 190
Mad Scientist, The, 352
Maharet (character), 297, 298, 303–307, 310, 325, 335, 343
Male Machine, The, 170
Marcel (character), 184–189, 222, 241, 337
Mardi Gras, 29, 324–325, 341–342
Marianna (character), 200, 202, 205, 252, 306
Marie (character), 184–186
marijuana, 96, 98, 124, 186
Marius (character), 112, 255–257, 260, 267, 303
  as continuous awareness, 256
  as moral voice, 256–257, 300, 307
  as vampire guardian, 254–255, 296
masks, 202, 231
masochism, 89, 115, 125, 213, 216, 218, 220, 223, 229, 230, 350
master, 220, 221, 222–223, 226, 230, 239–240, 350
"Master of Rampling Gate, The," 236–237
Mathis, Ginny (Hiebert), 61–64, 66–69, 73–74, 75
McCullers, Carson, 65, 84, 189
McKinnon, Catharine, 218
McNally, Raymond, 149
meaning, 78–79, 305, 308, 341
Michael (character), 329–331, 334–344, 350
Miller, Henry, 218
mirrors, 144, 150, 165, 309, 335
moral idealism, *see* Rice, Anne
Morrison, Jim, 261
"Mr. Justice Harbottle," 215
mummies, 255, 312, 320, 350, 352
Mummy, The, 40, 42, 314, 320–324, 335
Mummy, The (film), 33–34
mummy factories, 322
"Mummy Ghost, The," 39
Murphy, Billy, 26–27, 312
Murphy, Judy (O'Neil), 49–51
My One and Only, 262–263
My Secret Life, 218
mysticism, 27, 29, 341, 348
mythology, *see* Dionysus; Osiris

Nabakov, Vladimir, 87, 88, 89
nakedness, 231
near-death experiences, 334, 348
Nesbit, Lynn, 178, 182, 192, 215, 217, 229, 289, 319
New Orleans, 2–4, 18, 25, 26, 125, 143, 150, 167, 175, 179, 185, 232, 234, 254, 260, 275, 276, 278, 285, 287, 290, 298, 311, 312–313, 316, 318–319, 326, 330, 336, 338, 339, 342, 343, 348, 350
New Republic, 169
New York Times Book Review, 169, 191, 267, 291, 293, 314, 344
New York Times Magazine, 344
Newsweek, 344
Nicholas and Jean, 89–92, 95, 112, 115, 124, 125, 148, 198, 272
nicknames, 2–3, 10
Nietzsche, Friedrich, 62, 65, 69, 216, 252, 258–259, 261
nihilism, 62, 78, 171, 172, 250, 259, 299, 302, 303, 308, 310
nineteenth century, 171, 176, 178
Nixon, Richard, 106
North Beach, 82
North Texas State University, 66, 74
"Nose, The," 105
nothingness, 81

Oakland, 180
Oates, Joyce Carol, 242

oboe, 49
O'Brien, Dorothy, 53–55, 60–61
O'Brien, Howard:
  as poet and writer, 4–5, 24, 270
  Catholicism, 5, 19
  employment, 9, 22, 34, 55
  first marriage, 9–10
  growing up in Irish Channel, 4
  in merchant marine, 5
  in World War II, 11
  musical influence on Anne, 22
  relationship with Anne, 40, 65, 131, 152, 160, 168, 191, 214
  second marriage, 53, 55
O'Brien, Karen, 34, 38, 81, 168, 270
O'Brien, Katherine:
  alcoholism, 12–13, 23, 35, 41–44
  ambitions for children, 8, 15–22, 23, 42, 345
  as a girl, 5–6
  as literary inspiration, 247–248, 252–253, 283
  Catholicism, 8–9, 19–20
  childrearing practices of, 8, 15–22, 24
  death of, 45–48, 50, 273
  fear of dark, 12
  love of Dickens, 8, 17
  movies, 17
  storyteller, 17
  wedding, 9–10
O'Brien, Tamara, 22, 31, 36, 38, 40, 44, 46, 81, 121, 130, 131, 174
obsessive-compulsive syndrome, 157–158
"October 4, 1948," 13, 94
"Ode to a Nightingale," 151
Old Curiosity Shop, The, 5, 17
Oliver Twist, 5
Olsen, Tillie, 88
Omen, The, 171
Once Out of Nature, 351–352
On the Road, 49, 95
opposites, 22, 150, 279, 308–309, 327, 332, 346
Osiris, 257–258
Othello, 175
Other, The, 169
outsider, 63, 151, 172–173, 179, 204, 228, 230, 235, 267, 272, 331, 347, 350
Owen, Dr. Robert, 197–198
pain, as an element of writing, 182, 209
paradox, 20, 226–227
  as theme in vampire novels, 150, 172, 299, 302, 303, 308–309, 351
  as theme in *The Witching Hour,* 340–341, 343–344
Paramount, 168, 177, 264, 268–269
parents (literary theme), 48, 188, 273, 281, 283–284, 291
Paris, 156, 161, 179
parties, 83, 96, 114, 159, 175, 180–181
passion, 181, 220, 222
Pearl Harbor, 11
People Weekly, 266–267, 315
Percy, Dennis, 55, 63, 69, 79, 293
Phelps, Lynn, 56–57, 59, 61, 65, 67, 73, 76, 79, 82, 119
Philadelphia Inquirer, 323
Philip Street, 312
Phillips, Julia, 265, 268, 269, 270
physicality, 25, 30–31, 346
piano, 22, 38
Playboy, 194–195, 210
plays, 39
Poe, Edgar Allen, 140
poetry:
  influence on Anne, 16, 24, 83–86, 295
  readings, 84–85, 103, 174
  used by Katherine, 16
  used in novels, 273–274, 295
pornography, 89, 115, 211–244, 288, 299
  Anne's attitudes about, 89, 213–214, 224
  censorship of, 218–219
power, 159, 162, 170, 177, 201, 204, 205, 216, 223, 226, 231, 238–240, 273, 336, 339, 349, 350
prayer, 36–37
Preston, John, 237–238, 263–264, 265, 266, 291, 295
prism, 351
process, 96–97, 98–99, 146–147
Provosty, Lucy (Harper), 35–37, 48, 60, 94
pseudonyms, 210. *See also* Rampling, Anne; Roquelaure, A. N.
Publisher's Weekly, 169, 235

Queen of the Damned, The, 293–315, 319, 324, 325, 339
Anne's attitude toward, 311–312
autobiographical elements, 302, 305–306, 307–308
evil in, 301, 303, 307, 310
feminism, 301, 302, 307
moral philosophy of, 302, 306–307, 311
paradox, 302, 303, 308–309
publication date, 314
reviews of, 314–315
style, 303–304
symmetry, 308–310

Rampling, Anne, 225, 245, 289
Rampling, Charlotte, 225
Ramses (character), 321–322
Rank, Otto, 281
Reagan, Ronald, 106
Redbook, 210, 236
Redemptorist School, 2, 49, 313, 336
religion, *see* Catholicism; Rice, Anne; Transubstantiation
Renault, Mary, 169, 209
"Renegade, The," 40
reunions, 260–261, 288, 303, 349
reviews, *see novels by title*
Rice, Anne:
abstinence, 193–194
agents, 159, 160, 175, 178
alcohol, 23, 83, 103, 132–136, 182, 193–194, 280, 287, 348
alienation, 100–102
ambitions, 138, 140, 352
and art, 38, 50, 95, 140
being special, 38, 47, 53, 137, 138, 346, 348
book contracts, *see novels by title*
book tours, 168, 170, 193, 265–266, 344
born, 10
Catholicism, 19–21, 59
Chapter Thirteen, 120
childhood, 11–53, 204–205
children, 103, 104, 182
collaboration, 263–264, 270, 314, 323–324
college, 61–67, 80, 81, 84
and computers, 180, 295
death of daughter, 128–132, 146, 151, 158, 162–165, 166–167, 272, 311, 348
death of mother, 45–48, 143, 146, 164, 256, 272, 276–277, 287, 311, 339, 347
diary, 88, 151–152, 156
divided self, 225, 241, 349
dreams, 15, 111–112, 307–308
drinking phase, 132–136
duality, 49, 152, 226, 234, 253, 265–266, 279, 287, 349
editors, 190, 221, 229. *See also editors by name*
education, 18–20, 61–64, 66, 81, 95, 112
employment, 55, 59, 65, 67, 80, 92, 103, 136
erotica, *see* erotica
European trips, 179–180, 182, 344
excessive temperament, 37
fantasy life, 13–15, 30, 31, 37, 63, 87, 243, 246, 347
fears, 26, 32–33, 41–42, 100–102, 133, 215, 299, 330
feminine side, 57, 62–63, 211, 213, 214, 222, 241, 248, 253, 255, 281, 283, 306
feminism, 64, 71, 139, 213–214, 218–219, 238–239, 301, 309
first kiss, 60, 185
friendships, 62, 113–114, 139, 181, 183, 237–238
gay men, 63, 70, 105–106, 115–116, 195, 348
graduate school, 84, 95, 112–113, 121–122, 126
Haight-Ashbury, 67, 73, 78, 82, 104
homesickness, 59–60, 66, 71, 108, 116, 184, 313–314
and Howard, 40, 65, 131, 152, 160, 168, 191, 214
Howard Allen, 1–2, 10
humor, 114, 227
immortality, 322–323. *See also* Immortality
literary influences, *see* Dickens; Dostoevsky; Hemingway; M. R. James; McCullers; Renault; Shakespeare; Tolstoy; Woolf
loss of faith, 65–66, 130, 144, 153, 259, 347, 351
masculinity, 105, 152, 213, 222, 228–229, 234–235, 243, 245–246, 253, 255, 279, 286, 302, 303, 327, 348
masochism, 115, 213, 218
master's thesis, 122–126

moral light, 50, 247, 282
moral philosophy, 171, 247, 267–268, 306–307, 311, 321, 342–343, 349, 351
move to Texas, 55–60
move to San Francisco, 66, 76–77
move to New Orleans, 312–314, 318–319, 338
movies, 62
music lessons, 22–23, 38
names, 1–2, 10, 28, 58
need of a teacher, 64, 184–185, 246, 273
novels, *see by title*
obsessive-compulsive syndrome, 157–158
optimism of, 268, 282, 342, 343, 351
oral exam, master's, 121–122
oratory, 36–37
personality, 32, 43–44, 80, 84, 114, 138, 173, 181–182, 184, 319, 327
physical illnesses, 137
plays, 39
poetry, influnced by, 16, 24, 83–83, 295
political science major, 81, 84
pseudonyms, 210–244, 272–293
religious training, 19–21, 36–37
renaming, 1–2
and reviews, 192, 208–209, 266–268, 293, 315–316
self-confidence of, 32, 43–44, 46–48, 109
sexuality, 30–31, 63, 181, 211, 213, 233, 253, 279. *See also* bisexuality; homosexuality; sensuality; sexuality
as southern writer, 189–190, 316
Squaw Valley, 158–159, 161, 168
stories, 36, 39–40, 58, 68, 87, 105, 110–111. *see also by title*
and the supernatural, 140, 349
use of Catholic imagery, 96, 171, 226, 239–240, 252, 279, 292, 298, 300–301, 340
violin, 38
vision, 190, 285, 331, 339, 342, 352
vulnerabilities, 32, 195, 215, 265, 276, 347
wedding, 74–76
wholeness, 235, 317, 330, 347, 350
writing groups, 137–139, 156–157
writing habits of, 143, 149, 295
writing style of, 88, 90–91, 94, 95, 137, 143, 144–145, 183, 190, 192, 266, 295, 345
Rice, Christopher, 193, 294, 313, 338, 344
as artist, 208, 210–211, 318
born, 182
feelings about mother's work, 319
named, 182
personality, 182, 210–211, 318
writer, 270–271
Rice, Cythnia, 73, 127, 175, 179, 180, 181, 182, 234
Rice, Larry, 73, 81, 114, 115, 133, 136, 224
Rice, Margaret, 60, 76, 136
Rice, Michelle:
born, 104
contracted leukemia, 116–118
death, 128–132, 273, 293
illness, 117–121, 126–128
inspiration for Claudia, 154
naming, 104
personality, 104–105, 107, 127
Rice, Nancy (Diamond), 73, 76
Rice, Stanley:
Anne's love of, 57, 58, 60, 66–67
artist, 57, 79, 313, 318
courting Anne, 59, 72–74
death of daughter, 128–135, 167
education, 72–74, 81, 86, 92–93
employment, 72, 76, 80, 82, 92–93, 318
personality, 57–58, 76, 80, 83
poetry, 58, 72, 81, 83–86, 103, 344
poetry readings, 84–85, 103, 174
process, 96–97
as professor, 103, 318
responses to Anne's writing, 58, 92, 156, 217, 224, 229, 243, 344
wedding, 74–76
Rice, Stanley Sr., 60, 76, 136
Richardson High School, 56–59
Richardson, Texas, 55–61
Riley, Michael, 72, 75, 86, 92, 104, 105, 120, 127, 133–134, 137, 206–207
risk, 248, 262
Ritter, Jesse, 75, 149
ritual, 219–220
Rivers, Joan, 173
rock music, 250, 260–261

rock stars, 196, 250, 251
romance novels, 196
Romberg, Sigmund, 262
Rome, 87, 179, 182, 198, 202, 204
Roquelaure, A. N., 89, 215
Rosegate, 319
Rosemary's Baby, 169
Rosenman, Howard, 270
Rousseau, Jean Jacques, 172
Rowan (character), 327–328, 330, 334–342, 343, 349
Russell, Jeffrey Burton, 298

sado-masochism, 112, 212–213, 218–220, 222–223, 230, 233, 235, 238, 242–243, 335, 339–340, 352
St. Alphonsus, 2, 9–10, 313
St. Charles Avenue:
  2301, 6, 10, 60
  2524, 44, 50, 53
St. Joseph's Academy, 53–54, 333
St. Teresa of Avila, 36
St. Therese, 36, 195
saints, 29–30, 36, 115, 221, 258, 348
Salas, Floyd, 109–110
Salem's Lot, 171
San Francisco, 67, 73, 78, 79, 106, 181, 183, 195, 293, 324
San Francisco Bay Guardian, 191
San Francisco Chronicle, 195–196, 208–209, 221, 235, 267, 290–291, 293, 315, 323
San Francisco Review of Books, 169
San Francisco State University, 81, 84, 174
Sanitsky, Larry, 312
Sartre, Jean-Paul, 69, 124, 155, 158, 162, 172, 187, 226, 300
satanism, 162, 170, 266
Scott, Ridley, 270
"Scott and Zelda period," 132–136
scripts, movie, 177, 264–265, 268–269, 324
Seidel, Phyllis, 159, 160, 175, 177
self-realization, 203, 231, 233, 281, 307, 349–350
sensuality, 30–31, 144, 148, 181, 303, 333–334
seventies, 147, 170–171
sexuality, 30–31, 90–91, 106, 148, 211–220, 274, 288, 292, 303, 326, 333
  see also homosexuality; androgyny
Shakespeare, 8, 95, 112, 122
Sheppard, Gertrude, 9, 45–46
short stories, *see* Rice, Anne
significant form, 72
Simon & Schuster, 182, 192, 199
Sisters of Mercy, 20
Sisters of Notre Dame, 20, 49
Sisters of the Poor, Little, 37
sixties, 78–79, 82, 84, 104, 106–107, 126, 284, 292
slavery, 39, 186, 190
slavery, sexual, 214–216, 222–223, 225, 230, 239–240, 350
Sleeping Beauty, 120, 214, 311
Slickery fantasy, 13–14
Slusky, Joe, 114, 278
soap operas, 105
"Some Lamb", 117, 128–129, 131, 134, 167
Sonnabend, Casey, 83–84, 88, 98, 111, 156
Sonoma house, 294–295, 303, 312, 321
southern writer, 189–190, 316
"Space Patrol" fantasy, 14
Speak, Memory, 87
spirits, 304–305, 332, 338, 339
spirituality, 219, 220, 233, 305, 307, 310, 341, 346–347, 350
Spring Moon, 196
Squaw Valley, 174
Squaw Valley Writer's Conference, 158–159, 161
Stand, The, 312
Stephan, Ed, 69–70
Stern, Isaac, 38
Stoker, Bram, 149
Stooge, 113
Story of O, The, 89
Straub, Peter, 248
Streep, Meryl, 269
Strieber, Whitley, 248
Stuart, Shirley, 191, 208, 224
style, *see* Rice, Anne, writing style
subconscious, 96, 144–145, 150, 171, 173, 189, 209, 215, 229, 240–241, 244, 278, 280, 283, 331, 340, 346
submission, 148, 151, 219, 223, 225, 233, 240, 335
substance, 285, 288, 295, 306, 311, 332–333, 346, 349, 350
Sufferings of Charlotte, The, 89, 211, 222

Summer of Love, 106
supernatural, 27, 140, 263, 305, 332, 349
surrender, 148, 161, 194, 201, 202–203, 216, 218, 219, 220, 221, 226, 229, 236, 240, 241, 299, 349
Suzanne, Jaqueline, 196
Swift, Dennis, 328
symbolic violence, *see* violence
symmetry, 308–310

Taft Barish, 269
Talamasca, 298, 325, 326, 331, 336, 341
Tales of Rhoda, The, 115, 222
Talon, The, 58
Taravel Street, 104
Taupin, Bernie, 270
Teachings of Don Juan, The, 147
Texas Woman's University, 59, 61–66, 333
theater, 79, 161–162, 252, 258–259
"Thinker, The," 58, 88
Those Who Must Be Kept, *see* Akasha
Tolstoy, Leo, 113, 179, 192, 257
Tonight Show, The, 173
Tonio (character), 200–206, 222, 241, 337
transcendence, 201, 204, 217, 220, 238, 252, 268, 279, 282, 300, 327, 348, 349
Transfer, 88, 94, 95
trans-gender, 148, 203–204, 211, 230, 232, 233, 243, 253, 269, 287, 336, 350
transsexuals, 232
Transubstantiation, 28, 146, 217, 252, 258, 279, 306, 346, 350
transvaluation, 303, 308–311
Trianna Walker, 211–212, 272
Trickster, the, 326–327, 334, 340
Tristan (character), 217, 222–223, 238–241
truth, 277, 285, 289
Tulane University, 178
Tune, Tommy, 262–263
Turn of the Screw, The, 324
twins, 84, 201, 304–305, 310, 352

UFO's, 352
University of California-Berkeley, 92–93, 112–113
University of San Francisco, 79

vampire, 40, 43, 143, 145, 236, 251, 300, 350
  appearance, 151
  as alcoholic, 43, 153–154
  as androgyne, 148, 266
  as angel, 149–150, 250, 257, 309, 310
  as God, 171, 255–260, 261, 299–302, 308–311
  as metaphor, 145–146, 148, 149, 152, 153–154, 155, 156, 162–165, 169, 171, 174, 266, 267, 295, 299–300
  blood, 146
  conscience, 40, 148, 150, 153
  erotic, 148–149, 253
  evil, 145–146
  in folklore, 149, 171, 300
  immortality, 255
  mythos, 248
  sensuality, 143, 146, 147, 149, 253, 326
Vampire Chronicles, 257–258, 261, 266, 288, 299, 311, 319, 320, 351–352
Vampire Lestat, The, 38, 113, 244–270, 275, 281, 289, 290, 291, 293, 297, 299, 312, 314
  advance, 248
  Anne's attitude toward, 245–246, 262
  autobiographical elements in, 245–247, 252, 255, 256–257, 259
  Lestat as expression of Anne's masculine side, 245
  metaphors, 252, 258–259, 266, 267
  publication date, 265, 292
  reviews of, 266–267
  style, 254, 261–262, 299
  themes, 259, 267
Van den Daele, Lee, 70–71
vegetation gods, 257–260
Venice, 198, 200, 202, 206
Vesuvius, Mt., 201
victim, 43, 47, 49, 136, 161, 189, 201, 205, 213, 296, 310, 346, 350
Vietnam War, 78, 84, 104, 119, 250, 315
Village Voice, 213, 242, 291
violence, 232, 322, 335
  Anne's attitudes toward, 206, 212, 302

as evil, 250, 300–301
symbolic, 115, 190, 201, 213–214, 336
violin, 38, 197, 247, 252, 329
Vogue, 210, 236, 266
"Voice, The," 270
voices, three, *see* Rice, Anne, divided self
von Franz, Marie Louise, 351
vulnerability, 216, 223, 231, 238, 253

Wall Street Journal, 315
Warhol, Andy, 126
Warner Brothers, 270, 344
Washington Post, 169, 293
weather, as literary device, 94, 173
weddings:
Katherine and Howard, 9–10
Anne and Stan, 74–76
Weigand, Dr. William, 122, 126
Welty, Eudora, 24, 189
Whiteboy, 167
Whitehead, Bill, 221, 229, 237, 242, 293
Wilde, Oscar, 110, 143, 169, 207
will, *see* free will
Wilson, Victoria, 161, 173, 178, 199, 206, 208, 221, 272, 289, 312
Wiseman, Dr. Richard, 81, 174
Witchcraft in the Middle Ages, 298
witches, 304–306, 325–326, 327, 331, 344
Witching Hour, The, 20, 38, 42, 48, 121, 130, 131, 135, 216, 263, 298, 312, 313, 317, 324–344, 352
advance, 319
appearances, 343–344
autobiographical elements in, 325–330, 333, 334, 336–339, 342
and free will, 332, 334, 338
family, 326
imagery, 331, 332, 337, 340, 342
moral themes, 340
publication, 344
reviews of, 344
style, 331, 332, 337, 341, 342
witch trials, 331
witness, 131, 256
Woodstock, 107
Woolf, Virginia, 95, 122
World War II, 11
writers' groups, 137–139, 156–157
writing:
habits, 143, 149, 295
style, 88, 90–91, 94, 95, 137, 143, 144–145, 183, 190, 192, 266, 295, 345
Wyatt, Bob, 314, 320

"Young Goodman Brown," 140, 324